SONS OF THE
YELLOW EMPEROR

Also by Lynn Pan

In Search of Old Shanghai
Old Shanghai: Gangsters in Paradise
China's Sorrow: Journeys Around the Yellow River
The New Chinese Revolution

SONS OF THE YELLOW EMPEROR

*A History of
the Chinese Diaspora*

LYNN PAN

LITTLE, BROWN AND COMPANY
Boston   Toronto   London

First U.S. Edition

Library of Congress Cataloging-in-Publication Data

Pan, Lynn.
  Sons of the yellow emperor : a history of the Chinese diaspora /
Lynn Pan. — 1st U.S. ed.
  p.   cm.
  Includes bibliographical references and index.
  ISBN 0316-69010-4
  1. Chinese — Foreign countries — History.   2. Immigrants —
History.   3. China — Emigration and immigration — History.   I. Title.
DS732.P36   1990
951'.004924 — dc20   90-6258

10 9 8 7 6 5 4 3 2 1

MV-PA

Printed in the United States of America

For Henry Sacker
with love and gratitude

Contents

Maps and Illustrations

Preface

I was asked in the course of writing this book if I had any ethnic axes to grind. I have not, but since race is necessarily a theme of the book, and no one can be entirely neutral when it comes to race, I had better say something about myself so that the reader may judge for himself where my bigotries might be expected to lie.

I am one of the thirty million people whose historical experience I try to evoke in this book; I am part of the Chinese diaspora. I was born in Shanghai, was made an émigré by the terror campaigns of the Chinese Communist Party, and was educated, in a manner of speaking, in Hong Kong, British North Borneo and England, where I eventually established a base. I was going to say 'made my home', but that would suggest I had put down roots, whereas I often get the feeling when I'm in England that my real life lies elsewhere, though exactly where it lies it is difficult to say.

Shortly before he died, my father built himself a log cabin in the wilds of British Columbia. My sister lives in Hong Kong, married to an Englishman. My brother, who lives in Sabah (as British North Borneo is now called), is married to a second-generation Chinese immigrant there and his children speak neither Shanghainese, their father's language, nor Teochiu, their mother's, but Cantonese, English and Malay. Another sister and brother, victims of their transplanting, died young, killed by tropical disease and Borneo's primitive medical facilities. I have first cousins in Shanghai, Nanking, Taipei, Brighton, Sydney, New York and Boston, and more distant relatives in Florida and Brazil. I should say we're fairly representative, in our pattern of expatriation and adaptation, of a large proportion of overseas Chinese families.

I visited my cousin in Boston when I went to America to research this book. She is an immigrant success story, a realization of the American Dream; she made her first million before her thirty-third birthday and lives in a very WASP and very posh part of Massachusetts. To say that she chewed gum is perhaps to subscribe to cultural stereotyping, but that was what she did and what distracted my attention all the time we were talking, that and the fact that she said 'Is that right?' to everything I told her. She is warm and generous, and I like her immensely, but I find it hard to think of her as Chinese. An anthropologist of my acquaintance says that it's nonsense to talk of people as being more or less Chinese. Of course there is no norm of Chineseness, just as there is no norm of Frenchness or Englishness or Indianness, but what the anthropologist says is patently untrue on the level of subjective experience. Most Chinese Americans I met on that trip struck me as being far more exotically American than familiarly Chinese. If I were suddenly to find myself on the edge of nowhere, craving the company of the known and familiar, an Englishman appearing on the horizon would I think more nearly satisfy my need than a Chinese American.

That probably says something about my relationship to the English and to England, the country where I have lived longest. I have often been asked, though rarely by the British themselves, how I feel about Britain. I have a fairly long list of complaints, but if I were to be very brief my answer would be the same as the one I give to the question, also frequently put to me, of how I feel about China. I would say that it was summed up by the Chinese set phrase, *hen t'ie pu ch'eng kang*, 'O would that the iron would turn to steel'; it is a source of chagrin to me, in other words, that the country is not better and the people finer. This is not the answer of an indifferent immigrant, and it is true that while I am the world's most boring Brit basher, I hate England like a lover.

I have also been asked, again not by the British themselves, if I had ever run up against racial discrimination in England. Until I began this book, my answer was no; but writing this book has reminded me of an episode I thought I had put out of my mind, not for any discomfort it caused, but because of its insignificance to me at the time. I was at university, and a Canadian friend called Beverly asked me if I'd like to share a flat with her; she had seen one advertised that she thought would suit us. We went to see it together, and were shown round a lovely place by a very well-spoken, genteelly shabby widow who herself lived in the flat below. She said she would let us know, and the next day Beverly heard from her: the flat was hers, Beverly was told, if she found somebody white to share it with.

Beverly was quite distraught – unnecessarily so, I told her; she should simply take the flat and not worry about me. I wasn't being heroic, because I truly did not feel the landlady to be particularly unjust, and I felt neither wounded nor angry. To be fair to the landlady, I myself had made it a point never to share a flat with anybody English, because all the ones I'd lived with had wanted to buy their own milk, their own sugar, their own salt and so on instead of paying money into a kitty; I had put this down to English meanness, and had not contradicted a friend when he said that that was racialist of me.

For a while I shared a flat with a Jamaican girl. When we were flat-hunting in London I was the one who made all the appointments to view, because she felt that landladies mentally crossed Chinese off their list less readily than they did West Indians – I was less 'coloured' than she. And yet it seemed incredible to me that those signs you saw, ROOM TO LET. REGRET NO COLOURED, should refer to me.

I know now that if I was little aware of 'racial prejudice', it was because I felt so utterly comfortable in my Chinese skin; the more fool you, I thought of those who would spurn me on account of my origin. I also know that by no means all immigrant Chinese feel this way, and that the reason I do and they don't is partly to be found in our pre-migration experience.

British North Borneo had a substantial Chinese community. It also had Malays, Indians, Kadazans, Burmese and other Asian communities – each connected to the other by nothing save physical proximity, by the haphazard fact of its having been washed up on the same shore in a distant outpost of the British empire. Of the Chinese in the town where my parents had settled, Hakka speakers were the most numerous but not, in the opinion of us newcomers from Shanghai (the New York of China), the most superior. In fact, we rather looked down on them. To consider ourselves a cut above Chinese from other parts of China is a Shanghainese habit. It seems rather reprehensible in retrospect but I am thankful for the sense of self-worth it gave me, for without it I would have been a less culturally confident immigrant in England.

Coming from a far-flung bit of the British empire, I am, like many another immigrant in England, an ex-colonial. The imperial connection is a motif in the story of Chinese migration; and it was the British empire, above all, which dispersed the Chinese across the world. If I confine myself fairly closely in this account to the English-speaking world, it is partly for demographic reasons (Chinese migration there has been greater) and partly because the scale of the subject is such that I have had to be very selective. I am conscious on completing the book that it could be written all over again with its contents made up of entirely other matter. There could have been a chapter on immigration law and nationality. There could have been one on immigrant literature, on the Chinese in Japan or South America. An entire book has been written on immigrant Chinese farming in California, a subject that is barely mentioned in mine. It is not false modesty which makes me say that I am only too aware of my book's incompleteness as I reach the end.

Finally, a word about the spelling of Chinese names. No common system exists for rendering overseas Chinese names, the pronunciation of which varies considerably from dialect to dialect, and the romanization from one colonial setting to another. I have largely retained the commonly accepted local transliteration, rendering a name in its Cantonese dialect pronunciation, for instance, when its referent is Cantonese. For the rest I have fallen back on the Wade-Giles system of spelling, except for a handful of names with widely recognizable English forms, such as Canton, Peking, and Fukien; or which are more easily identifiable in their Pinyin romanization, such as Deng Xiaoping and Tiananmen. I know I can be thought old-fashioned for adopting Wade-Giles romanization, but its forms are less at odds with the local transliterations than those of Pinyin. I follow Chinese practice in placing surnames before given names, but make an exception of the names of Chinese in America, where the local convention is to reverse the order.

Acknowledgements

A book of this kind draws heavily and gratefully on existing literature, both scholarly and journalistic. Many of my debts will be evident from the notes and the bibliography.

Friends and strangers who have helped me in one way or another with the research for this book are too numerous for me to mention all by name. But I wish particularly to thank the following for giving me their time and in many cases their generous hospitality.

In Bangkok, Hat Yai, Pattani and Songkhla: Paul Handley, Phuwa-dol Songprasert, Ho Yun, Visit Mingwatanabul, Nopadon Aneckchai, Vichai Pipatananuglit and Liu Yong Chang.

In Berkeley, Boston, Los Angeles, New York and San Francisco: Ken Hom, Daniel Taurines, Darrell Corti, Alice and Henry Coolidge, Jay and Kent Wong, Russell Leong, Dolores Wong, Emma Louie, Him Mark Lai, Ruthanne Lum McCunn, Jack Tchen, 'Charlie' Chin, Charles Lai and Hu Ping.

In Fukien, China: Association of Returned Overseas Chinese in Ch'uan-chou.

In Hong Kong: Ip Kung Sau, Si Chung Mou, Vicwood Chong, Martin Cowley, Mike Horner, Robert Cheng, Jonathan Friedland, Margaret Scott and Dotty and Stan Shelton.

In Kuala Lumpur, Malacca and Penang: Andrew Sheng, Lim Suan Poh and Tan Siok Choo.

In London and Manchester: Jenny Lo, Simon Jones, Jamie Kenny, Catherine Stenzl, Hugh Baker, David Cesarani and Kimpton N'Dlovu.

In Manila: Lin Ch'uen Sheng, Fred Chua, Go Bun Juan, Betty S. Chua, Teresita Ang, James Ong Lepho and Ian Gill.

In Paris: Choi Hak Kin and Yau Shun-chiu.

In Semarang: Hoo Liong Tiauw.

In Singapore: Evelyn Chew, Pang Cheng Lian, Lim How Seng, Tan Sai Siong, Ho Lai Chan and Kealy Ho.

Thanks are also due to those who have given permission to quote copyright material:

Aitken & Stone Ltd: *The Middle Passage* by V. S. Naipul; Allen &

Unwin Australia: *No Man is an Island* by James Minchin; The Athlone Press: *Lineage Organization in Southeastern China* by Maurice Freedman; Bloomsbury Publishing Ltd: *The Reckoning* by David Halberstam; Cambridge University Press: *China and the Overseas Chinese* by Stephen Fitzgerald, *Conrad's Eastern World* by Norman Sherry; Capitola Book Company: *Chinese Gold* by Sandy Lydon; Chatto and Windus: *The British at Table 1940–1980* by Christopher Driver; Collins/Angus & Robertson: *The Struggle for Singapore* by Alex Josey; William Collins Sons and Co.: *The War of the Running Dogs* by Noel Barber; *Chinese Society in Thailand* by G. William Skinner, copyright © by Cornell University, used by permission of the publisher, Cornell University Press; André Deutsch Ltd: *Sour Sweet* by Timothy Mo; Duckworth Ltd: *Low Life* by Jeffrey Bernard; Editions Duang Kamol: *Letters from Thailand* by Botan; *Intellectuals and the State in Modern China* by Jerome B. Grieder, copyright © 1981 by The Free Press, a division of Macmillan, Inc.; Grafton Books: *The Magic Dragon* by Donald Moore; Hamish Hamilton Ltd: *The Proud Tower* by Barbara Tuchman; *Sunrise with Seamonsters* by Paul Theroux, copyright © 1985 by Cape Cod Scriveners Company, reprinted by permission of Hamish Hamilton Ltd, Houghton Mifflin Company and Cape Cod Scriveners Company; William Heinemann Ltd: *The Malayan Trilogy* by Anthony Burgess; Hong Kong University Press: *Proceedings of a Symposium on Southern China, South-East Asia and the Hong Kong Region* edited by F. S. Drake; *Peasants, Proletarians and Prostitutes* by Lai Ah Eng, reproduced with kind permission of the publisher, Institute of Southeast Asian Studies, Singapore; Kangaroo Press Pty Ltd: *Australian Mandarin* by Robert Travers; *Tripmaster Monkey: His Fake Book*, copyright © 1989 by Maxine Hong Kingston, reprinted by permission of Alfred A. Knopf Inc.; Him Mark Lai, Genny Lim and Judy Yung: their book *Island*; Ministry of Communications and Information, Singapore: *The Battle for Merger* by Lee Kuan Yew; Jan Morris: her book *Hong Kong, Xianggang*; Peter Owen Ltd: *Opium* by Jean Cocteau, trs. Margaret Crosland; Oxford University Press: *The Chinese in Southeast Asia* by Victor Purcell; Pan Books and the Schaffner Agency: *The Woman Warrior* copyright © Maxine Hong Kingston, 1975, 1976; Routledge and Harcourt Brace Jovanovich, Inc.: *World of Our Fathers* by Irving Howe; Times Editions, Singapore: *Singapore: Struggle for Success* by J. Drysdale; University of California Press: *Vermilion Bird* by Edward H. Schafer; University of Washington Press: *Chinese Women of America* by Judy Yung; *Immigrants and*

Minorities in British Society edited by C. Holmes, reproduced by kind permission of Unwin Hyman Ltd; Weidenfeld and Nicolson, New York: *The Star Raft* by Philip Snow; Yale University Press: *The Chinese in Philippine Life 1850–1898* by Edgar Wickberg.

While every effort has been made to trace copyright holders, the publisher would like to apologize to anyone who has not been formally acknowledged.

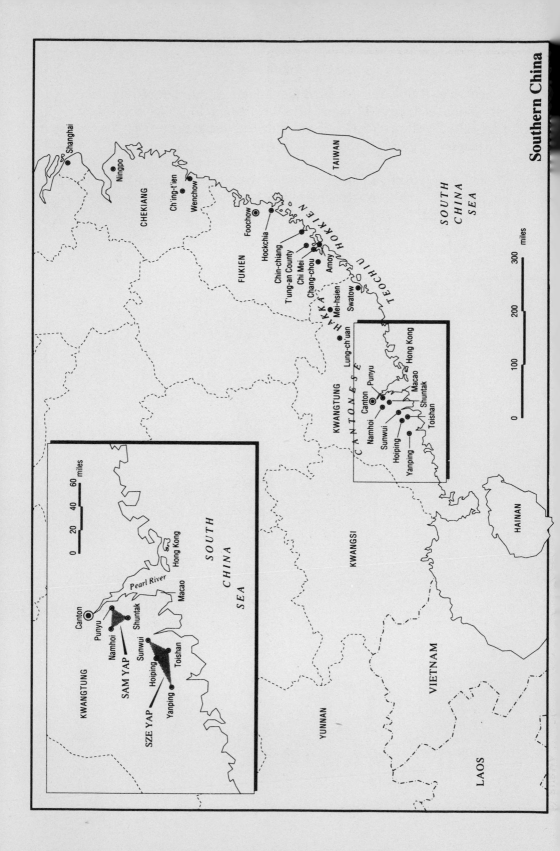

Southern China

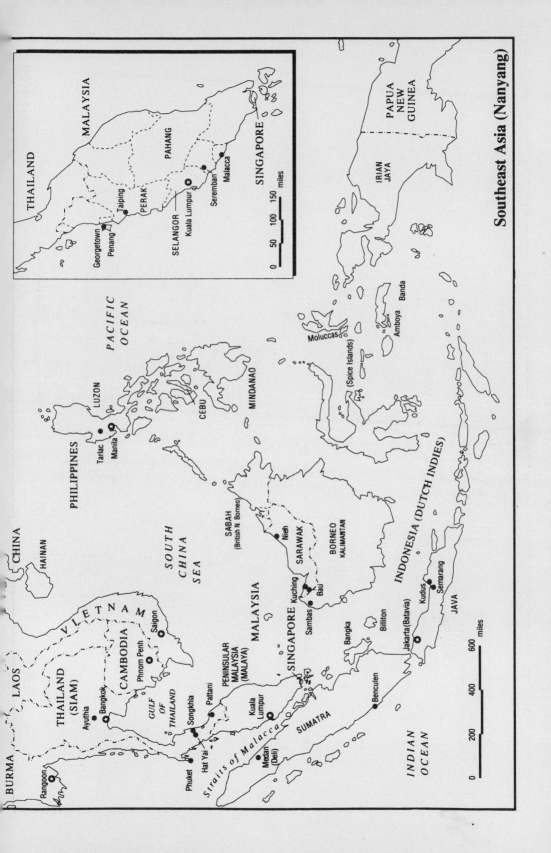

Southeast Asia (Nanyang)

PART ONE

c.1500–1870

CHAPTER ONE

Pioneers

Ch'en Jung-tse, born 1549, later moved to Luzon,
died and buried there in 1592.
Ch'en Shih-hsu, born 1643, proceeded to Jakarta to trade,
died and buried there in 1687.
K'o Ching-chou, born 1628, proceeded to Japan,
died and buried there in 1690.[1]

These are entries in the genealogical records of three families in Chin-chiang County, a spring of Chinese emigration in southern Fukien province. It is always hard to conjure up from the past the lives of the humble and forgotten, and we know nothing about these men beyond the bare facts of their birth and death and emigration. But we know something about the larger phenomenon of which they formed a part, and we may see them as forerunners, three of the millions of Chinese who settled in foreign lands over the centuries.

They were born in the Ming dynasty, the last but one of the imperial houses in China. The Ming was an empire of great *élan* and splendour, and it was during its first forty years that Chinese naval power reached an apogee. Between 1405 and 1433, in a spectacular display of seamanship, seven imperial expeditions sailed into the waters of Southeast Asia and the Indian Ocean, calling at some forty states and enrolling many of them as Chinese tributaries. The admiral who commanded these fleets was a brilliant navigator called Cheng Ho, a Muslim who held the post of Grand Eunuch of San Pao (Three Jewels). They were stupendous journeys, even judged by the standards of the twentieth century: each fleet is said to have included as many as sixty vessels and twenty-seven thousand men. The first of the voyages took them to Java, Sumatra, Malacca, Siam, Ceylon and the west coast of southern India. Later the fleets ventured as far as the Persian Gulf, Aden, East Africa and the south coast of Arabia. Made more than sixty years before Vasco da Gama rounded the Cape of Good Hope and discovered the Indian Ocean, Cheng Ho's expeditions, had they been fired by a zeal equal to that of their Iberian counterparts, might well have made the Chinese supreme in the seas between Burma and Goa. But the journeys proved a drain on the nation, and what Cheng Ho had started was never followed up. China never became a sea power, nor did it, as imperial European nations were later to do, sponsor colonies or movements of overseas migration.

What Cheng Ho did was to make so deep an impression on the imagination of the Chinese settled in Southeast Asia that he has been deified there, and the cult which formed around the name of San Pao Kung, Three-Jewel Lord, survives to this day. At home, in popular ballads and folk songs, the romance of these journeys took on a fabulous quality; and the exotic countries visited in Nanyang, the 'Southern Ocean', appeared as an alluring eldorado in the miraculous tales told to children.[2] Books were published, of which the most famous were *Treatise on the Barbarian Kingdoms of the Western Oceans, Marvels Discovered by the Boat Bound for the Galaxy* and *Marvels of the Oceans.* And yet to the seafaring Chinese of the southern coasts, Nanyang, the Chinese name for what we now know as Southeast Asia, was hardly *terra incognita*. It was where the commerce and contacts of the Chinese and Arab worlds intersected; the place where, for centuries, Chinese traders had sought the rare and exotic products cherished by the court and noble circles. Trade and tribute from Borneo, Malacca, Sumatra, Java and the northern islands of the Philippines had flowed along its seaways to the Chinese empire long before the journeys of Cheng Ho. But the admiral's expeditions must have opened the eyes of many more Chinese to the offerings and trading possibilities of the region.

As well as showing the flag, Cheng Ho's expeditions made it their business to gather tribute. Tribute grew out of the ancient distinction between Chinese and Barbarian. This was linked to the idea that the Chinese Emperor was the 'Son of Heaven', a sovereign who owed his position to the Mandate of Heaven. As the intermediary between Heaven and Man, the Chinese Emperor was universally pre-eminent; for just as there are not two suns in the sky, Confucius is supposed to have said, so there are not two Sons of Heaven on earth. The empire, the Chinese believed, must be universal and coextensive with civilization: they called it All Under Heaven, a term which they used (and still use) as a synonym for 'all the world'. Beyond the frontiers of the empire, or the civilized world as the Chinese knew it, were barbarian peoples who were only awaiting the time when they too would receive the benefits of the Son of Heaven's rule. And when the Emperor conquered the territories bordering the four sides of the empire, he was merely assuming control of what, as the ruler of All Under Heaven, he could legitimately claim as his.

Such a view of the world, evolved in the course of China's age-long encounters with the rude tribes about its borders, made for a distinct pattern of foreign relations: the empire recognized no other ruler as sovereign, and admitted no other state to equality. All other peoples were country cousins: vassals who, if they were to be admitted to the charmed circle of the Chinese scheme of things, acknowledged China's suzerainty and rendered tribute. Tribute-bearing missions were very well treated at the Chinese capital, handsomely housed and fed, feasted at the Emperor's table, and generously presented with gifts for themselves and for their rulers back home. But they were never left in any doubt about their inferior status, for once they found themselves at court, there was no escaping the ceremonial performance of the kowtow, a series of three separate kneelings and prostrations made to the sound of the usher barking 'Kneel!' 'Fall prostrate!', 'Rise to your knees!', 'Fall prostrate!', and so on.

On the face of it the Chinese court did not stand to gain much from the tribute system: its gifts and hospitality were, if anything, costlier than the offerings of local produce brought by the tributary missions. Exotic curiosities like the giraffes brought from Africa might have caught the Emperor's fancy, but they hardly benefited the imperial treasury. If the system paid, to the Chinese court it paid in symbolic, political and diplomatic kind. To the foreigner, it was a supremely convenient channel for trade. Trade was what brought the foreign embassies to the Chinese capital year after year, decade after decade; in the tribute missions were merchants acting either on their own behalf or as agents for their rulers, and much buying and selling would take place at the border and in the Chinese capital, where bazaars were held for this very purpose.[3]

All this was imperial trade, official trade. It was only a part, and an increasingly small part at that, of Chinese commercial expansion into the Southern Ocean. As the fifteenth and sixteenth centuries proceeded, as Chinese naval supremacy fell off from the peak represented by Cheng Ho's journeys, more and more hopeful private traders – the likes of Ch'en Shih-hsu in fact – were lured to take their chances overseas. Indeed private maritime trade never seemed livelier than in the sixteenth century, when the Ming, now grown insular and inward-looking, had all but withdrawn from the sea.

For much of the time, the private merchants who traded overseas did so in violation of imperial decree; until a system of licensed private trade replaced it in 1567, all private overseas trade was banned, and any Chinese merchant who ventured abroad made himself literally an outlaw.4 The scourge of the *wo-k'ou*, the 'dwarf pirates' of Japan, accounted as much as anything for the imperial policy. Not pirates in the strictest sense, since they never operated on the high seas but plundered the coastal settlements, these marauders were by no means all Japanese; though the campaigns were launched from Japan and backed by Japanese military equipment and know-how, Koreans, Vietnamese, Sumatrans, Malays, Portuguese and the coastal Chinese themselves all took part in the raids.

Furthermore, it was difficult to know where piracy ended and contraband trading began. Indeed, foreign trade was simply one vast smuggling operation, and many an adventurer was simultaneously a freebooter and a trader-emigrant. Many of the mandarins in the southern ports were persuaded to turn a blind eye – how else were the people to live? But official collusion was never total, and there were many who conducted overseas trade in open defiance of the law and then found themselves harassed and blackmailed on their return to China.

Some of the first places abroad to be settled by the Chinese were thus freebooters' lairs and havens. A well-known example was Taiwan, an island off the southern coast of Fukien province, not annexed by the Chinese empire until 1683. With the removal of the trade restrictions the well-beaten path between Fukien province and Taiwan was followed by merchants, hunters, artisans and farmers.5 Another favourite anchorage of the sea rovers was Pattani, a port in what is now southern Thailand. In the sixteenth century it served as the headquarters of a number of Chinese sea pirates, notably the notorious Lin Tao-ch'ien, a wanted outlaw who escaped to Siam from Fukien with a band of some two thousand men. These pirates became the nucleus of a Chinese colony in Pattani, from which port they and other buccaneer bands plotted their raids on the China coast, and there is a tradition that Lin married the daughter of a Malay chief and became a ruler himself.6

A fair amount of overseas Chinese settlement arose out of the junk trade, with the long-distance seamen putting down roots in the foreign countries with which they regularly traded. While most of the traders went to Nanyang as commercial birds of passage, some chose to become settlers. It was seaborne trade that gave life to the first of the overseas

Chinese communities of any size to be founded – the one in Manila, where silks and porcelain bound for the New World were exchanged for silver shipped by the transpacific galleons from Acapulco.

While reaching out eagerly to the trading opportunities in the Southern Ocean, the Chinese also had to emigrate to escape political troubles at home. In 1644, the house of Ming fell to alien invaders from the north, the Manchu founders of the Ch'ing dynasty. From the far south, where the resistance to the Manchus did not end for some decades, thousands of Chinese fled to Taiwan, the Philippines and other sanctuaries in Nanyang. Large numbers of Ming loyalists arrived and settled in Indochina, long a place of refuge for fugitive supporters of fallen Chinese dynasties.[7]

The chief challenge to Manchu supremacy came from Koxinga, the son of a Japanese mother and a Chinese trader-buccaneer from Fukien province. In Taiwan, which he made his base for his resistance campaign, Koxinga has remained a folk hero to this day. The campaign was a southern affair with a Nanyang dimension to it: Koxinga's father was one of those Fukienese traders who made a fortune from the trade with Southeast Asia; and Koxinga and other Ming loyalists fought the Manchus with the support they drew from Vietnam and the Philippines, the funds they tapped from the profits of the Nanyang trade, and the naval power they commanded from Nanyang shipping.[8] The Manchus couldn't know that they were seeing a pattern emerge that was going to repeat itself: if the southerners, exploiting their links with Nanyang, were the last Chinese to submit to their rule, it was also southerners who, with the support of sympathizers among the Chinese abroad, started the revolution that toppled the Manchus in 1911.

In the course of the protracted struggle against Koxinga, the Manchus decreed that all of the coastal regions be evacuated and the population moved several miles inland. This was the great Boundary Shift of 1661, when travel was banned and the southern coasts became a no man's land.[9] The Manchus looked to these measures to put the sea-roaming Ming loyalists out of reach of food and supplies and finally to break their resistance. They succeeded, but it was a tragedy for the local inhabitants, who saw their boats destroyed, and their villages and towns razed to the ground – an early instance of the 'scorched earth' tactics that virtually halted China's maritime trading activities and left the way open for the intrusion of European powers (Portugal, Spain and Holland) into East and Southeast Asian waters. The policy made refugees of the coastal inhabitants, and many of those who found themselves stripped of home and land left to make a new life abroad.

With the conquest of Taiwan, the Manchus lifted the restrictions on foreign trade, but by and large the government was averse to the emigration of its subjects. The Manchus, like the Ming rulers before them, were taking no chances: overseas colonies might become the resort of the disaffected and hotbeds of seditious conspiracy; sea captains might go and create independent and rebellious navies. The Manchus were also on guard against the pirates who continued to infest the coast and who posed such a danger to shipping that the wives and relatives the emigrants had left behind them in China were forbidden to travel abroad to join them.[10] If those who had managed to slip away had any thoughts of returning to China, the edict of 1712, which declared that the Chinese government 'shall request foreign governments to have those Chinese who have been abroad repatriated so that they may be executed',[11] soon made them think twice. The laws were like this for another one and a half centuries, give or take an amendment or two. As is clear from a regulation in force in 1799, all you had to do to be branded a rebel and enemy was to leave the country:

> All officers of government, soldiers, and private citizens,
> who clandestinely proceed to sea to trade, or who remove to
> foreign islands for the purpose of inhabiting and cultivating
> the same, shall be punished according to the law against
> communicating with rebels and enemies, and consequently
> suffer death by being beheaded. The governors of cities of
> the second and third orders, shall likewise be beheaded when
> found guilty of combining with, or artfully conniving at, the
> conduct of such persons.[12]

Strategic considerations played their part in the government's stand against emigration, but there was a Confucian streak to its policy as well. In the traditional ordering of society, the layers were, from top to bottom: scholars, farmers, artisans and merchants. There were periods in Chinese history when merchants were blatantly discriminated against, lumped with butchers and sorcerers and other despised groups, and forbidden to wear silk or sit the civil service examinations. Though money has a way of making a gentleman out of a merchant, and of blurring social distinctions, still the spectacle of animated trading rarely gladdened the heart of a true Confucian mandarin. The British empire showed what a commercial asset the British flag could be; the private Chinese trader, on the other hand, never had the assurance of official backing. Besides, it was probably quite difficult for the court, doubtless chauvinist to a man, to see why anyone should want to leave China at all.

Those determined enough to evade the emigration ban did. The laws were widely ignored and the seaways between the Southeast Asian ports remained busy with trade junks. The trading activities were given a boost by the arrival of the European powers on Southeast Asian shores, but it was not until the high colonial era of the nineteenth century, with the large-scale exploitation of the hinterland and the white man's assumption of imperial responsibilities, that the tides of Chinese migration to Southeast Asia were given their strongest impetus.

If the Chinese peopling of Southeast Asia in the nineteenth and twentieth centuries was the later phase of a Chinese commercial expansion that had begun much earlier, it was also the southward overspill of Chinese from their original homeland in central and northern China. The historical empire was much smaller than the 'China' that we think of today. Migration followed by colonization over the centuries had greatly extended the areas of Chinese settlement, Chinese culture and Chinese political power from their original core in the middle valley of the Yellow River. The Chinese world had grown ever larger by the absorption of what were once borderlands, and by the sinicization of their aboriginal inhabitants. The advancing frontier did not stop at the sea, but continued to offshore islands like Taiwan. Later it spread out of the southern shores still further along the trade routes to Southeast Asia. This southward movement throughout three thousand years of history, a historian has written, 'has something in common with the westward movement of American history and the eastward movement of Russian history'.[13]

Had there been national boundaries such as distinguish French, Italians, Spaniards and Portuguese in Europe, Chinese diversity would be much more obvious than it is. Repeated conquests by the barbarians of the northern steppes, migration, transfers of population or simple contacts between neighbours have led to much intermingling, and even the individual of recognizably Han (ethnic Chinese) identity is of very mixed ancestry. Mongols, Turks, Miaos, Yaos or Mon-Khmers could all have left a trace in his blood. The idea of foreign blood is highly distasteful to a people so strongly imbued with a sense of Chinese and Barbarian, Us and Them, and it was partly to show

how clean one's family record was, how indisputable the blood ties to the original Han core, that the Chinese became the world's most obsessional genealogists. Within two hundred years of the barbarian invasions of the third and fourth centuries, we learn, no fewer than forty-one systematic treaties on genealogy, the longest comprising 690 chapters, appeared in book form.[14]

That the Chinese were ancestor worshippers was another reason for keeping genealogical records. The Chinese devotion to parents would be judged neurotic in the West, but central to the pattern of Chinese society was filial piety, the reverencing of parents while they were alive, the worship of their spirits when they were dead. Any family rich enough to maintain one would have a clan hall or ancestral temple, bristling with spirit tablets arranged in order of generational seniority, each inscribed with the name of a male ancestor. Scrolls and plaques would look down from eaves and pillars, proclaiming the imperial academic degrees, public honours, citations and official ranks accorded the more illustrious sons of the family. Mottoes and exhortations left by departed ancestors would urge posterity to even greater glory. Here, twice a year, kinsmen gathered to conduct ancestral worship. These were grand occasions, with only men participating. They fostered a sense of belonging and continuity, and rallied individuals around a common focus of loyalty. All this was augmented by the genealogical record, periodically updated for the edification of the family.

Obviously, the further back the genealogy reached the better. To be really and truly Chinese, it was commonly believed, one had to trace one's ancestry to the progenitor of the Chinese race. The progenitor of the Chinese race was, and still is, held to be the Yellow Emperor Huang Ti, one of the culture heroes of Chinese mythology. It doesn't much matter that his existence is a matter not of attested fact but of misty legend; the Yellow Emperor still has his burial place in Huang-ling, a small town beside a Yellow River tributary in the ancient Chinese heartland. His shrine is still there, up a muddy climb from the town, standing silent among its little grove of old trees, yellow earth all around. When I was there I found that some overseas Chinese visitors had left a wreath. The black brush-strokes of the inscription read, 'To the father of our race'. It is hard to know whether these people thought themselves descended from the Yellow Emperor in a biological sense, or merely in a symbolic one, but it is extraordinary how many overseas Chinese will still produce genealogies to demonstrate to you their unchallengeable descent from Huang Ti.

Consider the Lo family, neighbours and close friends of my family in North Borneo. Jenny Lo, the eldest daughter, lives in London and works as a producer with the BBC. Her father, Peter Lo, is a lawyer and a former leader of government. His father, an orphan, arrived as a little boy with his elder brother from Lung-ch'uan, an enclave of Hakka speakers (of whom more below) in Kwangtung province. Family lore has it that the lads travelled as stowaways on a ship carrying fellow Lo clansmen to Hong Kong. That they finally found their way to North Borneo is not surprising, since Hakka speakers have been migrating there since the eighteenth century. They were converts to Roman Catholicism, and this is not surprising either, Lung-ch'uan being an area of zealous European missionary activity. I came by a copy of the Lo genealogy, and found the line of descent traced through a number of surname changes all the way back to the Yellow Emperor. This was not unexpected, because by then I had consulted Chinese clan genealogies in Bangkok, Manila, Hong Kong, Singapore, London and San Francisco, and I had found that, whether the surname was Chang, or Liu, or Wang, or Wu, all named the Yellow Emperor as their patriarch.

Besides Huang Ti, the Chinese have historically acknowledged Yen Ti, or Emperor Yen, as their founding ancestor. Yen Ti is better known as Shen Nung, or the god of husbandry, and is the one who is mentioned whenever Chinese medical science is discussed; for he was the one who, according to tradition, tasted the flavour of hundreds of herbs and brought medicine and pharmacology into existence. Every child who has been through Chinese school will have heard of Huang Ti or Yen Ti, and one would be an illiterate indeed if one didn't know that 'Descendants of the Yellow Emperor' and 'Sons and Grandsons of Huang Ti and Yen Ti' were synonyms for the Chinese race. Greeting an overseas Chinese, no matter how removed he may be from his ancestral roots, a native of China will say, 'Ah, but we're all Sons of the Yellow Emperor,' rather as one might say, 'We're all brothers under the skin.'

The theory that all Chinese are ultimately descended from a common ancestor rests on the tradition that the Yellow Emperor had twenty-five sons, fourteen of whom were given distinct surnames by their father. It is dimly supposed that all Chinese names are derived in some way from the fourteen created by the Yellow Emperor; and contriving to demonstrate a connection to these has kept clan genealogists busy for centuries. No one knows how many Chinese surnames there are, but a scholar who took the trouble to count the ones listed in two editions of a Ming biographical dictionary came up with the figures 3,736 and 4,657.[15] Some of these would once have been official titles or ranks in the family; others were place-names, the province or district of birth. Still others were royal family names bestowed by the Emperor as an honour on loyal ministers and barbarian chieftains. Many who bore Chinese surnames were not Chinese at all, but barbarians who, to enhance their social acceptability, substituted their polysyllabic tribal names for monosyllabic Chinese ones. All this made for confused genealogies. To assume that all those who bear the same surname share a common origin is patently absurd, but the idea that every Li, say, is related to every other Li from the same region has nevertheless a tenacious hold on the minds of the Chinese. As we shall see, one of the most remarkable of the social structures evolved by the immigrant Chinese were 'same-surname associations', groupings of men bearing a common surname. A consciousness of shared origin no doubt compensated for the feeling of being lost in a new country. My own experience probably resembled that of a typical new immigrant. Arriving in Manila to research the Chinese community, I made my way, as a first step towards penetrating the community, to the city's Chinatown, where Chinese signboards told me that there were same-surname associations about. Enquiries at one of these revealed the existence of a Pan Family Association. Now Pan is a common enough surname, no more unusual than Pugh or Paine. In no way was I related to the Pans in Manila, who were of southern Fukien stock, hailing from an altogether different part of China, but I was welcomed like a clanswoman all the same, invited to a 'clan' banquet and given every assistance.

Mobility has often prompted curiosity in uprooted people about their ancestry, and an ordinary transplanted Chinese, as anxious as the next man to appear a little less ordinary, was apt to take a greater pride in his origins than his cousins at home. Nor was mobility the only reason for the appeal of genealogy. An intense preoccupation with origins and identity is typical of people who live on the edge of things, away from the cultural or national centre; and Chinese emigrants, whether they ended up in Southeast Asia or in America, came overwhelmingly from Fukien and Kwangtung, both peripheral areas. In medieval times, even a Han might be despised by chauvinistic northerners if he had not been born in the Yellow River heartland.[16] In people of the far south, the feeling that north is best has persisted into our own times.

The two provinces which specialize in sending people abroad, Fukien and Kwangtung, lie next to each other. A glance at the map reveals Fukien to be a coastal area about the size of England, lying across the southeastern rim of the Chinese land mass, just above the Tropic of Cancer, and divided from the island of Taiwan by a narrow strait. To its northeast straggle the islands of Japan, to its southeast the archipelago of the Philippines. With mountains covering much of it, Fukien had little land fertile enough to reward intensive agricultural effort, and by about 1500 the province had less cultivated land per person than any other in China, its half-acre per head being roughly half the national average.[17] The annals show it to have been struck again and again by famine, 228 times in the seventeenth century, 158 in the eighteenth, a total of 888 times in the 844 years between 1068 and 1911.[18] Fukien was the home of some fine teas, but the crop had only to fail once and the fortunes of a tea-growing family would be devastated at a blow. You could almost tell how many people were going to emigrate by the size and quality of the ordinary harvests; in the villages they talked of a forty, thirty, twenty or nobody crop – meaning that the crop was such that forty, thirty or twenty of their clan would have to emigrate, or that the crop was so good that nobody did.[19] It was an uncertain living, made more uncertain by overseas market fluctuations; in the nineteenth century, for example, the replacement on Western markets of Chinese tea by the Indian and Ceylon varieties set off a wave of emigration.

The sea, though, was always there, and to the coastal Fukienese fishing and seafaring were obvious callings. The junk trade to Southeast Asia was not a creation from scratch, but grew out of the busy coastal shipping at home. Though it took guts to go adventuring in Nanyang, the sailors were hardly beginners; years of sailing to north China (over-land travel was rendered exceedingly difficult by south China's moun-tains) had done much to prepare them. We have it from Portuguese mariners that Fukienese pilots were the finest in East Asian waters.

In Chinese terms Fukien and Kwangtung are areas of fairly recent settlement by Han Chinese; they were cultural borderlands, places of in-migration by northern Chinese. Canton, later to become the provincial capital of Kwangtung, was a sort of colonial outpost of the Chinese empire. Today we think of Kwangtung as a province of China, but in the seventh and tenth centuries it was part of an entity stretching all the way to northern Vietnam, a territory about the size of California, known by the old name Nan-yueh, or, in the Vietnamese pronunciation, Nam-viet. The natives were not Chinese at all, but aboriginals of uncertain extraction. 'Southern heathen' or 'barbarian' were the names the Chinese gave them, the Chinese having never had any myths about the Noble Savage: savages were simply savages. The Thais, the Mon-Khmers, the Miaos with their dog and tiger cults – these were people who had somehow to be fitted into the Chinese scheme of things, to be absorbed and made Chinese. The whole picture, writes the historian Edward Schafer, 'reminds us strongly of California before the invasions of the Spanish and the Yankees'.[20] The bulk of the aborigines *were* sinicized, so that there are Cantonese today who, though they may call themselves Chinese, are actually more closely related in blood to the inhabitants of Vietnam, Laos and Cambodia than to those of northern or central China.

Racial stock, landscape, climate and historical experience have kept the people of Fukien and Kwangtung recognizably Fukienese and Cantonese. While the natives of Fukien struck Spanish visitors to the coast in the sixteenth century as 'white and well-built', the Cantonese were reported to be 'brown like Berbers'. They posed a distinct contrast to the people of the inland provinces, some of whom seemed to the Spaniards to be as light-skinned as themselves, and others to be 'more yellow and red' like the Germans.[21] Anthropometric measurements made in our own century show the Fukienese to be slightly taller and heavier than the Cantonese, though both are apt to be shorter and lighter than the people of the Yellow and Yangtze river valleys.[22] The aquiline form of nose, common among Chinese of the lower Yangtze valley, was found to be rare among the people of Kwangtung province, where a 'new form of nose', characterized by large nostrils and 'calling to mind the form of nose well known among some southern ethnical groups, let us say, of a Negrito origin', has been noted by anthropologists.[23]

But above all it is speech that distinguishes one community of Chinese from another. Linguistically northern China is a fairly homogeneous block, with the majority of people speaking one or another form of Mandarin, the language of Peking. But the south is a Babel, and if each were to speak only his own local dialect, a man of Canton and a man of southern Fukien would have as much difficulty understanding each other, or speakers of Mandarin and Shanghainese for that matter, as speakers of Portuguese, Spanish, Italian and French. A Mr Ch'en in Mandarin would be a Mr Tan in the southern Fukien dialect; a Miss Aw Boon Bee in southern Fukienese would be a Miss Wu Man Mei to a Cantonese. A common tongue gives its speakers membership of a mutual-help fraternity, and Mr Tan and Miss Aw are far more likely to meet kindness and indulgence where the southern Fukien dialect is spoken than where Cantonese is.

In Southeast Asia Miss Aw or Mr Tan, or any southern Fukienese, would be called a Hokkien (which is simply the local pronunciation of Fukien). One who originates from the area of the Pearl River delta in Kwangtung province would be called a Cantonese speaker or simply a Cantonese. But just to complicate matters, there's Cantonese and Cantonese. You could tell from a man's speech whether he is from a village in Sam Yap (Three Districts), the better-endowed counties around Canton, or from Sze Yap (Four Districts), the poorer and ruder area to the west of the delta. When an educated man from the Three Districts claims he can't understand a word of what a Four Districts peasant is saying, he is being snobbish of course, but also expressing a genuine difficulty. How is he to know that *doi*, for example, is really *tsai*, the word for 'bloke' in urbane Cantonese, or that *hyat* is really *sik*, his word for 'to eat'?

Compared to Mandarin the Cantonese tongue is remarkably conservative – in the sense that American English is conservative, resisting such changes as the long 'a' of 'can't' and 'path' that British English accepted more than a century ago, and clinging to the Elizabethan pronunciation of the vowel. And this, its relative closeness to archaic Chinese, is frequently invoked by Cantonese speakers, not without an element of defensiveness, as proof of their superiority. Seldom does one meet a people more persuaded of their own uniqueness. Forgetting the aboriginal genes that run in their veins, Cantonese are quick to claim that they are the most Chinese of Chinese, of a purer pedigree than the northerners whose blood has been tainted by intermarriage with Mongol and Manchu barbarians.

Yet another of the large emigrant tribes is the Teochius, a speech group concentrated in a crescent around the port of Swatow, only thirty-eight miles from the Fukien border in Kwangtung province. The Teochius had crossed in batches into eastern Kwangtung from Fukien between the ninth and fifteenth centuries. Teochiu folkways still show cultural links with Fukien's and as a dialect Teochiu is related to Hokkien.[24]

Southern Fukien was also the original home of the Chinese on Hainan, an offshore tropical island suspended, rather as Ceylon is from India, from the southernmost tip of Kwangtung province. In the eyes of any other people, Hainan, with its palm and coconut trees, might well have appeared as a paradise isle, but to Chinese from the cultural heartland, who could only think of it as a place of banishment and exile, it was a tropical inferno, the home of poisonous snakes, forest goblins and shoeless aborigines.[25] The island, poorly developed agriculturally, sent many of its people overseas; the Chinese settlers of Hainan had migrated to the island by sea in the first place, and now they went further in search of new lives in Nanyang, in the hope that they could fare better.

Contributing yet another strand to the patchwork of overseas Chinese speech and customs were the Hakkas, latecomers to the southernmost provinces, moving into Fukien and Kwangtung in two separate migrations: during the tenth century, and between the twelfth and thirteenth centuries. The Hakkas, whose name means 'guest families', have been described as the gypsies of China, people who live side by side with speakers of different dialects in enclaves scattered across six southern provinces, without a homeland of their own. They were a rugged lot, and even their women had to be hardy. Little wonder that the Hakkas were the only Chinese to refrain altogether from binding their daughters' feet into the 'golden lilies' that were *de rigueur* everywhere else. One thing Hakka women were not was dainty.

Men moving across great distances into an unknown landscape, assailed by the hostility of settlers who have preceded them, band together; and if Hakkas were (and still are) thought a very clannish people, they had good reasons to be. The banding-together took a palpably defensive form, in communal living and communal housing. Their dwellings, still to be seen today in a border area in Fukien province, are extraordinary constructions, rising out of the countryside like veritable fortresses, gigantic, multi-storied, round. They are built to a circular plan, with a thick outer wall of tamped earth pierced by tiny squint-holes, presenting a resolutely sealed and embattled look to the world. In the walled complex, an entire community, numbering six to seven hundred inhabitants, could be concentrated.

It was no easy matter to live among the Cantonese, to contend for land and water. Feuds were easily ignited in such an atmosphere, and there evolved a tradition of armed fighting between the migrant and the settler. We read of a period of prolonged fighting between the two in the years 1855–67, a war in which about half a million people are said to have lost their lives.[26] It is not hard to see why the Hakkas emigrated to Nanyang. In China they were pushed on to marginal land, hilly country rejected by those who had got there first.

The overseas Chinese world, then, was very far from a microcosm of the Chinese world, for they were mostly people from the two maritime provinces who migrated overseas, and few went from the Mandarin-speaking areas in northern China, and practically none at all from the western or far western provinces. Because migrants go where they are likely to find their own kind, the overseas communities evolved as places of strong linguistic affinities – Hokkiens with Hokkiens, Teochius with Teochius, Hakkas with Hakkas. Geo-history played its part in determining which group went where, as did patterns of shipping. As early emigrants to Nanyang the Hokkiens far outnumbered the Cantonese; this may be because, while the world converged upon Canton, the one Chinese port where the foreigner could almost invariably count on being admitted, foreign ships were not so ready to come to the coast of southern Fukien, where they could not always be sure of finding the ports open to them, and so it was the natives themselves who had to sail out in search of foreign commerce.[27] The Manchu rulers were presently to restrict all foreign merchants to Canton, so that all trade from southern Fukien came to be carried in Hokkien junks, by Hokkien seamen.

One can see from a glance at a map why Hokkiens predominated in Manila: with a good wind, it was just three days' sail by junk from a Fukien port to the Philippines.[28] By 1870, a regular and direct passenger service by steamer had been established between the southern Fukien port of Amoy and Singapore, and this probably explains why so many Hokkiens turned up in Singapore and in the places served by the Singapore port – Malaya, Java, Burma, Sumatra and southern Siam. Though they went to southern Siam in fairly large numbers, they were not drawn to Bangkok in central Siam, no regular direct passenger traffic having been established between that city and Amoy.[29]

Bangkok has long been the turf of the Teochius, and this has come of a pattern set in the second half of the eighteenth century, when Siam was ruled by the colourful Taksin, the son of a Chinese father and a Thai mother. Half-Teochiu himself, Taksin was happy enough to encourage the immigration of Teochius to Siam, assuring them of a predominance which has prevailed from those times to today. The Hakkas, found all over Southeast Asia, were the pioneers of Borneo, a destination others shunned. As for the Cantonese, the stream of their emigration flowed at its strongest to America, for the Pearl River delta had the advantage of Hong Kong on its doorstep, and as a conduit with many far-flung connections the port readily channelled migrants to the furthest shores. The preponderance today of Chinese Americans tracing their origins to the Four Districts, particularly to Toishan, harks back to those early movements. Lumpen workers, the human fodder of organized labour migration, were more plentiful there than in the richer Three Districts, where fewer hands were callused, and fewer needed to break their bodies in foreign countries.

Once a Chinese from a particular area had established a foothold in a foreign country, he either sent for, or else returned to China to fetch, a young son or nephew from his native village to share in the new opportunities – or, if he had achieved a measure of success, to help him with his business. As other relatives came over, so a community of families from the same native place was built up. Back in the village, emigration became a way of life, with son following father or nephew following uncle as a matter of routine, in a process specialists call chain migration. It was no accident that, in four Philippine provinces where census samples were taken in the nineteenth century, eight out of every ten immigrant Chinese were found to have originated from one of only four counties in southern Fukien; or that among the immigrants from this area, twelve surnames, chief among them Tan, were numerically predominant.[30]

It is a curious fact that a very small range of surnames is to be found among the Chinese abroad; one could count only forty-eight, for example, in the Singapore telephone directory in 1949;[31] and it is widely known among the Chinese in America that they are mostly called Wong in Stockton, Fong in Sacramento, Hom in San Diego and Tang in Phoenix. This has to do with the provenance of the immigrants, for Fukien and Kwangtung were remarkable in China for their great clan-villages. Whereas elsewhere in China clans (or lineages as they are called by anthropologists) were commonly but one component of a village, in Fukien and Kwangtung the clan *was* the village, with the members all bearing the same surname, and holding property in common. Some of the settlements were mere hamlets, others villages of several thousand inhabitants.[32] Not all of them went as far back as twenty or twenty-five generations, but a great many did, and a lineage that traced its descent to, say, the end of the sixteenth century would be considered recent. The symbols of clan continuity were the rites and paraphernalia of ancestral worship and the genealogical records. Many clans were interdependent, linking themselves through marriage, or on the basis of certain traditional alliances of surnames – the Changs,

Kuans and Lius, for instance, would get together on the strength of the fabled blood brotherhood of Chang Fei, Kuan Yu and Liu Pei, the three heroes of the historical romance on which whole generations of Chinese have been nourished, *The Story of the Three Kingdoms.*

The villages, then, were single-surname settlements; and, however remote the actual genealogical connections they traced between them, the assumption that they were ultimately descended from a joint ancestor made of the inhabitants, for all their differences of wealth and status, a united people. One clansman might be a rich landowner, another a poor tenant farmer, but in the eyes of outsiders they were one. Theirs was a combination of economic and political advantage, and they closed ranks in times of trouble. Trouble was endemic in Fukien and Kwangtung, where clans were always coming to blows and life was one long feud. These places had an unsavoury reputation for turbulence, and their people for a bellicosity so terrible that it had earned them a name for barbarism.[33] No visitor to the area could miss the warlike look of the villages, which were veritable garrisoned fortresses. One writer who wandered as far as the Teochiu homeland in the middle of the nineteenth century reported 'a state of chronic anarchy' in all the neighbouring country: 'the villages, towns, and hamlets were all walled, and each seemed prepared to fight with its neighbour. There were villages, certainly not a quarter of a mile distant from each other, both surrounded with distinct walls about sixteen to twenty feet high . . .'[34] The place was ungovernable, said the Viceroy of Fukien in a report to the Emperor, owing to 'the cruel, fierce, and quarrelsome dispositions and habits of the people'.[35] It was no better in the neighbouring province, where, reported the Governor in 1828, the law counted for nothing, the people delighted so much in litigation, and had so little 'regard for the preservation of life'.[36] The larger clans, he complained, simply seized the best lands and the most useful streams for irrigation at the expense of the smaller clans, whose women they also insulted. The most trifling personal slight could flame into a bloody affray, but by and large the fights turned on inter-village rivalries, and were occasions for adjusting the balance of power among the rural communities. These fights had implications for emigration, for it was often the fate of prisoners taken in them to be sold off as forced emigrants for coolie labour overseas. It could not have been mere chance that made the most notoriously belligerent places the most copious founts of emigration.

The villagers made their belligerence felt in two ways: in their private feuding, and in their rebelliousness against the state. The southerners exuded a lively disrespect for authority, and we have seen their refractory spirit reflected in the refusal to accept the rule of the Manchu founders of the Ch'ing dynasty. The spirit of anti-Manchu resistance, if not its substance, lived on through the southern provinces' secret societies, and the most dramatic repository of political subversion was the triads, a rubric that covered three similar but separate societies: the Heaven and Earth Society, the Three in One Society and the Three Dots Society – collectively known as the fraternities of the Hung Men, the Vast Gate. Their watchword, 'Overthrow the Ch'ing and Restore the Ming', gave them a suggestion of political dedication and allowed them to pretend to more than banditry, but while they found their initial following among the uprooted of the cities and trade circuits, migrants, boatmen and vagabonds, they also attracted pirates, smugglers and bandits. The triads' myth-history traces their origin to a monastery in Fukien, but they were probably founded by Hokkien immigrants in Taiwan,[37] where their initial purpose seems to have been one of self-defence in communal feuding; they first emerged as an agency of self-protection in the feuding between Chinese from different districts of Fukien.[38] In the succeeding decades their activities proliferated rapidly on the mainland, where they staged rising after rising, and where their martial-arts practitioners found ready patronage among the feuding villages.

'Tonight we pledge ourselves before Heaven that the brethren in the whole universe shall be as if from one womb, as if begotten by one father, as if nourished by one mother, and as if they were of one stock and origin.'[39] By this blood oath, pledged in the initiation ceremony, unrelated men were turned into ritual brothers, who were then expected to behave as brothers did. The secret society was a surrogate clan, and it was surely as a substitute for the families left behind that it found so welcoming a lodging in the immigrant Chinese communities. The arcanum of freemasonry – secret signs, passwords, initiation ritual, symbolisms, oaths, and other forms of hocus-pocus – had its fascinations and no doubt engendered romantic notions.

There was a clannishness evoking Sicilian *omertà*, but the spirit of fraternity was by no means universal, and wherever the triad lodges formed themselves, whether in Singapore or San Francisco, they were apt to do so in rival dialect groups. Grouping by dialect was the first and the most spontaneous of the characteristics of the overseas Chinese community, and the special sentiment of the emigrants for their home district was reflected in the remarkable network of native-place or dialect associations which they established in all the places in which they settled. The pattern of interlocking loyalties and enmities in Fukien and Kwangtung society – between dialect group and dialect group, triad society and triad society, clan and clan – could not be exactly replicated abroad, but the tendency to fission, as we shall learn, survived the journeys across the seas.

For all their regional separatism, though, the expatriate Chinese were completely united in their passionate attachment to their homeland. Seeing their stay abroad as temporary, many awaited the day when they could return to their villages in swank after making good – or, to put it in the Chinese way, 'go home in silken robes'. For commitment to one's native place, one's ancestral home, few people could beat the Chinese. The word *hsiang*, which can mean a village, the countryside, one's home town or native place, is one of the most evocative words in the Chinese language, far more emotive than its equivalents in English. The best-known of all Chinese poems, especially among expatriate Chinese, is the one which ends with the word *hsiang*, 'home', written by the famous eighth-century poet Li Po:

> So bright a gleam at the foot of my bed –
> Could there have been a frost already?
> Lifting myself to look, I see that it is moonlight.
> Lowering my head, I dream that I am home.

The Chinese rootedness in his own native place, and his deep dislike of leaving his ancestral home, were aspects of the importance he attached to family. His devotion to his home village was an extension of his filial piety. To show care for aged parents in life, to mourn them properly in death, to perform rites before the ancestral shrine, to make ceremonial visits to the family grave – these were a man's principal filial duties, virtually impossible to discharge if one lived away from home. The assumption that a man's moorings were fixed in his native soil lies behind the old saw 'Falling leaves return to their roots' – that is, a sojourner in a foreign land comes home in the end. Every family who had any means at all would have a graveyard of its own, and if a man should die away from home, no effort would be spared in transporting the corpse back to the ancestral tomb.

Underlying the damper laid on emigration by the law of the empire was the feeling that those who left Chinese shores to live abroad were somehow unfilial. When the Dutch sent the Manchu Emperor an apology for their massacre of Chinese in Batavia in 1740 (see Chapter Two), he is reported to have replied that he was 'little solicitous for the fate of unworthy subjects who, in the pursuit of lucre, had quitted their country and abandoned the tombs of their ancestors'.[40] If emigrants from south China did not spill all over Nanyang in greater numbers before 1860, it was partly because to most Chinese, 'Being away from home one *li* [a third of a mile] is', as the proverb has it, 'not as good as being home.'

CHAPTER TWO

East Meets West

A new phase in the story of the overseas Chinese began with the arrival
of Europeans on the Far Eastern scene. Hungry for empire, and with
profit as their lodestar, Europe's imperial powers stimulated commerce
in Nanyang, creating chances of profit for migrant Chinese traders at the
same time as they enriched themselves. The European movement was of
a different character from Chinese migration, which was never officially
sponsored and never impelled by motives of empire-building.

Portugal was the first European power to arrive, and broadly speaking the sixteenth century was the period of Portuguese power in the Far
East. Spices were its main object, and a prime motive of Portuguese
maritime activity was to gain control of the trade of the Spiceries,
a group of islands amid the cluster we now call Indonesia. Spices
were greatly sought after because the methods of stock-raising then
employed in Europe were such that it was difficult to supply the market
with fresh meat in winter, when the pastures would have become too
thin for the sheep and cattle to fatten, and dried or preserved meat was
much more palatable when heavily flavoured with clove, cinnamon,
pepper, nutmeg and mace. Obtainable only from faraway islands in
the Eastern seas, these substances were naturally cherished, and nearly
every sixteenth-century European explorer, missionary, merchant and
chronicler who ever spoke of Asia spoke of the spice trade.[1]

For a base from which to begin their systematic incursion into the
Spiceries, the Portuguese chose Malacca, a settlement on the Malay
peninsula. Malacca was where the maritime routes linking the Indian
Ocean with the South China Sea and most of the sea lanes and the
river routes of profitable commerce intersected. Its prosperity was
built upon its geography, for it stands at the point where the monsoon
winds meet. A navigator sailing up from the Spiceries could let the
northeast monsoon push him through the narrow straits between the
peninsula and Sumatra and usher him to his landing at the port of
Malacca. There, after discharging his aromatic cargo and reloading
his craft with the rich commodities of the Middle East, he would
wait for the winds to change and let the southwest monsoon drive

him home. The most beguiling of the great oriental emporia, Malacca had been enlisted by Admiral Cheng Ho as a Chinese tributary. The Chinese had been visiting Malacca since the seventh century, when large numbers of traders found their way to the peninsula via Siam, Cambodia and Taiwan. Most of them travelled back and forth between these places, but a handful remained to make their permanent home in the peninsula.

Meeting Chinese traders in Malacca made the Portuguese reach out to China. They sent an envoy to Peking to conclude a trade agreement with the Emperor, but the mission was a failure, and all commerce with the Portuguese was officially banned. Undeterred, Portuguese seamen resorted to illicit trade, an operation in which they were abetted by the Chinese of both the coastal provinces and Malacca. Later, in about 1557, they were tacitly given leave, though quite unofficially, to establish a permanent trading station at Macao as a sort of outpost of the main mart in Malacca.

The Portuguese had a difficult time of it in their Eastern outposts, fighting disease, corruption, tropical torpor and their Malay and Muslim enemies. Their power waned as the century wore on, and Spain appeared as a rival in the Eastern seas. On his celebrated journey round the world in 1521, Magellan had touched at Cebu in the Philippines, where he had raised a large cross and baptized eight hundred natives on a single Sunday morning.[2] But it was only with the conquest of Mexico, which gave Spain a base on the Pacific side of the American continent, that the successful colonization of so distant a region as Southeast Asia was possible. It was a Spanish expedition sailing from Acapulco, the first of the many crossings between Mexico and the Philippines, which overcame the local Muslim sultans and in 1571 founded the city of Manila on Luzon, the largest island of the archipelago.

The Spaniards had come into contact with Chinese traders in the Philippines, and these encounters, coupled with the allure of the rich China trade, bolstered the hope that Spain might conquer and convert China. Missionaries were forbidden to enter China; by converting the Chinese traders in Manila, Spanish friars hoped they might eventually evangelize China. There is much truth in the saying that the Spanish conquest of the Philippines was effected by the Cross rather than by the sword, for the colonization of the islands was indeed harnessed to an ecclesiastical purpose. Braced for living in the rural tropics among the backward peasants by their proselytizing zeal, the Catholic priests were all-penetrating. They were the prime agents of Spanish authority and European civilization, and so inseparable did Church and crown become that the colony was one day to be described as a 'friarocracy'.[3]

Those who saw missionary possibilities in the Philippines saw opportunities of profit too. That Manila was a natural entrepôt for the China trade, a convenient way station between the Chinese coastlands and the New World, was certainly a reason for the Spanish conquest of the Philippines. By the late sixteenth century, more than twenty Chinese junks were bringing the wares of the empire to the islands every year – gunpowder, saltpetre, beautiful silks and cotton fabrics, and luxury articles of brass, copper and carved wood. Year after year, decade after decade, merchandise was brought over by Chinese junks for the two annual galleons that sailed to Mexico from Manila. The galleon trade was a thriving concern and it was the Chinese who handled the trans-shipment of silk and silver. The Spaniards simply waited for the yearly monsoon winds to bring the Chinese junks to Manila, where the cargoes of silk and other luxury goods were loaded on to the galleon bound for Mexico; on its return journey the Manila galleon brought Mexican silver to pay for the goods, and again it was the Chinese who carried it back to China. Later the junks were to be eclipsed by Western shipping, but no matter what the cargoes and vessels were, or which routes were taken, the trade would continue to be controlled by the Chinese, whether at the Manila end or at the Fukien and Hong Kong end.[4] Space in the galleon was divided into shares of a fixed size, and in selling these to shippers the Spanish community found plenty of scope for self-enrichment. The Chinese were happy enough to provide an outlet for all this money, and besides junk owners and sailors, retailers, artisans and market gardeners flocked to Manila.

To the southwest, the shores of what was to become Indonesia were, in the first half of the seventeenth century, becoming familiar with the greed and ambitions of a rival European power, the Dutch. The instrument of their power was the Dutch East India Company (Vereenigte Oost-Indische Compagnie, voc), a trading company that was also a state, the founder of modern South Africa and the progenitor of modern Indonesia. By capturing Malacca from the Portuguese in 1641, the voc had gained control of the vital straits, and by concentrating its naval power in the waters of the Indonesian archipelago it secured a virtual monopoly of the production and trade of the precious spices.

The main centre of the voc's trade was Batavia, one day to become the modern Jakarta, on the northern coast of Java. In Java the Dutch traders found themselves rivalled by the Chinese, who had been frequenting these shores in their junks since the twelfth century, and who had established busy ports and prosperous seasonal colonies in the archipelago.5 To extract what they could from the islands under their authority, which was widening with time and military conquest, the Dutch needed more labourers than were already settled in the Indies. For the peopling of the archipelago, some thought that no race in the world would do them better service than the Chinese. How the Chinese were to be brought to the archipelago is suggested by this note from one Dutch governor to another in 1623: 'it is requisite by this present monsoon', it said, 'to send another fleet to visit the coast of China and take prisoners as many men, women, and children as possible . . . for the peopling of Batavia, Amboyna, and Banda; . . . the ransom of the Chinese to be set at sixty ryals apiece; but by no means you must not suffer any women to return to China, or any other part out of the Company's jurisdiction, but with them to people the same.'6

Another blank space that had to be filled with labouring bands of Chinese was the Dutch colony at the Cape of Good Hope, founded in 1652 by Jan van Riebeeck of the voc. The Cape Colony, along with the Dutch settlement in Ceylon, became a sort of Botany Bay to which the undesirables of Batavia, vagrants and felons of Chinese as well as Indian and Javanese stock, were transported. Van Riebeeck's successor was no less eager for Chinese labour; in a letter he wrote to the authorities in Batavia in 1662, he said that he could do with twenty-five to thirty dirt-poor Chinese with knowledge of farming. He was not fussy; all he asked was that each Chinese work-horse be capable of doing the work of fifty African indigenes. Another letter besought Batavia to send free emigrant and convict alike, or any Chinese who could set his hand to tilling, carpentry, plaster work, bricklaying or pottery. The numbers of Chinese arrivals were never large, though exact figures would be difficult to determine, when the same man could appear as OnKo, OnKonko, Oguanko, Loguanko or Hoguanko in the records, which, naturally enough, were not unduly fussy about spelling.7

Yet another colony the Dutch tried to fill with Chinese transportees from Batavia was the island of Mauritius off the east coast of Africa. They failed there, and after they had abandoned it to pirates it was left to the French to colonize the island in the eighteenth century.

In Southeast Asia, the Dutch command of the sea routes was presently to be challenged by the British, who were beginning their moves to secure the eastern flank of their empire in India and to protect their routes to China. In their conquest and penetration of Nanyang, the British, dazzled by the still more glittering prizes of India, were slower off the mark than the Dutch. But theirs was the world's first industrial nation, their maritime ambitions were growing, and in England there were already empire builders in the making who were looking ahead to the time when they might advance the eastern frontiers of the British imperial domain. With the acquistion of the beautiful island of Penang in 1786, the British gained their first foothold in Malaya. No sooner had they begun clearing the undergrowth for settlement than the first Chinese migrants started arriving.

The most remarkable of the British expansionists was the young Stamford Raffles. On a green hump of virtually uninhabited jungle rising out of the sea at the foot of peninsular Malaya, Stamford Raffles, empire builder *par excellence*, founded the great port of Singapore. In 1824, five years after the Union Jack was hoisted over the island, Singapore was ceded in perpetuity to the British East India Company. Two years later Malacca, Singapore and Penang were formed into a single administrative unit called the Straits Settlements. Malacca had been Dutch, but in a deal between the Netherlands and Britain, it had been swapped for Benculen, a British outpost in Sumatra.

With its excellent deepwater harbour Singapore was an exchange port that could hardly fail, and it quickly achieved supremacy in the vigorous seaborne commerce of Southeast Asia. 'In little more than three years', Sir Stamford Raffles proudly wrote, 'it has risen from an insignificant fishing village to a large and prosperous town, containing at least ten thousand inhabitants of all nations actively engaged in commercial pursuits which afford to each and all a handsome livelihood and abundant profit.'[8] This, he added, may be considered 'as the simple but almost magic result of that perfect freedom of Trade which it has been my good fortune to establish'. Within five years of its birth Singapore had a Chinese population of well over three thousand. Coming at first from Malacca, the only Straits Settlement territory with a long-settled population, Singapore's Chinese migrated increasingly from China itself, after the arrival of the first junk from the southern Fukien port of Amoy in 1821.[9] Encouraged to settle in Singapore by its British founder, they were nearly as numerous as the Malays and were soon to surpass them – so evolving Singapore's most permanently distinctive feature, the predominance of the Chinese race.

The Chinese, in a strange and unforeseen way, were also partly responsible for the extension of British rule in peninsular Malaya. The British had not been in a mood to be embroiled in the internal politics of the native states, or to be lured into new colonial annexations; but Chinese feuds in the tin mines of Perak forced them into expansion. Tin having been discovered in many parts of Malaya, Chinese miners belonging to rival brotherhoods had flocked to the peninsula. The rival factions soon came to blows, their quarrels flaring into open warfare and threatening to spill over into British Penang. The pressure on the British grew, until they found that they could no longer hold themselves aloof from turning larger parts of peninsular Malaya into British preserves.[10]

While events were putting the British in control of large parts of Southeast Asia, the French, not to be left out of the scramble for Asia, were advancing into Indochina. They occupied Vietnam, Cambodia, and last of all Laos. Though there already lived tens of thousands of Chinese in Indochina when the territory fell to France, their numbers were to increase substantially under French domination.

The French East India Company had tried to people their colonies in the western Indian Ocean with Chinese transported from Southeast Asia. Having annexed the island of Réunion, they had occupied Mauritius (which they renamed Ile de France) in 1721, and there had optimistically founded Port Louis to be used as a base for attacking the British in India. The French cultivated sugar cane, originally introduced from Java by the Dutch, but while they could ship slaves over from Madagascar and Mozambique to work the plantations, they could not keep them – the slaves kept disappearing into the forests. Was there a people better fitted to take the place of these reluctant labourers than the Chinese? This was a rhetorical question which the Comte d'Estaing, a French admiral, put to himself shortly before he shanghaied three hundred Chinese from the Sumatran port of Benculen to Mauritius. The scheme proved flawed, however, for not only did the Chinese not work with uniform zeal, they could not be persuaded to work at all. It wasn't as though they were badly treated; indeed, the French employed cajolery rather than force, bribing them with regular rice rations, supplies of beef, salt pork and even brandy; but the Chinese simply refused to truckle to their European masters, and had to be sent back to Benculen the year after.

But it was an altogether different matter if they came of their own free will. The thousands that arrived in Mauritius in the mid-1780s – a happy time for Port Louis, then thriving as a vital way station on the route to India and the Far East – offered a sharp contrast to the sullen, unwilling abductees of forty years before. Brought by English, Danish and French ships from the port of Canton, these made themselves useful as carpenters, tailors, blacksmiths, cobblers and sugar plantation workers;[11] and an outward sign of their commitment to Mauritius was the *camp des Chinois*, a small Chinatown that came into being in Port Louis.[12] Chinese immigration was encouraged by not only the French but also the British to whom the island was ceded in 1819, after the Napoleonic wars. A Chinese settler, a trader called Log Ahime, was commissioned by the first British Governor of Mauritius to go and arrange for the movement of Chinese migrants to the island. A man of wide experience, some of it gained in China itself, the Governor knew to tempt them with offers of land on which to build their tombs and temples.[13]

In much of Southeast Asia Chinese immigrants followed on the heels of the European advances, and 'it could almost be said that Chinese trade followed European flags'.[14] Only Siam stood apart from the general pattern. Chinese traders and immigrants had been converging upon that kingdom in increasing numbers in the sixteenth and seventeenth centuries, when no Europeans had been around. In deciding how best to run their lucrative trading monopolies, the Thai kings took the practical step of employing Chinese seamen, factors, warehousemen and accountants. Colonies of Chinese merchants sprang up all around the Gulf of Siam; in Ayuthia, the capital, the main street in the Chinese quarter (called China Row by English writers) boasted some of the finest homes and buildings in the city.[15] At the time the Chinese were not considered foreigners by the Siamese, and there were even Chinese officials serving at the Siamese court. Actors and entertainers from China were very popular with the Siamese courtiers, and the King's chief physicians were Chinese.

Chinese trade more than held its own when Siamese doors were opened to Western commerce. A treaty negotiated by Sir John Bowring and signed in 1855 with Siam – ruled at the time by the progressive King Mongkut, whose reign was to become the basis for the popular twentieth-century musical comedy *The King and I* – granted commercial rights and other privileges to Britain and heralded a considerable expansion in foreign trade. But the Chinese, who were already there in considerable force when Bowring arrived – he put their number at around one and a half million[16] – gamely met the Western challenge and even profited from it.

In Southeast Asia as a whole, the flow of migration thickened with the expansion of economic opportunities, and wherever there were metals to be mined, sugar to be planted, pepper and gambier to be cultivated, there Chinese settlements would be established. Nanyang was presently mottled with Chinese communities – communities like the ones in the Malay peninsula, where tin and rubber had attracted large numbers of Indian and Chinese immigrants, brought in by the shipload from south India and south China; or the ones in the tin-rich islands of Bangka and Billiton, where the mineral rights, ceded by the Sultan to the King of England, were contracted by His Majesty's representatives to the Chinese.[17] From trading enclaves in coastal ports and inland capitals, the Chinese penetrated to riverine colonies in remoter areas, in places where they lived lives of terrible hardship, with nothing but mangrove swamp and impenetrable virgin forest for miles around.

These were changing times, times of widening horizons and expanding economic opportunities. The spread of European colonial rule was paralleled by a shift in gear in the movement of Chinese abroad. A British or French flag meant different things to different people, but to many a Chinese emigrant it connoted trade, protection, and a pressing demand for his services. If, during the initial phases of Chinese movements abroad, the overseas settlements were mostly small, there was now, as Southeast Asia underwent a period of quickened transformation under Western colonialism, a vastly greater volume of emigration. Products needed to feed Western industrialization, such as tin, tobacco, and later, rubber, could not be supplied fast enough; nor the manpower required to work the mines and plantations. The opening of the Suez Canal in 1869 greatly accelerated the process of development, and teeming communities of Chinese migrants came into being to lend their energies to the growing economies. The great waves of Chinese migration had begun.

To grasp what it meant for the Chinese to find themselves living under European domination in Southeast Asia, one must think of the West as a newcomer and remember that at first its power inspired less awe than it was to do later. The early maritime commerce of the Europeans was grafted on to the thriving Chinese junk trade, and to muscle in on it some of them had to interfere with the established shipping and the commercial arrangements the Chinese had with the local sultans and princes. China did not share their thirst for territorial expansion, and offered them no political competition, but establishing mastery over the overseas Chinese was still not always easy. A display of force was often necessary.

Long before Magellan opened the way to the Spice Islands with his epic voyage, long before the Philippines was named for the Emperor Charles V's son Philip, the heir to the Spanish throne, embassies bearing tribute had been arriving from Luzon in China. The first of the Chinese settlements, in any meaningful sense of the term, was the one planted by the Fukien seafarers in the Philippines. The place had been brought within the sphere of Chinese authority by Cheng Ho's expeditions, and the Ming Emperor Yung Lo had sent an official to govern Luzon in 1405. But when they hoisted their flag over the island group, founding the city of Manila in 1571, the Spaniards did not find themselves forestalled by China, for by then the Chinese court had lost its imperial enthusiasm. What resistance they met came from Chinese traders, who sailed up in their junks and greeted them with a great warlike display – beating on drums, playing on fifes, and firing rockets and cannons.[18] Later Manila was very nearly taken by the famous Chinese pirate, Lin Tao-ch'ien, the ruler of the coastal Siamese port of Pattani.

Animosity between Chinese and Spanish was to be a running theme of the Philippines' colonial history. The Chinese, whom the Spaniards called 'Sangleys' – from the southern Fukienese word *sengli*, meaning 'trade' – did not have an easy time of it in Manila, subjected as they were to irksome taxes and restrictions, and drafted into forced labour as rowers of Spanish galleys. There is no doubt that the name Sangley carried pejorative overtones, and in Spanish usage it was almost always followed by the world *infiel*, 'infidel'.[19] The Spaniards concentrated them in a fenced-in quarter built under the guns of the fort, a ghetto called the Parián, the better to control them. Spanish exactions and oppression repeatedly aroused Chinese violence, and in the Ming annals we read of Chinese rowers seizing a ship and killing her Spanish captain because he had whipped them so harshly that several of them had died.[20]

The Spaniards did not do anything for themselves, and it was the Chinese who supplied all their wants, as traders, carpenters, tailors, cobblers, locksmiths, masons, weavers, craftsmen of every kind, and even bakers. The Chinese were an economically necessary but resented community, and Spanish policies towards them lurched from acceptance to suspicion, from the velvet glove to the mailed fist. One minute the Chinese found themselves very welcome, the next minute they were anathema. This was to become a recurring colonial pattern throughout Southeast Asia, where imperial powers, whether Spanish, Dutch or British, began by being eager for Chinese immigration and ended by being hostile or ambivalent.

One could easily draw an analogy between those Chinese traders in the Philippines and the Japanese of today: they could sell you everything and you could sell them nothing. Even the raw cotton that was grown in the Philippines was taken to China and brought back woven.[21] To buy Chinese silks, porcelain, bronzes and jade, Spanish galleons from Acapulco brought to Manila cargoes of silver coins and bullion in such quantities that the Mexican dollar became the medium of exchange in the international trade of the Far East. The Chinese were paid in pieces of eight, and would accept no other currency. The thought of all that money falling into Chinese hands, of all that wealth being drained from the islands and the Mexican treasury, was naturally displeasing to the Spanish, and from time to time the government snatched at remedies; one of these was to forbid the Filipino natives from wearing Chinese fabrics.[22] Between the Chinese and the Spaniards, a constant sense of distrust and menace hovered, a state of tension in which violence could easily be triggered off.

Into this arena of uneasiness stepped three Chinese mandarins on 23 May 1603. Their purpose was vague, but they emanated an unmistakable importance, wearing all their insignia of office, and carrying their box of seals and patents just as they would in China. Led ashore and accepting as only their due the homage paid to them by the Chinese residents, they presented a letter to the Spanish Governor explaining that they had come to investigate a hill of gold and silver, as yet unexploited they understood, of which the Chinese Emperor had heard tell. They bore themselves with the dignity befitting the emissaries of All Under Heaven, moving through Manila as though it were Chinese territory, and administering floggings as they saw fit. The Spaniards did not quite know what to make of it. Was it a curtain-raiser to a Chinese takeover of the Philippines? A sense of disquiet spread among them, a fear that secret Chinese forces were assembling. Taking immediate precautions, the Governor issued orders for all the Chinese on the island to be registered, and for the men to be divided and housed in groups of three hundred.[23] The Chinese, for their part, felt that a Spanish attack was imminent, and there came from the Parián, shortly before midnight on the eve of St Francis's Day, the sound of war gongs being beaten. They marched on Quiapo and Tondo, leaving the pueblos ablaze and large numbers of Spaniards killed. They then decided to advance against the city, and might have stormed it had they not been thrown back – by the apparition of St Francis on the walls, the priests later said.

Spaniards burst into the Parián, falling upon some Chinese and sending others fleeing to the interior. The Governor offered terms and a suspension of hostilities, but the Chinese, suspecting a trap, took no chances and killed the envoy. At this, the Spanish Governor assembled his army and laid an ambush to starve the Chinese into submission. Battles followed, and Spanish vengeance was terrible. In an appalling massacre twenty-three thousand Chinese were slaughtered, and no looters plundered Chinese property more rapaciously than the Spanish soldiery.[24] Later some Spaniards had cause to regret the killing of so many Chinese, for, as one of them lamented, they found that they had no food and 'no shoes to wear, not even at excessive prices'.[25]

These inconveniences proved brief however, for soon the Chinese were back, and the Parián once more became a hive of activity. Many settled along the southern shores of Laguna de Bay, earning their livings as farmers and market gardeners. As before, the Spaniards found it hard to resist squeezing the Chinese; and when, in 1639, the latter were faced with increased taxes, they rose in revolt again. It was the cultivators of Laguna de Bay who started the insurrection, the first victims of which were the Mayor of Laguna and the local priest. Burning and plundering, the mob came down the Pasig River to the city, where, joined by the Chinese of the Parián, it crumbled before the Spanish forces. Bands of straggling Chinese roved the country, burning a church here, attacking a native village there. They were armed with spears, or bamboos to which were attached the knives they were accustomed to using to harvest their rice. The rising had begun in November; by March it had reached its limit. When seven thousand Chinese surrendered to the Spaniards, to be punished by being sent to the galleys as rowers for the Governor's expeditionary fleets, Luzon had been littered with the corpses of between twenty-two and twenty-four thousand Chinese.[26] Three hundred natives had lost their lives in the disturbance, but only fifty Spaniards had lost theirs. When the tumult died, the Spaniards celebrated the completeness of their victory with a pageant led by the Governor, and as it marched triumphantly through the streets, with drums beating and trumpets tooting, the *Te Deum* was sung in churches all over Manila.

But again the Chinese were missed, and again they came back, bringing new life to the Parián, where some fifteen thousand of them were to make their homes. Did they feel more secure? Anti-Chinese feeling was by no means dead, but if it was not seen in the context of the past massacres probably few Chinese gave it much thought. In 1662, however, their days again darkened, and for a time it looked as though they were in for a third wholesale massacre. Like the mission of the three mandarins, the immediate cause of it was an absurdity. In that year Koxinga, the famous Ming loyalist who had ousted the Dutch from Taiwan just the year before, sent a letter to Governor Manrique de Lara protesting against Spanish oppression of the Chinese residents, noting particularly the massacre of 1603, and imperiously demanding that the Governor submit to his rule immediately. Besides being insufferably impertinent, Koxinga's demand seemed to the Spanish to suggest conspiracy and collusion among the Sangleys. A sense of impending doom came over the Chinese as, nagged by fears of an attack, the Spaniards in Manila prepared for a move against them; extermination and expulsion seemed likely. Some of the Chinese drowned as, fleeing the Parián, they tried to swim across the river; others took their own lives or rushed to hide in the hills. The scene was set for panic and violence, and might have ended in carnage if the Jesuit missionaries hadn't pleaded for the Chinese, and if the Governor hadn't kept his head. He allowed a specified number of Chinese to return to Manila by a certain date, and told the rest to go back to China. The fate of the escapees was inevitably death, the Spanish troops hunting them down and despatching them. The leaders were caught and publicly executed. It was about this time that news of Koxinga's death was brought to the Philippines. The threat of an invasion, if it was ever very real, passed away.[27]

The possibility of repatriation lingered, however, and from time to time the King of Spain decreed the expulsion of the Chinese. In the autumn of 1762, when the English captured the city, the Chinese cooperated with them and took their side. They did not foresee that Manila would be handed back to Spain just two years later, nor the terrible punishment that they would earn for their disloyalty. No sooner were the Spanish installed than orders were given for all Sangleys to be hanged.

Like the Spanish, the Dutch were to have second thoughts about the Chinese. Jan Pieterson Coen, the founder of Batavia and the Dutch empire of the East Indies, had wanted to see his colony peopled as much as possible by the Chinese, who had traded and lived along the coast of Java for centuries, and who could always be relied on to deliver pepper supplies in sizeable quantities. When able-bodied Chinese did not come of their own accord, Coen sent ships to various trading stations and the southern Chinese coasts to kidnap them. 'There are no people who can serve us better than the Chinese,'[28] thought Coen, who also knew that Chinese immigration could only enlarge Batavia's share of the alluring junk trade. The Chinese trader dealt with not just the Dutch but the English and the French, and was canny enough to play one off against the other. To divert the Chinese junks to Batavia, Coen blockaded Manila, Macao and other parts of the Chinese coast; and to tempt the Chinese to settle there, he offered them tax concessions. The privileges enjoyed by the Chinese did not cease with Coen's death in 1629, and for several decades the Dutch seemed to let the Chinese be.

But if the junks brought trade, they also brought people – an ever growing stream of them. This began to bother the Dutch, and in 1690 the first of a series of restrictive regulations was brought in. The aim was to make life more difficult for arrivals after a specified date, and, to differentiate old immigrants from new, a distinction was drawn between Chinese who wore their hair in the old style, with 'a puff and a knob'; and those who dressed it in the style more recently imposed by the Manchus, with the front half of the head shaven and with the remaining hair plaited into a queue. The regulations grew stricter as time went on. Against payment of a specified sum, one could be issued with a residence permit, but only by showing oneself to be a 'useful inhabitant' and not a loafer; anyone not in possession of a permit would be considered an illegal immigrant and put in chains. Numbers of roaming undesirables were rounded up and shipped off to Ceylon or the Cape of Good Hope. Inevitably, given the poor quality of many of the Dutch civil servants, the regulations became a source of extortion and blackmail, and even perfectly law-abiding Chinese became fodder for the money-grubbing officers entrusted with the issue of permits.

The Chinese were seething with discontent, needing only a spark to ignite them. The spark came in July 1740 with a rash decision by the Dutch authorities to deport all unemployed Chinese to work in the cinnamon gardens of Ceylon. Soon a rumour went round that the deportees were thrown overboard the minute their ships left Java, and within a few months of their decision the Dutch found a rising on their hands. From up-country, where many Chinese had fled, there presently came stirrings of rebellion. News of this reached the Dutch governing body, the Council of the Indies, but it was greeted with scorn by some of the members, who thought that the Chinese, the most cowardly of races, would never dare to attack the city. They were mistaken, of course, for though it is true that the rebels proved poor soldiers – many of them were mere ruffians and vagabonds – they were as capable of rioting as any aggrieved people. They marched on the city in three formations,[29] better provided, as one Dutch report observed, 'with cymbals and banners than with cannons and rifles'.[30] They engaged with Dutch mercenaries the night they arrived outside the city walls, but were forced to retreat in the morning.

Inside the walls, the Dutch had ordered the Chinese to surrender all their weapons, down to the smallest kitchen knife. They were thus a sitting target for the armed mob that the Dutch now let loose upon them – sailors, soldiers, and what the Dutch themselves called 'the low-class masses'.[31] These took a terrible revenge, and for a whole week the frenzy of slaughter and looting went on unchecked. Those who called it mass murder were not exaggerating, for no fewer than ten thousand Chinese were killed, including men in hospital and prison.[32] In Dutch colonial history the episode came to be known as the Batavian Fury. The tragedy was repeated all over Java, the Council of the Indies having voted for an open season on the Chinese, an out-and-out pogrom.[33]

With the advantage of historical perspective, one could see that this was not a confrontation pure and simple, if only because it had behind it the economic rivalries of the Dutch and the Chinese. The Spaniards were crusaders, missionaries rather than merchants. Not so the Dutch, whose imperial adventure had no higher purpose than the amassing of Eastern fortunes. Moreover, they saw wealth as a limited commodity: the more others had of it the less there would be for them. It had suited them to have the Chinese as their commission agents, but not as their rivals. To root them out was to rid oneself once and for all of a nagging threat. The VOC thought that it had outgrown the Chinese middleman, for spices were no longer the prizes of world commerce, and the island's economy was to surge on sugar, coffee and other plantation crops. For their part, the Chinese could not accept that the Dutch should have it all their own way. In hindsight it seems an unequal contest, but to the Chinese at the time it did not seem so unbalanced; they did not think their Dutch masters beyond challenge. Their outlook was altered by the experience of the massacre, and their circumstances changed: from 1740 onwards they were confined to ghettoes – in Batavia within range of the city's guns.

The Dutch had not begun their incursion into the Outer Islands of the Indonesian archipelago when a Chinese mining community took shape in the gold fields of western Borneo. The Chinese had been brought in by the Sultan of Sambas, the leading local principality, but since 1760, when they decided that they had had enough of the Sultan's exactions, the miners had been running their own affairs, the Sultan claiming only a share of the gold.

One may imagine the place from the writings of the succeeding century, such as Joseph Conrad's novels and the reports of European naturalists and explorers. This was the 'white man's grave', nothing but jungle, swamp and river, the inhospitable home of malarial mosquitoes and tropical fevers. It was inhabited by tribes of different stock, among them the Land Dyaks, gentle folk who lived mainly on dry ground; and the Sea Dyaks, riverine people who went about by canoe and who took to marauding with gusto. If the West knew these people at all, they knew them as headhunters – as indeed they were, for it was standard practice for their young men to go off by themselves to collect some heads to impress the girls they wished to marry.

If the taking of heads was a sign of virility, the owning of big Chinese pottery jars was a symbol of riches and aristocratic status. Hoards of Sung dynasty (960–1279) ceramics have been found in Borneo, brought by enterprising Chinese traders who ventured up the rivers to exchange their jars and beads for edible bird's nests, hornbill beaks and other jungle produce. At the river mouths they dealt with Muslim Malays and their chieftains, settlers who took advantage of their strategic location to make a handsome living from river tolls and tributes, and who were to evolve a string of sultanates (Sambas being one of the most important) along the coastal fringes.

This, then, was the setting in which the classic Chinese frontier institution, the *kongsi*, took root and flourished. Part government, part cooperative and part secret society, the kongsi in its various guises would become a feature of all expatriate Chinese communities. (The word means 'company', but the visitor to modern Nanyang may hear it used of a dialect or native-place association.) In the gold fields of west Borneo a kongsi which began as a small partnership of miners could go on to become, through conquest of rival kongsis or through amalgamation, a large federation with many districts or sub-districts beneath its authority, forming a semi-state. The miners were mostly Hakka-speaking, and the kongsi, which consisted of one or more groups of families sprung from the same clan, each with its own leader or elected district representative, was developed from the structure of Hakka villages in South China.[34] Seats on the governing body went to the settlement's richest and most influential men, and these were frequently leaders of a secret society, one of those brotherhoods that the world was to know as the triads.

Lo Fong Pak, the best known of the kongsi headmen in west Borneo, was a member of the Heaven and Earth Society. He arrived in about 1772 with about a hundred fellow Hakkas from Kwangtung province, and was soon engaged in clearing jungle, digging wells, building houses and developing mines. He was a natural leader, endowed with a gift for organization and with enormous vitality. It was under his command that rival settlers were quelled or absorbed, and the kongsi's territory extended. In his hands the community seemed to function like a highly organized Chinese village, governed with more sophistication and democracy than you might suppose, and stimulating the immigration of more Hakka speakers to Borneo.[35] When he died, a tablet was raised for him in the kongsi house, and sacrifice offered to him on appropriate days. There grew a legend of his magical powers of taming crocodiles, and he himself was revered like a deity.

The kongsi survived his death, and had four more headmen before fading out under Dutch pressure. The fifth headman to rule Lo Fong Pak's kongsi became a powerless pensioner of the Dutch, and when he died his masters simply took possession of his territory. By 1857 the Dutch had, in effect, dismembered all of west Borneo's kongsis. The advance of their influence took place against a background of struggles between warring kongsis and Chinese clashes with the indigenous peoples. All these contributed to the waves of Chinese emigration from Sambas to neighbouring Sarawak, that part of Borneo which political accident had placed under the authority of the British.

In Joseph Conrad's novel *Lord Jim*, the eponymous hero comes to Patusan and there finds his vocation, bringing peace and order to the valley and becoming ruler of the indigenous people. In creating Lord Jim, Conrad had been inspired by the exploits of James Brooke, the first of the White Rajahs of Sarawak. It was with this English adventurer that the Chinese had now to come to terms. They did so, after a fashion, in the great rising of 1857.

James Brooke, a man much given to impetuous opinions, had first set eyes on the Chinese on a trip to Singapore and had hated them on sight, writing of them that 'Their habits are the most filthy, their dress the most unbecoming, their faces the most ugly, and their figures the most ungraceful of any people under the sun.' 'When they move,' he went on to say, 'they swing arms, legs and body, like a paper clown pulled by a string, and to sum up, all their colour is a dirty yellow, nearly the hue of a Hindustani corpse.'[36] What a contrast they posed to the graceful Dyaks, much more one's idea of the Noble Savage. Brooke responded to the beauty of the Dyak dances with an enthusiasm that he could never feel for the jerky Chinese. He felt the Chinese to be the white man's competitors, to be watched with care, and the natives to be his wards, to be protected against interlopers and exploiters, whether Chinese or English. Brooke later modified his opinion of the Chinese and welcomed them as colonists for his new and growing realm, even engaging a Cantonese to be his own steward.[37] Kuching, his capital and chief trading port, was to rely greatly for its prosperity on the skills and industry of its Teochiu, Hokkien and Cantonese immigrants.

Much less tractable, however, were the Hakkas who worked the gold mines in and around Bau, a settlement in the upper reaches of the Sarawak River near the border with Sambas. The kongsi which governed these mining camps was a branch of a kongsi in Sambas, the main source of the Chinese influx into Bau. Having always been a self-governing entity, it did not see why it should salute anybody else's flag, and if it recognized the Rajah's overall suzerainty, it did so only vaguely. If Kuching represented one kind of power, Bau, in its own eyes, constituted another. It minted its own coins and maintained its own judicial structure, and while Kuching in 1857 had only eight hundred Chinese, Bau had more than five times that number.[38]

Rivalry between the two flared into warfare in February, sparked some say by the Rajah's protection of a Hakka adulterer whose death the Bau authorities had decreed, adultery being a capital offence in the kongsi. Others say that the Rajah's measures against opium-smuggling stoked the fire of the Hakkas' resentment. Opium-smoking was both a part of the baggage of habits Chinese emigrants took with them when they left home, and a device for palliating the harshness of a life lived in an alien country without the company of women and the consolations of family. It had been made a government monopoly, and when Sarawak's tax collectors discovered a fall in the legal import of opium, at a time when Chinese immigration was increasing, they rightly suspected illegal trafficking from Singapore and neighbouring islands.

The Hakkas might also have been stirred by the news of British-Chinese clashes in Canton, and emboldened by the rumour that the Rajah was in bad odour with the British government for the way he went after the Dyak pirates and headhunters.

The Rajah was asleep in his house, The Grove, when a troop of Chinese carrying muskets, spears and a blazing torch came yelling and firing across the grounds. From a bungalow in the grounds dashed young Nicholetts, just eighteen and newly recruited to the service. He was struck down by the Chinese, who, believing he was the Rajah, cut off his head, stuck it on a spear, and brandished it all night like a trophy. As they were gathering around Nicholetts's body, Brooke rushed to a creek and swam under the bow of a boat which had brought the rebels, later making his way to the house of a trusted Malay official, the Datu Bandar. The Chinese force was divided into two parties, one aimed at capturing the Rajah, the other at taking the stockade. The latter was defended, not very successfully, by a hot-headed Irishman called Charles Adare Crymble with four Malays. He, too, had to run for it in the end.

The remaining English cast of this drama was small. There was Arthur Crookshank, in whose care Brooke was wont to leave the government during his own absences from Sarawak. He was attacked in his house but managed to escape and later to join the Rajah, while his young wife of a few months was struck down and left for dead. There was Mr Middleton, the Inspector of the Police, who also succeeded in slipping out of his house but whose wife was left there hidden in a water jar in the bathroom. There she heard her two sons murdered, the elder boy decapitated (his head kicked across the room like a football) and the younger flung screaming into the flames, the Chinese having set their torches to the house. There was breezy Bishop MacDougall, into whose mission-house fled all the remaining Europeans of the town: six men, nine women and eight children. They were there all night, waiting for an attack by the Chinese. None came, but when dawn broke seven rebels approached the bishop and, to his surprise, informed him that they had no quarrel with the English, only with the Rajah and his government.

Having captured Kuching, the Chinese summoned the bishop, the Datu Bandar, a private merchant called Rupell and Ludvig Verner Helms, director of the Borneo Company (a British company formed to advance the Sarawak government's commercial interests), to a meeting in the court-house. There the head of the kongsi was seen squatting on his haunches in the Rajah's chair, presiding over a roomful of scowling and gesticulating Chinese. The headman began by listing his grievances: the heavy taxes, the ill-treatment, the insufficient dignity accorded to the Chinese. From now on the kongsi would rule the country, with Helms and Rupell as co-Rajahs perhaps, and the Datu Bandar taking charge of the Malay section of the community. The kongsi would do it from Bau, to which the rebels proposed now to retreat with all their booty. They wanted an assurance that no boat would be sent upriver in pursuit, and a contract, sealed in the appropriate fashion by a scattering of cock's blood, was drawn up to embody that pledge. The meeting was then brought to a close with tea and cigars, and a shaking of hands. The attack sputtered on, in skirmish and looting, until off the rebels went the next morning, withdrawing upstream with their plunder.

Some hot-headed young Malays pursued them, capturing a Chinese boat and killing some of its passengers. They were beaten off, but the counter-attack prompted the Chinese to halt their retreat and to sail downriver again to retake the town. Half Kuching was left a smoking desolation. The Grove burnt down completely, and nothing was left of the library which James Brooke had lovingly assembled. The Raj seemed utterly doomed, and the distraught Rajah, not fully recovered from a bout of malaria, was heard to say in a moment of blind panic, 'Offer the country, on any terms, to the Dutch!' But in fact help was just around the corner, and it came in the shape of a Borneo Company steamer, the *Sir James Brooke*, sailing unexpectedly up the coast at the eleventh hour, in the manner of the last-minute rescue in a good adventure yarn.

'*Kapalapi* [the fire ship]*! Kapalapi!*' the Malays shouted, jumping and dancing with joy. The Rajah boarded her at once, and a few hours later the vessel swung into sight of Kuching. The Chinese opened fire, but their nails and bits of rusty iron were no match for the ship's eighteen-pounders, and away they fled, 'like wild hares in March,' reported an observer, 'some dashing up the road, others running through the bazaars, affording practice for the riflemen on board'.39 Meanwhile the Rajah's nephew Charles Johnson arrived from the interior, bringing armed Sea Dyaks and Malays who itched to pursue the Chinese into the jungle. In a bid to prevent excessive bloodshed, the Rajah invited the Sea Dyaks on board the *Sir James Brooke*, hoping thereby to detain them. His guests were indeed distracted by the mechanical marvels that they saw, but they were thirsty for revenge, and could not be restrained for long. Now they showed their colours, as their canoes quickly caught up with the Hakka rebels. Desperate, the rebels took to the jungle, and while some of them stumbled their way to the border, others in their hopelessness hanged themselves. Clothes, dead bodies, silver and other looted valuables bestrew the track left by the retreating Hakkas. Bau lay in ruins. About a thousand Chinese were killed, but some 2,500 made it to Sambas, more than half of them women and children.

Some of the Kuching Chinese fled the country, not because they were in any way guilty of complicity, but because the Malays were not 'in the humour to distinguish one Chinese [pig]tail from another'.[40] Every now and then, Dyak headhunters could be seen cleaning and smoking Hakka heads over their fire in the bazaar, taking all the more pleasure in their task when there were Chinese spectators about. On James Brooke the clash left scars that would never quite heal. When, some months later, news of the Indian Mutiny reached Sarawak, the Rajah, whose childhood was spent in Benares, was deeply shaken, feeling as stung by it as he had been by the Chinese rising.

He wrote of it that it was the madness, 'the stark staring folly of the attempt which caused it to succeed'.[41] His biographer, too, seemed bemused by it, describing it as 'the most absurd and causeless rebellion that ever occurred'.[42] They both wrote without the advantages of historical perspective, and so did not grasp the deeper implications of the affair. To us it seems not so causeless, the instinctive protest of a people who did not recognize the power of Victorian imperialism, and were not reconciled to European supremacy at all. After 1857 no political autonomy of the kind exercised by the Hakka miners at Bau was ever enjoyed by any kongsi again. The struggle was a duel of destinies, in which was decided which was the stronger: the kongsi or the Raj; the Chinese or the white man.

CHAPTER THREE

Floodtide

The greatest waves of Chinese emigration began in the second half of the nineteenth century, with more than two million people moving from their homeland to the Malay peninsula, Indochina, Sumatra, Java, the Philippines, Hawaii, the West Indies, California and Australia between 1848 and 1888.[1] There were certainly enough of them that would leave China if they could. A long period of internal peace that began in the nineteenth century had produced a phenomenal population explosion – a doubling from 150 million to three hundred million and a further jump to about 410 million by 1850.[2] In a country where there had appeared no new kinds of material, technical or political improvement to absorb the proliferation of people, such numbers made for destitution, popular demoralization, corruption, apathy, and the breakdown of public order and personal morality.

China was violently changing, under the stresses of overcrowding and Western penetration. After centuries of trade with China, the West had at last found something it could sell the Chinese in large quantities: the tons of Bengal, Patna and Malwa opium unloaded by clippers on the China coast were helping to pay for Britain's further colonization of India, and to right the adverse balance of payments entirely in its favour. But force of arms was necessary to put the traffic on a legal and unrestricted basis, and to open China up to British commerce and ambitions. A British expeditionary force landed in China in June 1840, and for the next fifty or so years a defeated China found itself driven, step by step, into relinquishing its claim to universal overlordship of All Under Heaven.

'A war more unjust in its origin, a war more calculated to cover this country with permanent disgrace, I do not know and I have not read of.' Thus the young Tory Gladstone. The British flag at Canton, he continued, 'is hoisted to protect an infamous contraband traffic; and if it were never hoisted as it is now hoisted on the coast of China, we should recoil from its sight with horror.'[3] The Treaty of Nanking which concluded the first Opium War was imposed upon the Manchu court at gunpoint, and by signing it China agreed to the cession of the island of Hong Kong to Britain and the opening of five treaty ports – Canton, Amoy, Foochow, Ningpo and Shanghai – to foreign trade and residence. Close on the heels of the British came the French and the Americans, demanding similar concessions. That the gunboats were introducing China to capitalism, that the war marked the start of a profound change in the way the Chinese saw the world and accommodated to it, was a historical insight not yet spelt out, but in hindsight we can see that since the earliest appearance of European profit seekers in the Eastern seas, it had been an impulse of Western capitalism to breach the walls of All Under Heaven and to urge it to a different style of trade and foreign relations.

The opening of the treaty ports in 1843 and 1844, while it brought many an overseas stranger to China's shores, also summoned countless Chinese out of their poor and overcrowded villages. The arrival of many more foreign vessels in south Chinese waters was one of the great social facts of Manchu China, and the mass exodus of the populace was its partial result. Hordes of Chinese crossed the oceans from the quays of the treaty ports.

Overcrowding apart, there were soon other reasons for leaving. The period of domestic peace ended with the Taiping Rebellion, the most dramatic and devastating of the insurrectionary movements to erupt in the mid-nineteenth century. Led by a strange sect of Hakka converts to Old Testament Protestant Christianity, the rising swept across sixteen provinces and destroyed more than six hundred cities, and it was a full fourteen years before it was suppressed by the imperial forces. Never before in the two hundred years of Manchu rule had the empire been so horribly ravaged.[4] Other uprisings followed, driving streams of refugees southwards. Probably sixty million people died in all, and it was against this backdrop of death, destruction and faltering imperial authority that the mass emigration of Chinese took place.

People left in batches, under headmen they called *k'o-t'ou* or *towkay* (the latter term still to be heard in Malaysia and Singapore today, as an epithet for the owner of a shop or business). Old returned emigrants themselves, these headmen acted as emigration brokers, going into the villages to recruit passengers and matching them up with employers abroad. Emigrants leaving for North America, Australasia, Singapore, Malaya and Thailand went under the credit-ticket system – a system which derived its name from the fact that each emigrant obtained his passage on credit, the *k'o-t'ou* or ship's captain to be reimbursed on arrival at his destination by friends or relatives, or by an employer for whom the emigrant had to work until his debt was paid off. The emigrant boarded the receiving ship holding a ticket giving his name, age, place of origin and port of destination, and stating whether his passage had been paid in advance.[5] It was an old, well-established system of organized labour recruitment, probably first used by the Chinese colonists of Taiwan.[6] It presently became an organized international trade, involving passage brokers and emigration agencies in many of the world's ports. (The Wells Fargo Bank History Room in San Francisco displays a credit-ticket contract signed in 1849 between a party of Chinese labourers and an English company in Shanghai.)[7]

The system was subject to countless abuses, and many emigrants found themselves bondmen to unscrupulous extortioners. It was big business for the brokers and shipowners, who were not merely reimbursed for the passage money they advanced but paid a handsome commission for every able-bodied immigrant they landed. It could be shady as well, for emigration was technically illegal, and Chinese officials at the sending ports had to be bribed to permit it, and because so many of the brokers were powerful figures in underworld secret societies. As the volume of emigration increased, so the emigrant ships became more and more overcrowded, and on arrival at their destinations all too many vessels disgorged dead, dying, sick or half-starved passengers.

People shipped under credit-ticket procedures are usually described as 'free emigrants', to distinguish them from coolies or indentured labourers, but actually it is difficult to draw a definite line between the two systems of emigration, and to ask (as some writers have done) whether or not the Chinese in America were coolies is to pursue a fruitless line of enquiry. The bond blurred into the free. Emigrant shaded into coolie. (The word 'coolie', originally the name of an aboriginal Gujarat tribe of India, and extended to mean transient labourer or hireling, contributed a new term, *k'u-li*, 'hard strength', to the Chinese vocabulary; application of the word to Chinese contract labour was easy, for 'coolie' was already in use among foreigners in China for menial workers and house servants.)[8]

Chinese coolie emigration under the contract system, begun in earnest in 1845, was established on the ruins of the African slave trade. Slavery had been abolished throughout the British possessions, and two years before the start of the Opium War the last bondmen of the empire had been freed by their masters. Faced with a desperate shortage of manpower on their West Indian plantations, European merchants were looking to replace the African slave with the Asian indentured labourer, Chinese or Indian. The treaty ports were points of ingress for both the opium and coolie trader, and often the men who helped to advance the sale of the one were also working to promote the other.[9]

A British Guiana planter, on a tour of the British empire's Eastern possessions, thought he had found what he was looking for in the Chinese labourers he came across in the Straits Settlements. Their strong physique, their eagerness to make money, their history of toil from infancy, their relative freedom, compared to the Indian, from religious inhibitions and the kind of prejudice that might prevent them from marrying local women – all these qualities suggested that Chinese coolies would meet the needs of the West Indian planters.[10] It was true that they were not so easily disciplined, that they were likely to demand higher wages, and that they would 'no more bear ill-usage than an English labourer', but on the whole they seemed superior to the Indian coolie. Lord Stanley, Secretary of State for the Colonies, was inclined to agree: the Chinese would set the emancipated Negroes, who were apt to wander off the plantations into the interior, an 'example of continuous and industrious application', and would probably prove to be better workers than any other race.[11] If India sent many thousands of indentured labourers across the world, China sent even larger numbers.

Chinese coolies took the place of African serfs, and yet you would never guess, from this remark by Lord Russell (Prime Minister of Britain in 1846–52 and 1865–66), that coolie labour had any analogy with slavery: 'By judiciously promoting emigration from China, and at the same time vigorously repressing the infamous traffic in African slaves, the Christian Governments of Europe and America may confer benefits upon a large portion of the human race, the effects of which it would be difficult to exaggerate.'[12] And yet there were barracoons in Chinese ports as grim as any to be found on the African coast, and the horrors of the coolies' voyages rivalled those of the infamous Middle Passage.

Humanitarianism was definitely not a trait of the coolie agents, British firms like Messrs Syme, Muir and Co., or Tait and Co. Nor were they mere shady operators, working in the dark. James Tait, the biggest shipper of coolies from the treaty port of Amoy (the chief outlet of the early contract trade), was no doubt helped in his unsavoury business by the fact that he was simultaneously a British subject; the consular representative of Spain, Holland and Portugal; and the one-time employer of the acting-consul of the United States. Not a few of the most important agents then are still well known names in the Far East today, firms such as Boustead, Guthrie and Jardine Matheson. Some were actually authorized by their home governments.[13]

They procured their emigrants through local Chinese recruiters – the so-called coolie crimps – who were paid so much a head for the men they brought to the barracoons or the receiving vessels. If false promises had been made to tempt people into selling themselves, no questions were asked. Debt, gambling losses, or simply hunger drove many men into signing away their freedom. Others had been taken prisoner in the violent clan fights of Kwangtung and Fukien, and then sold by their captors to the prowling agents. We read of a receiving station in Amoy where hundreds of them were gathered together, 'stripped naked, and stamped or painted with letters C (California), P (Peru), or S (Sandwich Island [Hawaii]) on their breasts, according to the destinations for which they were intended'.[14] The medically unfit were rejected, but the able-bodied were given contracts and then packed aboard ships that were nothing but slavers. Thousands died on the voyage, but once ashore, those that lived would work out the years of their contracts until they became free settlers or, if their luck held, they found the means to sail for home.

The first batch of Chinese coolies to be shipped abroad under a foreign contract was the one which a French vessel took from Amoy to the Isle of Bourbon (Réunion) in 1845.[15] Within a few years, human cargoes had left for Cuba, Australia, Peru and the Caribbean sugar colonies. Between 1847 and 1862, American agents shipped six thousand Chinese to Havana each year.[16] Each passenger would have signed a contract with the emigration agent, but one wonders if he understood what he was signing. Besides, if the contract was printed in English on one side and Chinese on the other, the two did not always say exactly the same things. This may be seen at the Mitchell Library in Sydney, where twenty-one of the contracts signed in 1851 between Chinese labourers and an Australian contractor called J. B. Simpson are preserved:

Term of Years	5 years
Wages per month	3 dollars [one dollar = four shillings sterling]
Weekly rations:	
Sugar	1 lb
Flour	8 lbs [English version gives only four]
or Rice	10 lbs [Chinese version gives flour or rice]
Meat	9 lbs [Chinese version gives eight]
Tea	2 oz [Chinese version gives unlimited]
Wages commencing	From the date of arrival
Advance	8 dollars
Advance deducted from	
the monthly payment	0.5 dollars [Chinese version gives one dollar][17]

Whoever coined the common Chinese simile for the coolie trade – 'the buying and selling of piglets' – had a good idea of its squalor. As competition for Chinese labour intensified, so abuses multiplied. The Chinese coolie was exploited by unscrupulous men at every turn: tricked, decoyed, hustled or simply kidnapped by his recruiter, and then terrorized and tortured – by being plunged into a cold river, or tied up by the thumbs, or beaten up – into agreeing to emigrate.[18] Potential 'piglets' were subjected to every kind of trickery, as many of those shipped to Cuba by Portuguese and Spanish agents were later to recall:

> We were induced to proceed to Macao by offers of employ-
> ment abroad at high wages, and through being told that the
> eight foreign years specified in the contracts were equiva-
> lent to only four Chinese, and that at the termination of
> the latter period we would be free. We observed also on
> the signboards of the foreign buildings the words 'agencies
> for the engagement of labourers', and believed that they
> truthfully described the nature of the establishments, little
> expecting that having once entered the latter, exit would be
> denied us; and when on arrival at Havana, we were exposed
> for sale and subjected to appraisement in a most ruthless
> manner, it became evident that we were not to be engaged
> as labourers, but to be sold as slaves.[19]

The barracoon in Macao, many transportees to Cuba reported, 'was of great depth, and, at the time of punishment [inflicted on those who attempted to escape], as an additional precaution to prevent the cries being overheard, gongs were beaten, and fireworks discharged, so that death even might have ensued without detection; and witnessing this violence, there was no course open to us but assent.'[20]

The crowding on the receiving vessels, whether lorcha or American clipper, was appalling, for it was obvious that the more people the shipper could cram into his craft, the greater would be his profit; and even if some of the passengers were to die on the voyage, it still made better business sense for the trader whose ship could legitimately carry three hundred men, say, to take on board six hundred and lose 250 on the way than for him to start with the proper number and land them all safely.[21] Coolies were commodities, barely human beings. A short story by Joseph Conrad, *Typhoon*, makes this point through an exchange between a character called Jukes and the captain of a steamship carrying two hundred Chinese coolies back to their village homes in Fukien province: upon Jukes's suggestion that the ship, which had run into a terrible typhoon, changed direction to make the journey more comfortable for the passengers, the Captain said:

> 'Passengers? . . . What passengers?'
> 'Why, the Chinamen, sir,' explained Jukes . . .
> 'The Chinamen! Why don't you speak plainly? Couldn't
> tell what you meant. Never heard a lot of coolies spoken of
> as passengers before. Passengers, indeed! What's come to
> you?'[22]

Many of the coolies would be in chains, and if a fire should break out the captain and crew would simply abandon ship, leaving their human cargo to die in the flames or smoke or be trampled to death in the stampede for the hatches. The vessels were truly floating hells, the conditions of which no modern traveller can really imagine. In the mid-1850s the death rates among the coolies transported to the New World ranged from fifteen to forty-five per cent; of the more than 140,000 Chinese who sailed for Cuba, more than sixteen thousand died at sea.[23] If sickness, hunger, thirst and suffocation didn't kill them off, the orgies of flogging soon did. The ones who could no longer endure the suffering simply threw themselves into the sea.

Those who lived to describe the voyage spoke of people being shut up in bamboo cages in the hold, or chained to iron posts, or, if they looked particularly strong, being fettered down in irons. The masters of the vessels took no chances, for thoughts of mutiny could never be absent. Men suspected of mutinous intentions were often shot or hanged. Every now and then captive passengers took their revenge by murdering crewmen and rioting, though successful mutinies, given the heavy security, were few.[24] The first of the mutinies was aboard the

American ship *Robert Browne* in 1852. The Captain found he had a
rebellion on his hands when, subjected to cumulative sufferings, from
being flogged to having their bodies scrubbed with sea water and their
queues forcibly cut off, the Chinese rose against the officers and for a
time took command of the coolie carrier.[25]

Meanwhile, back at the emigration ports, just to go out into the streets
was to be fallen upon by the coolie crimps. In Canton, now the chief port
of the coolie traffic, matters came to a head in 1859, when an angry mob
killed some of the kidnappers. This convinced the British residents in
Canton that there could be no respect for foreign flags and no security
for foreigners while so scandalous a wrong as the coolie traffic was seen
to be a European responsibility. The British were in the happy position
of being able to do something about it, for although Canton was run
by the rather colourless Governor Po-kuei in name, in reality it was
governed by the Allied Commission, a European body presided over
by Harry Parkes, the Chinese-speaking British Consul who had made
it his business to vet Po-kuei's proclamations in a back room. Parkes
held the prevailing British view on Chinese emigration – that it should
be freed but regulated. The view reflected Britain's larger purpose in
China, which was to get it to follow the British style of free trade under
a rule of law, the better to do profitable business with it. So when Mr J.
Gardiner Austin, Immigration Agent General of British Guiana, arrived
in Canton that year with a scheme to establish a system of voluntary
emigration, Parkes was ready enough to support him.

Within three months of Austin's appearance on the scene, Po-kuei
issued a proclamation. This was a revolutionary document, because
although it merely conceded that amongst the densely crowded population of Kwangtung province some might be compelled by want to seek
a livelihood beyond the seas or to accept employment by foreigners,
and that such people were now at liberty to do so provided that they
emigrated of their own free will, it signified the first official recognition
of the right of the Chinese to leave their homeland and settle abroad.[26]
The British had won their point. By admitting that law and tradition
must be 'subservient to the exigencies of social change and progress',
the British minister Sir Frederick Bruce suggested approvingly,[27] the
Chinese authorities showed that they had come to their senses, that
they had adopted 'in short, the mobility of European in lieu of the
rigidity of Chinese statesmanship'.[28]

Emigration was now legalized, at least locally. In Canton, British
and Chinese officials were jointly to run a British Emigration House

to be established for the recruitment of a regular stream of emigrants from the overcrowded country round about to the half-empty spaces of the British colonies. French and Spanish Emigration Houses were presently licensed and established. But it still remained for the legalization of the trade to be rendered national. The events of the following year soon gave Britain the awaited opportunity.

In many ways the first Opium War and the Nanking Treaty of eighteen years before had been inconclusive; the Western powers had not achieved all that they wanted, and they had been looking to impose their will on the refractory Chinese by any available method. Making the most of minor incidents, British forces, presently joined by the French, had started the second Opium War with a bombardment of Canton in 1856. The allies had then pushed north to bring the imperial government at Peking to terms. The final phase of the war had seen the Anglo-French forces charging into Peking, and looting and burning the Emperor's famous summer palace.

The victors then dictated another charter for the expansion of foreign privileges in China, the Convention of Peking of 24 October 1860. Besides ceding to Britain the Kowloon peninsula opposite Hong Kong, among other things, this treaty had an emigration clause inserted into it by the British and French plenipotentiaries, a provision that was to have for British colonial history consequences unforeseen at the time of its drafting. The Emperor of China, this particular article declared, would command every provincial authority to proclaim that 'Chinese choosing to take service in British colonies or other parts beyond the sea are at perfect liberty to enter into engagements with British subjects for that purpose, and to ship themselves and their families on board any British vessel at any of the open ports of China.'[29] (The provision, only reluctantly acceded to by China, served British purposes usefully enough in 1860, but it was not to be so useful when the Chinese government invoked it as an argument against the exclusion of Chinese immigrants from British possessions three decades later.) Such rules as were necessary for the protection of Chinese emigrants, the treaty went on to say, would be worked out by the provincial authorities and the representatives of Her Britannic Majesty.

These terms were secured not only by Great Britain, but by France, Spain and, eight years later, the United States. An Act of Congress had made it a crime for any American citizen or vessel to engage in the coolie trade;[30] but Anson Burlingame, a former US ambassador to China whom the Chinese had appointed as their roving envoy, took it upon himself in 1868 to negotiate a treaty which provided for the sending of Chinese consuls and labourers to America. Although the Chinese were not consulted in advance, the treaty, in words of a suitably American ring, represents both the United States and the Emperor of China as having recognized 'the inherent and inalienable right of man to change his home and allegiance, and also the mutual advantage of the free migration and emigration of their citizens and subjects respectively from one country to the other for purposes of curiosity, or trade or as permanent residents'.[31]

The coolie business, then, was rendered fully official. The Chinese government, for their part, tried to secure better terms than were provided by the Convention of Peking: the employers could surely give the emigrant a free return passage at the end of his service, they thought, and shouldn't the period of indenture be limited to five years? An Emigration Convention setting out these and other conditions was signed by Britain and France in 1866, but neither country could bring itself to ratify it, in face of the vehement objections raised by British planters and French merchants. Nevertheless, it formed the basis for the Chinese government's policy towards emigration for the next three decades.

But such rules as were devised to control the trade were flouted by foreigners and Chinese alike, and ships still cleared from the seaports with coolies who had been shanghaied or decoyed. Besides, to evade the rules in force in Canton, it was easy enough to shift operations to places beyond the control of the Chinese authorities – to Macao and Hong Kong, for example, both foreign settlements. Macao's reputation as a coolie market was particularly tainted, and few coolies who left it were voluntary emigrants. The effect of the Chinese insistence on enforcing the Emigration Convention, it seemed, was to give new impetus to contract emigration from that Portuguese colony, raising the number of barracoons there from about eight or ten to nearly forty within a year.[32] The British voiced objections, sending letters to Lisbon, but they could scarcely tell the Portuguese to put their house in order when the Portuguese could so easily wag their finger at what went on under the British flag in Hong Kong.

By the mid-1860s, steam had taken the place of sail, and scheduled steamer services were running between south China and Nanyang ports.[33] This facilitated the great waves of Chinese expatriation, which were to swell to millions before they began to ebb in 1930. Years were to pass before the edict of 13 September 1893 revoked the imperial ban on Chinese emigration and made it possible for Chinese expatriates to return home at will, but from the docks of Singapore to the plantations of Cuba the sight of the Chinese coolie working with ant-like industry, his bare back shiny with sweat or black with mosquitoes, was already inescapable.

Mass emigration from China, like mass emigration anywhere, required the juncture of bad times at home with good times abroad. Expatriation was the resort of the desperate, but large numbers of Chinese were also tempted out by news of boom and gold rush in distant countries. When the Cantonese called San Francisco Gum San, Gold Hills, and Australia Sun Gum San, New Gold Hills, they were being quite literal. Among those who set sail from the Four Districts of the Pearl River delta in Kwangtung province, travelling by raft or junk down inland waterways to take the steamship across the Pacific from Canton or Hong Kong, thousands went in search of undreamt-of wealth in the gold fields of California, New South Wales and Victoria.

When in 1848 gold was discovered near Yerba Buena, a sleepy Mexican village the world knows today as San Francisco, Chinese settlers had been in the area for a whole decade. But the pioneers were mostly Cantonese traders from the Three Districts of Namhoi, Punyu and Shuntak; the greater hegira, of optimistic fortune hunters and credit-ticket labourers, had its source in the poorer villages of Sze Yap or the Four Districts, namely Toishan, Sanwui, Hoiping and Yanping.

In they came, these multitudes of Sze Yap Chinese, streaming into the fabled land of gold and opportunity, over twenty thousand passing through the San Francisco custom-house in 1852 alone.[34] Of those who made the long journey in search of pickings, some worked for themselves, some for Chinese contractors, and others for American companies. Convulsed with gold fever, the booming San Francisco became so acutely short of labour that miners found it cheaper to send their dirty clothes on a clipper to Hong Kong or Honolulu to be washed than to pay for them to be laundered locally. The idea of importing Chinese labour seemed self-evident.

To the peasant in Toishan or Hoiping, America was the best of all places to be, never mind the animosity of white miners who drove Chinese prospectors out of the best claims and forced them to work areas others had abandoned, never mind the racially discriminatory laws to which Chinese were subjected. The advertising handbills distributed

by American clipper companies, the ones which did such good business
out of bringing emigrants over, were enough to make one dizzy with
dreams: 'All Chinamen make much money in New Orleans,' one of
these declared, 'if they work . . .'

> Chinamen have become richer than mandarins there. Pay,
> first year, $300, but afterwards make more than double. One
> can do as he likes in that country. Nobody better nor get more
> pay than does he. Nice rice, vegetables, and wheat, all very
> cheap. Three years there will make poor workmen very rich,
> and he can come home at any time. On the ships that go there
> passengers will find nice rooms and very fine food. They can
> play all sorts of games and have no work. Everything nice to
> make man happy. It is a nice country. Better than this. No
> sickness there and no danger of death. Come! go at once.
> You cannot afford to wait. Don't heed the wife's counsel or
> the threats of enemies. Be Chinamen, but go.[35]

The emigrant, upon arrival, registered with the appropriate native-
place association, the Three Districts immigrant with the Three Districts Association, the Four Districts immigrant with the Four Districts
Association, the official of which might well be his creditor or his creditor's agent. There were, by 1862, six of these associations, which later
combined to form the Chinese Consolidated Benevolent Association,
an umbrella organization perhaps better known to Americans as the
Six Companies. This kept tabs on every incomer, and no credit-ticket
emigrant could leave American shores without a nod from the Six
Companies. At its best it was a mutual aid society; at worst, the
heads were little better than Chinatown racketeers; in later years the
company's infiltration by chapters of secret societies, called 'tongs' in
America (the word meaning 'hall' or 'parlour' in Cantonese), was to
cast a shadow on its reputation.

The immigrant's first nights were likely to be spent in the company's
boarding-house, and it was there too that he arranged for part of his
wages to be remitted home and for his body to be shipped back to China
should he meet with mishap in America. Only after these important
matters were settled did he proceed to the diggings. Later, if he struck
lucky, he might be glimpsed entering a Chinese shop on the waterfront,
bringing his gold to be made into ornaments, belts and chains which
could be sewn into his clothes and taken out of California to China
under the noses of American customs officials.

The earth had to be fickle indeed to discourage the Chinese prospectors. 'It's dogged as does it' might be their motto, as they picked over ground judged poor or exhausted by white Forty-Niners, or scrabbled about deposits that needed the patience of Job to work. By the 1860s, when the boom had bottomed out, two-thirds of the mine workers in the states west of the Rocky Mountains were Chinese. In states such as Oregon and Idaho, as many as six out of every ten miners were Chinese. Of the Chinese at Auburn, an Oregon gold town, a writer has remarked that they 'patiently panned the gulches until there was scarcely an ounce of gold in the tailings of other days . . . when the Chinese miners had gleaned the last meager clean-up of dust from the gulches, the story of Auburn was ended.'[36]

Gold hunters found their way north to Canada, and by the winter of 1858 had formed their own community, a Little Canton, in Victoria.[37] In California the gold rush was flagging, but the state was soon caught up in a new enthusiasm, the building of the first American transcontinental railway. In June 1861 the Central Pacific Railway Company was established to lay a track eastward from Sacramento, while a rival company, the Union Pacific, was to start from Omaha and work westward until the two tracks met up. The Central Pacific had the harder task, for the line from Sacramento had to cross the massive granite slab of the Sierra Nevada, and mile after arid mile of the Nevada and Utah deserts. The Irish immigrants hired for the job had no heart for it. A worried Charles Crocker, one of the railroad barons, decided to try out fifty Chinese – miners, laundry men, domestic servants, labourers and market gardeners. You wouldn't think, from their diminutive build, that they would be much good at it, but the Chinese proved such satisfactory workers – so 'quiet, peaceable, patient, industrious and economical', the President of the company was to observe[38] – that the Central Pacific had twelve to fourteen thousand of them on its payroll before the project was finished.

Another quality they demonstrated was ingenuity. To drill holes in rock faces or to light dynamite, they hoisted themselves up and down cliffs in wicker baskets they wove from reeds, working pulleys. Blizzards buffeted them, explosives wounded them, snow chilled them and avalanches buried them, but they were little daunted by the hazards of their job or by climatic extremes, and lost few days to illness. An untold number lost their lives: a newspaper in 1870 reported that twenty thousand pounds of bones, the remains of some 1,200 railroad workers, were shipped to China for interment. As railroad builders they recognized no superiors, and it was cheap Chinese labour that later helped bring railways, including the Canadian Pacific, to the North American west.

At a time when labour was scarce and expensive, white Americans were pleased enough to hire Chinese workers. Chinese coolies in Cuba were brought over to work the sugar-cane plantations of Louisiana, where colonies of Catholic Chinese from the Spanish Philippines presently also sprang into being.[39] Agents contracting with Southern planters brought Chinese workers to substitute for Negro labour in the cotton fields of Arkansas and Mississippi, and discharged Chinese railway construction crews were found to make 'excellent' harvest hands – ones who could be 'depended upon to go to work on *Monday mornings*' – in the Monterey Bay region.[40] They were people to whom hardship and long hours were no novelty, and, with the completion of the transcontinental railway in 1869, they took to other trades and callings, becoming cooks, laundry men, houseboys, barbers, grocers and market gardeners. They performed prodigies with the region's agriculture, its sugar-beet and fishing industries. Yet the mark they left is not immediately obvious, and they are not explicitly mentioned in the local and regional histories. But, notes their historian in the Monterey Bay region, 'if you hold each page to the light you can make out a faint pattern. The longer you look, the stronger the pattern becomes. The Chinese are in the very paper, they are the watermark.'[41] Many had come to the Gold Hills hoping to better themselves on the diggings, but they did not lose their sense of purpose when gold wealth grew evasive.

California was not the only eldorado. In 1851, a Forty-Niner who had spent his last dollars on a passage back to Sydney from San Francisco struck gold in Australia. The discovery of gold in New South Wales and Victoria brought a rush of immigrants from southern China, shiploads of either contract coolies brought in to ease the labour shortage, or gold seekers coming on their own account or under the credit-ticket system. A newspaper in Hong Kong noted in 1854 that 'within the last three months [January, February, March], upwards of 2,100 have departed for Melbourne, thus showing what attention Australia is exciting among the Chinese . . .' Chinese passage brokers were driven 'to such utmost straits' that 'European ships condemned years ago as unfit to carry cargo are readily purchased at enormously high prices and fitted out for passages.'[42]

In October 1848, the *Nimrod*, a 234-ton barque, brought 120 Chinese labourers from Amoy to Sydney through the agency of James Tait. The odd Chinese carpenter and houseboy had preceded them many years before, but the arrivals on *Nimrod* were probably the first Chinese to come to New South Wales as a group.[43] They were followed by many others, for Australian squatters badly needed pastoral labour in appreciable quantities.

After 1851 fewer contract labourers were landed, but the number of credit-ticket emigrants setting out from the Pearl River delta (and particularly from the Four Districts) shot up, reaching some 11,500 in Victoria in 1855, and nearly 12,500 in New South Wales in 1858.[44] In the mining camps they pitched their tents and led as Chinese a way of life as they could. And just as migrants to California drifted north to Canada, so Chinese in Australia found their way to New Zealand, the first rush from Victoria starting in 1866, after gold was discovered in Otago.[45]

In both Australia and New Zealand, the influx of Chinese released, as large-scale immigrations are inclined to, a spring of racialist emotions. 'Mongolian filth' and 'locusts' were two epithets hurled at them by hostile members of the local population. One day in 1861 more than a thousand white miners sallied out to attack the Chinese miners at Lambing Flat with pickhandles, spades, bludgeons and hammers, led by a band playing

> Rule Britannia! Britannia rule the waves!
> No more Chinamen shall land in New South Wales![46]

Measures were taken to restrict the inflow of Chinese, and these were later to evolve into the White Australia Policy.

Australians were not the only hosts to express a distinct revulsion against the Chinese; doors were later to be slammed against the immigrant flood in other receiving countries. But all that still lay in the future. In the 1860s the floodtide had only just begun. In Hong Kong and Macao ship upon ship awaited its living cargo. The nineteenth century, the age of the great migrations, saw the dispersal of the Chinese across the world on a scale unprecedented in Chinese history.

PART TWO

1870s–1920s

CHAPTER FOUR

Shores

They went to Africa, they went to South and Central America, they went to the south Pacific and Melanesia. They went to work in virgin territory across the world. Though the mass of the Chinese emigrants were labourers, some went in search of trade or turned themselves into traders. Most lived by the sweat of their brow, and some not so much by their skill or wits as by a general competence to turn their hand to anything.

African shores offered some a labouring life, others a trading one. In Mauritius, life led many Chinese unerringly down to the market-place in Port Louis, and an English visitor to the colony in the 1860s was reporting that 'a Chinaman's shop' could be found 'in every out-of-the-way nook and corner of the island'.[1] Among the Chinese in Mauritius, the Cantonese had at first predominated, but they were overtaken by the despised Hakkas from Mei Hsien (Plum County) towards the last years of the nineteenth century. The two did not leave their differences at home, and Mauritius was to share with other overseas Chinese communities the familiar theme of feuding between Hakkas and Cantonese.

By then, Mauritius's economy having gone into decline, English voices were calling for a stop to Chinese immigration; unless they thinned out, these voices said, the Chinese would be driven to crime or beggary. But the Chinese were lucky to have a champion in the Governor Sir John Pope-Hennessy, who sprang to their defence before the colonial assembly in 1885:

> Go into the little shops of the Chinese in this town, and what
> do you see? At the end of the shop you will see in the evening
> – you will notice it in the evening, but it is there all day –
> a little lighted lamp. That is a lamp before their altar. They
> have their own forms of religion. It is not for us to stigmatize
> their religion because we ourselves may believe that we have
> a purer form of faith . . .
> We all know that at almost all the crossroads of the island
> are to be seen the well-built stone residences and shops of

the Chinese that have sprung up within the last few years;
and those Chinamen undoubtedly manage to sell the poorer
classes of this community cheap and simple goods which the
poor people wish to buy . . .[2]

Actually the Chinese knew as well as anyone that it would be hard
for the economy to absorb more newcomers. They could mope, or
they could venture further afield. The community leaders, the heads
of guilds and native-place associations, were all for reducing the influx
by onward migration, and the years between the 1880s and 1930s
were a time of considerable traffic, with Chinese leaving Port Louis
for Réunion, the Seychelles, Madagascar and South Africa – any
shore where better prospects beckoned. Port Louis became a place
of transit, a way station where Chinese newcomers were broken in to
foreign or European ways. The change from sail to steam had made
movement easy, and whereas many people used to suffer and die at sea,
now great imperial shipping lines like Méssageries Maritimes and the
Union Castle Line landed Chinese immigrants in fighting shape. There
was a constant coming and going of migrants between Mauritius and
Réunion, the direction following the ups and downs of the islands'
economic fortunes.

Madagascar, colonized by France in 1896, came to harbour the third
largest overseas Chinese community in Africa.[3] Chinese began arriving
the year after its colonization by the French, who were keen to settle
it with coolie labour. The first batch, mustered with the help of the
authorities in French Indochina, came from Kwangsi, the province
whose southern border marches with that of northern Vietnam.[4] In
Madagascar it was Chinese coolies who built the first roads and laid
the first railway, but this did not prove their fitness as pioneers, for
while many managed to make it back to China after they had fulfilled
their contracts, large numbers died at sea or, if they survived the
voyage and did not run away, were enfeebled or wasted by disease.
The hardship of those years was part of the common stock of Chinese
coolie experience across the world. The mortality rate was high among
the contract labourers, and the Chinese community that took root
in Madagascar came not so much of coolie importations as of free
immigration – of traders, seekers of opportunity or pursuers of profit
from both Mauritius and China. It was a distinctly and self-consciously
Cantonese community, many of whose members had migrated to escape
the increasingly overbearing Hakkas in Mauritius.[6]

As elsewhere, the migrants became middlemen. Barefoot Chinese were presently found in the remotest corners of Madagascar, spending their nights in the open and buying up coffee, vanilla and cloves (for resale in the towns or for export) at harvest time. There was much to attract Chinese traders to Madagascar: not the least of its local products was *bêche-de-mer*, the prized edible sea slug in which the western Indian Ocean abounded, and which the Chinese settlers fished and profitably exported to China. We later hear of native Africans in the hire of Chinese companies diving for sea slugs in Tanganyika.[7] It was sea slugs, so goes a local story, that drew Chinese migrants northward to Zanzibar, and from there to the shores of eastern Africa.

Following their nose, they pushed their way into other parts of Africa, often arriving in the newly colonized territories 'hot on the heels of the Europeans themselves'.[8] There were Chinese far in the interior of Africa, and in central and southern Africa. Transient colonies of them helped to lay Africa's earliest railways – in Belgian Congo, in Portuguese Mozambique, in French West Africa. 'I cannot get over the conviction', wrote a nineteenth-century German colonial administrator, 'that if it is possible for Central Africa to be opened up, it can only be accomplished by means of the Chinese . . . a few hundred Chinese established in any suitable place – under the direction of practical Europeans – would form a better nucleus for the colonization of Africa than any number of Indian elephants and ironclad steamers . . .'[9] Similarly, German imperialists in Tanganyika were convinced that for their coffee and tobacco plantations, Chinese labour was 'the only possibility'.[10]

To Lord Milner, High Commissioner and Governor of the Transvaal, Chinese labour was 'our only hope'. In conquering the Transvaal from the Boers, the British had acquired, in the highlands around Johannesburg, the largest deposits of gold in the world. The security of the vast amounts of speculative City money sunk in the gold fields of Witwatersrand (or the Rand as it was commonly called) hinged crucially upon the assurance of an adequate and steady supply of labour, but this the native Africans did not provide. 'We must', Lord Milner wrote, 'call in the aid of the Asiatics,'[11] a temporary but for the time essential expedient if the mining industry, prostrated by labour shortage, was to be resuscitated and, as Winston Churchill put it, South Africa was to 'turn her back upon the dark past'.[12]

The idea of importing Chinese miners was by no means universally welcome, though, for what safeguards were there against a repetition of the Natal experience? In that other British colony in southern

Africa, there had been introduced Indian indentured labourers who had afterwards entered trade and skilled employment, threatening the white population with a great deal of unwelcome competition. What was to stop the Chinese from doing the same? Whites in the Transvaal were afraid that unless the incoming labouring gangs were barred from trade and kept in rigorous submission, Johannesburg would end up as a Chinatown[13] – as one of them put it, 'It is simply absurd to suppose that we are going to have Asiatics in this country and be able to prevent them from following any trade.'[14]

But the mine owners were insistent. It was, as *The Economist* put it, a matter of pounds, shillings and pence.[15] In 1903, a Mr Ross Skinner was sent to California and the Far East to see if he could find a remedy. Mr Skinner concluded after investigations in California, Canada, Korea, Japan and China that 'the better class' of Chinese coolies would be suited to the mine owners' purpose, for as a race the Chinese struck him as 'docile, law-abiding, and industrious people . . . most easily led if matters were fully explained to them', though inclined to prove 'most stubborn' if new ideas or methods were thrust upon them without due explanation through the headman.[16] No sooner was Skinner's report delivered than negotiations were started with the Chinese government. Recruitment was undertaken on a grand scale, with emigration agents and their subcontractors rounding up people in not just the usual coastal areas but further afield, in the northern province of Shantung, the birthplace of Confucius and the home of some of China's tallest, burliest and hardiest men. In March 1904, 9,668 men landed in Durban, the first of a seven-year gush that, at its highest annual count, totalled almost 51,500.[17]

For all their careful stipulations, neither the Anglo-Chinese Labour Convention, signed by the Rand authorities and the Chinese government, nor the contracts of service drawn up in triplicate proved a guide to how the coolies would be treated by their masters in South Africa. If they had left their native shores with dreams of digging for gold in Africa, the reality in no way matched their expectations. To say that their life in the Rand was purgatory would perhaps be to exaggerate things, but one need only look at the casualty figures to realize its harsh exactions: of the 935 deaths in the first year, nearly four hundred were due to homicide, suicide and accidents.[18] Upon arrival they were quartered in special compounds, where they were to live in prison-like conditions for the duration of their three-year contracts, segregated from other humanity, ringed around by corrugated iron and wire fencing and kept under close surveillance by sentries and inspectors. No provision was made for their recreation, though if Christian they received the attention of the South African Baptist Missionary Society and the Salvation Army; but minds not instructed in the truths of Christianity were left to rot with boredom.

Some of the white overseers treated them little better than prisoners; others they conciliated by bribery: 'The Chinese is an adept,' reads an annual report of the labour department, 'and having gauged the character of the white inspector with whom he is brought in contact, he treats him accordingly. Collusion and corruption were thus common.'[19] Not everyone acquiesced in his fate, and desertions were common – they numbered no fewer than 1,700 in a single month in 1905;[20] recaptured absconders were fined or flogged with a whip of rhinoceros hide and had their heads clamped in a cangue, a wooden collar riveted around the neck. Some escaped coolies never got very far and merely ended up losing their way; others sneaked out to try their luck at trade; yet others wreaked violence on settlements in the surrounding country.[21] There were instances of runaways raiding Boer farmsteads, breaking into houses, and derailing trains. The consternation that these caused confirmed in many an anxious European his dread of being swamped by the Chinese, in whose formidable numbers and tenacity he perceived a threat to white supremacy.

But there was not much chance of that when, as well as being excluded from skilled employment, Chinese coolies were sent back to China the moment their contracts expired. No, if they made any impression on Johannesburg, it was by the part they played in reviving the productivity and profit of the Rand gold fields. They did more than meet a labour shortage; their competitive presence put a pressure on the blacks to return to work, and as the Transvaal prospered, so more white immigration was stimulated. It is doubtful if they themselves gained much by their expatriation; often the need to resort to opium and gambling to blot out the harshness and tedium of their existence defeated their intention to save as much of their hard-earned wages as they could, and they returned to China no better off than when they started out.

The landslide victory the Liberals won in the British General Election of 1906 was instrumental in ending Chinese contract immigration into South Africa. Winston Churchill, who became Under-Secretary of State for the Colonies, declared that the importing of Chinese labourers would cease and that no law would be entertained which sanctioned any condition of service smacking of servility – though of the contract entered into by the Chinese coolie, he had said, 'It cannot [undesirable as it may be], in the view of His Majesty's Government be classified as slavery in the extreme acceptance of the word without some risk of terminological inexactitude.'[22]

The Liberals had thundered against coolie labour and had made it an election issue, causing the emotive cry of 'Pigtail!' to be heard up and down the constituencies. Could any issue be turned to better account for the ends of the Liberals than that of 'Chinese slavery'? That the Liberals themselves had authorized the import of Chinese coolie labour into British Guiana and Trinidad in 1904 was conveniently forgotten in the screams for the Tories' blood. It was powerful stuff, the picture of wretched Chinese cooped up like serfs in the compounds, the posters showing Chinese coolies in chains, Chinese being flogged, the parades of manacled sandwich-men dressed as Chinese slaves. Cartoons of a Chinese coolie in a straw hat, captioned TORY BRITISH WORKINGMAN and thrown on a lantern screen at political meetings, elicited the outraged howls they were designed to provoke, from a working-class audience which 'could not have told whether it howled from humanitarian indignation or fear of the competition of cheap labour'.[23]

The new Liberal government restored the Boers to power and supported them in their moves to terminate coolie labour, which had been a British enterprise and had never commended itself to the Boers. Besides, the influx of Chinese had occurred at a time of growing white hostility to Asians. The noticeable increase in the numbers of Asian pedlars and merchants added more grudge to the antipathy of white shopkeeper towards brown or yellow trader, and voices were raised for curbs to be put on their further expansion. In 1906 the Transvaal government published a particularly humiliating ordinance, the Asiatic Registration Act, requiring fingerprints of every Indian and Chinese resident. This put the Asians on the defensive, for they saw the law as only too clearly a device of white discrimination, and they decided to resist. They were led in their defiance by a young Indian lawyer, Mahatma Gandhi.

Common oppressions make common causes, and there formed an alliance of the Indian and Chinese communities. Gandhi worked closely with the chairman of the local Cantonese Association, Leung Quinn. When Indians demonstrated their defiance by burning their trading licences and registration, so, encouraged by Leung Quinn, did Chinese. Leung, a free immigrant who had arrived in the Transvaal in 1896, was repeatedly arrested, but he fought on gamely, until ill-health from too many prison sentences forced him to stop. It was, had he but known it, a battle he could never win, for this was the country that was to give birth to that most baleful of racialist philosophies, apartheid.

The Chinese went early to Central and South America and to the West Indies. They went under Portuguese auspices to Brazil, where a transient colony of several hundred tea growers, perhaps the first settlement of Asians in the New World, was established in 1810.[24] They went, as hopeful merchants for the most part, to Mexico, Guatemala, Panama, Ecuador, Venezuela and Costa Rica.[25] But it was the coolie trade which took the bulk of the Chinese to the New World, with shipload after shipload reaching Cuba, Peru and Demerara in British Guiana in the years between the 1840s and 1870s.

It was a very unlucky coolie who found himself transported to Cuba. A great deal came to be known of the hardships and cruelties suffered by the coolies there, for in 1874 the imperial government in Peking despatched a commission of enquiry to Havana. It was a delegation of three which arrived in the Spanish colony: a Chinese educational officer, Mr Ch'en Lan-pin; a Mr A. Macpherson, Commissioner of Customs at Hankow; and a Mr A. Huber, Commissioner of Customs at Tientsin. Besides calling on the consular representatives of various European countries, these gentlemen visited barracoons, jails, plantations and sugar warehouses, interviewing Chinese coolies personally and receiving their petitions.

Their findings make grim reading. For a start, it turned out that no fewer than four-fifths of the coolies had been decoyed or kidnapped. On landing, they were herded like cattle into a barracoon – by 'foreigners on horseback, armed with whips', according to one of the testimonies offered to the commission[26] – or held at a quarantine station where their queues were cut, and where they awaited inspection by prospective buyers. At the 'men-market' where they were offered for sale, they were divided into three classes and had all their clothes removed so that the buyers could size them up and ascertain the amount of work that could be extracted from them and hence the price to be offered for them.

Nine out of ten coolies ended up in sugar plantations; others were sent to work on farms or coffee estates; in sugar warehouses and gas works; in bricklayers' or washing establishments; on railways; on board cargo boats; in bakeries or cigar, shoe, hat, carpenters', stone-cutters'

and other shops; as domestics or as municipal scavengers. Some of
these places were no better than torture chambers, where whips and
rods were in constant use, 'and maimed and lacerated limbs [were]
daily to be seen'.[27] Confinement or the lash were used as punishment
with machine-like regularity. On the plantations, the overseers cracked
whips the three- to four-foot-long lashes of which were made of 'the
muscles of oxen dried in the sun'.[28] The food rations, consisting of
potatoes, bananas or maize, and rarely any meat, were miserably scanty
– as one testimony put it, 'The administrator who gives only four
unripe bananas a meal, is considered an able servant, and if he gives
only three he is regarded as still more efficient'.[29] And yet the coolies
were made to labour up to twenty-one hours out of the twenty-four,
with the workday beginning in the middle of the night, from three
or four a.m., and continuing up to the following midnight, with only
an hour off for the midday meal. Those who lagged or fell sick were
beaten, quite often to death. Benignant masters were not unknown,
but they were an exception; the whip-wielding overseers left lacerated
and bleeding backs wherever they went. Stripped of all hope, abused
beyond endurance, many Chinese were driven to hang themselves, cut
their throats, swallow opium, or jump into wells or sugar cauldrons.

'The agreement-term expired,' asked the commissioners, 'what
becomes of the coolie?' One of the coolies spoke for many when he
told the commissioners what happened when his eight years were up:
'I imagined that I could seek employment elsewhere, but my master
chained me and flogged me and forced me to engage myself for six
years.'[30] The chances of their being set free or returning to China
were slim in the extreme, for, if they were not coerced into working
for another term or sent to labour without wages on public works
when their contracts expired, they were all too frequently defrauded
of the money they had saved for their passage home. A man had only
one way out of this bondage, and that was by dying. Dead, he was
tossed into a hole, his bones dug up in due course and used, just
as the charred bones of oxen were, for the refining of sugar. As one
testimony put it, 'It is certain that for us there will be neither coffin
nor grave, and that our bones will be . . . burnt with those of horses
and oxen and to be afterwards used to refine sugar, and that neither
our sons nor our sons' sons will ever know what we have endured.'[31]

But their plight did reach the ear of Chinese authority, thanks to
the commissioners' chilling report, which was published in Shanghai
in 1876 and which horrified its readers. The acrimonious exchanges

which ensued between the governments of Spain and China had international reverberations and a broadly happy denouement. The Spanish authorities freed 43,298 coolies, about a third (the rest having perished) of the 126,000 who landed in Cuba between 1847 and 1877.[32]

Cuba was the nadir, but there were coolie shores with reputations almost as unsavoury. Peru was also investigated by a Chinese delegation, and found guilty of enormous outrages against the imported coolie. Between eighty and a hundred thousand of these were landed from 1849 to 1874 to feed the hunger for labour in the haciendas.[33] They arrived in two waves, with the numbers reaching a peak in the 1870s. Between the two, recourse was had to the natives of the Hawaiian islands, but these had 'died like flies that had been poisoned'.[34]

On arrival at Callao or Paita, Peru's seaports, the ship and its passengers were inspected by officials – but only perfunctorily, for the traffickers were usually men of substance and high social standing. Sometimes a single planter would have contracted for the entire shipload of coolies; but cargoes not disposed of in this way would be offered for sale on board or at the pier, with the men lined up for their physiques to be looked over by the prospective buyer, to have their biceps squeezed, their ribs poked at, and their bodies twisted around 'like a top'. There was, wrote a contemporary spectator:

> a look of bewilderment on the Chinaman's face while undergoing this process – that is to say as far as his Mongolian features are capable of expressing such emotion. But it is not always so, for there are some smart perky coolies who are only too anxious to show off their points . . . Brothers or cousins are always eager to get together, and if this doesn't suit the views of the purchaser, John is sometimes very decided, and often gains his point by dint of Celestial eloquence and signs.[35]

Most of the coolies were destined for the sugar plantations, but many were employed in railroad building and factories, and as household domestics. A local poet, Juan de Arona, conjured up their ubiquity along the Peruvian coast in a Spanish verse which, freely translated into English, goes something like this:

> There is no place where you do not find the Chinese,
> From the sacking of guano,
> To the cultivation of the valleys;

From waiting on the tables
To cleaning the streets.
He is even the servant of the commoner,
And there is no activity – you understand? –
On which he does not diligently embark.
And the people of the country?
They are thinking of becoming gentry![36]

Of all the places where the Chinese were set to work, the most dreaded was doubtless the guano beds. The excrement of sea-fowl found in islands off Peru and profitably used as a natural fertilizer, guano had enriched the country more than any other export item for over a quarter of a century. An American Consul to Peru reported in 1870 that the Chinese put to labour on the guano islands had to clear a hundred wheelbarrow-loads of the deposit a day, and that those who were too weak to stand up were made to work on their knees to pick the small stones out of the guano. It was vile work, a harrowing picture of which has been left us by an English observer sent to investigate the guano industry for British holders of Peruvian bonds:

> No hell has ever been conceived by the Hebrew, the Irish,
> the Italian, or even the Scotch mind for appeasing the anger
> and satisfying the vengeance of their awful gods, that can
> be equalled in the fierceness of its heat, the horror of its
> stink, and the damnation of those compelled to labour there,
> to a deposit of Peruvian guano when being shovelled into
> ships.[37]

The harshness of the job was made worse by the cruelty of the task-masters, who used the lash to exhort the coolies to greater effort. The prospect of drudging in this inferno from day to day, month to month, year to year was dire enough to drive some of the labourers to take their own lives; guards had to be posted around the shores to prevent suicidal coolies from hurling themselves into the sea.

On the plantations, trees replaced the sea as a means of escape, and the number of hangings was an index of the shrivelled wills and broken bodies. It certainly did not help that the hacienda owners played on the racial antipathy which the local blacks, Indians and mestizos felt towards the Chinese, using these people, in a conscious application of the principle of divide and rule, to offset the strength of the Chinese. 'Negroes themselves had been slaves,' notes the historian Watt Stewart, 'and they are said to have regarded the Chinese as their successor and to have enjoyed cracking the whip over the yellow labourer as it had once been cracked over them.'[38]

The exactions and abuses bred fantasies of vengeance, and hatreds easily inflamed into insurrection and violence. The first of the coolie risings occurred on a September evening in 1870, when a planter and his three dinner guests were surprised at their supper by the sudden appearance of a band of belligerent Chinese. Armed with machetes, knives, guns and lances, these fell upon the diners and slaughtered them, and then made off with everything of value they could find in the house, including, we are told by a despatch from the United States Consul, fifty good horses. The rising spread, and in one town, whose citizens took refuge in the church, the women 'suffered a terrible fate, their persons were violated, and their bodies cut into pieces, their heads cut off and placed on poles, and shown to those inside the church'.[39] The next town, though, was ready for the rioters, and put up so spirited a fight that they covered the road with the bodies of the Chinese.

Social critics and observers friendly to the Chinese blamed the risings on the callousness of the hacienda masters. Public opinion crystallized against the planter class and its ill-treatment of the Chinese. Was it so surprising that they rebelled? 'Everyone knows', wrote one newspaper editor in 1876, 'that these frequent uprisings are bloody and impotent protests against horrible wrongs.'[40] Others excoriated the Chinese. That the number of 'free' Chinese – coolies who had fulfilled the terms of their contracts – was growing was a cause of considerable public unease, for they were seen to be the fomenters of risings and potential trouble-makers, beyond the control of the plantation masters.

The ratio between contract labourers and 'free' Chinese was shifting, for forced immigration was drying up. The last shipload of contract labourers had sailed into Callao in July 1874, the year Portugal succumbed to British pressure and decreed an end to Chinese coolie emigration through Macao.[41] Other arrangements would have to be made if Peru was to be assured a continuance of Chinese immigration. What was more, it would have to contend with the ire of the Chinese government, in whose view Peruvians were no better than the Spaniards whose venality had been so clearly attested by the Cuba Commission.

The Peruvian government sent a mission to China. Considering the odds against it, the treaty it succeeded in concluding with the imperial government was nothing short of a diplomatic triumph. Among other concessions, Peru won from China (happy to be relieved of the crush of its own population, if incensed at the way its citizens were treated abroad) the recognition of the right of its subjects to emigrate if they so chose; Peru would still get the manpower it needed, but this would now be voluntary. Ironically, so many Chinese were to enter the country that in the first decade of the twentieth century measures had to be adopted to restrict further immigration.

In Lima, to which the Chinese tended to gravitate, there had long evolved a Chinese quarter, an early example, to judge from what was written of it by a minister of the United States to Peru in 1874, of the Chinatowns that Chinese emigration would spawn across the world:

> Streets fronting on the large markets or those leading to them
> are filled by Chinese grocers, tailors, shoemakers, bakers,
> butchers, and other tradesmen so much so that walking
> around seeing the people, their shops and signs you could
> easily imagine that you were in a Chinese town.[42]

Many Chinese became converts to Catholicism, and when they died were allowed burial in Christian graveyards – the US diplomat noticed 'several niches in the costly part of the ground with Chinese inscriptions' in the Santo Tomás Church in Lima.[43] There may still be found in Lima today Chinese graves dating from the nineteenth century. One spotted by an English visitor to the Chinese cemetery in Lima in 1987 goes back to 4 September 1891, and you could tell from the Chinese inscription that the deceased, one José Asau, had been buried there by the native-place association to which he belonged.[44]

Hawaii was another shore. Called T'an-hsiang Shan (Sandalwood Mountains) in Chinese, it was a harbour and refuelling station for the ships that traded in Hawaiian sandalwood and other commodities between the south China coast and North America. The Chinese went there early: they were already living there by the late 1820s. But mass migration began later, stimulated by large-scale commercial sugar production. The Chinese, coming from a country where sugar had been made for centuries, in fact pioneered this, though it was Americans and Europeans who made it the industry it became – it is said that the first Chinese sugar maker, Wong Tze-chun, arrived in Hawaii in 1802 with a rudimentary sugar mill and boiling pans on a vessel engaged in the sandalwood trade.[45]

Here, too, Chinese indentured labour met a manpower need. The first batch comprised Fukienese coolies shipped from Amoy, speaking a dialect so different from that of the Cantonese shopkeepers already settled there that, for the two to converse, they had to resort to Hawaiian speech. But the Fukienese were to prove a transient community, for later almost all the immigrants came from a few coastal districts in Kwangtung province. From 1876 to 1885, a time of simultaneous expansion in sugar and rice cultivation, they arrived in Hawaii at the rate of about 2,600 a year.

Opportunities abounded in Hawaii, and those not employed on the sugar or rice plantations earned their livings growing coffee and pineapples; farming fruit and vegetables; raising poultry, pigs and horses; fishing and whaling; or making honey and even *awa*, the narcotic drink much favoured by Hawaiians. Immigration gave many a Chinese the chance for a decent, even a comfortable, life. Some made fortunes, like the man who became Hawaii's Taro King, Lum Yip Kee. Lum was a Cantonese immigrant who arrived as a nineteen-year-old in 1884. He worked for four years as a taro planter, then returned to China to marry. Subsequently he put in some years in Saigon, affiliated to a Chinese firm, and returned to Hawaii at twenty-seven. He operated two taro plantations, and he did this for seven years, helped by relatives and fellow villagers newly arrived from China. On one of the plantations, he presently set up a factory for converting taro into *poi*, the food basic to the Hawaiians' diet. There also followed a diversification of business into importing and general merchandising, the main outlet of which was located in Honolulu's Chinatown. The company's main warehouse was destroyed in a Chinatown fire, and Lum Yip Kee lost a considerable sum of money. Nothing daunted, he returned to China to do some business with the Chinese suppliers, and at the same time to visit his wife and family. When he returned to Hawaii in 1902, he brought his family. Three years later, in partnership with another Chinese, he established the Oahu Poi Factory, one day to become the largest in Hawaii. There followed another factory, then another, until Lum and his partner had all of the poi market at their feet.[46]

There was also Chun Afong, who was made a noble of the kingdom and who raised a dozen children on his considerable fortune. In 1889 he left his white Hawaiian wife, Julia Hope Fayerweather, and returned to China, where he remained for the rest of his life. It was on the life of Chun Afong that Jack London based his story 'Chun Ah Chun'.[47]

Not so lucky was Chang Wah, who was born in 1866 in the same district in Kwangtung province as Lum Yip Kee, the sixth of fourteen children, in a family hard-up enough to have considered the sale of some of its offspring. When he was ten, he did what he must – he started working in a neighbour's rice fields; but in his mind was a frail hope, the hope of bettering himself in the Sandalwood Mountains of which he had heard tell. What, he suggested to his parents and relatives, if they put up the money to send him there, so that by his remitted earnings they might all benefit? A number of buffaloes and many of their chickens had to be sold to finance his journey, but eventually he was on his way, arriving in Hawaii in 1890.

He had heard from fellow passengers that there was a Chang from his native village running a rice plantation in Oahu; and sure enough there was. He found work there, and was set to tasks that elsewhere might be shouldered by a beast of burden, but he was pleased enough with the job, and remained in it for ten years, receiving nine dollars a month on top of board and lodgings. At the end of that time his employer sold his business and returned to China, and Chang Wah went to work for another planter. He was paid the same, nine dollars a month.

After five years of this, he finally moved on. Earnings were higher on the sugar plantations, and as a cane cutter and piece contract worker he could make about a dollar a day. To work a little harder, a little longer, to save some more – this has ever been the impulse of migrants. Chang was no different, but after ten years of strenuous work on the sugar plantation his physical vigour was no longer what it had been, and he had to switch to lighter work in the rice fields. But by then he had saved enough money to go into business for himself, and with a Chinese friend for a partner he started a rice plantation of his own and prospered. Those were palmy days; in those days he could call himself a rich man. But they did not last, for a dip in the price of rice was to signal the collapse of his business, and to return him to the poverty of his earliest years in Hawaii. Too old now to make a fresh start, Chang Wah found himself having to live off relief, regretting all the while that he had not sold out and returned to China when the going was good.[48] The later typecasting of the overseas Chinese as successful entrepreneurs obscures the fact that failure was very much a part of the migrant's experience.

Lum's and Chang's was a familiar vocational odyssey, from working for others to working for oneself. Though large numbers of coolies ended their lives as coolies, some became not only their own men but their own bosses. Though it was the coolie traffic that dispersed the Chinese across the world, such settlements as were brought into being could only have survived with commerce as their *raison d'être*.

In many a frontier society settled by the Chinese the travelling trader in native products was very often the vanguard; after him would come the shop, the settlement, the town. Few corners of the world remained strangers to the Chinese tradesman; no place was too far or too exotic for the Chinese migrant. There are many illustrations of this: as good as any is Papua New Guinea.

New Guinea was annexed by Germany in 1884, and run by the German New Guinea Company until 1899. German New Guinea consisted of the Bismarck Archipelago, a scatter of islands which included Neu Pommern (New Britain), and the northern stretch of what is now the New Guinea mainland, which they called Kaiser Wilhelmsland. The Germans were quick to tap the Far East for the manpower needed to settle the shores of Kaiser Wilhelmsland, and to make them productive with coconut and tobacco plantations; indentured Chinese and Malay labourers were brought over from Singapore and Sumatra, hundreds arriving each year, and subsequently from Hong Kong and China. It was a harsh and often brutal world in which the newcomer found himself, and if the diseases to which he fell prey didn't finish him off, the dire working conditions soon did – the mortality rate was high, as much as sixty per cent, for example, among the ones who arrived in 1891 and 1892.[49] Of those who survived, only a small number remained after their contracts expired. The scheme was judged a failure, and no lasting Chinese settlement arose from it.

And yet Papua New Guinea was one day to have a half-Chinese for a Prime Minister – Sir Julius Chan, who came to power in 1980. Julius Chan's father was a prominent Chinese merchant and plantation owner who had married a woman from the Tanga Islands, to the northeast of New Britain, and the future Prime Minister had attended a Chinese school before going on to a European one. The Chans, whose surname was one of the three commonest in the New Guinea Chinese community, went back a long way, to a time before the importation of contract coolies into Kaiser Wilhelmsland. In those days there were Chinese working for the Germans in the Bismarck Archipelago, some thirty of them, employed by German firms as carpenters, housekeepers, cooks, copra buyers and trading agents. Sailing around the coasts, by themselves or in the company of Germans, pioneering Chinese traders transacted business with the native villagers, exchanging steel, salt, cloth, knives, mirrors and beads for copra – playing very much the part, in other words, of many of their compatriots in Southeast Asia. Some were bird of paradise shooters; others were labour recruiters, travelling from village to village to sign up native contract workers on behalf of their German masters. In the course of doing this they introduced the native to Pidgin; to the use of shotguns; to fruit and vegetables such as pawpaw, cucumbers and taro; and no doubt to a few bad habits. The encounters were not always happy, and cases of Chinese being murdered by the islanders were sometimes reported.

It is probably safe to say that the pioneers were Chinese from Singapore, for the regular shipping services that began operating between Europe and New Britain in 1894 invariably called at this port. It was only later that migrants came straight from China. Aside from a sprinkling of Hainanese islanders, the earliest arrivals were villagers from either Toishan or Hoiping, two of the Four Districts which provided, it may be recalled, the great bulk of Chinese immigration to the United States. Later they were joined by Hakkas, and Cantonese from the Three Districts.

The very first Chinese to settle in the Bismarck Archipelago appears to have been Lee Tam Tuck, better known as Uncle Ah Tam, an illiterate but clearly canny character who came to New Guinea with some German traders and became a considerable businessman, owning two shipyards, a wholesale and retail shop, a hotel, several plantations, a gambling den, a brothel and an opium-house. Most newcomers went to him for their first job, and almost every Chinese who ever lived in the Chinese quarter had had him for a landlord at one time or another.[50]

New Guinea did not beckon with gold and riches the way California or Australia did, but it was a place where failure was not inevitable. Chinese migrants were good at making the most of things, however unpromising; good at taking life as it came, and doing what they must. 'I'm a dead duck,' thought Seeto Soon, a nineteen-year-old immigrant to New Guinea in 1909, when he first set eyes on the place, so much more backward than he had imagined. He wanted to turn round and go straight back to China; but when his father, who had preceded him to New Guinea, berated him, and told him that he would just have to put up with it, he did, and it was twelve years before he saw China again.[51]

In those days migrants expected to go home, if not to marry, then to retire. Emigration was not a permanent transfer. If there were many arrivals in New Britain in the years between 1903, when Chinese immigration of any size began, and 1914, when it was occupied by Australia, there were also many departures. The inflow in 1903 was largely of carpenters, encouraged to come to the Bismarck Archipelago to help construct a new wharf the Germans had planned for a harbour on New Britain; the harbour was later to burgeon into the township of Rabaul, the capital of the German New Guinea. The opening of regular shipping services between New Guinea and Hong Kong by the line Norddeutscher Lloyd made the journey more direct than it might have been. For an immigration middleman the Germans had the ever efficient Uncle Ah Tam; they made it worth his while, paying a fee for each immigrant he brought in.

They also leased him, for a nominal rent, seventeen acres of land in Rabaul, a town by and large built by the Chinese. On those seventeen acres rose Chinese shops, laundries, restaurants, bakeries, homes – in other words a Chinatown. This was how an Australian observer was to describe it in 1919:

> It is as if a little East-Asiatic township, by some magic power, has been transplanted to New Britain . . . Although most of the shops neither impress by size nor cleanliness, but are just what one would expect in a Chinese quarter, there is plenty of excuse for everybody to go there . . . Over and above all, Chinatown is Rabaul's busy, unruly corner – where people rise early – are always on the move – and go to bed late. While after sunset the European quarter becomes quiet, and the streets look empty and desolate, life in Chinatown moves on – intense – rapid – and wicked.[52]

It was said that Chinese businesses, open till all hours, threatened the European firms with 'grievous competition'.[53] This was not a new story, nor was its corollary, the introduction of measures to curb their activities. Australia, when it assumed control of New Guinea, pursued an exclusive policy, barring the Chinese from leasing land, from participating in certain areas of economic life, and from living or trading in certain areas. The Chinese, more than a thousand of them, were confined to Chinatown, an area no larger than a quarter of a square mile; and in 1926 all Chinese houses beyond its ambit were removed. But still the Europeans complained: 'One cannot smell the flowers in the [nearby botanical] gardens,' grumbled a letter-writer to the *Rabaul Times* in 1928, 'because of the odour that arises from the contiguous Chinese houses.'[54] A policy of racial segregation saw to it that whites and Chinese did not mix in public places, and there were parks, schools, hospitals, cemeteries, gaols, theatres, clubs and even boats where neither Chinese nor blacks were allowed.

When New Guinea became an Australian Mandate in 1921 Chinese immigration was officially terminated. No longer was New Guinea a welcoming shore, and in the succeeding years its Chinese population dwindled, to pick up again only after the Second World War.

The story of the Chinese dispersal would not be complete without some mention of the movement of nearly two hundred thousand men to France in the First World War, for, though nearly all were repatriated, a few became permanent immigrants, either then or later.

There was a crying need for men to engage in non-combatant work on railways, roads, dockyards, forests, fields, mines, factories, and so on in France, and to free the French and British for front-line duties. Where were these men to be had? British minds turned not unnaturally to China, recalling the indentured labourers sent not all that many years before to the gold mines of South Africa. In 1916 the British government decided to form a Chinese Labour Corps to serve in France, and to organize its recruitment and movement along the lines that had been adopted in the case of the Transvaal labour importation, while avoiding any suggestion that it was what the Liberals had called it in the 1906 General Election – Chinese slavery. It was thought that, by employing Chinese workers in France, English men would be relieved not only to go to the front but to return to London, Liverpool, Southampton and other British ports, where their services were urgently needed. To send the Chinese to England, on the other hand, would be to invite a clash with the trade unions over the matter of coloured labour.

The British learnt that the French had forestalled them, and were already starting to enrol men in emigration agencies in Shantung, Shanghai, Canton and other places. It was hoped in some British quarters that those who had been repatriated from the South African mines could be re-enlisted into the Chinese Labour Corps and form its nucleus, and it was not hard to decide on Weihaiwei, a small British-leased territory at the northeastern end of the Shantung peninsula, as their chief recruiting centre. Apart from its being British, Weihaiwei had a ready-made depot – the 'coolie barracks' erected, though never used, by the Witwatersrand Native Labour Association of Johannesburg for shipping labourers to South Africa.[55] And there was perhaps no better recruiting ground than Shantung, the men there being 'extremely hardy, used to a climate range of, say, anything over 100 degrees in summer to 10 degrees below in winter; always cheerful and hardworking, they had no inhibitions, caste or religious taboos . . . which have caused so much trouble in India'.[56] Later it proved expedient to widen the catchment area and move the main depot to Tsingtao, a port with better communications on the southwestern coast of the peninsula. Chinese emigration agents did the actual recruiting, backed up by newspaper publicity and announcements handed out at tea-houses or posters stuck in front of fairgrounds and temples.[57] There was no shortage of candidates, for Shantung had a population almost the size of that of France, with a territory only a quarter as large. Thousands signed up, as rumours of good food and wages spread. Families left behind were promised an allowance – to the delight of many wives, and especially to the one who told a missionary: 'The British government is splendid; not only have they taken away my worthless husband but in addition they pay me ten dollars a month!'[58]

The coolie (this was what he was officially designated in the three-year contract he signed with the British government) was to be paid just over half of what a British private received, namely one French franc per day. This being four times what he would have earned in Shantung, a British commentator remarked that the Witwatersrand barracks 'are today the gateway to an Eldorado'.[59] If the British were thought to be generous, the French were even more so, offering a net pay of F2.50 a day, as well as extra on Sundays (F7.70) and bonuses for overtime, 'assiduousness' and 'economy', to the extent allowed French workers engaged in the same work. And while the British paid a monthly sum of $10 to the labourer's family back home, the French paid $30.[60] A British Foreign Office memo described the French wages as 'fantastic'.[61]

What was perhaps even more fantastic was the amount that the Chinese labourers managed to save. This is of course a constant of immigrant life: whatever they do, whichever way they adopt, scrimping every penny or working overtime at every opportunity, immigrants save. Those savings are their future. In nineteen months, we learn from a note by the Chinese Minister to London in May 1919, the 130,000 men in France had deposited fifty-one million francs in French banks, representing a savings rate of F20.65 per person per month. Of the total deposited, perhaps sixty-nine per cent came from the workers in British employ, the ones stationed in northwestern France, where the cost of living was lower; these men would have saved an average of twenty-five francs per month.

Boarding a boat built in Newcastle, the first contingent of the Chinese Labour Corps left Weihaiwei in January 1917, disembarking in April at Le Havre, whence they were taken by train late in the same evening to Noyelles-sur-Mer, by the River Somme.[62] There, behind the fighting

front, they passed their first night, in a type of camp with which many
hundreds were already familiar, having been first introduced to it in
South Africa. The Chinese brought over by Britain were intended only
for the military zones in Flanders and France, and so were sent to the
seaports up and down the coast from Le Havre to Dunkerque and the
battlefields between Cambrai and Ypres. Those recruited by France,
on the other hand, were scattered over a wide area – the length of the
coast from Brest to Marseille, inland from Rouen to Le Creusot, and
along the battlefront from Arras to Verdun – employed not only on
public works but in factories and private companies, a deployment to
which the English trade unions would never have agreed. Unlike the
British-employed, they were not subjected to strict military discipline,
and by and large they enjoyed greater freedom, for instance to go about
as they pleased on their days off – in Rouen two were once spotted
relaxing in the Rue Martainville, wearing what seemed like 'ill-fitting,
semi-secular, frock-coats, over black silk robes and straw boaters,
and carrying umbrellas'.[63] Reflecting on the difference in French
and British approach, the YMCA secretary for Le Creusot wrote:

> From my observation the Chinese labourers with the French
> were more contented than those with the British. Besides dis-
> cipline, the difference in the attitude of the officers towards
> the labourers was also an important factor. The French
> officers were much less race-conscious. They were more
> democratic in their manners and took a more paternalistic
> interest in the labourers. The British stood on dignity as
> officers, and perhaps as white men, most of the time.[64]

To a patronizing Englishman, what *were* these men but 'great big
boys' no older 'than ten years in character – very amenable, easily managed with kindness and firmness, and loyal to the core if treated with
consideration'? 'They bear', this same observer remarked, 'nothing but
dislike for anyone who is afraid of them. A dog is the same.'[65] They
were terrific workers, you certainly had to give them that. Watching
them unload equipment upon their arrival in Boulogne at three o'clock
in the morning, a British officer said that they 'worked like Trojans
. . . beating all other white battalions'.[66] Reports of their performance
abounded in praise – here is one of many: 'The spectator got the
impression that there is no irony in the remark that the Chinese actually
love work.' Of all the nationalities working for the British Army, the
Chinese seemed the most efficient – you could tell this from a 1918

report to the War Office setting out an 'order of utility' for the coloured labour employed: '1. Chinese; 2. Fijians; 3. Cape Coloured; 4. South African Natives; 5. Egyptians; 6. British West Indians; 7. Indians.'[67]

There were exceptions. One of the Chinese interpreters, living up to the stereotype of the Shanghainese dandy, was described as 'almost useless', wearing a new suit every other day and drinking only champagne.[68] Nor were the Shantung men always so predictable. They are not known for their cleverness, compared to the wily southerners, but they can be ingenious enough, though not always in the way wished for by their employers – as when they tried to steal a side of lamb by dressing it up in standard issue Labour Corps garb and marching it out of the work area wedged between two labourers.[69]

When first recruited, the Chinese workers, as citizens of a neutral power, were not supposed to engage in any military operation or indeed be exposed to any danger, but in August 1917 China entered the war, and then no one felt like sticking very closely to the letter of the agreement. The danger was in any case already there, in places close to the fighting such as Calais and Dunkerque, and from aerial bombing and long-distance shelling. Chinese could be found in the field, digging trenches, exhuming and reburying the dead of war, giving their food and cigarettes to the wounded and sometimes, in the middle of clearing up the battlefields, getting injured or killed themselves by an unexploded bomb or grenade.[70] They could not help but be drawn into the fighting, and there circulated several versions of a story of a Chinese attack upon German prisoners of war. This is the story which the writer Angus Wilson, who was told it by his father, worked into his novel *Late Call*. In the book it comes out as the reminiscences of an officer, Arthur Calvert:

> No, he's a very good fighting man, your Chink. We had a few labour-detachments of them with us in Flanders, you know. And they spoiled for a fight. Not like our ancient and honourable ally the Pork and Cheese [Cockney rhyming slang for Portuguese]. I was in charge of a crowd of Hun prisoners of war at the time. Order to protect them. Protect them my Aunt Fanny! Well, the Boche 'planes came over – it was late in '17 – and straffed these poor bloody Chinks to hell. The next day I was sitting in the mess when the sergeant comes in, 'Major Calvert, sir. Come at once. The Chinks have run amok!' 'Course when I came out the German prison compound wasn't there. Blown to smithereens. Just a

bit of wire and guts left. The Chinese were quite open about
it, 'German killee Chinese. Chinese killee Germans.' They'd
chucked a couple of bloody bombs at them. The Colonel
went mad when he heard about it. 'You must make an
example of them, Calvert,' he said. 'If you'll excuse me,
sir,' I told him, 'I'll do no such thing. You can't blame
them. It's their philosophy.' Well, the long and short of it
was that we had a hell of a row, but I managed to get the
thing taken to higher ranks. In the end – laugh this one off
– it got up to the C.-in-C., and gor blimey, if he didn't come
down on the side of yours truly. 'Calvert's perfectly right,'
he said, 'it's the Chinese philosophy. Its all in Confucius.'
That's their equivalent of Jesus Christ, you know.[71]

The dead were buried in England and France; the wounded and
sick were usually sent back to China. For the most part, the others
were repatriated when their contracts were completed, the shipments
beginning in the autumn of 1919. Carrying their rifles back from the
front as souvenirs, some were taken to England, where they remained;
among them were those maimed in action and at sea.[72] Nearly two
thousand of those employed by the French renewed their contracts,
which differed from the British ones in allowing the labourer to stay
on in France if he wished. A number of Chinese had married French
girls – the number of mixed marriages was not great, as the French
government was to prohibit it – and these too became settlers. (Two,
Lu Hou-tcheng, who set up on his own as a maker of car-seat covers
after a spell working for Le Creusot engineering works, and Tsang
Kuong-pio, who once ran a restaurant near the Bastille, were awarded
the French Legion of Honour in 1989.) Back in China many of the
repatriates had trouble fitting in, for they had seen something of the
world, their horizons had widened, and they felt like men on the move
rather than stuck in a groove. Large numbers were to become migrants a
second or third time, the British colonial police service providing a path.
For long years afterwards, you could guess the origins of many guards
and policemen in the British-run International Settlement of Shanghai
and in the British colony of Hong Kong from their physiques, for who
but the men of Shantung would be so tall and so sturdily built?
Across the seas, nearly two thousand of their compatriots lie in graves
near Folkestone and at Plymouth in England, and in cemeteries on the
French coast. The largest of these is the one near Noyelles-sur-Mer, by
the Somme estuary. A signpost in English, TO THE CHINESE CEMETERY,

points the way. The Michelin Guide has an entry. Enclosed by a low stone wall, shaded by cedars and maidenhair trees, here are laid out the graves of 838 Chinese. An imposing monument inscribed with Chinese characters and surmounted by a flaring Chinese tile roof honours their memory. The Chinese touch is said to have been conceived by the architect of the Imperial War Graves Commission in France, and to have inspired the admiration of Sir Edwin Lutyens, creator of New Delhi and principal architect for all the cemeteries in France.

CHAPTER FIVE

Limehouse and San Francisco

It was the trade with China and the ships of the East India Company that brought the first Chinese to England. In London Chinese sailors were spotted as early as the eighteenth century, as recorded in this newspaper article dated 27 July 1782: 'Coming through Stepney on Sunday evening, at a public house', the *Morning Chronicle* reports, a journalist saw a 'genteely dressed' person in a public house doing his best to annoy a Chinese who was sitting on a bench and minding his own business:

> he strove first to provoke him by the most insulting lan-
> guage, which he bore with surprising patience; he then
> made remarks on his dress, at which the people, who were
> collecting very fast, imprudently laughed, and encouraged
> him to proceed; he next took hold of the Chinese man by
> the hair, though repeatedly requested by the genteeler part
> of the spectators to desist: deaf to reason, he imprudently
> continued to aggravate him, by pulling his hair, which at
> length so incensed him, that he immediately ran in doors,
> and fetched out about a dozen more, who in an instant armed
> themselves with short bludgeons, kept by them seemingly for
> the purpose, for they had a large knob at one end, which they
> held in the right hand; the other end was up the sleeve that
> you could scarce perceive them armed; their hair they tied
> round their heads in an instant, and rushed out in a body,
> but did not attempt to molest anyone, only formed a ring
> for the two combatants . . .

In London there was a shifting society of foreign seamen, Chinese and Lascars, who had disembarked to take up shore life or to wait for the next sailing.[1] Small as it was, the colony of Chinese reflected the occupational specialization by dialect and locality of other overseas Chinese communities: the firemen, boatswains and seamen were Cantonese, the cooks were from Hainan Island, and the stewards from the treaty port of Ningpo.[2] Chinese seamen jumped ship to settle not only in London but in Liverpool, Cardiff, Bristol and Glasgow. There were very few of them to begin with – seventy-eight in 1851, 147 in 1861, and 202 in 1871;[3] but their number increased after 1865, when several Liverpool shipping companies, most notably Alfred Holt's Blue Funnel Line, began trading with China and employed Chinese crew on the China run.[4] By 1881 the number of Chinese in British ports had risen to 665, and by 1911 to 1,319. Many earned their living servicing Chinese sailors, running laundries, shops, groceries, restaurants and lodging-houses.

In London they were concentrated in Limehouse Causeway and Pennyfields, two narrow streets of slummy houses in the boroughs of Poplar and Stepney. 'Limehouse' came to mean 'Chinese' in the way that other parts of the East End (such as Whitechapel) meant Jewish. That this was a Chinese quarter is still remembered today in the names of some streets in east Stepney, such as Pekin, Nankin, Canton and Ming. Badly bombed during the blitz, the quarter did not survive the war, but 'Limehouse' is still evocative of vivid images. Because of its association with the Chinese, Limehouse has always existed, as colourful places do, as a kind of journalist's and novelist's fantasy, all opium dens and gas-lit mystery. Two generations of Britons and Americans found their views of the Chinese coloured by it, for Limehouse had entered that most powerful of preservatives, popular fiction.

In 1911 a prolific English novelist called Arthur Henry Sarsfield Ward was commissioned to write a thriller about the Chinese criminal underworld in Limehouse. Writing as Sax Rohmer, he created the most potent of the 'Chinaman' fictional villains by publishing *The Mystery of Fu Manchu*, a novel that ran to more than forty editions in Britain and America, and spawned some thirteen sequels. Fu Manchu was 'the Yellow Peril incarnate', the evil genius plotting to take over the world. Whether or not we are to believe Rohmer when he said that the character was inspired by a chance view of a well-dressed, unusually tall Chinese he saw getting into a limousine in Limehouse Causeway on a foggy night, there is no doubt that Limehouse's reputation had something to do with its creation.

That reputation owed its unsavouriness to opium, or more accurately to the imagined squalor of a Chinese opium den. The habit had not always appeared degrading to English eyes, and an early description of opium-smoking in the East End, an 1868 account of the Prince of Wales's visit to a den, lacked the luridness of later depictions. It was at the home of a Chinese-English couple, Chi Ki and his wife: 'Chi Ki keeps open house for opium smokers, and his chief customers are the sailors who arrive at the London ports. Sometimes, I was informed, trade was so slack that no more than two or three customers would apply all day long; while at other times it was as much as Chi Ki could do, distilling and frizzling and frying, to keep the smokers going.'5

A different picture of opium-smoking emerged with the publication of Dickens's *Mystery of Edwin Drood* (1870), and as various magazine articles in the popular press succeeded in surrounding it with a haze of mystery and evil. Readers were transported to the dark world of drugs and saturnalias, in unspeakable dens where, swirled about by thick brown opium fumes, the recumbent forms of smokers lay this way and that in the strangest poses. People also took their images of opium-smoking from Oscar Wilde's *The Picture of Dorian Gray* (1891), and came to believe that the opium den was the place to head for if it was depravity you were after. The thrills of penetrating the unknown drew the curious to the Chinese lodging-houses of Limehouse, but they did not always find what they had been led to expect, for the picture of a few Chinese seamen quietly settling down to their pipes in a front room did not quite square with the highly coloured clichés. Perhaps, some of them concluded, there was no such thing as an opium 'den' at all, and a reporter sent by the *Morning Advertiser* came away from one in 1884 with the impression that 'it was not repulsive. It was calm, it was peaceful.'6 But people can read into things what they wish, and there were observers who saw something menacing in the very passivity of the pastime; one, a late-nineteenth-century writer and lecturer on morphine addiction called Dr Benjamin Ward Richardson, thought that the outwardly placid opium smokers were actually 'very dangerous under those circumstances . . . they might rise up, and be mischievous to anyone who might perform an experiment upon them, however simple it might be'.7

Others were capable of greater detachment, finding the vice less objectionable than that of the gin palace, and urging recognition, as one writer in *The Times* did, of the fact that all the 'dens' in the two Chinatown streets 'together will not furnish from one month's end to another any such spectacle of "degradation" or rowdyism as may be seen nightly in almost any public house'.8 When Walter Besant looked into one in the course of writing his book *East London* (1899), he had expected, because such places had acquired a symbolic status as haunts of evil, to experience 'a creeping of the flesh at least'; instead, to his great disappointment, the place turned out to be 'neither dreadful nor horrible'.9 In reality opium-smoking among the Chinese seamen was simply a daily routine, as unremarkable as lunch or breakfast: they would get up at seven or eight in the morning, have their two pipes, and then go off to work. Hardly a Chinese lodging-house was without its extra beds for smokers.

But as public attitudes hardened, and as the law got tougher, so the Chinese were obliged to smoke their opium in greater secrecy. Under the Pharmacy Acts of 1868 and 1908, only qualified pharmacists were allowed to sell opium, but the drug could be bought over the counter, and laudanum, an opium derivative, was widely available throughout Britain. To control Chinese opium-smoking, new by-laws had to be brought in; these were passed in 1909, introducing compulsory licensing of seamen's boarding-houses and providing for the withdrawal of the licence of any lodging-house keeper who permitted opium-smoking on his premises.

There were raids, there were prosecutions; but if the police were looking for dens with a fixed address and clientele, they did not find any, for the venues were always shifting, and when they entered a suspect house, they would often find it empty, or occupied by new tenants who naturally had no inkling of the identity or whereabouts of the previous tenants. Sometimes a knock on the door would be answered only after a long delay, time enough to hide the pipes and the opium and to cover up the evidence. An early-morning raid of twenty-nine Chinese houses in Limehouse in 1912 – eleven of them licensed, eighteen of them not – found evidence of opium-smoking in eleven of the unlicensed places, but this was only because the other houses had kept the police waiting outside while they tidied up inside. The Chinese could sometimes bribe their way out of a conviction; the local police were not above using a little discretion – 'probably got a couple of bob now and again', we are told by an old Limehouse resident, an Englishwoman who lived with a Chinese until his deportation in 1928.10

By an enormous mischance, the Chinese in Limehouse caught the unwelcome attentions of the Quaker, Church of England and nonconformist zealots of the anti-opium movement, a moral crusade directed more at Britain's part in the iniquitous Indian opium trade with China than at the smokers at home, it is true, but which felt its conscience to be engaged by the 'helpless slaves to this expensive indulgence' in England too. The Society for the Suppression of the Opium Trade had been founded in 1874, slowly gaining strength until, with the Liberal victory of 1906, it found its convictions backed by an anti-opium majority in Parliament. Just as missionary frustration in China had been an original ingredient of the movement – the Chinese had some justification for resisting conversion by foreigners who came up the China coast in opium clippers and distributed Bibles along with the drug – so the suppression of the vice in the East End was seen to be a Christian duty for England and the occasion and means of immigrant Chinese betterment. 'Vile, unhabitable tenements,' cried the movement's propagandists, 'transformed into the homes of vicious, ruinous indulgence . . . constitute a pitfall and trap to many of those simple Easterns . . . Has England no duty here? Have those ill-paid servants no claim to our care?'[11]

Before long, these anti-opium sentiments found themselves riding a wave of strong anti-immigrant feeling; this was directed chiefly at Jewish immigration, but the Chinese did not escape its ripples. Visible and vulnerable, they were an easy target for racialist reactions, and their fondness for gambling and opium did not help. Indeed, such was the climate of hostility that you could easily believe, without suspecting bias or stigmatization for a moment, what an ex-policeman said of the Limehouse Chinese and their opium dens in 1904: 'oriental cunning and cruelty . . . was hall-marked on every countenance . . . Until my visit to the Asiatic Sailors' Home, I had always considered some of the Jewish inhabitants of Whitechapel to be the worst type of humanity I had ever seen.'[12] Now he knew it was those little yellow men with slit eyes and devious smiles.

Drugs had glamour, all the same, and there were people in London's theatrical and artistic circles who loved their opium or cocaine – loved it all the more for its suggestions of adventure, hedonism, Bohemia and daring. And who catered to this clientele? The East End Chinese, it was generally believed. Among the rich it was very much the thing to go pottering around Chinatown. Alarmed observers saw this in sinister terms, as the taking-hold of the white population by oriental vices.

They were confirmed in their fears when a succession of well pub-licized drug scares between 1918 and 1922 traced white middle-class experimentation with drugs to the East End. One was provoked by the death of a London shipping merchant, Walter Gibson, from an overdose of morphine in his Baker Street flat; the Chinese who had sold him the drug in Limehouse was later given a month's hard labour and expelled.[13] Another revolved around the death of a young nightclub dancer called Freda Kempton from an overdose of cocaine. Brilliant, or Bill Chang, the owner of a restaurant on Regent Street, was convicted and jailed for having supplied the drug. Upon his release, Chang moved his business to Limehouse, much to the discomfort of the local Chinese, who feared and hated him, and who breathed a sigh of relief when he was caught with cocaine in his possession and deported.[14]

The most dramatic case of all was that of Billie Carleton, a celebrated performer on the stage of the Haymarket Theatre, found dead in her bed from an overdose of cocaine on the morning after a ball she had attended at the Albert Hall. She had been given the drug by a theatre dress designer called Reggie de Veulle, not a Chinese, but the fact remained that she had been with a friend to Limehouse to smoke opium. And apparently it was the Scottish wife of a Limehouse Chinese who prepared the drug at one of de Veulle's opium-smoking parties. The newspapers were well informed on these parties, which were held at de Veulle's flat off Piccadilly and were unhesitatingly described as orgies – occasions on which, we are told by *The Times*, 'the men divested themselves of their clothing and got into pyjamas, and the women into chiffon nightdresses'.[15] This was only to be expected, the readers must have thought, as they mentally added sexual debauchery to their stock of opium clichés. An acute sense of uneasiness spread, and the spectre of a criminal mastermind in the image of Arthur Conan Doyle's Moriarty, a Chinese super-crook stalking 'the mean streets of the East End' with the names of prominent people 'constantly on his lips', was raised in many an English mind.[16]

Cunningly, Sax Rohmer worked the case into one of his stories. Though he said that it was 'not inspired by, nor . . . distantly concerned with, any cause célèbre, recent or remote',[17] his novel *Dope. A Story of Chinatown and the Drug Traffic*, written at a time when he was living in Limehouse, has clear echoes of the Billie Carleton case, with characters recognizably modelled on her circle, including a Mrs Sin Sin Wa, or Lola, the wife of a one-eyed Limehouse Chinese who organized opium parties.

Translated into French, German, Spanish, Italian, Dutch, Portuguese, Swedish, Greek, Polish, Hungarian, Czech, Japanese and even Arabic, the novels of Sax Rohmer, presently to be adapted into radio serial plays and Hollywood films, turned Fu Manchu into a household name and distributed the stereotypes of Chinese torture, mercilessness, craftiness, and villainy across half the world. Almost without knowing it, British and American children picked up their notion of Chinese character from the films and stories of Fu Manchu, invariably portrayed with 'menace in every twitch of his finger, a threat in every twitch of his eyebrow, terror in each split-second of his slanted eyes'.[18]

Several factors coalesced to undermine the position of the Chinese community in Britain in the period before the Great War. English attitudes to Chinese migration were deeply coloured by the importation of indentured labourers into South Africa, an issue, as we saw, of enormous consequence in the general election of 1906.

The chorus of voices raised against coolie labour in South Africa was confused, combining humanitarian protests with arguments against capitalist exploitation, and giving expression at the same time to a deeper fear and distrust of aliens. The yellow faces of the pictures on the hoardings, noted a contemporary observer, aroused 'among very many of the voters an immediate hatred of the Mongoloid racial type and this hatred was transferred to the Conservative Party'.[19] The distinction was blurred between the coolies in South Africa and the Chinese seamen and laundry men at home. Nor were the Chinese the only aliens to be abhorred in the campaign. That there was a great deal of Jewish money in the South African diamond and gold mines brought out the bigot in some of the campaigners, and one detects undertones of anti-Semite hostility in the representation of the Tory government as the dupes of Jewish financial interests.[20]

Unfortunately for the Chinese, they represented cheap labour, people who accepted any work at any wage. They always seemed to survive, however low the pay, however harsh the conditions, however much work was extracted from them. That one of the pack-ponies on Sir Ernest Shackleton's expedition to the South Pole in 1908–9 was nicknamed 'Chinaman' was an indication of how widely that view was held.[21] 'You know, we know and they know', remarked the *Cardiff Maritime Review* in 1911, 'that the Chinaman isn't worth a toss as a seaman; that his only claim to indulgence is that he is cheap.'[22] The British seaman did not disguise his distaste for the Chinese, and attacked them in print whenever he could, although in fairness to him it should be noted that the Chinese, on top of being a threat to his livelihood, were strike-breakers. So much did they arouse Welsh ire that all of Cardiff's thirty or so Chinese laundries were attacked in a night of rioting after the seamen's strike of 1911.

In Liverpool, the Chinese minority caused locals some disquiet in 1906, though neither the city's Chief Constable nor the city council's commission of enquiry, specially appointed to report on the morals, habits and economic aspects of the Chinese presence, could put their finger on any particular cause for this unease. The sanitary standards of the Chinese, reported the commission, seemed satisfactory enough. Perhaps, the Constable thought, it was the competition they offered the city's laundries and boarding-house keepers. Chinese laundries were not popular; in London five years before, the prospect of having one spring up on North Street had inflamed the residents of Poplar into 'a state of ferment'. The place was besieged by a great crowd all day, reported the *Evening News*, and brickbats and stones were hurled against the shutters and doors. Later, under cover of darkness, the dozen or so Chinese inside the house escaped.[23]

But laundries did not attract as much attention, or give as much offence, as sexual liaisons between Chinese men and white women – not actually a criminal offence, admitted a commission of enquiry which looked specifically into this matter in London in 1910–11, but 'undesirable from an English point of view'. Evidence offered by a Miss Robinson, the headmistress of a London school, of two cases of Chinese men cohabiting with teenage girls had excited, if not fascinated horror, at least enough concern for the enquiry to have been started. That there was 'conclusive' evidence of the 'seduction of girls by Chinamen' had been a finding of the Liverpool enquiry too, based on three cases of intercourse between Chinese men and English minors. The apparent preference of Chinese men for young girls, 'especially those of undue precocity', was remarked upon, but what was not realized was that the girls probably did not seem under-age to the Chinese, in whose own country girls were customarily married at fifteen or sixteen.

Blandishments on the part of the Chinese there might have been, but sexual coercion there was not; contemporary accounts suggest that the women were willing enough. It was the opinion of the detective inspector sent to investigate Miss Robinson's complaint in Limehouse, an area he had policed for three years and knew well, that 'the Chinaman if he becomes intimate with an English girl does not lead her to prostitution but prefers to marry her and treat her well'.[24] Newspaper-men might speak of 'Limehouse Lures', but there were at least two things to be said for a Chinese husband. He was no roistering sailor, for one thing; you could count on him to be sober always. And for another, there was nothing penny-pinching about him. Why, said a writer in the *Evening News* in 1920, a Chinese man allowed the sisters of his English wife to be quartered upon him without any protest (because, one may assume, he looked upon them as family, and on the whole the Chinese don't think of family as spongers). It was the lotus-eating life, the writer concluded, even more than the 'atmosphere of Eastern mystery', which lured so many white girls to Chinatown, for no women in the East End had so much leisure as 'John Chinaman's wife or housekeeper'.25 The husband even did the cooking – one guesses because he disdained English fare.

'White girls are not hypnotized – they go willingly to the yellow men,' a newpaper-woman had observed just the week before. Mainly they were 'girls of a low type' who married Chinese men, the writer said, poor little 'gutter-sparrow' girls from Cardiff, Birmingham and other provincial towns. Was there any difference between a white husband and a Chinese one? the reporter was interested to find out. No, her informant told her: 'A White'll black yer eye. A Chink'll cut yer throat.' But she added, 'They treat you all right if you be'ave yourself. They like you to look flash and to go and 'ave baths and all. So long as you don't shame their face you're all right. What I mean is: if you take up with a Hong Kong man, you mustn't make friends with a chap from Shanghai, or you're for it.'26

At the time the Chinese men in Britain outnumbered Chinese women by something in the order of eight to one, so it was hardly surprising that they miscegenated. Evidence of these mixed unions survives in some of the headstones of the East London Cemetery at Grange Road, as in the one whose inscription reads, IN MEMORY OF A DEAR DAD WONG BING (1881–1962) AND MUM IVY BING (1915–1973). (In the ordinary course of events Ivy Bing would have been called Ivy Wong, but in England as elsewhere, Chinese family names and given names were sometimes muddled.)

That it was mostly working-class English girls who married Chinese fitted well with the notion that the Chinese were an inferior people; a better class of women would have preferred their men white. These attitudes found their echoes across the seas in California, where a decade and more of sinophobia had succeeded in giving to the Chinese, in the eyes of the writer Bret Harte, 'an abiding consciousness of degradation – a secret pain of self-humiliation in the lines of the mouth and eyes'.27 They seldom smiled, he thought, and their laughter 'is of such an extraordinary and sardonic nature – so purely a mechanical spasm, quite independent of any mirthful attribute – that to this day I am doubtful whether I ever saw a Chinaman laugh'.

Robert Louis Stevenson was horrified by the contempt in which white Americans held the Chinese immigrants, whose forbearance in the face of the cruellest insults he could only admire. 'A while ago it was the Irish,' he noted in his book *The Amateur Emigrant*, 'now it is the Chinese who must go.'[28] White Americans declared them 'hideous vermin', he reports, 'and affected a kind of choking in the throat when they beheld them'.[29] Whoever coined the phrase 'Chinaman's chance', an expression which entered the vocabulary round about this time, and which meant 'not much of a chance at all', knew what the Chinese were up against. While paying higher taxes than anyone else, no Chinese in California could testify against a white man, and none were eligible for American nationality. They could do nothing right: if they did not bring their wives from China it was because they 'had no regard for the family, did not recognize the relationship of husband and wife, did not observe the tie of parent and child',[30] and preferred the company of prostitutes; if they were stoic and docile they were nothing better than slaves; if they were too cowed to come out of their shell they were aloof and inscrutable, and if they were not easily roused to battle they were incapable of normal human reactions. Indeed they were a debased form of humanity, often referred to as Mongolians – a term which, by no means fortuitously, evoked children afflicted with congenital mental deficiency.

It would be tedious to list all the outrages against the Chinese and to reproduce the invective against them that periodicals like the weekly *Illustrated Wasp* poured into the ears of their readers. It was a hysterically racist time. 'Lynch him! Kill the greasy slave!' were the cries that rent the air at a rally. A great outburst of anti-foreign feeling had climaxed two decades before, when the Know-Nothings, as the xenophobes came to be called in the 1850s, resorted to mob violence against Roman Catholics and immigrants. But the movement against the Chinese was broader, longer lasting, and infinitely more successful in achieving its ends.

It no doubt ran deeper because the Chinese were much more noticeably alien; in fact no immigrant group could be more different, and in degree of foreignness opium-smoking far exceeded stout-swilling and St Patrick's Day carousing. Could anyone exemplify more exactly the unassimilated alien than the Chinese, the very negation, in his fidelity to the ways of his ancestors, of the Melting Pot? The idea of immigrants of all nations melting into a new race of men had been at the heart of the American self-image from the Republic's very beginning. By casting doubt, however unintentionally, upon this profoundly American conviction, the Chinese made themselves many enemies.

There were reasons for the wave of anti-Chinese feeling beyond the normal gut reaction to aliens: its rise traced the graph of California's economic malaise. The boom days were over; cycles of economic depression, overlapping with a flood of poor immigrants arriving off crowded ships from Europe at New York, left the country badly shaken and gave a sense of defensive sourness and uncertainty to the 1870s and 1880s. It is true that the Chinese had held jobs the white man had shunned, but now there was not enough work to go round, and all the while, wagonload after wagonload, the now completed railroad was bringing more out-of-work people from the east coast of America. The seeds of hostility and violence were already there, in the fact that, though they were only a twelfth of the state's population, by 1870 one out of every four workers in California was Chinese.[31] If white labour unions were incensed by big business – and large fortunes had indeed been made out of the factories and railways – the Chinese, by accepting low wages, were seen to abet the venal exploitation of the greedy capitalists and to compound the widespread hardship of the times.

A popular song of the day gave voice to the resentment against the Chinese:

> O workingmen dear, and did you hear
> The news that's goin' round?
> Another China steamer
> Has been landed here in town.
> Today I read the papers,
> And it grieved my heart full sore
> To see upon the title page
> O, just 'Twelve Hundred More!'
>
> O, California's coming down,
> As you can plainly see.
> They are hiring all the Chinamen
> And discharging you and me;
> But strife will be in every town
> Throughout the Pacific shore,
> And the cry of old and young shall be,
> 'O, damn, "Twelve Hundred More."'

So it went on like this for a few verses more, to arrive at the conclusion that 'This state of things can never last/In this, our golden land.'[32]

By the summer of 1877, the unions' grievance had reached its flashpoint, and at nightly mass meetings in San Francisco, crowds were whipped up to a pitch of murderous excitement by inflammatory speeches. The most inflammatory of the speakers was Dennis Kearney, the Irish founder of the Workingmen's Party and a rabble-rouser with a hellfire style of oratory. 'Judge Lynch is the only judge we want,' he has been quoted as saying. 'The monopolists who make their money by employing cheap labour better watch out!' his spellbound audiences were told; 'they have built themselves fine residences on Nob Hill and erected flagstaffs upon their roofs – let them take care that they have not erected their own gallows.'[33] People worked themselves up into a state of fury with the cry 'The Chinese Must Go!', while anti-coolie clubs sprouted in the working-class neighbourhoods of San Francisco. The campaign reached its terrible climax on 23 July, when a rally of about ten thousand agitators assembled in the Sandlot, the popular tribune of San Francisco. Two gunshots rang out, and two protestors fell. This set off a night of rioting, with bands of young men roaming the streets, wrecking Chinese laundries, randomly taking Chinese lives, setting fire to Chinese properties, and pitting themselves against the police who tried to stop them.[34] On the third night, the mob took its vengeance on the docks of Pacific Mail Steamship (the place where thousands of Chinese immigrants had arrived off their boats, and where numerous Chinese seamen were employed), setting a nearby lumber yard ablaze and battling with the firemen who came hurrying to extinguish the conflagration.

As the years passed the violence flared from town to town, mining camp to mining camp, community to community; a map of the riots shows outbreaks in fifty-five places in nine western states.[35] If it was not destruction of one kind, it was destruction of another. Chinese were driven out of their homes, booted out of town, put on barges and told never to return; or else they were stabbed, or shot, or hanged from balconies. Chinese were terrorized from California to Nevada, from Oregon to Washington. There was little that the Chinese legation could do, beyond seeking compensation for individual material losses on behalf of the victims. The anti-Chinese movement had quickly become an instrument of local and state politicians, whether Democrat or Republican, for it did not take much political astuteness to see that a full-blooded display of sinophobia and anti-monopoly sentiments could win votes. A string of frankly discriminatory laws was enacted, barring Chinese employment in any state, county, municipal, or other public work, 'except in punishment for crime'.[36] Not all of these laws went unchallenged by the Chinese, and some of them were to be declared void or unconstitutional, but still most Chinese acquiesced in their fate, too crushed and confused to stand against the tide of American vindictiveness.

The Chinese did have their champions: rail barons and manufacturers who needed their labour; traders with China who wanted to keep on the good side of their customers; Christian missionaries who wished to convert them; or simply people, the best of the white Americans, who helped out of kindness and a sense of fairness. Nevertheless, it proved beyond the capacities of these people to stop the United States Congress from taking a step it had never taken before, the adoption of an immigrant policy altogether new to American thinking: the passage of the infamous Chinese Exclusion Act on 6 May 1882, a law which all but banned the future immigration of Chinese workers.

The act, which did not apply to teachers, students, merchants and tourists, proved difficult to enforce, for it was easy for an aspiring immigrant to get a certificate from the Chinese officials declaring him to be a member of one of the exempt classes, a student, say, or a trader. Cases came to court too of Chinese visitors circumventing the law to find jobs and settle in the country. In 1884, the Exclusion Act was tightened, making it harder for labourers to pass themselves off as merchants (the word now so defined as to exclude hucksters, pedlars, and dealers in fish), and closing loopholes.

Chinese labourers already in the United States were assured of the right to leave and re-enter, but this right of re-entry was cancelled four years later, when a further hardening of heart resulted in the passing of the Scott Bill. The effect of this was to prohibit the return of Chinese workers who had temporarily gone abroad, including the twenty thousand who at the time happened to be visiting China, and the six hundred who were already on their way back to America. The appeals of those who found themselves turned away upon their arrival counted for nothing, nor the intervention of the Six Companies, which rustled up the money to challenge the constitutionality of the new act in the courts. It was the law of the land, and it satisfied the racial mood then current all over western America. Judged by other standards though, the Scott Act was an ignominious piece of legislation. Almost exactly two years before, a gift from France, a monumental sculpture by Frédéric Bartholdi, was unveiled in the presence of President Grover Cleveland (he who was to put his signature to the Scott Act) on an island in New York harbour. Known to all the world as the Statue of Liberty, this dramatic work of engineering greets the immigrant as he sails in through the harbour, like a beacon to the open and ample bosom of America. Few could write about it without quoting the famous lines of Emma Lazarus inscribed in bronze upon its pedestal:

> Give me your tired, your poor,
> Your huddled masses yearning to breathe free,
> The wretched refuse of your teeming shore.
> Send these, the homeless, tempest-tost to me,
> I lift my lamp beside the golden door.

Setting the Exclusion laws beside the noble symbolism of the Lady of Liberty brings out the incompleteness of American generosity, not to say the hollowness of the American ideal of openness and equality. What the acts did was to mark off a race and then close the golden door on it. They showed America's self-image to have been deeply faulty.

From the warnings of impending doom in California, you would hardly know that, even at its peak in the 1870s, the Chinese population represented no more than four and a half per cent of all immigrants.[37] A demonology re-animating the old idea of the Yellow Peril had been created to stir up white anxieties about being engulfed by Chinese hordes sweeping all before them by sheer numbers and powers of endurance. Penny-press pamphlets and cartoons expressed it, such as the one which showed an endless row of marching Chinese and told you that 'If all the Chinese in the world were to march four-abreast past a given point they would never finish passing though they marched forever and ever. (Based on US Army Marching Regulations)'.[38] Everybody knew that there was a staggeringly large number of them, and the reason they were so numerous – so popular belief had it – was that they were uniquely fitted as a race to endure any hardship, to bear any amount of pain, and to survive on less than other human beings; and the reason they were like this, according to the testimony of some physicians in San Francisco, was that their nerve endings grew further away from their skin than was the case with the white races. From their own inability to feel pain, it followed that they could inflict it on others without any hesitation. From this, it was but a short step to the clichés of Chinese cruelty and Chinese torture.

So Fu Manchu found plenty of eager takers when he crossed the Atlantic from London. It was a two-way traffic, and some of America's fears had long been shifted to Britain, where 'the Chinese question', it was felt, would before long become almost as urgent. You had to be ready for them, warned a European journal quoted by *The Times* in 1878 – soon steam navigation would be transporting the Chinese 'at fabulously low prices to all parts of the world', and they would 'end by fixing themselves among us like the Jews . . .'[39] In the two succeeding decades, the number of Chinese in the United States fell to between less than half to just over one per cent of the immigrant population.[40] The ones who remained in San Francisco – many had fled east – were isolated as never before, keeping well away from their persecutors by living in the cave of their own fossilized culture, in Chinatown.

There Arnold Genthe found them in 1895, and captured the feel of their existence – the humdrum and the festive, the old and the new, the hopeful and the miserable – through the lens of the small 'detective' camera he had acquired specially for this purpose.[41]

Arnold Genthe was a young German born to a cultured family of distinguished academics in Berlin. With a doctorate in philosophy under his belt, he had come to San Francisco to become a tutor to the son of the Baron von Schroeder. He was enchanted by the city, but he was particularly fascinated by the Chinese quarter; and it was his wish to convey how exotic it seemed to his European fancy that launched him upon his successful career in photography. Ignoring the advice of his German guidebook to visit it only in the company of a guide, Arnold Genthe spent hours and days alone, roaming its streets, lurking in its corners, haunting its courtyards, becoming such a familiar presence that his subjects no longer shied away startled down cellars or into doorways. He was not to know that he was recording it all at a specially poignant moment of its history, that the old world did not have long to go before it would be brought abruptly to an end, once and for all, by the great earthquake and fire of 18 April 1906.

There were some ten blocks of it, surveyed to the north by the splendours of Nob Hill, the luxurious mansions and hotels of those at the top of the social heap. Just round the corner, to the north, were the Italian North Beach area and the tawdry night-life of the Barbary Coast. The southern approach, along Sacramento Square, offered booths for target-shooting and houses where white prostitutes sat behind half-open windows awaiting business. Half-way along the eastern perimeter lay Portsmouth Square, which in those days still had its Robert Louis Stevenson memorial statue, and which, on a fine morning, looked just made for the picnics of Chinese babies and their mothers or nannies.

Genthe saw San Francisco's Chinatown as a 'Canton of the West', and he depicted it as such – a place with hardly anything American about it. The style of many of the brick buildings was Italianate enough, it is true, but Chinese signs and lanterns orientalized them, and there were plenty of spectacles to assure the seeker after exoticism that it was indeed different. There was surely nothing American about the way its citizens dressed, and what could seem more foreign than the queue which all the men wore, the butt of so much American derision, and the object of the childishly cruel teasing of that well-known rhyme?

> Chink Chink, Chinaman, sitting on a rail,
> Along comes a white man and cuts off his tail . . .

The pigtail was imposed on the Chinese by their Manchu conquerors, and rightly abhorred by patriots as a hated symbol of subjugation; but curiously enough the Chinese abroad cherished it as a badge of their Chinese identity, and regarded any attack on it as an insult; it maddened them to have it forcibly cut off. This was as true of San Francisco as it was of Singapore or any other overseas Chinese community.

What distinguished San Francisco's Chinese from their cousins in Canton, though, were the black felt Homburg hats they wore to shield their heads and eyes from the glare and heat of the Californian sun. Their attire was otherwise utterly Chinese: wide-cut, cotton-wadded tunics with overlong, rolled-up sleeves and the traditional frog buttons; pyjama-like trousers; and cloth shoes with thick white soles. Genthe liked to visit Chinatown on a feast day to portray for his audience the Chinese in all their finery: the local swells in their dark satin robes and caps of fine woven silk; the women with their pomaded and shiny back-knots; the little girls, the most gorgeously attired of all, with pompons bobbing, tassels trailing, and beads of pearl and ruby dangling from the embroidered flowers of their elaborate headdresses. See them tottering there on their raised platform shoes, shoes with soles like egg-cup stems, a Manchu fashion designed to give women who did not bind their feet the titillatingly wobbly gait of those who did. That the women were dressed in tunic and pantaloons and the men in robes was different enough from American practice for it to be thought worthy of mention by those who saw it as a case of men wearing skirts and women trousers, and as further proof that the Chinese did everything backwards.

Such vivid scenes there were for a photographer to record, for all the shabbiness of their setting. You find yourself stepping into the thick of it as you leave Portsmouth Square behind you and, sauntering up Clay Street in the early-morning fog, come upon the shops and markets of Dupont Street (now renamed Grant Avenue). The markets are already busy, with the fruit and vegetables arriving on horse-drawn carts, and the pedlars setting up shop on their established bit of doorstep or pavement. Bob Lim, the dealer in animal remnants, clatters up with his wagon, offering the pig intestines, cow stomachs, duck and chicken feet, and other scraps that he and his brother have salvaged from the slaughterhouse where their father works. Chinatown really does seem to sell everything, and there are grocery stores, such as the one at 621 Jackson Street, which seem like something straight out of Canton, with the sausages, ducks and hams hanging from hooks on metal racks; the shelves of dried foods and fresh vegetables, bitter melon, Chinese cabbage, chives and lettuce; the barrels of pickled vegetables; the glass cabinets of bottled, packaged and tinned goods imported from China. Still more surprising, in a setting so unmistakably Cantonese, is Tung-t'ai, at 900 Dupont Street, the provision store selling specialities from the eastern Chinese cities of Soochow and Hangchow.

Picking your way eastwards into Washington Street, you soon come within smelling distance of Washington Place, better known to the locals as Fish Alley – or, in Chinese, the Street of Virtuous Harmony. Here a fishmonger, his pigtail wrapped around the crown of his head to keep it out of the way, goes about his daily business, surrounded by wicker baskets of shrimps and trayfuls of heaped fish. In the shop a few doors down a butcher and his assistant are plucking the feathers of freshly killed chickens. Chinese faces go by, and one man stops to chat, not much bothered it seems by the uncomfortable feeling of dankness about the place, the dankness of fish, wet cobblestones, horse dung, spit and the ever muffling fog from the bay.

Back now along Washington Street, and there are at least four establishments to catch your interest. There is the office of the *War Kee*, the first successful Chinese weekly to be published in Chinatown, at 803 Washington Street, a little to the west of Dupont Street. There is the Red Cassia Theatre, at number 814, one of two lively theatres in Chinatown, each seating audiences of several hundred – the rich merchants in boxes reserved for them, the rest on bare wooden benches – and periodically staging performances by celebrated actors from China. Further west, at number 830, there hangs the sign of the pawnshop Hong Lee (Cantonese for Pervasive Profit), conveniently located at the junction with Ross Street, the street where all the gambling-houses are. Finally, at 871, there is the Chinese Tea and Herb Sanatorium, which used to be patronized as much for its nostrums as for the attentions of the late Dr Li Po Tai, who is said to have seen between 150 and three hundred patients a day, and who, not altogether surprisingly, died a very rich man indeed. There is no shortage of pharmacies in Chinatown, and those who think they could do with a tonic or an aphrodisiac will find what they want in a potion of pickled wildcat, chicken and snake. This last, reputed to be a great booster of courage, sells well whenever a tong fight is in the offing. You can sometimes glimpse, in a dark corner down an alley, a yet-to-be-skinned wildcat hanging by its hind legs next to an unplucked fowl. Wildcats don't come cheap, and the wildcat-meat dealer Wing Chew, who disappears into the mountains every now and then to bag one, knows that he is on to a good thing.

Back now on Dupont Street and its junction with Jackson Street, and here you meet your first tourist, eyeing the costly Chinese vases (or are they spurious antiques?) at the Chinese and Japanese Curio Store at number 924. Tours of Chinatown start from the Globe Hotel on the other side of the intersection, and already the sidewalk is beginning to thicken with white tourists, clusters of caped ladies chattering among themselves and perhaps brushing the dust from their long, sweeping skirts. Compared to the Chinese passers-by in their loose-fitting garments, these women have a bundled look, strongly suggestive of whalebone, crinoline and hoops. The Chinese find 'this American fashion of mopping the streets with the skirts of ladies' dresses' very nasty and not at all to their taste.[42]

For their part, the Americans find the place as dirty as they had imagined it, and see evidence of the Chinaman's primitive standards of hygiene in the ill-swept sidewalks, the muck-lined kerbs, the debris that swirls around you, the slops that ooze from kitchens. You don't see any dustmen in Chinatown, but you do see a paper gatherer, a poor shuffling scavenger whose job it is to pick up any litter with writing on it and put it into the wooden deposit boxes with which Chinatown is dotted. The paper is burnt in special incinerators, and the ashes collected and taken on boats to be flung into the ocean beyond the Golden Gate Bridge. All this because, with their immemorial reverence for the written word, the Chinese cannot bring themselves to throw away paper with writing on it the way they would scraps of ordinary rubbish.

The dirt is only to be expected, in a place where large numbers of people are uncomfortably accommodated in cramped, forty- to fifty-year-old houses. Space is at a premium, and to make more room people put up extensions and turn cellars into living quarters and eateries. Balconies are added, and enlivened with potted plants. Many a roof is hung with washing. Homes have beds folded from walls. Down behind Jackson Street, across from Cooper Alley, there fester the tenements of the very poor of Chinatown, living communally to blunt the edge of their shared misery, and huddling for comfort around the wooden shed which passes for their kitchen in Ta-t'ien-ching, or the Big Courtyard. The most conscientious housewife can hardly maintain a decent home in a place like this. It is so unspeakable that it has even gone into the guidebooks, which call it the Palace Hotel to raise a few laughs among their readers.

Do not, however, judge the prosperity of a Chinatown dwelling by its façade. Buildings with a humdrum exterior along upper Clay and Sacramento Streets sometimes secrete four- to five-bedroomed apartments of unbelievable opulence. Here live the rich merchants surrounded by the emblems of their success: bejewelled wives, deferential servants, carved crystal in one ebony cabinet, porcelain and ivory in another, and against a wall of the drawing-room, that statutory status symbol, a sofa. These are almost the only people lucky enough to have families in Chinatown, allowed by law to bring their wives over from China. A family is not something you can take for granted here, and children are consequently deeply cherished. The fathers in Genthe's pictures look distinctly fatherly, unashamedly carrying their always exquisitely dressed babies; and though we mustn't assume all children to be as well looked after, we see no ragged urchins playing rough in the streets. In Chinatown only the rich are family men. For the rest, there are the solaces of Ross, Duncombe, Bartlett's and Sullivan's Alleys.

Night-time is when you should visit these places, for then the alleyways come alive, and just wandering among the all-male crowds is a unique experience. If some of the men strike you as poor lonely creatures, that is because they are isolated individuals, condemned to a womanless, unfamilied existence. Others look relaxed and cheerful, a hard day's work of garment-sewing or shoe-making behind them. There may be migrant workers among them, men who labour a six-month season in the orchards, farms and ranches, and scrape through the winter sleeping in their overcrowded lodgings in shifts. There is a touch of pathos to them, as they parade down the alleys to what they think will prove to be the best moments of their day or week. Behind rows of solid, iron doors – 'clanked swiftly shut', Genthe tells us, 'at the approach of the police'[43] – the evening passes all too quickly in sessions of gambling. For the outsider, who has heard all about the tongs controlling the alleys, a hint of menace lends excitement to the scene. To a susceptible European, they have an irresistibly oriental tinge and live up completely to their guidebook legend – revisiting Chinatown many years later, when all the mystique had been swallowed up by asphalt, noisy cars, bright lights, and crowds in American clothes, Genthe was to feel sentimentally nostalgic for 'the old mellowness of dimly lit alleys, the mystery of shadowy figures shuffling along silently . . .'[44]

In the cold light of day, though, there is nothing irresistible about Ross Alley, and for a taste of more vivid street life, the visitor would do better to head for Waverly Place, in the heart of Chinatown. T'ien-hou, the goddess of heaven and protector of sailors, fishermen, travellers, actors and prostitutes, has her temple here, at number 33. Huge, decorated lanterns hang by the doorway, which opens spaciously above a pillared staircase. Picking your way through the small children sitting and standing on the front steps, you venture inside, and find there the teak tables of the T'ien-hou altar, which are virtually sagging with the weight of the heavily ornate paraphernalia they bear, vessels, carvings, censers and assorted offerings. The altar is a perfect image of the Chinese taste for over-rich ornamentation.

In China temples are the focus of much social life, and Waverly Place, too, has the feel of a hub. It is where the itinerant vendors like to ply their trade, away from the hurly-burly of the main thoroughfares. There is hardly a trade, hardly a mode of retail that cannot be found within the confines of Chinatown. Pedlars and street stands sell toys, peanuts, dried lychees, poultry, cigars, sweets and Chinese narcissus. Fortune tellers sit at their collapsible wooden tables offering to divine your life or to prophesy whether you are going to be lucky at the gaming tables. Big Ox, a well-known figure often to be seen at Waverly Place, performs a martial-arts routine replete with poles and broadswords prefatory to selling you a herbal medicinal rub for injuries sustained in a fight or a fall. Modest basement canteens serve workers their down-to-earth snacks, beef porridge or other kinds of *congee*, fish and *wonton*. Barbers, who carry on their thriving trade one after the other down the sidewalks – giving rise to the nickname of Waverly Place, 'the fifteen-cent street' – do what Chinese barbers deftly and proudly do the world over: shave and scrub your forehead, clean your

hair, replait and oil it, remove stray hairs on the face, and scrape your
ears clean. Among Americans hairdressing is not usually imagined as
one of life's central rituals, but the queue wearer is bound to take the
matter more seriously.

Not all of Chinatown's vendors are Chinese, though, and if you
hang around long enough you may come across the Jewish balloon
man around the corner on Dupont Street. His balloons, helium-filled
and stencilled with the figures of animals, are a great favourite with the
children. You would hardly know, from the way he and Chinatown's
inhabitants behave towards each other, that whites and Chinese have
been such embittered enemies; but then it is not so much by Jews as by
Irish and Italians that the Chinese have most harshly been used. There
is room for white pedlars in Chinatown's tourist trade, and there is even
said to be a Jewish shop on Dupont Street, one owned by two German
Jewish brothers who speak fluent Cantonese and who are known to the
neighbourhood as the Sa-ling brothers.

Some of the best-known foreigners in Chinatown are Christian missionaries, and the Presbyterian Mission House on Sacramento Street,
to which every ill-used Chinese girl is likely to be introduced sooner
or later, blossoms under its director Donaldina Cameron, she who
is called Lo-mo ('mother') in Cantonese. Donaldina Cameron is a
determined woman who makes it her business to rescue mistreated
Chinese girls from their employers or families; hardly is a case reported
or rumoured than she is there with the police, making her surprise visit
by scrambling across rooftops if need be. Her heart must lift at the way
some of these girls turn out, growing up to lead lives of great devotion
to the mission and to Christianity. Chinatown is not so impervious to
Christian proselytization as you might suppose from its temples and its
cultural separateness. The influence of the Christian churches, for good
or ill, is considerable. Where but in these churches can a Chinatown
man or woman attend proper English classes? At times when there
is nowhere else to go, the churches alone provide a welcome, doing
much for the old and the lonely by organizing regular social functions.
They play a prominent part in acculturating individual Chinese to
American society; immigrants who strive to assume American ways
find themselves brought into membership of white society through
conversion to Christianity, and to go Christian is commonly to go
American.

Inevitably Chinatown changed, but it took more than missionaries
and do-gooders to alter its most rooted aspects. In the event it took

nothing less than an earthquake. This fateful event occurred in the dawn hours of 18 April 1906, and within three days Chinatown was reduced to rubble. Lapped in flames and plundered by looters (many of them Italians from the adjoining quarter), building after building collapsed, dispersing the inhabitants throughout the city. Where to rehouse the Chinese became a matter of some concern to the authorities – and much alarm and indignation to the residents and property owners of Presidio, in whose neighbourhood it was thought to resettle the Chinese. Just the thought of the Chinese smells that the summer breezes would waft to their doors were a Chinatown to spring up in their midst was enough to make these people nervous. The authorities saw their point, and moved the Chinese to a farther corner of the Presidio. For the Chinese, every day of that April was an ordeal; the authorities were no help, and white looters who made off with Chinese possessions got away with it. In the end the Chinese found their own solution, the landowners among them repossessing their properties and rebuilding them, so that in due time a new Chinatown arose out of the ashes of the old.

Miraculously, Arnold Genthe's photographs of the old Chinatown survived the catastrophe, though thousands of his other negatives were gone. A loss that was to prove beneficial to the Chinese was the destruction of the immigration records of US Customs. This gave thousands of illegal immigrants their chance to claim residence rights and to apply to bring their families over from China. The Chinese population grew, and time tempered the uncompromising Chineseness of Chinatown. Yet attitudes outlive stone and brick. The Exclusion laws continued to cast their shadow, and it would be many years before the Chinese were accepted as people more or less like anyone else.

CHAPTER SIX

Immigrant Society

Just as Italians, Greeks, Irish, Poles and other migrants shunted back and forth between the homeland and the overseas destination before they finally came to rest in one country, so Chinese emigration was a temporary absence from home, or at least was thought of as such by those who went abroad. And just as Southern Europeans regarded their expatriation as a short-term proposition, so Chinese migrants expected to go home after staying five years, ten years, or after they had made some money and could return to their native village in 'silken robes'.

Indeed, then as now, there was scarcely an immigrant group anywhere in the world that did not talk of going home eventually. Some did just that. Many did not, and for these 'the myth of return' soon became a consoling form of self-deception. Nor was it unknown for returned migrants to re-migrate when they found their native village to be not quite the place it had appeared during the years abroad, when it was seen sentimentally through nostalgia's prism.

'Sojourners', American social scientists came to call these impermanent migrants, using the term to mean people who spend many years of their lifetime in a foreign country without being assimilated by it. The term was developed by a Dr Paul C. P. Siu in a classic study of the Chinese laundry man in America, the 'ethnocentrist par excellence' as he called him,[1] and it became a great favourite with writers on the immigrant Chinese, who used it in the mistaken belief that the sense of impermanence marking the sojourner was somehow uniquely Chinese. At a time when immigrants were commonly expected to discard their old ethnic identities and surrender themselves wholeheartedly to the embrace of America, the Chinese immigrant's unwillingness to sink deeper roots was held against him; he was seen to sit on the fence, not committing himself. To regard oneself as essentially transient did seem an unpromising formula for the newcomer's integration into his host society, but it was (and still is) an attitude common to pioneering migrants, whether Chinese, Irish, Sikh, Italian or Pakistani. And since many returnees re-migrated, to talk of 'sojourners' as a category distinct from 'settlers' is to draw artificial boundaries.

It was perfectly natural for the first generation of immigrants to harbour mixed feelings about their continued expatriation, and it was only with the emergence of a second generation – the native-born, or at least native-educated, children of immigrant parents – that the vacillation, the sense of displacement, was overcome. But however many Chinese might have dissolved or disappeared into the host society, the replenishing of Chinese settlements with fresh tides of immigration ensured that there were enough first-generation immigrants around to keep the communities looking and feeling Chinese. The newcomer or 'greenhorn' marked the boundary between greater or lesser Chineseness. He was a distinct figure, creature of another world, and it was no accident that special words were used to describe him, to set him apart – *sinkeh* (Hokkien for 'new arrival') in the Straits Settlements, *totok* ('foreign-born, pure-blooded immigrant') in Indonesia, 'FOB' (Fresh Off the Boat) in America.

So at the same time as there was a return movement, there were inflows of new immigration, with men from the old village being called to join or replace kinsmen already established in the new country. The 'chain migration' thus established between an overseas destination and a handful of villages in the homeland meant that instead of arriving in a random scatter, migrants were related, if not by blood, then by ties of a common dialect or place of origin. Migrants tended to bunch together by clan or provenance, so that in America, for instance, one discovered soon enough that Pittsburgh's Chinatown was the turf of the Yee clan, Chicago the Moys', Denver the Chins', and so on.[2]

Migration to America was extremely popular, and had the country been more welcoming larger numbers of Chinese would have made their way there; the circumstance which gave it its restrictive character was of course the passage of the Chinese Exclusion laws, by which the United States clanged shut its doors to the Chinese worker. Nevertheless, though it took some ingenuity, and some money, Chinese continued to enter the United States as illegal immigrants, smuggled across Canadian or Mexican borders or through chicanery – in 1901, for example, it was estimated that fraudulent entrants were arriving at a rate of twenty thousand a year.[3] The Chinese were to be helped in these practices by the destruction of the city's records in the San Francisco earthquake and fire of 1906, which made it impossible to establish who was a legal resident and who not. A citizen could travel in and out of the country as he pleased, and any children he fathered abroad could become citizens by American law. When a Chinese applying to bring his family over

from China swore that he had been born in the United States, who
was to contradict him? It did not take the Chinese long to think up the
'slot racket', an illegal scheme which worked in this manner: during
his visit to China, a Chinese-American citizen eligible for re-entry into
the United States would announce the birth of a child, usually a
son, whether or not such a thing had occurred; in this way he created
a 'slot', one he could sell to anyone who wanted to emigrate to America,
making the transaction through friends or relatives or even a broker.
Those fictitious offspring, entering the United States under surnames
not their own, were called 'paper sons'.

The United States Immigration Bureau got wise to this practice, and,
in an attempt to stop it, built an immigration detention centre on a wild
island in the middle of San Francisco Bay, the notorious Angel Island,
in which to hold new arrivals for questioning. People said it was another
Ellis Island, the receiving station to the southwest of Manhattan where
transatlantic immigrants such as Jews, Poles, Italians, Austrians and
Hungarians awaited their fate, joyous at having reached the Promised
Land, fearful of being debarred and deported. It is true that one immigrant receiving station was much like another – there were the waiting
rooms, the barracks, the kitchens, the hospital wards, the docks, the
customs-houses, and so on; also true that for all too many newcomers,
the long waits, the medical inspection and the legal interrogations were
a bewildering and harrowing experience. But Ellis Island was never the
prison which Angel Island became for the many Chinese who were
detained there, for weeks or sometimes for months, as they waited to
be called for questioning and to hear the authorities' decisions. We have
been left mementoes of those long, monotonous and despairing hours:
the poems which they wrote or carved into the wooden walls of the
detention barracks. They are there still, and could move the susceptible
visitor. Here is a translation of some lines from one of them:

> The day I am rid of this prison and attain success,
> I must remember that this prison once existed.
> In my daily needs I must be frugal.
> Needless extravagance leads youth to ruin.
>
> All my compatriots please be mindful,
> Once you have made some small gains, return home early.[4]

On Ellis Island, men could be seen with little slips of paper in their
hands rehearsing other arrivals in the answers they were to give and the

lies (unnecessary in many cases) they were to tell when they came up for interrogation.[5] On Angel Island too, arrivals impersonating merchants, students, travellers or the sons of Chinese-American citizens would have memorized their crib sheets, the ones that described their native village and their fictive family histories in every detail. A paper son could be found out if his story didn't tally with the one given by his putative relatives. You had to have your wits about you, for no minutia was too small for the immigration officials. How many steps are there in your house? one prospective immigrant was asked. Did it have a clock? Where did you sleep in the house? Which position do you sleep in? And even if you got all the answers right a check for trachoma, hookworm, filariasis, liver fluke and lunacy could find you unfit for admission.[6]

The ones who did succeed in crossing the few hundred yards of water that separated Angel Island from their new home were received by kinsmen if they had them, or by the native-place association if they did not. It did not much matter that the newcomer had no true conception of the future lying in wait for him beyond Angel Island; that magical moment when he stepped out of its confines was partly savoured as a realization of a dream, the dream of the Gold Hills, and as an escape from drudging in the fields in China. To old-timers, his optimism might seem to border on folly, for what lay ahead were years of struggle, when his only reward, his only hope, was that he might last until he had earned enough money and could go home to Toishan. He was convinced that he would not have to stay in America for long – that was his defence against loneliness. He knew he was not wanted. Why, then, should he bother to learn about the new country or its language? He would work like a slave, for if he were ever to stop working the people at home would 'stop eating'.[7]

As for the kind of work he did, the choice was not wide – like his relatives and friends in America, he either earned his living as a 'chop suey man' or in a hand laundry. The laundry – the 'eight-pound livelihood', as they called it, after the eight-pound iron they used – was a protective economic niche, an isolated self-contained pocket in the larger American society. The laundry man was the 'no tickee, no shirtee' 'Charlie' of contemporary cartoons and movies.[8] In 1920, three out of ten Chinese who worked in the United States were employed in laundries, and there were Americans who had come across Chinese only because of the Chinese laundry. Lord Bryce, travelling in the United States in the 1880s, thought that most American cities looked the same, with the 'same wide streets, crossing at right angles . . . the same shops, arranged on the same plan, the same Chinese laundries with Li Kow visible through the window'.9 And the story goes that at a very smart club in New York where waiters were pointedly rude to customers, the Chinese ambassador was once handed a bag of washing.

The laundry man who planned to stay only three years quite often found himself staying thirty. He was chained to the laundry (he even lived in it), and the menial job that was supposed to be the stepping-stone to self-employment remained a menial job. His muscles ached. His wants were few and his tastes inexpensive, but if he was weak-willed his savings were dissipated in gambling. His sex-life consisted of hasty consummations in seedy hotels or brothels. Letters from home were only ever after two things: 'man or money', his return or his remittances.10

His plight found its echoes all over the world, in all the places where the Chinese settled. For a similar picture of dashed hopes and back-breaking work, one could, for example, go to Singapore. Between the 1880s and 1920s this 'Eastern port', as Conrad has called it, underwent spectacular growth, sucking in streams of migrants and acquiring the features of a boom 'coolie town'. From Conrad's descriptions, we may reconstruct what the newcomer would see as, put ashore from the boat which brought him from Fukien, he wanders into town from the quayside. To the east, past the bridge which spans the Singapore river, lies the tree-lined Esplanade, and on it stand the Hôtel de l'Europe and the Gothic St Andrew's Cathedral, more splendid than anything our sinkeh has ever seen before. 'Native craft' – Malay praus, coasting boats, Chinese sampans – lie 'moored in clusters . . . jammed up together . . . covered with mats . . . among the confusion of high sterns, spars, masts, and lowered sails.'11 But the newcomer shuns the bridge for a crowded thoroughfare on the west side of the river, one that is 'as narrow as a lane and absolutely riotous with life', where 'the tightly packed car of the cable tramways' navigates 'cautiously up the human stream, with the incessant blare of its horn'. Here he recognizes, with a leap of heart, the shops of the Chinaman yawning 'like cavernous lairs'.12 All the streets he would come to know like the back of his own hand.

Suppose our sinkeh was a native of northern Fukien, speaking a minority dialect called Hockchia. How would he fit into Singapore's Chinese community, which was dominated by speakers of southern Fukien dialect, or Hokkiens? The Chinese community had its own hierarchy, and Hockchias, who were a kind of out-caste, came near the bottom of it. Every Chinese in Singapore knew what Hockchias did for a living: they, and their cousins from Hengwah, the county that adjoins theirs in Fukien province, were rickshaw pullers. For just as one thought of ice-cream parlours when one thought of Greeks in America, or clothing stores when one thought of Jewish immigrants, so rickshaw-pulling was linked to Hockchias and Hengwahs in Singapore.

The rickshaw was a Japanese invention, but the Chinese rickshaw coolie quickly became a commonplace figure in the Asian urban land-scape – 'Chinese rickshawalas awaiting custom at the roadside', we read, 'were a familiar part of the Chowringhee scene' in Calcutta, to which the vehicle was introduced by members of the Chinese community.[13] Rickshaw-pulling was no job for the weak of heart or the elderly – many were the men who, barely past the age of forty, simply dropped dead between the shafts from cardiac arrest, sunstroke or sheer exhaustion. Nor was it much of a path to prosperity – out of ten pullers, perhaps only two owned their rickshaws. It was a walk of life in which one's strength was everything; lose it through age or disease and you were as good as dead.

Rickshaw coolies lived in airless and dirty lodging-houses, eighteen or nineteen to a room, some dossing down in shifts, some sleeping on the floor, often under benches that passed for beds. Tiny cupboards hanging from the rafters stored the remains of their last meal.[14] Not surprisingly, many pullers were afflicted with energy-sapping gastric diseases. It was no way to live. To keep themselves sane they smoked opium – while only two out of a hundred rickshaw sinkehs were opium users when they arrived in Singapore, nine out of ten Hockchias became addicts after landing.[15] Venereal diseases, easily transmitted in a population of male migrant labourers with only brothels to go to for sexual release, added their portion to the cycle of ill-health, loss of energy and income, despair and suicide. Those that road accidents did not kill quite often finished themselves off, some using a stout piece of rope to hang themselves (usually in their cubicle in the lodging-house or the latrine at the back, generally in the hours between midnight and dawn), others by swallowing opium, yet others by taking a razor to their throats.

Each new immigrant found himself re-enacting in part the experience of the preceding ones, his life locked quickly into the institutional structure and the allegiances of the overseas Chinese community. The affinities of the Chinese were to their own home towns and fellow provincials; and despite a uniform appearance to outsiders, their overseas settlements were intensely varied within. The linguistic and temperamental differences between the Cantonese and Hakkas, for instance, might seem insignificant to Anglo-Saxon Americans or Spaniards, but they were fiercely important to the Chinese themselves. Loyalties were well knit and local; a strong comradeship bound together the speakers of a common dialect, blunting the edge of their homesickness and their feeling of alienation.

The nearest thing to a Chinese native-place or dialect association in the West would be the Jewish *Landsmannschaft*, a lodge made up of people coming from the same town or district in the old country. Like the Landsmannschaft, the dialect association was partly a mutual aid society, partly a club-house, and partly a place to go to to re-immerse oneself in one's Chineseness. The Chinese had an unsurpassed ability to organize for practical ends, and though voluntary associations are common to all immigrant enclaves, perhaps no ethnic minority had as enormous an appetite for them as the Chinese.

In China they were adumbrated by the clubs and guilds which merchants formed on the basis of geographical origin and trade – the two were very often related – when their business required them to live in cities to which they were not native. The region they represented could be as small as a single county or as large as an entire province. They were parochial organizations, each keeping much to itself, concerned to protect its domination or monopoly of a particular trade or occupation from interlopers, and little interested in the other guilds and associations. The overseas Landsmannschaften also had elements of the charitable societies, the *shan-t'ang*, that existed in cities in the old country to provide the indigent sick with free medical care and the destitute dead with coffins and burial. And they looked back too to a tradition in the mining valleys of China (such as the copper-mining areas of Yunnan, the province bordering northern Burma), in which a man with means brought together fellows from the same lineage or speech group to work the mines together as a joint endeavour, creating a kongsi.[16] As used of the mining communities in Borneo in the eighteenth and nineteenth centuries, the term 'kongsi' referred to a large social and political grouping, but in the Straits Settlements it came to be used of any clan or dialect association.

There was an undoubted religious flavour to the dialect associations, whose club-houses kept shrines to their own local heroes and tutelary deities; the immigrants, rural folk for the most part, were a superstitious lot, much given to supernatural explanations of ordinary matters. In Singapore, the Temple to the Holy Mother and Empress of Heaven and the Hokkien Association were practically synonymous, the one a forerunner of the other, serving as a club-house for the Hokkien community, which had done more than any other speech group to bring it into being.

The dialect communities were subdivided on the basis of a common surname into what were called 'clan associations'. The Chinese would hate to hear it said that by going abroad they had forgotten their origins, and the aims of these associations were to provide facilities for the worshipping of ancestors, to promote the well-being of clansmen and their harmony, and to preserve the records of the clan's accomplishments. It was not always blood ties or geography, though, that bound a Khoo to another Khoo, or a Chan to another Chan. Clansmen did follow other clansmen to the overseas communities, but it was parts of a single-surname village in Fukien or Kwangtung that transplanted themselves overseas, not the entire lineage. Abroad, it would be a small clan association indeed that recruited only genuine family members. Properly speaking it was a same-surname club rather than a kinship organization; yet though the blood tie was more imagined than real, the feeling of kinship was there. The members claimed descent from a common ancestor, and this was easy enough to do, when on paper all Chinese descent lines could be traced back to the Yellow Emperor if the genealogists really put their minds to it. 'The attention bestowed by the Chinese on their deceased ancestors,' noted John Francis Davis, the author of a nineteenth-century work on them, 'and the prevalence of clanships, or extensive societies claiming a common descent, give to the lower orders some of the feeling which in England belongs only to persons of family, but which has characterized the Scotch people very generally.'[17]

The clan association was a home from home, and life for the uprooted immigrant was greatly eased by it. At its most practical it was a welfare agency and a settler of disputes; on a subtler level, and as an organizer of the rituals of ancestor worship, it assuaged the member's nostalgia for the old country, helped to perpetuate descent lines, satisfied the need for a sense of closeness to one's origins and prolonged one's memories of home. In a community always in danger of being diluted by forces in the outside world, the clan association served as an oasis of Chineseness.

It *looked* Chinese for a start. To see this for ourselves, let us go

to Georgetown, where some good specimens still stand. This British
tropical creation on the island of Penang, lying three miles off the
mainland Malayan coast, has about it the gentle feel of an English
provincial town; yet it is intensely Chinese in parts, with temples
and kongsi built to the architectural styles of Fukien province. Few
travellers to Penang miss the Khoo Kongsi, so much does it look like
something out of a willow-pattern plate. It was no good being one of
the Five Big Clans (namely the Khoo, the Yeoh, the Cheah, the Tan
and the Lim)[18] if you didn't build a kongsi grand enough (detractors
would say ostentatious enough) to bring people to a halt with gaping
astonishment. It would be a proper symbol of the family's standing in
society, and it would have a double roof like the ones you saw atop the
imperial buildings in Peking. Sadly, the structure burnt down in 1901,
before it was even occupied, and a somewhat less ambitious building,
if still a very impressive one, was raised in its place.

If you confront it head-on, you will see a fantasy of a roof, Fukienese
Baroque in the profuseness of its ornamentation, with ridges swirling
into elaborate 'swallow tails', and flying eave corners sweeping into
intricately carved animal shapes and curlicues. Perched on the roof are
no fewer than six free-standing, medallion-like sculptures, each a boatload of figures, evoking perhaps the prominence of the sea in the story of
the immigrant Chinese. Beyond the portico, doorways and curtain walls
are set between pillars wrapped around with polychromatic dragons,
and illuminated by decorated Chinese lanterns glowing with gilt. Once
inside, it is quite possible to succumb to the illusion that you are now in
a temple in southern Fukien rather than one in a British outpost near the
Equator. Two things, however, give the game away. Entrance to the
temple is gained through a projecting porch, and this has no prototype
in China, but seems to owe more to the style of Anglo-Indian design.[19]
Second, the kongsi is a two-storey building, with a lower floor that is
visually and structurally European. These deviations from the Chinese
norm have persuaded an architectural writer that the Penang kongsi
was a unique creation of the Straits Chinese.[20]

Something that *would* be altogether familiar to the visiting Chinese
from the homeland, though, is the structure facing the kongsi across
the courtyard, a permanent stage such as you would find in many
Buddhist monastery complexes in China, where religious festivals were
celebrated with theatrical perfomances. Many an immigrant Chinese
heart must have lifted when the time came each year for the Khoos
to sponsor an opera or a play at their theatre.

The big clans probably vied with each other to build the bigger and more spectacular kongsi, so they did not flinch from the cost. The Cheahs, whose famous clansman Cheah Chen Eok presented the city with its clock tower to commemorate Queen Victoria's diamond jubilee in 1897, built themselves a kongsi almost as impressive, a two-storey affair with a balustrade of wrought iron running across the façade and distinctly European-looking gargoyles projecting from the top of the pilasters on the lower floor. The Yeoh clan-house has a roof almost as extravagantly decorated as the Khoos', perched with as many of those sculpted Noah's Arks. The Tan clan-house has these barges too, only instead of figures they carry clusters of architectural forms topped by a foliated knob, a bunch of leaves springing away above.

The kongsi houses the ancestral shrine, the spirit tablets and the commemorative plaques which back in Kwangtung or Fukien would be held in the clan hall or ancestral temple. In the main hall of the Khoo Kongsi, a tablet exhorts clansmen to 'Faithfulness and Frugality'. Halls of fame to the side display gilded plaques inscribed with names in black Chinese and English lettering, followed by such suffixes of accomplishment as 'Bachelor of Medicine and Surgery, University of Manchester, UK', 'B.Sc. (Civil Eng.), University of Dundee, Scotland', and 'Barrister-at-Law, Middle Temple'.

A different style of kongsi can be found in Manila. I have already mentioned the Pan Family Association there. This is in Suite 1601, State Center Building, 333 Juan Luna Street, Binondo, rather than in a detached Chinese temple. There being not very many Pans in Manila, the association is a modest affair, where instead of tablets honouring degree holders the walls are hung with the ads of the members' companies: MANILA PLASTIC PRODUCTS, LILY'S PEANUT BUTTER MADE BY NEWBORN FOOD PRODUCTS INC. The members themselves have Spanish names: José and Domingo Acosta, to name just two from the list of donors to the association.

From its exterior the Lim Association seemed little different, housed on the fifth floor of a modern block on Ongpin Street. But step inside, and you can tell at a glance how much bigger and more consequential a clan the Lims are in Manila's Chinese community. A full-length portrait of the clan's founder, a bearded gentleman wearing a Chinese robe with a sash and badge crossing his chest, stands to one side of a box-like structure, one of a pair flanking the central ancestral altar. The altar is elaborately carved, with a black wood frame enclosing gilded panels that would put a European visitor in mind of the retables of Hispanic Catholic churches.

For a truly magnificent specimen, you should go to the Chua-Ko Association, whose premises take up the top three floors of a modern building on Juan Luana Street. There is no missing the self-assertiveness of this two-surname association, with its considerable membership, its enviable look of wealth, its marble floors, its ebony furniture, its orchestra of Chinese instrumentalists and its well stocked library of books and periodicals from Taiwan. FIRM ROOTS BRING FORTH LUXURIANT BRANCHES, one of its tablets says, certain of the importance of pedigree. Among the deceased clan worthies whose names are emblazoned on walls, one notes a Chua Bun Wah, a banker and clearly a model member, commended by Chiang Ching-kuo, President of the Republic of China (Taiwan), for his tireless efforts on behalf of the anti-Communist cause. Banks of spirit tablets, tiered like rice terraces, remember the dead. Before one of these, a descendant has thoughtfully placed a garland of jasmine, a plate of steamed buns, a cup of tea in a tumbler, tins of pickled lettuce and lychees, a tin of Del Monte peach halves, and, this being the Philippines, a bottle of San Miguel pale pilsen.

To its critics, the kongsi was a very repository of Chinese clannishness and parochial narrowness, an impediment to the unity of the community. Memories of clan feuds at home did not grow dim with expatriation. Abroad, the animosities were exacerbated by business rivalry. Common speech was a bond beyond class, but while it gave each group a sense of tight cohesiveness, it splintered the larger community. In the Philippines, long the domain of the Hokkiens, the popular reputation of the Cantonese stood low; and yet while the Hokkiens thought them frivolous and unstable, they thought the Hokkiens crafty and untrustworthy. In Singapore, a Hakka didn't marry a Teochiu, nor a Cantonese a Hokkien. In Siam, the different speech communities struck a nineteenth-century English writer, George Windsor Earl, as being so strongly opposed to each other that it was 'as if they belonged to rival nations' – a view echoed by the Reverend Howard Malcom, who observed a couple of years later that 'the variety of their dialects drives them to clan-like associations, which not only keep them reserved and cold toward each other, but often engage them in animosities'.[21] As well as being at loggerheads with one another, the different speech groups in Siam had their own favourite gods: the Teochius and Hakkas their Pen-t'ou Kung, linked in legend to the father of Thai boxing, and the Hokkiens their Holy Mother and Empress of Heaven, the sailor's patron deity. Preferring to remain separate even in death, each had its own cemetery, the Cantonese graves clustered in one centre, the Teochiu in another.

The divisiveness of the community was well recognized by the colonial authorities; when a Chinese Advisory Board was set up in the Straits Settlements in 1889, the British knew to relate the representation of the five main speech groups – Hokkien, Teochiu, Cantonese, Hakka and Hainanese – to the population of each.[22] Adroit practitioners of the method of 'divide and rule', the British would have been happy enough with this state of affairs if it hadn't grown so violent. The violence came of the involvement of the secret societies.

Secret societies were organic to overseas Chinese communities. The two had gone together from the very beginning, with the immigration business; it was by organizing themselves into syndicates that immigration brokers were able to acquire, control and dispose of coolies in large numbers. Cho Kim Siang, for example, was at once a coolie trader and the leader of the five-thousand-strong Ghee Hin, a Hokkien-speaking triad society in Malaya and Singapore. Acting as a coolie agent for at least seven European companies, he did a roaring business recruiting labourers for Deli in northeast Sumatra and Australia.[23] The secret society, with its command of *samsengs* ('thugs'), was perfectly suited to bring refractory coolies into line and to stop them from absconding.

From the first the British acknowledged the fact of its usefulness as a means of social control, and there is much truth to the description of the triads as an *imperium in imperio*. In the early days of British rule the Chinese largely governed themselves, dealing with the imperial power through community leaders or headmen. A string of such men – called *Kapitan China* in Malaya, *Luitenant, Kapitein* and *Majoor* in the Dutch Indies, *Nai-amphoe-jek* ('the Chinamen's district officer') in Thailand[24] – ran the affairs of the Chinese communities and answered for them to the governing power. They were special people, singled out for their wealth and influence, and advantageously placed by their official position to receive government contracts or favours. Secret societies stood behind them, and all too often the *Kapitan* was simultaneously a triad chief and the head of his dialect community. The secret society and the Landsmannschaft combined to form his power base, and it was frequently hard to tell where one ended and the other began.

The British left well alone; they could not, however, do so for long. In 1867 Penang was paralyzed by gang warfare. Here is how, under

the headline 'Boom in Coffins', the *Penang Gazette* described it in its
edition of Sunday 4 August 1867:

> There is now a big sale in coffins! After the warfare between
> the rival secret societies, the Ghee Hin and the Toh-Peh
> Kong, reliable sources have revealed that many members
> have been fatally wounded. A Chinese carpenter (Ghee Hin)
> formerly employed in the Convict Establishment led Charles
> Edward Anderson, overseer in the Convict Establishment,
> to the Kongsi House in Church Street. On the lower floor,
> carpenters were busily constructing mass-produced coffins.
> Many occupied coffins lined the front of Pitt Street Temple
> this evening.

Something would have to be done to end this mayhem, and also to put
a stop to the mischief down by the Singapore quays, where coolies were
constantly being poached from the depots and free immigrants were
brazenly set upon by triad thugs to be sold off as indentured labourers.
The solution the British came up with – and it was an inspired stroke
– was the appointment in 1877 of William Pickering, a well-known
scholar of Chinese, as the first Protector of Chinese. The Protectorate
began by addressing itself to the abuses of the credit-ticket system and
to the exploitation of the Chinese labourer at the hands of the mine and
plantation owners, but over the years Pickering interested himself in
arbitrating disputes between rival societies and speech groups, and in
this way undermining the power of the secret societies.

Now there was somebody other than the triad chief for the Chinese
to appeal to for protection; there was the colonial government, in
the guise of Mr Pickering. A contemporary joke about him alludes
to his popularity: nothing charmed the Chinese more, it went, than
'Mr Pickering . . . going about the villages playing on his [bag]pipes,
Chinese tunes mayhaps. He quite won their hearts like Orpheus of old
and the result was that the Chinese became most tractable.'[25]

In 1890 the secret societies were outlawed in the Straits Settlements,
but they were suppressed in theory only, and in fact the old villainies
lingered on in many spheres of immigrant Chinese life. In three of
these the triads remained supreme: in the control of the opium excise
farm, in gambling and in prostitution.

Widely used by native rulers before the coming of the Europeans,
the excise farm system, under which a person (the farmer) paid the
government a fixed fee for the exclusive right to sell a particular service

or commodity for a specified period, had been successively adopted by the Dutch and the British – what better way to assure themselves of a steady flow of revenue without the burden of administrative costs than to lease the sole right to sell opium and spirits and to operate lotteries and gambling-houses to the highest bidder for the monopoly? The revenue farm was a colossal money spinner, for the government as well as the successful bidder. In Siam, the opium, rice spirits, gambling and lottery farms provided up to half of the total state revenue in the late nineteenth century, and it could justly be said, writes the historian William Skinner, that 'while the country depended on Chinese virtues for the expansion of commerce and industry, the government relied on Chinese vices for the expansion of public revenue'.[26]

The opium farm was ubiquitous in colonial Asia, from the Dutch Indies to British India, and an opium business in one country was much like an opium business in another. In Nanyang partnerships or syndicates of the richest Chinese vied for it, and it was rare to find an opium farmer who wasn't backed to the hilt by a secret society. The successful bidder very often consorted with high government officials, for whose cooperation he would have paid handsome gifts. Everyone knew him, for he was very likely the headman of his community, the Kapitan China or the Majoor.

It would be strange if the Chinese didn't smoke opium; Britain had gone to war against China to sell it to them. It is said that the overseas Chinese took the habit with them when they emigrated, but that doesn't explain why the emigrant indulged in it more than the stay-at-home. In San Francisco's Chinatown no less than forty per cent of the adult population smoked it.[27] In mid-nineteenth-century Singapore as many as a third of the adult Chinese population were addicts, and about as high a proportion was found among the Chinese in Malacca when the matter was looked into in 1881; this was far in excess of the ratio in China itself.[28] It was mostly the labouring classes and the artisans, the coolies, the carpenters, the blacksmiths, the barbers, the boatmen and the gambier planters who smoked the drug, and this is not surprising, for opium was the poor man's friend – the easer of pain, the salve of overworked muscles, even the surcease from the numbing boredom and the nagging ache of homesickness. It was the 'ultimate siesta', as Jean Cocteau has called it, and he should know. 'One of the wonders of opium', Cocteau has said, 'is to transform instantaneously an unknown room into a room so familiar, so full of memories, that one thinks one has always occupied it. When addicts go away they suffer no hurt because of the certainty that the delicate mechanism will function in one minute, anywhere.'[29] The docklands of London, the sugar plantations of Cuba, the tin mines of Malaya, the jungle trading posts of Borneo – all could be made as familiar as the villages of southern Fukien or Kwangtung. What was more, opium must have helped to allay sexual starvation as well, since in those days it was only men who emigrated, and every single overseas Chinese society was in great want of women. The Chinese opium smoker was no De Quincey, pursuing hallucinatory visions; he merely wanted the drug to kill his pain and give him a good night's sleep.

The opium farm not only fed the habit but made it grow. The more widely the vice spread, the greater were the profits that accrued to the farmer and the colonial government. Small wonder, then, that in Singapore the number of licensed opium shops (where cooked opium, or *chandu*, was retailed to the consumer) leapt from forty-five in 1848 to five hundred in 1897.[30] In Malaya's tin districts, a creditor or financier could usually expect to get the labour he needed because he was also the opium farmer, with a ready supply of the drug to be advanced to the coolie, who soon found himself in thrall. It was the same story on the plantations, where the opium distributors were the owners themselves, and the newly recruited coolie was encouraged to develop a craving so that he could be paid part of his wages in chandu.

Triad power was hardly uppermost in his mind when an addict walked into an opium-shop, but in fact he was stepping into the thick of it, for the business was suffused with it, and it was secret-society gangsters who, when the monopoly came up for bidding, terrorized rival contenders into withdrawing, and wreaked vengeance on the smugglers and poachers who infringed the monopoly. There was much opium-smuggling into Singapore from the Dutch colonies, from Hong Kong, Amoy and Swatow, and it was a good guess that the organized rings of the secret societies were involved.

So much of the addicts' pay went on opium – as much as two-thirds, some reports said[31] – that those poor wretches who wanted to make their pile before hurrying home to Fukien or Hainan all too often found their savings depleted and their date of return indefinitely postponed. The guilt ground them down as much as the hopelessness. Opium was a scourge all right, and it gnawed at the social conscience.

There arose a movement to suppress it, the chief champions of which were two physicians who had been educated in England, Dr Yin Shut Chuan and Dr Lim Boon Keng, and who saw opium-smoking as the shame and the stigma of the overseas Chinese. By 1910 the struggle for the abolition of the opium-farming system in the Straits Settlements had been won, and the government took over the sale of the drug itself, bringing an unfettered commercial enterprise under public control. Thailand had done away with it the year before, bringing to an end the huge profits of the opium farmer.

When they were not smoking opium the Chinese immigrants, especially the ones who toiled the hardest, were likely to be gambling. The men loved to chance their luck, loved it all the more for having nothing much else to do with their leisure hours. The native enthusiasm for gambling did not merely survive the journey from the home country; as an antidote to boredom and loneliness, it positively blossomed. There is also this, that the man who emigrates, who goes abroad to seek his fortune, will be a gambler at heart, a seeker after quick money. Money is what will ensure that he can go home 'in silken robes'. But all too often gambling, by ruining the unlucky, is also what puts paid to such dreams.

It didn't much matter where they were – in Singapore, Bangkok, London or San Francisco – the Chinese played the same games. Games like *pai-ke-p'iao* (called *puck-apu* by those who wrote about it in England), a numbers game, and *fan-tan* were constants, and have remained so into the 1980s. 'It is nothing more or less than *odd and even*,' wrote an onlooker at a session of fan-tan he came upon in 1873 in Peru:

> The parties who play, sit down on the ground with a handful of beans &c between them, and one, taking out a few, stakes his money, or other available property, on the fact as to whether they are odd or even in number. The lookers-on invest according to their fancy, and the beans or grains of maize, or coffee, as the case may be, are carefully counted one by one . . . The operation is gone through with a bit of stick . . .[32]

Compare this description with these notes I took of a game of fan-tan I watched in a gambling den in London's Gerrard Street one Saturday afternoon in 1988: 'The croupier, a young, buxom woman wielding a chopstick, scoops up a bowl of buttons from a tub, empties them on to the table, takes the buttons away four at a time, using the stick to brush them aside, until only one, two, or three buttons are left. The player stakes his money on how many of the beads are left, winning or losing large sums of money in the blink of an eye.'

Lotteries were popular, and in Thailand the *hua-hui*, a game in which players stake on thirty-six animals and the prize is thirty times the amount of the stake, was a revenue farm in itself. The drawing of the lottery was held twice a day, and one heard tell that until the winning animal out of the thirty-six was announced, normal business could not resume. In Singapore you could not move for the crowd of men, women, children and domestic servants that thronged Hong Kong Street, *the* place for the hua-hui lottery.

Deeply enmeshed in all this were the secret societies, which quarrelled, and sometimes killed each other, over the huge profits to be made from running gaming-houses and from the associated racketeering. In San Francisco, it was mob chiefs like Little Pete, Big Jim, Tom Chu and Wong Yow who controlled the gambling clubs, of which there were more than three hundred in Chinatown alone.[33] Anyone who dropped by at Wong Yow's own house on Waverley Street would find the whole place given over to gambling.

For it wasn't as though you could pick up a newspaper at the end of a ten- to sixteen-hour working day and find the entertainment page offering a hundred and one things to do. There was no home to go to either; in San Francisco's Chinatown, the crowding was so dire that two or three men slept on each bunk in shifts. Licit sexual delight and wifely tenderness were denied most men – commonly quoted sex ratios of Chinese women to men were 1 to 10, 1 to 14 or, in America, even 1 to 20.[34] When people observed that the great majority of the Chinese females in San Francisco in the nineteenth century were prostitutes, we may take what they said for a fact. In the Straits Settlements, too, the scarcity of women lowered morality. The bulk of women there, remarked the ever observant Victorian colonial administrator J. D. Vaughan, 'are purchased in China from their parents by bawds and panders, and have to repay their purchase money and other advances by prostituting their bodies, for years it may be. The lives of slavery and debauchery these poor creatures lead, ending often in disease and death, is something horrible to contemplate.'[35]

Could anything else be expected? The men themselves had suffered a similar fate at the hands of coolie crimps and immigration brokers. Of course they could become a colony of homosexuals; there was no reason why homosexuality shouldn't be as pervasive among these womanless males as among prisoners or the convict transportees in Australia.

Yet it seemed not to have been the preference; certainly reports or rumours of homosexuality did not reach the ears of the authorities. There were apparently 'dark and nicely Victorian references' to a 'more than normal degree of sexual perversion' among the coolies in Peru,[36] but the absence of any reliable account of it in the literature couldn't have been just oversight or discretion.

Prostitution, though, is another matter. Along with opium, the organized traffic in prostitutes was what gave the overseas Chinese such a bad name; there was scarcely an American comment on Chinatown, rarely a description of the Chinese community, that missed the chance to bring up the subject – newspaper stories about it bore headlines like 'Her Back was Burnt with Irons', 'Confessions of a Slave Dealer' and 'Story of Girls Shows Working of a Chinese Ring'.[37] Some of the American men really knew what they were talking about when they brought up the 'Chiney ladies', 'moon-eyed pinch foots' and 'she-heathens' in their conversations, for Chinese prostitutes in California served white customers as well as clienteles of their own kind, the faded ones offering themselves pathetically to passers-by from behind barred windows in cubicles or 'cribs': 'Lookee two bits, feelee foor bits, doee six bits.'[38]

In 1870 seven out of ten Chinese women in San Francisco were prostitutes, and until about 1907, there were 22.5 whores to every 100 inhabitants in Chinatown. Females were precious commodities, bitterly fought over by rival gangs in the notorious tong wars so luridly written up in the local newspapers. When a girl ran away, tong hitmen called 'highbinders' (a term used of a member of the Irish banditti and extended by the New York police to any hoodlum) were employed to go after her. Once that happened, the girl had to be prepared for the worst, for highbinders were aptly dubbed 'hatchetmen': one girl, Yellow Doll to her fans, was found chopped into pieces in 1876.

Things were no better in Malaya or Singapore. Brawls frequently broke out in brothels, because all you had to do to get up the nose of a rival secret society was to go and create a disturbance at a bordello under its protection. Dialect complicated matters here as everywhere. Because most prostitutes were Cantonese or Teochius who favoured their own kind, men who did not speak these dialects were apt to feel slighted and discriminated against, and once stung to the quick they could be, and often were, inflamed into violence.[39]

The complications of speech and secret society on which the structure of immigrant Chinese colonies rested could be seen in the terrible

killings that ensued from a clash between the tongs of the Three
Districts and those of the Four Districts in San Francisco. In 1894
a Four Districts man was arrested for murder. The Three Districts
people, who considered themselves a cut above, refused to defend
him. Already smarting at their rivals' superiority, the Four Districts
men retaliated by boycotting all the Three Districts shops and forming
their own merchants' guild. Enter Little Pete, Three Districts mobster,
showing his colours, and before long fifty Four Districts men are dead.
Twelve Four Districts tongs merged to avenge their deaths, their taste
for blood sharpened, their hatred for the Three Districts people more
bitter than ever. They would get Little Pete, they would. And get him
they did, riddling him with bullets in true mob style in 1897, while
he was at the barber's and his bodyguard was out getting a betting
sheet.

The tribal differences tearing Chinatowns apart were to lead a distinguished visitor to conclude that civic responsibility was not a general
trait of the Chinese people. The visitor was Liang Ch'i-ch'ao, one of
those reformers who believed that China would have to be radically
changed before it could become strong; the slavish mentality of the
Chinese people, the corruption and degeneration that afflicted their
country, he had concluded, were an illness that could not possibly be
cured 'without taking the medicine of liberty'.[40] In 1903, he made a
tour of American Chinatowns, and what he saw there of the clannishness and parochialism of the overseas Chinese, their lack of public-
spiritedness, their submission to the tyranny of tradition and their
exploitation by criminal gangs, was enough to make him think twice
about championing liberty on behalf of the Chinese people. Heaven
knows the Chinese were an oppressed nation, weighed down by centuries of autocratic rule, but here were Chinese living in a democratic
system, and they were no fitter for majority rule.

The American newspaper-men reporting his visit were their usual
breathless selves – 'Dream of Big Republic Thrills All Chinatown',
'Leong [Liang Ch'i-ch'ao] Rouses Latent Patriotism of Meek Mongolians', 'Oriental Mark Antony Tells Chinamen How They Have Only
Been Slaves' were some of the headlines[41] – but Liang himself felt
anything but excited. 'No more am I dizzy with vain imaginings,'
he was to conclude. 'In a word, the Chinese people must for now
accept authoritarian rule; they cannot enjoy freedom . . . Those born
in the thundering tempests of today, forged and moulded by iron

and fire – they will be my citizens, twenty or thirty, nay, fifty years hence. *Then* we will give them Rousseau to read, and speak to them of Washington.'42

Liang was a disciple of the famous K'ang Yu-wei, an evangelical scholar who, back in China, had urged upon the young Emperor Kuang-hsu reforms of the kind adopted by Peter the Great in Russia and by the leaders of the Meiji Restoration in Japan. The Emperor had been all ears. Much attracted by the notion that China might become stronger if it were more modern, more like Western nations in the way in which it was governed, Kuang-hsu had decreed a dizzying spate of reforms in the summer of 1898. How distasteful all this must have been to the conservative court officials may easily be imagined, and Kuang-hsu's powerful aunt, the terrible Empress Dowager T'zu-hsi, had been persuaded to intervene. Before long she had taken over the reins of government and placed her nephew under house arrest. Had he not fled to Japan, K'ang Yu-wei would have been beheaded.

K'ang became a wanderer, travelling in search of support from one foreign nation to another. In Victoria, Canada, he founded Pao-huang Hui, the Society for the Protection of the Emperor, whose aim it was to impress upon Chinese people the world over that reforms to transform China into a modern constitutional monarchy must be revived. Because he found his backers among the rich of the overseas Chinese (including the heads of the secret societies), K'ang made it a simultaneous aim of the Pao-huang Hui to better the commercial and legal status of the Chinese and to elevate them to a level 'equal to that of any other civilized race'.

Every other Chinatown in North and South America came to have its chapter of the Society for the Protection of the Emperor. In San Francisco's Chinatown you could tell when the members were meeting, for posters would be stuck up in the streets. The mood would be very far from mellow, for the buds of Chinese nationalism, here as elsewhere in the Chinese world, were about to burst. K'ang was the first of several well-known Chinese from China to persuade their overseas compatriots that being Chinese was nothing to be ashamed of, and that their future was linked to the destiny of their mother country.

What he worked for was the establishment of a modernizing constitutional monarchy, not the downfall of the dynasty. So had the secret societies, which seemed ever more like mobs of gangsters, forgotten their original inspiration, the overthrow of Manchu rule? Well, not quite. It is well known that the 1911 revolution in China, heralding an end not only to the 268-year reign of the Manchu dynasty but to an empire reaching as far back as 221 BC, had its share of secret-society plotters. Just as tongs had rallied to the cause of reform espoused by K'ang Yu-wei, so, when the idea of a constitutional monarchy gave way to the idea of a republic, they had sympathized with the revolutionary crusade of Dr Sun Yat-sen.

Dr Sun, one day to be known as the father of the Chinese Republic, was born to humble peasants in a village near Canton in 1866. His elder brother had emigrated, as was customary in the village (one of those places at the home end of the migration chain), to Honolulu, and it was there that the younger Sun went to join him when he turned thirteen. Sun studied at an Anglican missionary school and then at Oahu College, and would have gone on to the United States if his brother, afraid that he might convert to Christianity, hadn't stopped him. So in the end it was in Hong Kong that he completed his medical studies, and where he turned Christian after all.

As much as anything, his expatriate experiences convinced Dr Sun that he must rid China of its corrupt rulers. Why was the contrast so stark between Hong Kong and his home district, only fifty miles away – the one so prosperous and well ordered, the other so backward and stagnant? He thought that the difference could only be one of government, British here, Manchu over there. He did not doubt that revolution was the answer to China's ills; the only question was how.

By seeking the help of the secret societies, someone whispered in his ear. The seed, once planted in his mind, began to flower. He began to travel far and wide, becoming that familiar type, the émigré plotting revolution abroad, and finding his readiest supporters among perimeter people – the expatriates, the Christian converts, the members of secret societies. To strengthen his hand, he joined a secret society, the Hung Men (the Vast Gate), in Honolulu, and it was as an office-bearer of that organization that he was welcomed into the Hung Men in the United States when he went there in 1904. He was at his most comfortable among people who had spent many of their years abroad, and it was among the overseas Chinese that the first revolutionary party was born. In August 1905, he inaugurated the Chinese United League – later to spawn the Kuomintang, the Nationalist Party – in Japan, pledging to found a republic in China. And so he proved the Manchus right in their fears of several centuries before, when they banned travel abroad out of a wish to preclude all possibility of overseas insurrection.

He had some trouble winning support in the Chinatowns in America, because there he had been forestalled by K'ang Yu-wei, preaching a message of reform. Well might he feel unloved in San Francisco, where the Chinese were so enthusiastic about the Society for the Protection of the Emperor that when its headquarters burnt down in the great earthquake of 1906, the money to rebuild it (some coming from well-heeled businessmen, some from the tongs) was collected within a matter of months.[43] But much of that loyal ardour lost its focus in 1908, for the Emperor Kuang-hsu died that year, and with his death went the rationale for the Emperor Protection Society.

Sun Yat-sen's became the most popular cause around, and as he travelled from one Chinatown to the next, finding his supporters in the network of secret societies, revolutionary cells sprouted, donations spilt forth. Uncounted amounts of money came the way of the revolutionary cause, money to arm risings, to run subversive magazines. It would not be too much to say that without the support of the overseas Chinese, the overthrow of the dynasty would have been achieved later and possibly in a different manner. Revolution as a means of national salvation was a theme to which the overseas Chinese responded with ardour, and the Kuomintang was to enjoy their allegiance until well into our own times. One day to be called the 'Mother of Revolution', the overseas Chinese had evolved their nationalism the quick way, by being aliens in a foreign country.

CHAPTER SEVEN

The Jews of the East

Here and there in Nanyang, far up a muddy river, the interior of a steamy island would open out into a jungle clearing. Around the clearing would lie impenetrable forests, with lianas strangling the tree trunks and snakes slithering across the roots. In the blazing noonday sun, the hot air would steam like a sodden blanket. The place would look listless and deserted, but for a plume of smoke from a solitary, rickety hut. Those who found their way there would know the hut to be the *kedai*, the little general store selling every imaginable thing from dried fish to pots; and here, sitting naked to the waist outside it, with tiny rills of sweat running down his sun-brown back, was the *towkay*, the Chinese who owned it.

This classic picture of the Chinese trader was, with only slight modifications, to be encountered in country after country in Nanyang. 'In the most secluded hamlet,' noted a British observer in Siam in 1898, 'and in the deepest jungle, wherever men are gathered together', there would the Chinese be, 'doing the chief share of the work, and taking the largest slice of the profits'.[1] The account which the famous Isabella Bird gave of her travels in Malaya in 1879 spoke so often of the ubiquitous Chinese that she felt duty-bound to explain: 'I have written a great deal about the Chinese and very little about the Malays, the nominal possessors of the country, but the Chinese may be said to be everywhere, and the Malays nowhere.'[2]

To go to the markets gathered on the Chao Phraya river in Bangkok was to enter a Chinese bazaar. The flotillas of houseboats, half home and half shop on the water's edge, were Chinese.[3] 'There are of course, many Siamese employed in various kinds of domestic or official work,' notes a British observer in the closing years of the nineteenth century, 'but in the streets nearly every workman is Chinese.' 'Isa-kee! Isa-kee!' one of them bawls as he comes staggering along the road, carrying two heavy pails at the ends of his bamboo pole.[4] 'Isa-kee' being his rendering of the English word 'ice-cream', the vendor, sweat streaming down his bare body and soaking the cloth around his loins, does a roaring trade outside the city's schools when the little boys are let out at recess.

All over Southeast Asia, it was a Chinese who sold you a drink, a chicken, a needle, a lamp, a catty of rice, a length of cloth, a bag of spices – a quantity of anything, in fact, that was essential to everyday living. The Chinese were good at marrying surplus to scarcity, and vast numbers of them were involved in distribution. Long before retailing was everywhere seen to be a Chinese monopoly, Chinese merchants and pedlars were making money at a rate which far exceeded anyone else's.

The King of Siam, Rama VI, was one day to write an essay denouncing the Chinese as the Jews of the East; but he was by no means the first to draw the comparison. Almost three centuries before, a Sir Thomas Herbert, whose travels to Sumatra, Malacca and other places began in 1621, observed that the huge contingents of Chinese traders who came in their junks every January to trade with the English, Dutch, and other nations were 'too subtle for young merchants, oftimes so wedded to dicing, that, after they have lost[,] their whole estate and wife and children are staked; yet in littel [*sic*] time, Jew-like, by gleaning here and there, are able to redeem their loss; if not at the day, they are sold in the market for most advantage'.[5] In the late eighteenth century another traveller to Java, a Dutch admiral called Johan Splinter Stavorinus, noticed how most of the sugar mills were run by the Chinese and was no less reminded of the Jews of Europe when he observed the way they conducted their business.[6]

'Quick-witted for chances, markedly self-interested, purpose-like, thrifty, frugal, on the whole regarding honesty as the best policy, independent in manner as in character, and without a trace of "Oriental servility"' was how they struck Isabella Bird in Malaya.[7] In Java it was the same story. Whether he was a footsore pedlar or a portly millionaire, the whole of 'a Chinaman's life in Java' was devoted to 'the making of bargains'. He was a merchant with 'his whole heart, his whole soul and his whole understanding', we are told, who 'could as soon leave off breathing as leave off buying and selling'; his very thoughts might be 'noted in figures'.[8] Could anyone exemplify more exactly the self-made man than the Chinese who began as a pedlar and ended as the owner of a general store? At first you saw him trudging along selling soap, sewing-cotton, combs and matches. After a few months you would find him selling sarong cloth and thin silks. Next time you saw him, he would have a panting helper in tow. He would soon have his shop, and, venturing into that well stocked establishment a few years later, you would glimpse his wife and 'be astonished at the size of the diamonds in her shiny coil of hair'.⁹ He would have a great many things on his mind, not the least of which was his plan to send his son to Europe in one of his own ships and get him admitted as a student at Leiden University.

One thing they certainly did not mind doing was soiling their hands with commerce; but as well as a furious sense of opportunism, the Chinese had another advantage. A quality they were frequently credited with was cleverness, and if they were detested for their fondness for profit, they were often admired for their quickness and dexterity. 'They are so skilful and clever,' remarked Domingo de Salazar, a Spanish bishop who worked among the Sangleys of the Parián in Manila in the last decades of the sixteenth century, 'that, as soon as they see any object made by a Spanish workman, they reproduce it with exactness . . . and I think that nothing more perfect could be produced than some of their marble statues of the Child Jesus which I have seen.'¹⁰ They made prettier things than were made in Spain, noted the bishop; and, perhaps even more to the point, they could make everything more cheaply.

Familiar generalizations made about the Chinese in Hong Kong and other places in the present century – that they could make you a fake Gucci bag or an IBM computer almost as good as the real thing, that they would sooner work for themselves than for a wage – are adumbrated in a story which Bishop Salazar relates. A bookbinder newly arrived from Mexico sets up shop in Manila and engages a Chinese who had offered his services to him. Without his master noticing it, the Chinese watches the bookbinder at work, and when, in a very short time, he has mastered the secrets of the craft, the Chinese hands in his notice and sets up a bindery himself, becoming 'so excellent a workman', says Bishop Salazar, 'that his master has been forced to give up the business, because the Sangley has drawn all the trade'.

Chinese masons built the city walls of Manila, as well as its finest churches, monasteries and hospitals, and among other useful things they introduced to the Philippines were the first sugar mills with vertical stone crusher and iron boiling pans, the extraction of saccharine juice from sugar cane and the working of wrought iron.¹¹ In Siam it was a Chinese who, around 1890, pioneered the process for producing the clean, white rice that was so much more remunerative than the older variety.¹² In the west coast tin states of Malaya the immigrants were credited with having introduced new mining methods;¹³ and in their contribution to the development of the resources of Penang and Singapore, the Victorian colonial administrator J. D. Vaughan thought that they equalled or even surpassed the Europeans. In the Straits Settlements, Vaughan wrote, 'The Chinese are everything'; 'they are actors, acrobats, artists,' he began listing, and went on to name a total of 110 separate occupations, from clerks and cashiers to vagabonds and thieves.[14] In Thailand there was scarcely a soul who would not go to a Chinese artisan if he wanted anything made or mended, from shoes and bracelets to boats and cupboards.[15] In Georgetown, Malaya, Isabella Bird went into the bank and found only Chinese clerks, into the post office and saw only the same, went into the P&O office to see to her berth to Ceylon and 'it was still a Chinaman, imperturbable, taciturn, independent, and irreproachably clean'.[16]

What marked the overseas Chinese, above all, was their capacity for hard work and their physical power of endurance, and even Stamford Raffles, for all his initial antipathy to the commercial cunning of the Chinese in the Dutch Indies, observed that while 'the Arabs are mere drones, useless and idle consumers of the produce of the ground', the Chinese 'must be admitted to be industrious'.[17] No one worked harder or with more sustained stamina than the sweating Chinese labourer, clearing jungle in Borneo or cutting sugar cane in Hawaii. And no one had fewer holidays than the Chinese shopkeeper: in the Straits Settlements Chinese stores were open every day of the year except Chinese New Year's Day.[18] The Chinese were not infrequently compared to ants, which they were said to resemble by the way they overcame difficulties by the force of numbers, and by their 'persevering and unconquerable industry'.[19] The furious vitality of the overseas Chinese was to impress itself vividly on the impressions of successive generations of observers. Enter one of the three or four Chinese quarters in Batavia, one of them said, and you would suddenly find yourself in what seemed 'another quarter of the globe', a place where the streets fairly hummed with traffic, and where people moved with 'an energy and briskness never seen among the Javanese'.[20] Twenty years before, Kipling had reported that neither at Penang, Singapore nor Hong Kong did he see a single Chinese asleep while daylight lasted, adding that

> If we had control over as many Chinese as we have natives
> of India, and had given them one tithe of the cosseting,
> the painful pushing forward, and studious, even nervous
> regard of their interests and aspirations that we have given
> India, we should long ago have been expelled from, or have
> reaped the reward of, the richest land on the face of the
> earth.[21]

But perhaps it was the lack of cosseting that spurred them, for in helping people too readily one could encourage their helplessness. The Chinese did not succumb to tropical torpor, for they were driven by that appetite for self-advancement, that dream of fortune which is itself an immemorial impulse of emigration. Grit and gumption, drive and perseverance – these are typical immigrant qualities, by no means confined to the Chinese. As well as being unusually successful in adapting themselves to new conditions, the Chinese possessed obvious advantages, such as the strength of their historical tradition; for although the majority of immigrants sprang from the lowest levels of Chinese society, being impoverished peasants, riff-raff, or worse, still the empire from which they originated antedated the Southeast Asian societies in civilization and commercial development and greatly exceeded them in wealth and sophistication. From the beginning, the Chinese 'were playing against the natives with loaded dice'.[22] Besides, there was no network like the network of Chinese connections, which joined market to market through clan or family, and assured the Chinese middleman that, wherever he happened to be, whether at home in China or abroad in Southeast Asia, there would always be plenty of cooperation on tap.

One loses count of the number of times the overseas Chinese's extreme thrift, their other hallmark, prompted comment, and it is true that they were great ones for deferred gratification, always concerned to put something by for tomorrow and for the advancement of their families. They were great savers. In this they differed from the natives of their host countries in Southeast Asia, who, if you held up a prosperous Chinese as an example of what you could do if you tried, would probably not get the point. And why should they? Unlike the Chinese they had not known those extremes of poverty and want, that knife-edge of survival which had impelled the tides of migration. Their values were different, they prized material success less obviously than the Chinese, and it was certainly no part of their ambition to become their own masters at any price. For the most part the Westerner found it easier to warm to the gentler natives than to the hard-headed Chinese, but to reckon one Chinese to be worth four Malays in application and initiative was a fairly characteristic British assessment.[23] And even to say 'that the Chinese make as good emigrants as the British', notes Isabella Bird, 'is barely to give them their due'.[24]

Set against the simpler practices of the natives, the commercial skills of the Chinese seemed positively innovative. If there were two ingredients to the success of the Chinese retailer, they were his satis-faction with a low profit margin and his readiness to provide credit. We have it from Bishop Salazar that these practices appeared early: '[The Sangleys] make good bread and sell it at low cost; and although this land possesses much rice, many now use bread who did not do so before. They are so accommodating that when one has no money to pay for the bread, they give him credit and mark it on a tally. It happens that many soldiers get food this way all through the year, and the bakers never fail to provide them with all the bread they need . . .'[25]

But even natural merchants are nothing without the right opportu-nities. Chinese immigrants were people who reached the right place at the right time. It is as hard to imagine Southeast Asia without Chinese commerce as it is to think of Chinese economic success without the background of Western capitalist development against which it was achieved. Energy, industry, thrift and acumen could only get the immigrants so far; to go further, they needed the opportunities of a capitalist arena, and this the Western imperialist provided. It was not exactly a case, as the old cliché has it, of the Europeans holding the cow while the Chinese milked her, but it is certainly true that as European capital stimulated the exploitation and export of primary products, and as the hinterlands were brought under European order, so there were more jobs for the Chinese commercial agent or middleman to do, more customers for the Chinese retailer to sell to, and more territory for the Chinese as a whole to range in.

We see this in the Philippines, where the profound changes of the nineteenth century – the opening of Manila to the trade of the world, the influx of European factory manufactures (the textiles of Manchester and Glasgow being particularly visible), the development of export crops like sugar, abaca (Manila hemp) and coffee – gave the Chinese middleman new frontiers across the archipelago. Under the new economic exigencies, the Spaniards reversed their policy of prohibiting Chinese immigration, and whereas the activities and mobil-ity of the Chinese had hitherto been hedged about with many irksome restrictions, now they were free to choose their occupation and place of residence. Now they were everywhere, as purchasing agents, whole-salers and distributors, tapping the trade of the provinces, selling local produce to European buyers for export to world markets (having in many cases processed them first), distributing foreign imports all over the islands, and generally opening up communications and binding the natives closer within the overall economy. The Chinese agent was capable of what the European was not, namely the legwork needed for penetrating the last nook and cranny of the interior.

How to organize his sprawling business was a challenge that the Chinese merchant met through the *cabecilla* system, a network in which a wholesaler at the centre – this would usually be Manila, where the foreign business houses were also located – had his rural agents stationed across the islands, to retail his goods through a general store, the so-called *tienda de sari-sari*, and to buy up crops for him to sell to the foreign exporters. It was the prudent practice of the cabecilla to use his relatives – especially young nephews or cousins who, as minors, were not legally liable for debts under Spanish law – as his agents, as it was the agent's practice to keep the name of his cabecilla a secret from his local creditors, so that debts could seldom be chased beyond the outstation. The Chinese sari-sari stores, open all the time, were hubs of trade in their respective areas, serving as places where raw produce might be delivered and collected, and where barter and purchases (by native producers having crops to pledge for credit or cash loans) might be continuously and profitably transacted.[26]

It would be some years before the Chinese themselves became bankers and financiers; and it was the Europeans, most notably the British – first among the foreign trading nations in the Philippines – who provided the credit and the capital for much of the Chinese business. Indeed, the relationship between the Chinese and the British merchants was close enough for one Spaniard to describe Manila's commercial scene as being marked by a 'special Anglo-Chinese seal', and for another to complain that, 'From the commercial point of view, the Philippines is an Anglo-Chinese colony with a Spanish flag.'[27] Under an arrangement which redounded profitably to both parties, the Chinese retail agent took a small amount of goods on credit, made a partial repayment of his debt once he had sold them, and then, on the strength of the repayment, asked for a still larger advance. That way, he built up a business with no capital at all. The pattern lay at the heart of Chinese business success in Southeast Asia, and it was to persist into recent times. The idea that it was better business to operate on a small profit margin using somebody else's money has been found to prevail, for example, in twentieth-century Sarawak, where the Chinese would, as the saying went, 'Buy [an article on credit] for ten [dollars], sell for seven, give back three, keep four' – a seemingly uneconomical practice, but one which allowed them to do business without money.[28]

Elsewhere, too, the economic dominance of the overseas Chinese was only too apparent. In Java Chinese immigrants were masters in trade and money-lending. When sugar and rubber became big money earners in the Dutch Indies, they expanded into the areas which fed off the plantation economy, collecting produce for export, retailing goods, and providing credit to peasants and smallholders, who often found themselves pledging their next crop. They got the better of the indigenous traders not only by their own commercial acumen, vigour and greed, but by the opportunities presented to them by the Dutch system of farming out various monopolies or rights – for levying road and river tolls, taxes and customs duties; for fishing; for the preparation and sale of salt; for buying up all the native produce, and so on – to the highest bidder. The Chinese were the ones who did the actual collecting, sending the Dutch the proceeds after subtracting a share for themselves. It also happened that large tracts of land, whole villages leased from native chiefs and princes, fell into their hands, and these they ran with all the power of feudal lords, using the labour rights thus acquired to grow sugar and other crops.[29]

They were often ruthless in their exploitation, always contriving, as Stamford Raffles has remarked, 'to reduce the peasants speedily to the condition of slaves';[30] and we may be sure that the contractors and money-lenders among them took as much as they could get – 'like bloodsuckers', noted an eighteenth-century Dutch observer.[31] What they took, their detractors were always to complain, they would not put back, for they were only temporary residents, out only to enrich themselves and their families back home. And when it came to exacting their due they were regular Shylocks, missing no opportunity to impose more stringent conditions on the native debtor at the first infringement of the letter of a contract. They certainly did not endear themselves to Stamford Raffles, who, when he governed Java during the British occupation of that country between 1811 and 1816, wrote of the Chinese that they were 'in all ages equally supple, venal, and crafty', concurring with an official Dutch report from Batavia that they were 'a dangerous people', indeed 'a pest to the country'.[32]

All the same, the great European trading firms could not have got at the mass of the native producers and consumers without their Chinese intermediaries. As the historian Victor Purcell put it: 'All that the natives sold to Europeans they sold through Chinese, and all that the natives bought from Europeans they bought through Chinese.'[33] The Chinese middleman was the filling in the colonial sandwich: 'One finds him everywhere; one needs him everywhere; one must therefore accept him, while limiting as far as possible the bad effects of his role.'34 A Captain Sherard Osborn, a British traveller in Malayan waters in the late 1830s, was one of the people who thought that, for all their Jew-like qualities, Chinese emigrants were indispensable throughout the colonies, and 'better conducted subjects Her Majesty Queen Victoria nowhere possesses'.35

Elsewhere in Southeast Asia much the same thing happened. In Thailand the one sure way of picking up the nuances of the local market was to work through a Chinese middleman, and the European traders who came in increasing numbers to cash in on the opportunities created by the free trade provisions of the Bowring Treaty knew what they were about when they engaged Chinese compradors. Like their counterparts in China, these canny commercial bridges between Western merchant houses and local Thai business became very grand indeed, amassing great fortunes from their sales commissions and rising to positions of power in the Chinese community.

The Chinese were pre-eminent in the rice business, the biggest prize of all in Thailand.36 Western steam mills, when they first appeared, did indeed pose a challenge, but the Chinese learnt fast, and once they had mechanized their own mills, importing installations and engineers from England, they became every bit as efficient as their competitors, giving rise to the British Consul's lament in 1879 that 'It is impossible under the conditions of trade prevailing in the East for the European to compete with the astute Chinaman in this particular business.'37 In that year there were as many Western steam mills as Chinese ones; by 1912, only three Western mills were still in business, the rest having closed or passed into Chinese hands.

By and large the one livelihood the Chinese were happy to leave to the natives was subsistence farming. In spite of Spanish encouragement, farming never ranked high among Chinese pursuits in the Philippines; and in Siam rice cultivation remained the preserve of the Thais, though the Chinese immigrants were keen enough market gardeners and plantation wage labourers. For a peasant people, the immigrants were reluctant ploughmen, and this was more than a matter of local laws against land alienation, or of the lack of capital for investment, or even of the absence of wives and children to help work the farms; this was a question of a peasant determining to lift himself up from poverty, by going for the kind of work that paid best. After all, it was to escape the hardships of the village, where life was too near the soil, that he had emigrated in the first place; and in leaving his country, he looked to leaving country life as well. A farmer remained a farmer, whereas a pedlar could dream of becoming a shopkeeper. His was a move to better things, like that of poor villagers converging upon the city in a twentieth-century developing country; and it was in ports and capitals that the Chinese, their eye to the main chance, found a focus for their entrepreneurial activities.

There they achieved a commercial pre-eminence far out of proportion to their numbers. And yet, of the millions who left their villages to seek their fortune abroad, only a fraction found it. It is true that the bulk of the internal trade of most countries in Nanyang was in Chinese hands, but it has to be remembered that a trader could be anything from a pedlar to a tycoon, and that pedlars were far more plentiful than tycoons. Most Chinese businesses were small-scale, family undertakings; the largest enterprises remained European. These immigrants were after all starting from scratch. There was scope for the hardy pioneer to try his luck, but there was not always the capital to do it, and only a very few individuals were ever able to muster enough money to enter into business on the European scale, to overtake the robuster European plantation owners or merchant houses as the dominant element in a country's economic life.

One could only save so much through frugality and careful husbandry. For the rest, one looked to one's kinsmen or sworn brothers. Membership of a clan or dialect association often paid off in contacts and sponsorships. There were also the rotating credit associations, a common way of raising at least some of the capital necessary to start a business. This was a traditional lending institution. The tradition has never lapsed, and today it continues to occupy a place in Chinese business life, providing an alternative to banks and modern means of finance. (The practice is not peculiar to the Chinese; it is also used, for example, by Jamaican immigrants, who call it 'partners', in England and New York.)[38]

The age did throw up some big-time Chinese capitalists, magnates of the prominence and calibre of John D. Rockefeller and J. P. Morgan. But all these got their real start under some form of government sponsorship, and made their first fortunes from monopoly farms, trading or mining concessions, or rights to perform certain services. I have already mentioned the Chinese tax-farm operator in Java. In Siam, before the Bowring Treaty abolished it, a system of royal trading monopolies governed the import and export of a range of goods into the country. The King farmed out many of these monopolies to Chinese merchants – one Chinese merchant held no fewer than ninety of them.39 The treaty might have hit the Chinese hard had new farms not been created to make up for the losses in government revenue. As it happened, they greatly benefited from the change. Among other things, the Bowring Treaty confirmed the opium monopoly, allowing the drug to be imported free of duty and the sole rights to its local distribution and sale to be sold to the opium farmer. This was an entirely Chinese concern, for the law forbade the Siamese to smoke opium; any Thai caught doing so was punished by being made to pay the Chinese poll tax and to wear a pigtail.

Values were coarser then, and the fact that he made money from a vice did not much disturb the conscience of the opium farmer. But there was a tradition of philanthropy among Chinese men of substance in Southeast Asia, and guilt on some less than conscious level might have been at the bottom of it, along with ostentatiousness and magnanimity. A readiness to give to charities was one of the hallmarks of the overseas Chinese, and schools, hospitals and temples received generous donations. The near did not necessarily receive priority over the far, for the Chinese gave to the needy abroad with as free a hand as they did to local causes. They sent money to those who suffered the great earthquake in San Francisco, for example, and they raised funds to relieve the lot of the coolies in the Transvaal. Huge sums went to succour the victims of natural calamities in China, and no appeal from Amoy or Swatow, or any of the other emigrant sending societies, was likely to go unanswered. In 1906, one famous multi-millionaire even offered to start a voluntary subscription among the world's Chinese to help pay off China's colossal national debt.40

Many gave to win social approval, or to vie with a rival. A public pledge of a sum by one millionaire was an invitation for another to name an even higher figure. If they did good, the overseas Chinese liked to be seen to be doing good. Hospitals bore the names of benefactors; temples carried plaques covered with the names of donors, complete with the sums given – all, as like as not, in inscriptions of gold. To read them was to know who the prominent businessmen were, who were always in the papers, who were looked up to as community leaders. But there was more to Chinese giving than public recognition; there was the knowledge that if they did not look after each other no one else would. It was part of the immigrant's instinct. It went with the remittances, the assumption of responsibility for the material support of the relatives back home. Charity began at home, but it did not end there, and all might be forgiven a rich businessman if, besides looking after his own, he shared enough of his prosperity with society.

Such, in general, were the characteristics of the Southeast Asian Chinese magnate. Three men, in particular, epitomized them. Thio Thiaw Siat, Loke Yew and Oei Tiong Ham were giants of their age, exemplars of a type of immigrant Chinese that crops up again and again in the diaspora's history.

In Penang, on a rocky slope surveying the bustle of Georgetown, there stand in tiers the buildings of Kek Lok Si, the Buddhist Monastery of Supreme Bliss. The temples, gaudily repainted, are thronged with sightseers and look at first sight to be nothing more than a tourist attraction; but the historical traveller will find it interesting to discover that the monastery, created in 1885, holds a gilded shrine in which is kept a memorial statue of Thio Thiaw Siat.

Thio was a benefactor of the monastery. He was the star of overseas Chinese business stars, one of the few to achieve success on the Western capitalist scale. He was a Hakka from Kwangtung province, and was only seventeen when he left in 1858 to make his fortune in Batavia. We know very little about his family, and today it is difficult to winnow the truth from the legend, but his father is said to have been an educated man, one who, having passed an imperial examination, earned his living as a village teacher.[41] Of the favourite stories later told about Thio Thiaw Siat, one says that he showed so little promise as a child, not learning to speak until he was about seven or eight, that his brother-in-law made a bet that if Thio were ever to achieve fame and fortune, he would hang the lanterns in front of his house upside-down. He lost his bet, of course, and had to invert his lanterns much abashed when Thio came home a grandee.

In Batavia he earned his keep as a water carrier for a dealer in sundries. A river ran under the shop, and it was there that he bathed every day, frequently sitting on a protruding stone to scrub himself, as it had been drummed into him that to avoid the local fevers all new immigrants must wash themselves three times a day. In this way, goes another favourite story about Thio, he caught the eye of the shop owner's daughter. Thio was a sinkeh, a greenhorn, and this was a point against him; but she let it be known to her family that it was he, rather than the better-established suitors for her hand, that she wanted to marry. To make him worthy of his daughter, Thio's prospective father-in-law lent him money to start his own shop. Did he perhaps believe that the young man, nineteen at the time, would go far? He was not alone in his foresight. The stone on which Thio sat to wash himself, it later turned out, was no stone but the hump of an old crocodile, one that was seer enough, so legend says, to spare the life of a man destined for greatness.

There is ambition, luck and effort in the story of every self-made man. It was Thio's good luck to marry the boss's daughter, and he was also fortunate in having arrived in the Dutch Indies at a time when the range of opportunities offered a young man of astuteness and energy was widening. But it was his own efforts which put him so far ahead of his fellows. He did not stop at trading in foodstuffs; he became a provisioner for the Dutch Army and Navy, and, we may assume, cultivated the colonial authorities. These were plantation years. The Dutch Indies was bursting with projects. Coolie labour? Thio could supply it. Managerial supervision? Thio could see to that too. Some very lucrative contracts came his way, and he also succeeded in bidding for the opium, tobacco and spirits monopolies. He started his own coconut and rice plantations, with Dutch capital backing him; and when Sumatra was added to the Dutch domain, the development of the whole of the northern half of that island came under his sway too. He naturally had a greater share of the revenue farms there than anyone; and it was one of his companies that planted Deli (modern Medan) with rubber, tea and coconut palms.[42]

Sumatra and the Malayan peninsula are separated from each other by the narrowest of water passages, the Straits of Malacca. Once the wave of Thio's business interests had broken on Sumatran shores, it was inevitable that it should splash on to Penang and Singapore. Imperial borders meant little to him, and it was expressive of the cosmopolitanism of his business empire that he was for many years a major shareholder in the Penang and Singapore opium syndicates. One enterprise simply led to another. Backwards and forwards along the coastal routes went his steamers, flying the Dutch flag and enjoying, with Dutch blessing, a virtual monopoly of the shipping between Penang and Deli. When Thio himself sailed into a harbour, he knew for certain that he would be respectfully saluted.

The best known of the stories about him concerns a voyage. Three of his employees were to travel with him from Singapore to China, one of them his own doctor, a German. He sent a man to buy four first-class tickets on a German steamship, but was told that only his

1. A typical example of the circular, fortress-like communal dwelling of the Hakka people in Fukien province

2. Nineteenth-century Chinese on board the steamship *Alaska*, headed for the gold fields of California

3. A Chinese fire brigade, Deadwood, South Dakota, 1888

4. Chinese working on the railroads,
Monterey Peninsula, California, in 1889

5. A Chinese village in a coconut plantation in 1890s Singapore

6. Children in San Francisco's Chinatown, turn of the century.
Photo by Arnold Genthe, who entitled it 'An Afternoon Siesta'

7. Ross Alley, San Francisco's Chinatown, 1890s.
Photo by Arnold Genthe, whose title for it was 'The Street of the Gamblers (by day)'

8. Chinese men posing
amid European props
in a studio in
Singapore, *c.* 1900.

9. Studio portrait of a
Nonya dressed in
Malay style in
Singapore, *c.* 1900

10. José Rizal in Madrid, 1890, aged twenty-nine

11. Thio Thiaw Siat, overseas Chinese magnate (1840–1916)

12. Mary Bong,
Chinese frontierswoman
in Alaska (1880–1958)

13. A Chinese nanny
with her blonde
European charge
in Singapore,
early 1900s

14. Singapore waterfront, *c.* 1900. Note the row of rickshaws awaiting custom along the embankment

European doctor was eligible to travel first class – second class was thought quite good enough for Chinese. Thio was not a man to take this lying down, or to ignore the slights of colonial society. What he did next was characteristic. He placed an advertisement in the European press announcing plans to start a steamship service catering only to Chinese; what was more, it would carry passengers and cargo at half the German tariff. The managers of the German company dismissed this sneeringly as a hare-brained scheme, until they discovered who was behind it and how large a business concern he commanded. Deciding that a rival line presided over by the likes of Thio was competition they could ill afford, the managers quickly apologized and invited the Chinese magnate to travel first class. But only the complete removal of the colour bar would satisfy Thio, and it was not until the salons and smoking rooms of the Imperial German merchant fleet were open to all Chinese that he withdrew his challenge.[43] The tale is told with relish in almost every Chinese account of Thio's life, for what subject people could resist the thought of one of their own kind standing up successfully to the haughty Europeans?

That he was very conscious of being Chinese was perhaps the second most significant thing about him, the first being his gift for making money. Nanyang was a frontier society that rewarded hard work to a degree undreamt of by the Hakka or Cantonese poor in China, but what was wealth without recognition? In China superior people did not acquire wealth as an end in itself. Long before Europe printed its first book, the Chinese bureaucracy had recruited its officials through competitive literary examinations. Academic degrees had enormous cachet in China; they were like magic, the one unequivocal gauge of social worth. If one was a degree holder one became an office holder, a member of an acknowledged élite. So desirable was this status that *arriviste* merchants were prepared to pay huge sums to buy it, with the inevitable result that a roaring trade in degrees and brevet ranks developed. Here was a way in which wealth could be converted to prestige. It was one which many rich overseas Chinese employed to raise their social standing; photographs of the time show them looking solemn in their mandarin robes, adorned with the symbols of imperial honours they had won by their donations to their homeland. Thio was Chinese enough to desire such signs of status. He was awarded many, the Manchu court showering him with higher and higher honours until, in early 1905, he was allowed to wear the button of the first rank and became a supreme mandarin. It was like being elevated to the peerage in England.

The court had at first not much concerned itself with the overseas Chinese, shrugging off all responsibility for those who managed to leave Chinese shores in defiance of the imperial ban on emigration, and treating the returnees disgracefully. But times had changed. The ban, it was realized in some quarters of the government, hurt China's interests. As the Chinese minister to England put it in a memorial to the Manchu throne, 'To drive fish into others' nets, or birds into others' snares (says Mencius), is not clever policy, but it is what we have been doing for England, Holland, and other countries. These get Chinese labour and great towns spring into being on desert islands. Foreign countries thus turn us into instruments for their aggrandizement. We, the while, drive away Chinese skill and the profits of it into their arms.'44 China had been prised open by European might, and for a time it had seemed to Chinese officials that only foreigners possessed the capital and expertise to usher their country into the modern age. But it now occurred to some of the more progressive mandarins that the help of the overseas Chinese might be enlisted. China at that stage of its industrial expansion needed merchant entrepreneurs, and the merchant entrepreneur was the type *par excellence* of the Nanyang Chinese emigrant. Besides, the Chinese in the tropical European colonies were better acquainted with Western ways than their compatriots at home, and they appeared a soft touch.

On 13 September 1893 an imperial edict proclaimed that all Chinese emigrants in foreign countries would be allowed to return home at will. The right of Chinese subjects to travel freely outside China was at last recognized. People like Thio were encouraged to contribute to the material progress of their homeland and to make China part of the sweep of their commercial empires. British Hong Kong, the foreign concessions in the treaty ports, their own native ports of Canton, Swatow and Amoy – these became home bases for the enterprises of the overseas Chinese. And as the imperial government took an increasingly sympathetic interest in its distant subjects, consulates were opened both for the better protection of the Chinese abroad and for the furtherance of China's interests. In 1893 Thio was made the first Chinese Vice-Consul of Penang, and in 1896, with Queen Victoria's approval, the Chinese Consul General in Singapore.45 Through Thio, the Manchu government could get at the Chinese in Java and Sumatra; he himself wielded enormous influence there, and the Kapitein of Medan, another man of wealth and substance, just happened to be a cousin of his. Singapore itself became a convenient centre for China's purposes in Nanyang, a place from which it made its bid for the expatriate's cultural loyalties. It was sufficiently successful in this for the British to feel uneasy. Many prominent Chinese in Singapore professed themselves to be loyal subjects of Queen Victoria, but, when a statue of Her Majesty, financed by subscriptions from the Chinese, was unveiled at Government House in early 1899, more than a dozen Chinese worthies attended the ceremony wearing their mandarin gowns and badges of imperial Chinese office.[46]

Thio operated on a grand scale in China, involving himself in railway construction, mining, agriculture and manufacturing. He did much to kindle overseas Chinese interest and investment in China, and to bring capital and venture together. In those days railroad building particularly fired overseas Chinese enthusiasm, but the undertaking for which he is best remembered is the Chang Yu Pioneer Wine Company.[47] The scheme had its origins in a conversation he had at the French consulate in Java, in which it was observed that Chefoo, in northern China's Shantung province, was ideally suited to grape-vine growing. In 1860, during the second Opium War, French and British troops had jointly marched on the area, and the French Consul, a veteran of the expedition, recalled that the soldiers had tried to make wine there. Had the French stayed, the Consul remarked, they might well have started a winery. Much taken with the idea, Thio was to put it to the test some twenty years later. Assured that a glassworks in Shanghai could make the winebottles, he set about finding himself a cellar master. When he took up his consular appointment in Singapore, a German doctor he met there was able to put him on to a licensed Dutch wine maker. The experiment began, and the Dutch master came back from Chefoo with a sample product the very same year. British and Dutch chemists called in to test it pronounced the wine immature, but Thio went ahead and bought two thousand grape vines from America as well as large tracts of land in Chefoo.

Thio himself laid out all the initial capital, importing the necessary machinery and building the winery before selling shares in the company in 1898, three years after it was launched. By then it had weathered its first setback, the discovery that the Dutch cellar master was not really as qualified as was at first believed. Luckily, by approaching the Consul of the Austro-Hungarian Empire, Thio was able to secure the services of the Vice-Consul, Baron von Babo, a wine expert. Almost the first thing the baron did upon assuming the reins was to deplore the choice of American grapes and to import 140,000 foreign vine shoots. Only about a third survived the long journey to China, but this was supplemented the following winter by half a million more imported seedlings from just about every wine-producing country in the West. Before long, the hillsides behind Chefoo were covered in grape. Under von Babo, who remained in charge until after the First World War, the company flourished. The winery is still there, a nationalized enterprise complete with Party secretaries, producing brandy, vermouths, red wines and even Chinese herbal liqueurs. On a visit to Chefoo, now called Yen-t'ai, in 1982, I was shown around its cavernous underground cellar and its enormous, hundred-year-old wine casks. The founder continues to be honoured as a patriotic overseas Chinese, and though the name of the firm has been changed to the Yen-t'ai Wine Company, many locals still know it as Chang Yu.

The fall of the Manchu dynasty in 1911 and the advent of the Republic did not much affect Thio's relationship with his mother country, whose industrial and commercial aspirations he continued to support with a mixture of patriotic concern and opportunism. In 1915, when he was seventy-five, he did a prodigious job of promoting China in America. Much publicity attended the fifty-day tour, with the *New York Times* calling him 'China's Rockefeller' one minute, and 'the J. P. Morgan of China' the next. With his sprawling interests – in rubber, coconut, American cotton, tea and coffee plantations, a bank, a glass-making plant, coconut oil factories, a textile mill, salt, cattle, mining, shipping and general commerce – he was just the sort of prodigy Americans would take to their hearts. Was he worth US $100 million, or $200 million? the papers enquired. Did he, upon arrival in San Francisco, really cash a letter of credit for $200,000 to use as spending money? He looked interesting, wearing a long mandarin's gown, huge spectacles, a derby hat and American shoes; and he had an interesting proposition to make to Wall Street.

American investment in China was what he was after, and the idea of establishing a bank, to be jointly financed by American and Chinese industrialists, and linked in some way to the creation of a new transpacific steamship line, was what he had in mind to sell to the Americans. 'We have much wealth,' he was quoted as saying, 'but we have little money.' He himself was to put up the money for the bulk of the Chinese stake, but financiers in the United States were less forthcoming – 'the years of American dominance in Asia had not yet come', commented a historian[48] – and the bank never materialized.

One day in New York Thio begged off a banquet at which he was to meet John D. Rockefeller, Jr., and got his English-speaking son to attend in his stead; he felt tired and wanted to stay in his hotel room to rest. Less than three months later, he died at his home in Batavia. There was not a spectator in the crowd which turned out to watch the funeral procession – and almost the entire Chinese community in Batavia did – who did not gain a vivid impression of Thio's importance. Over a thousand mourners took part in the obsequies. Dutch and British flags were lowered to half-mast. And when the procession ended the coffin was taken down to the pier and put on board a ship sailing for Penang and Singapore. From there the coffin was carried to Hong Kong for trans-shipment to China; for of course Thio was to be buried, as every overseas Chinese would wish to be, in his own native village.

He left behind him homes in Java, Sumatra, Penang, Singapore, and north and south China. Thio was one of those overseas Chinese who might be in Peking one week, Medan, Batavia and Hong Kong the next; crossing from city to city as though political boundaries did not exist. They were a cosmopolitan lot in those days, 'jet-setters in a pre-airplane age'.49 One of Thio's contemporaries was a British citizen at the same time as he was a Chinese mandarin; another might be a British subject, a Dutch kapitein, and a holder of a Manchu title simultaneously. Sooner or later they discovered the advantages of conducting business under the Union Jack. The British interfered less with their colonial subjects' affairs than did the Dutch, and Chinese businessmen set themselves up in Penang and Singapore rather as tycoons establish offshore bases today. The multinational spread of the interests of these Chinese meant that even their munificence crossed imperial boundaries. Thio is credited, along with a number of his contemporaries, with having founded the region's first modern Chinese school, the Chung Hua School in Penang, in whose main hall his statue still stands. And it was Thio, the very first person to be awarded an honorary Doctor of Laws degree by Hong Kong University, who, by an annual gift of working funds, kept the institution's floundering Faculty of Arts going in the difficult early years.

It is hard to say where he was domiciled, he was so incessantly on the move. But the lovely island of Penang seems to have had a special claim on his affections; certainly it was there that he built himself his most splendid residence, a mansion large enough, it was thought, to house nine generations of future descendants. It was a house in the Chinese style, built on two floors and roofed with glazed tiles imported from China. Inside the encircling brick wall, porcelain pots of dahlias, chrysanthemums, roses and camellias ringed a large pond.⁵⁰ Grimacing stone lions guarded the massive front doors. Inside, two staircases, one on each side of the central courtyard, led up to the rooms on the upper floor and the inside verandahs. The verandahs were screened with ornamental iron grille-work, the sort one found in Chinese-Portuguese houses of the same period in Macao, and pillared with cast-iron columns ornamented with flutes and Corinthian scrolls and topped by carved wooden birds and flowers. For all its foreign influences, though, the house was a cultural statement in its Chineseness. Indeed, it is said to be an exact replica of a family mansion in China, and squads of master craftsmen were brought to Penang from China to build it.

It still stands, looking as though nobody has been interested in it for generations, on Leith Street, crying out for a conservationist to save it from further dilapidation. I ventured inside it during a visit in late 1987, and managed to get as far as the corridors linking the central apartments to the side wings before a man stepped out of the shadows to tell me off for trespassing. Beyond, in the rear of one wing, I caught a glimpse of a beautiful cast-iron spiral staircase picked out by a sun shaft from above. The empire that Thio built withered with the death of its founder, and the house seems to have been allowed to go to seed, divided up among too many down-at-heel families. The ancestral hall, facing the central courtyard, feels dingy and derelict, but the blackwood altar, once overlooked by big Chinese lanterns with glass panels framed in gold, is still there, the wall behind it hung with the faded portraits of Thio and three of his consorts. The oldest-looking of the three one guesses to be his principal wife. She is richly dressed in Indonesian or Malay style, while the second is attired in Manchu fashion. The third is strikingly beautiful, and may have been the most cherished of his seven concubines.⁵¹ Something extraordinary was that, as I took a closer look at the altar, I distinctly made out a finger of incense smoke: joss sticks were burning, proof that someone, somewhere, still cares to preserve Thio's memory.

An overseas Chinese magnate of a similar sort was Loke Yew, another of those people who arrived in Nanyang with nothing but the proverbial bundle of clothes and pillow, and then turned themselves into millionaires in the way of the best rags-to-riches legends. The only son in a family of five, Loke was a Cantonese of humble birth who landed on the Singapore docks in 1858 as a poor boy of eleven. He went to work in a shop on Market Street and, in four years, succeeded in saving $99. With the capital he opened a shop of his own. But he was meant for bigger things; five years later, he left his shop in the hands of a manager and set out for the Malay states on the west coast.[52]

Tin had been discovered on the west coast of Malaya, and though conditions in the fever-ridden mining camps were gruesome, and the coolies who worked there had only an even chance of surviving the first year, Chinese immigrants, fired by dreams of striking it rich, were coming to the peninsula in droves. Larut, Loke Yew's destination in northwestern Perak, was the focus of just such a rush. The Chinese were doing prodigies of work in the mines, introducing new techniques and increasing production, but their influx was bound to be disruptive to the native Malay population. There was suddenly far more wealth around than there ever used to be, and the Malay chiefs who drew tribute and royalties from the Chinese soon came to blows over the richest fields. All this was complicated by enmities within the Chinese community, with the Hakkas ranged against the Cantonese, and the Hai San secret society against the Ghee Hin fraternity. Between 1862 and 1873 quarrels between the factions flared repeatedly into open warfare.[53] The British in the Straits Settlements had not wanted to intervene, or to be lured into new colonial annexations, but when the Chinese animosities were further confused by succession disputes among the Malay chiefs, and the climate of lawlessness threatened to slide into anarchy, Her Majesty's Government deemed it wise to step in.

In January 1874, three groups of men met on an island off the Perak coast, one consisting of a section of the Malay ruling class, another of the leaders of Hai San and Ghee Hin, and the third comprising British officials. The meeting heralded the creation of British Malaya, for it was agreed then and there that Perak would receive that familiar British imperial figure, a Resident 'whose advice must be asked and acted upon on all questions other than those touching Malay Religion and Custom'. The best advice, historians were later to note, might well have been 'Get rid of the Chinese'. But getting rid of the Chinese, they went on to observe, 'was the last thing the British had in mind'.[54] On the contrary, the key to the agreement reached between the two main groups, the Malays and the British, 'is supplied by the silent presence of the third, the Chinese miners and merchants'. Between them, the British and Chinese would transform Malaya, shifting the ethnic and social balance of the peninsula. The fateful significance which the Chinese had for Malaya cannot be over-emphasized, for as well as prompting the extension of British imperial authority there, they brought a working society into being and helped change the place economically and socially.

Loke Yew arrived in Larut a little before the Pax Britannica. The Hai San and the Ghee Hin were at each other's throats, and Loke Yew found himself a profitable niche supplying food to the troops; like many another keen seizer of opportunities, Loke knew war to be a good time for making money. Those were confused but heady times, when men risked enormous stakes and won spectacular fortunes. Loke Yew's first undertakings in tin were profitable enough, but his fifteen years in Larut were not without their sudden catastrophe, when the secret societies took to arms once again and mayhem disrupted mining. A brutal attack by the Hai San on their unsuspecting Ghee Hin rivals in 1872, followed by a retaliatory blockade of the Larut coast by the Ghee Hin, brought tin exports to a halt and left Loke Yew ruined. Once more, he took to supplying food to the fighters, steering his riverboat up hazardous jungle waters.

This was when the British came into the picture. With peace, and the opening up of lower Perak and the growth of its southern neighbour Selangor, the west coast of Malaya began to approach the prime of its fortunes. In the tin fields the heads of secret societies, like union bosses in the West, continued to command the loyalties of all mine workers, and this gave them control of mining for a quarter of a century after the British established political authority over the Malay states. Western interests found it impossible to break in, and for many years a European could only do business in the Malay states by financing a Chinese partner. Indeed, it was said that any Chinese who invested in an English umbrella and a good jacket could get credit from an Englishman.[55] But the high noon of empire was approaching, and by the last decade of the century their capital and mastery of technology would have placed the Europeans ahead of their Asian competitors. Chinese family enterprises, however large or dynamic, were no match for Western public joint stock companies.

Britons, Malays and Chinese all benefited from the rise in general prosperity, but only men of the heroic dimensions of Loke Yew became millionaires. He acquired acres of rubber plantations; he had a stake in the opium revenue farm of Selangor;[56] everything he touched, it was said, turned to gold. He could see how the wind was blowing, and how he could link his destiny with that of imperial Britain. He invested in more than an English umbrella: he acquired English manners and became a great favourite of the British. They called him *towkay*, Hokkien for 'head of family or business', a term used in colloquial speech in Malaya to denote a man of property or wealth; one British observer described him as 'a Chinese captain of industry' and compared him favourably with the famous Andrew Carnegie.57 He was further inducted to Englishness when he took his family on a tour of Europe in 1902 and stopped by London for the coronation of the new King.

He knew what it took to breach the barricades of British racial bigotry. When a new railway through the Malay states opened, many Europeans had been averse to admitting Chinese to the first-class carriages. Loke Yew's response to this was to get a free manual printed, providing exact guidance on 'Etiquette to be Observed by All Chinese First Class Passengers'. The instructions are telling, and include the following:

> You are requested to be polite and courteous to ladies and relinquish your seats to ladies if the carriage is crowded. Never allow a lady to stand.
> Staring at people (especially at ladies), expectorating, talking in a loud tone of voice, laughing loudly – all are considered ungentlemanly and bad manners.
> Your hat should be removed when you enter a carriage in which there are ladies.
> Your feet should not be placed on the cushions with or without shoes.
> Your jacket, shoes and socks should not be removed nor should you expose your limbs.
> You should not smoke in carriages if ladies are present.
> Only small packages must be put into first class carriages and anything that has an offensive smell should never be brought into a carriage.58

Loke Yew's ability to adjust himself to British ways was reflected in some of his business ventures; for example he had an Englishman for a partner in one endeavour, a private motor mail service, and he became a large shareholder in an old, thoroughly Scottish engineering and shipbuilding company, Messrs Alexander, Hall and Company of Aberdeen.

Loke Yew was not a gentleman by birth, but his wealth and philanthropy placed him in the very first rank of society. He was nothing if not generous. Hospitals, schools, the famous Raffles College,

Hong Kong University – all these came within the immensely wide sweep of his munificence. For his support of higher education he was awarded an honorary degree by Hong Kong University, and he is remembered to this day in a hall named after him in that institution.

Another donor to Raffles College was Oei Tiong Ham, the Sugar King of Java; he, too, gave money to education, and today a building of the University of Singapore still bears his name. Born the eldest son of a Chinese immigrant from Fukien, Oei was a second-generation Chinese who spoke Chinese less well than Malay and Javanese. His father had fled to Java from Amoy, where he had joined the Taiping rebels in an unsuccessful fight against the Chinese imperial forces. Starting as a pedlar in Semarang, a port town in central Java, the elder Oei had made his money importing dried fish, tea and silk from China, and exporting sugar and tobacco from Java. The young Oei inherited the family firm, the famous Handel Maatschappij Kian Gwan (Establishing the Source – of riches, it is understood), when the founder died, so he was not exactly a self-made man, but while Loke Yew began with nothing and came to be one of the richest men in Malaya, Oei began with something and expanded it to considerable multiplications of that. When he died of a heart attack in 1924, aged fifty-nine, he was said to be worth two hundred million Dutch guilders.[59]

Though he did not earn his success the hard way, Kian Gwan would not have been the household name it is if the younger Oei did not revolutionize it in a series of bold and far-sighted diversifications. There was no Chinese sugar producer in Java to compare to him, and there was scarcely anything the island produced that he did not trade in, from kapok and rubber right through to tapioca and tea. He invested heavily and successfully in steamship navigation, and in 1906 established his own bank in Semarang. He controlled the opium monopoly, of course; and, in keeping with the familiar pattern, was Majoor of the Semarang Chinese. He was of far more than local significance, however, for though he spoke no English, his far-flung business empire included branch offices in Mincing Lane, London, and Wall Street, New York.[60] In all his undertakings he was never daunted by the matter of scale.

He did not invest in China, nor did he feel its sentimental pull.[61] Like Loke Yew, Oei felt the fascination of the modern world; almost the first thing he did when his father died was to take his wife and two daughters on a trip to Europe – where, as it happened, his carriage won second prize at a May flower festival.[62] Motor cars, when they first appeared, greatly appealed to him, and he sent over to England for a Lancia; with its dark, heavy upholstery, the limousine could not have been less suited to Java's tropical climate, but nothing daunted, he imported an English chauffeur to drive it.[63] If one sweated in it – and one did, profusely – that was the price one paid for stylishness. He dressed himself in European style (always in colonial whites, down to his handmade shoes), and in so doing he defied the Dutch ruling that all Chinese in Java wear Chinese clothes.[64] He was the first Chinese in Java to cut off his queue, and by employing the finest lawyer in the colony, a Dutch baron, to argue his case he got the authorities to grant him freedom of residence and to agree to his moving out of the Chinese ghetto into the European section of town.[65] In their new home the Oeis lived a life of 'fairy-tale opulence',[66] entertaining visiting celebrities such as the King of Siam[67] and the Crown Princes of Denmark and Greece.[68] Like many another overseas Chinese, though, Oei was to find British Singapore more to his liking than the Dutch Indies; and he moved there permanently when his estranged wife left him to live in London. Oei, who loved women with a sensual casualness, had eighteen acknowledged concubines and a total of forty-two children by them. One of his sons took over the reins of the business empire when he died, but he was not the man his father was, the going was harder now, and the company eventually passed to other hands. During the Second World War it was taken over by the Japanese when they overran the Indies, and it was later confiscated by Sukarno, the President of the new Indonesian republic.

It was a kind of gold-rush era that Oei, Loke and Thio lived in, one where a fortune awaited the bold and enterprising. Asked the secret of his success, Thio once said, 'I exploit to the full what the land has to offer; I follow the changing times. What others cast off I keep; what others want I supply.' He bought cheap, he went on, and sold dear; and he knew how to prevail against the unexpected. Then, in the terse style of classical Chinese, he expressed in seven short words the cornerstone of his dramatic achievement: 'Industry and frugality; picking the right men'.[69]

To Oei on the other hand the right men were lucky men, for he was certain, born gambler that he was, that luck was part of his success. Oei had strong speculative instincts, and an unerring sense of timing, but it is also true that fortune favoured him. He was lucky, for example, in his first backer, a retired German ex-consul living on one of his father's estates. The German wanted to buy the house he was renting, but the elder Oei wouldn't consider it. One day, when the younger Oei came on one of his rent-collecting rounds, the German made him a proposal: suppose he were to advance Oei a sum of money to invest as he pleased; if Oei increased it ten times or more, would he promise to turn the house over to him the moment he inherited it? Oei accepted promptly, and with ample money in hand he acquired land to start sugar plantations. Sugar held out good prospects – prospects which he realized with spectacular success through the introduction of modern machinery and management methods. When the German got his house, Oei was well on his way to becoming the single richest individual in the Indies.

He saw his chances and he took them. His daughter (of whom more in another chapter) remembers him telling her, as he showed her round his palm-tree plantation in Singapore, 'Other people see trees when they look at this plantation. I see money. Palm trees cost nothing, they simply grow; but they bring in money.'[70] It was not the money as such, but the risky manipulation of it, that he found exciting. But what kept him at the top was a readiness to use European advisers and managers and to experiment with new ideas and technology. Europeans were scarcely his superiors when it came to commercial adroitness, but their cooperation was nevertheless essential to his success. He bribed them unashamedly; whenever a government functionary came to call, his daughter recalls, 'Papa invariably sent him away with a batik sarong for his fat Dutch *mevrouw* – housewife'; and hardly a day went by without him sending his bearers around the city with gifts.[71]

As we shall see, the fact that many of the wealthiest Chinese derived their wealth from connections with the colonial powers would provide fuel for resentments which would find expression a generation or two later in hostility and discrimination on the part of the indigenes. Also, what helped their rise to riches, the interweaving of Western and Chinese interests apart, was a conspicuous commercial aggressiveness which, as it appeared to their victims and competitors at any rate, seemed to suggest that they were prepared to subjugate all to the main chance, and that the golden calf was a central part of their creed. In 1914 there was published a document, allegedly from the pen of the King of Siam, Rama VI, which said that in so far as money matters were concerned the Chinese knew neither morals nor mercy; Mammon was their only god, and for money they endured any privation and performed the vilest deeds. The document, as we have seen, was entitled *The Jews of the East*.[72]

CHAPTER EIGHT

Hybrids

In 1841 or thereabouts, a twenty-four-year-old native of T'ung-an County in Fukien province left the shores of southern China for the Philippines. With him was his six-year-old son Co Giok Kuan, presently to be baptized by the Spaniards and named José I. The father, known to the Spaniards as Martin Co, was a child himself when he first set foot on Luzon. He had grown to manhood there, and it was probably with some savings that he had, as was customary, returned to his native village to marry and to have children. He had then re-migrated, as was also customary, taking with him his second son.

Settled in Manila, José I became a carpenter. But there must have been an entrepreneurial streak in him, for when we next hear of him he had become a contractor in the trade. In the 1870s he married a Spanish mestiza (the offspring of a Spanish and native union) and had three children by her, Ysidra, Melencio and Trinidad. He then went on to acquire some land in the province of Tarlac, and it was there that the family made its home and its fortune. José I dealt in sugar and rice – it was a very good time to be doing that – and he was a money lender to boot. His estates expanded, as, lacking the cash to repay him, some of his debtors offered land in lieu. Locals remembered him as a tall, fair-skinned man of substance, often to be seen riding a horse accompanied by his assistant, and who could doubt the ampleness of his means when, towards the end of his life, they saw him travelling to Manila by car, no less, when everybody else took the train?

When it was time for Melencio to marry, he chose for his wife a Chinese mestiza called Tecla Chichioco. Tecla added her share to the family coffers by doing an archetypically Filipino-Chinese thing, running a sari-sari store. Melencio's two sisters never married; Trinidad was no more than thirty-five when she died, but Ysidra lived to be ninety-three. Ysidra was a businesswoman through and through, charged with life and commercial drive, and she became one of the richest women in her time by dealing in rice, sugar, and *gango* (small dried shrimps), and by money-lending. Later she was to found a private bank, the Philippine Bank of Commerce: not for nothing was she the daughter of a Chinese.[1]

At some point the family had Hispanicized its name to Cojuangco. The 'juang' could have been a rough Spanish rendering of the last syllable of José I's Chinese name, Co Giok Kuan. The second 'co' was a Hukkien contribution, a polite suffix (*ko*, 'elder brother') which, when it appears as an ending in a Filipino surname today – and it does so in a great number of names – nearly always signifies a Chinese derivation. Chinese mestizos commonly Europeanized their fathers' names by slurring the components into one another, so that, when the Chinese name might have been Uy Tin Leng, say, the mestizo surname would be Uytinleng – or, if Uy Tin Leng was popularly known as Uy Leng Ko (Elder Brother Leng), his mestizo offspring would call themselves Uylengco. Sometimes the Chinese components would be dropped altogether, and the descendants of Carlo Gonzales Uylengco would simply assume the surname Gonzales.[2]

Melencio Cojuangco, who died tragically of a heart attack in 1909 when he was only thirty-eight, had four sons: José, Juan, Antonio and Eduardo. His eldest son José, who came also to be known as Don Pepe, took up law and married into a consequential political family. Left a great deal of money by his aunt Ysidra, he was also to enter politics. He fathered six children: Pedro, Josephine, Teresita, Corazón, José Jr (Peping) and Pacita. The name of his fourth child came to be known far outside Luzon, for she married Senator Benigno Aquino, who it was widely thought would one day become the country's president. As the whole world knows he was assassinated in 1983, and his widow, the great-granddaughter of Co Giok Kuan and Cory to the nation, became the President of the Philippines. Among those who came to Manila to congratulate her and to make a sizeable donation to her new government were delegates from the World Kho (Co) Clan Association, whose members ramify over Southeast Asia and North America and which claims her as a kinswoman. Mrs Aquino is an eager cook, and it is perhaps a measure of the Chinese element in the Philippines that her speciality, the dish she used to prepare for Benigno Aquino for his birthday, is Peking duck.[3].

While in Fukien in 1987, I went one morning to her ancestral village. Hung-chien-ts'un, a village of 2,400 people, is an hour and a half's drive from Amoy. There was scarcely any traffic on the narrow road, but peasants could be seen working bareheaded at a distance. It proved easy to find the village, because you had only to say, 'the President of the Philippines' and passers-by would wave you in the right direction. It was nearly noon when I arrived at the village square, and only old men were about, the young were all at work in the fields. A traditional Chinese house of a colourful Disneyland picturesqueness caught my eye as I got out of the car; but it was not, as I had thought, the Cojuangco home; it was the house of another native son made good, a Co Bun Tiong, the owner of a trading company on Manila's Ylaya Street.

'The Co family,' I enquired as the old men crowded around.

'We're all Cos here,' one of them said.

'Well, Corazón Aquino's kinsmen . . .'

'That's me,' the speaker smiled, showing four gold teeth. So immense and so extraordinary did the gulf between him and Cory Aquino appear that it was a shock to hear it simply stated that he was her *t'ang-shu*, 'paternal uncle'.

His name was Co Guan Hing, and his grandfather was José I's younger brother, left behind in the village by Martin Co when he went back to the Philippines. He was sixty-seven, a tall, deliberate man with sombre eyes and a large forehead. Silent and shy, he led me along a stone path to where he and his wife lived. It was a rustic house, with walls of a concrete grey. On the wall facing the door, over a square table holding a thermos flask and a tray of those tiny teacups one knows to be traditional in the area, were two strips of red paper inscribed with a couplet. On the two side walls were framed collages of family photographs, in each of which was included a xerox copy of a *Time* magazine cover portrait of Cory Aquino.

As his wife dispensed sweets, the kind reserved for weddings and New Year festivities, Mr Co brought out a book of writings on T'ung-an's local history and showed me the chapter on the Cojuangco family.4 He then told me an extraordinary story. This was by way of proving that he really was a relative, for when Cory Aquino's eldest brother and closest political adviser, José Peping Cojuangco, came to visit in the course of his official tour of China, Co Guan Hing's half-brothers had tried to pass themselves off as the Cojuangcos' Chinese kin. Mr Co's father had died when he was only four months old, and his mother had remarried into another Co family. She had two sons (the half-brothers Mr Co mentioned) by this marriage, and though they are not related by blood to the Cojuangcos, they had wanted to claim kinship with the Philippines' presidential family. In this they were abetted by the branch Party secretary of the village and the officials of the county, who were friends of the half-brothers and who, on the day Peping Cojuangco was due to arrive, took it upon themselves to 'kidnap' Mr Co and place him under house arrest for the duration of the visit. The corners of his mouth drooped in dolefulness as he told me this extraordinary story.

Later, on my insistence, he took me to see the Co clan temple where, I had read in a Manila Chinatown newspaper, Peping Cojuangco had made obeisance to his ancestors. Dating from the Manchu dynasty, the temple was a cruder specimen of the dozens I had seen in Penang and Singapore. Unpainted and seasoned by time, it looked more beautiful, certainly more organic. I found it to be a shell – when Mr Co unfastened the padlock and opened the doors, light alone filled the room.

The mixed origins of the Cojuangco family hark back to a time when Chinese overseas settlements were all-male affairs. Interbreeding was commoner among those earlier immigrants than among the later generations, and cross-bred offspring – the mestizo of the Philippines, the *lukjin* ('child of a Chinese') of Siam, the *metis* of Cambodia and Indochina, the white-Chinese *injerto* and the black-Chinese *chinocholo* of Peru – were found wherever the Chinese settled. Indeed, it was the belief of Charles Brooke, the white Rajah of Sarawak, that the best race for the advancement of Borneo would be the offspring of Chinese and native intermarriage: 'The mixed breed of Chinese with the Malays or the Dyaks', he wrote, 'are a good looking and industrious race, partaking much more of the Chinese character than that of the natives of this country. This mainly arises from the education and early formed habits which are altogether Chinese; and in religion and customs they likewise follow, in a good measure, the paternal stock.' The mixed race, he went on to say, 'is worthy of attention, as the future possessors of Borneo'.[5] It was not one of his more prescient predictions, for racial cleavages were to widen in the succeeding century; but earlier practices had brought whole races of half-castes into being, and today there are countless Southeast Asians who have some trace of Chinese blood in them.

In New Zealand Chinese immigrants married Maori women.[6] In Peru, we are told by the United States minister Richard Gibbs in 1874, they 'intermarry with the lower class of whites, mestizas, and cholas [Indians], and by these are looked upon as quite a catch for they make good husbands, industrious, domestic, and fond of their children. While the cholo husband is lazy, indolent, often a drunkard and brutal to his wife.' He adds, 'I often meet children in the streets whose almond shaped eyes show their Chinese origin,' and who would almost certainly be brought up as Christians.[7] In Trinidad, they frequently intermarried with Creole women; and in Mauritius too, 'the connections of Creole women with Chinese', the British Governor Sir Arthur Gordon reported in 1881, 'are more numerous than those with the Indians'.[8] In Madagascar they had children by Malagasy women, themselves the offspring of racial crossing between Malays and Indonesians. And there were Chinese who formed relationships with African tribal women, producing racially mixed children of whom the pale-skinned, slant-eyed Joseph Kasavubu, the first President of what had been Belgian Congo before its independence in 1960, is said to be a famous example.[9] In Liverpool, when the Aliens Restriction Order of 1914 excluded all Chinese women under forty years old, there was a good deal of racial crossing between Chinese and English – of twenty-two Chinese men investigated in Liverpool in the early 1920s, five had Chinese wives, eight had English wives or partners, seven had wives in China, one was unmarried and one recently widowed.[10]

One of the most famous of the offspring to be produced by a Chinese-English union was Lesley Charles Bowyer Yin, better known as Lesley Charteris, the writer, creator of 'the Saint'. Born in Singapore in 1907, Lesley Yin (who took the name Charteris legally in 1928, the year he became an American citizen) was the son of Dr Yin Shut Chuan, last glimpsed in these pages organizing the anti-opium movement. Dr Yin, who had begun his career as a colonial government interpreter attached to the Police Court, studied medicine in America and England before returning to Singapore to partner Dr Lim Boon Keng, another well-known anti-opium public figure, in private medical practice.[11]

By and large the children of mixed marriages were sent back to China to be brought up as Chinese: foreign they might be, but barbarian they would not. This practice brought into existence a race of half-castes who looked, say, African or Siamese, but who were linguistically and culturally entirely Chinese. In the home village these children quite frequently discovered they had half-brothers and sisters, the offspring of their father and his village wife. For it was not at all uncommon, as long as he could afford it, for an emigrant to have two wives, one he left in the home village to look after his parents and to manage the family's affairs, and another (usually a local woman in his place of residence) he took to help him with his overseas business.

Chinese men found it to their advantage, for example, to marry Thai women, for the traders in that country, the shrewder and more practical members of the population, were the womenfolk, not the men. There was a great deal of intermarriage between Chinese and Thais in the nineteenth century, and among Siamese families whose residence in Bangkok dates back a couple of generations, you don't have to dig deep for a Chinese ancestor. Chinese concubines – daughters of ennobled Chinese – crop up here and there in the genealogy of the Siamese royal family, and right up to the twentieth century the Thai Kings themselves acknowledged Chinese blood in their ancestry.[12] As for the Siamese women, their predilection for Chinese men went back at least as far back as the fifteenth century; we have it from members of Admiral Cheng Ho's retinue that whenever one of them 'meets a Chinese man, she is greatly pleased with him, and will invariably prepare wine to entertain and show respect to him, merrily singing and keeping him overnight' – to the delight, what's more, of her husband, only too pleased that his wife should find favour with the Chinese.[13]

The children of Chinese fathers and Thai mothers melted into the larger racial pattern, and were regarded as indigenous quite as much as Chinese. If a lukjin wished to be Thai, Thai he became. The half-breeds did not constitute a class apart, and in this they differed from the offspring of mixed marriages in other Southeast Asian countries. In the Philippines, Java and Malaya, people of mixed blood formed a community of their own, marked by an altogether separate identity. Over centuries of immigration and intermarriage, each of these countries has nurtured a distinct hybrid minority – the Philippines its half-indio (indigene) and half-Chinese mestizos; the Dutch East Indies its half-Javan and half-Hokkien *peranakan*, or 'locally born foreigners'; Malaya, and especially Malacca, its half-Malay and half-Hokkien Babas, often referred to as the Straits Chinese.

The mestizo in the Philippines had an india for a mother, and either a Spaniard (usually a creole from the New World) or a Chinese (usually a Hokkien) for a father. In the Philippines as in Latin America, the Spaniards believed in dividing their subjects into separate administrative categories, and just as 'indio' and 'Chinese' were legal labels, so mestizos of india-Chinese parentage, as the majority group among half-castes in the Philippines, were a distinct legal entity, with political rights and a social standing of their own. Each paid a different rate of head tax, with the indio paying the lowest, the Chinese the highest, and the Chinese mestizo an amount half-way between the two.[14]

The conquistadors saw Spanish Catholicism as the one factor that would unify these disparate people socially. The Spaniards took their

Catholicism seriously, their friars working to spread the faith among the indios; to keep the indio and Chinese apart, to their way of thinking, was to separate the faithful from the infidel. Nevertheless, though the native population was their chief concern, the Spanish Church and Spanish culture were open to all comers, Chinese included. What was more, the Spaniards saw the intermarriage of converted Chinese and indias as the best route to racial integration, and rewarded Catholic Chinese who took local wives by giving them tracts of uncultivated land in Manila's suburbs.

The Iberian experience with the Moors and the Jews had convinced the Spaniards that converting the Chinese to Catholicism, as well as segregating and repatriating them, was one way of getting on top of them. It seemed to the Spanish conquerors only common sense that, if their Catholic convictions were imposed on indigene and immigrant alike, the Chinese would be hispanized along with the natives. That the whole process could be speeded up by intermarriage seemed equally obvious to them. The Dominican friars were especially eager to convert the Philippine Chinese as a first step towards breaking into China, a venture in which, they hopefully supposed, the educated Chinese mestizos could help them. Missionaries were banned in China, but if they consistently protected the Chinese against the persecution of the Spanish officials, and word of this reached the ears of the Manchu court, might this not, the Dominicans reasoned, help to advance their cause in China?

It paid to be a Chinese convert, for acceptance of baptism could immediately earn one a Spanish godparent (who was at once a bondsman, a patron, a creditor and a protector in legal matters) and such privileges as reduced taxes, land grants, and the freedom to reside almost anywhere – all of which were denied the unconverted Chinese. We mustn't think that all who agreed to be baptized were insincere, but it can't be denied that many were simply feathering their nest. Everybody, including Captain Alexander Hamilton, an English visitor to the islands in the early 1700s, could see what they were about. 'All Chinese who go there for commerce', the captain reports, 'get a little brass image hung about their neck, with a string of beads in their hands, and learning to cross themselves, cry *Jesu Sancta Malia* (for they cannot pronounce Maria, because the letter R is excluded from the Chinese alphabet [*sic*]'; but once they have cheated the Spaniard and taken their leave of Manila, he goes on to say, 'at their passing by a mountain dedicated to the Virgin Mary, they throw their beads overboard, and thank the Virgin for her kindness to them'.[15]

And yet, shrewd as they were, and quite remarkably when you consider how much they could gain by it, few Chinese adopted Christianity. The Spaniards certainly didn't make things any easier for them when, to make sure that only the truly faithful were baptized, they decreed that the converts cut their hair and that their return to China be forbidden. Understandably, the Chinese found this hard to take, since the Manchus had made the wearing of pigtails mandatory for all subject Chinese; to men who still dreamt of taking themselves and their fortunes back to their home town for good one day, to be prohibited from going to China was to find life robbed of its meaning.

Many of those who were none the less tempted into a religion they would not otherwise practise took the names of their sponsoring Spanish godparents, coupling these with their own to form combinations of such splendid quaintness as José Castro Tan Yaoco or Carlo Gonzales Lim Sengco.

The Chinese mestizo did not speak any Chinese, the language having in any case degenerated in the market-place of Manila into a patois of Hokkien, Cantonese and Tagalog (the native speech). There were rich snobbish mestizos who would have you know that their fluency in the Spanish language was quite the equal of anybody's in Mexico or Madrid, that they were staunch Catholics, and that they would side with a Spaniard against a Chinese any day. In time these people evolved a subculture of their own, something neither indio nor Chinese, but a blend of values and manners peculiar to itself. On the other hand, the proverbial business acumen of their forefathers did not disappear as completely as other Chinese features, and in the mid-eighteenth century large numbers of mestizos were able to profit from the expulsion of unconverted Chinese – by whom they had hitherto been overshadowed – to become men of great wealth and social prominence. Indeed, it is agreed among historians that the economic and social ascendancy of the mestizos was the single most significant social phenomenon of the century between 1750 and 1850. They had their own settlement in Manila, Binondo; and though they were only five per cent of the population at the start of the nineteenth century, they were concentrated in areas offering the best chances of economic advancement and they represented the most dynamic element of Philippine society.[16]

In the trades and professions, they were generally more prosperous than the pure-blooded indigenes, and they were less than modest in their demonstrations of this. The principal traits of the mestizo, decried an English naval officer in 1828, are 'vanity, industry, and trading ingenuity'. Money, he goes on to observe, 'is their god: to obtain it they take all shapes, promise and betray, submit to everything, trample and are trampled upon: all is alike to them, if they get the money: and this, when obtained, they dissipate in lawsuits, firing cannon, fireworks, illumination, processions on feast days and rejoicing, in gifts to the churches, or in gambling.'[17]

They found their economic dominance challenged in the mid-1800s, when, in a change of Spanish policy, bars against the Chinese were lowered and the Chinese population, which had hitherto been limited to about five thousand, surged to three or four times that number with renewed Chinese immigration. The emphasis in the Philippines had shifted from the galleon trade to export crops, and large quantities of sugar, tobacco, abaca and coffee were finding markets in Europe and America. There were profitable openings all over the islands, and into nearly all of them the new immigrants went. Many mestizos retreated before these more vital people, yielding their control of the wholesale and retail businesses to the new arrivals, and shrewdly shifting their interests to export crop production and landholding.

These profound social changes threw up large numbers of rich landowners among the Chinese mestizos. Living ever more grandly, these mestizos, who could scarcely pride themselves on aristocratic pedigree or cultural superiority, saw to it that landed wealth was the gauge of social worth in Philippine society. Their critics would say they were a flashy people, sometimes excessively so. Rich Chinese mestizos were famously fashionable, and to go by portraits of the mid-nineteenth century, mestizo couples dressed in the style of the day were very well turned out indeed, the man in a top hat and a knee-length, frilly cuffed *caisa de chino* shirt hanging outside his trousers; the women in a plumed hat or mantilla, a blouse and a long skirt, and a shawl edged in broderie anglaise around her shoulders.[18] (To keep people in their place, a law had been passed to mark by dress and privileges the various classes in Philippine society, and while Spaniards were allowed to wear ties, mestizos and indios were not: the loose, open-necked shirts the latter were obliged to adopt were to beget the attractive national dress of the Philippines today, the *barong tagalog*.)[19] If they gaze out of the pictures with a certain hauteur, it is because they were the trend-setters of the day: where the Chinese mestizo went, there the indio followed. If in their manners they were more Spanish than the Spaniards, well, this was only to be expected of a people who lacked firm cultural roots themselves, who thought themselves better than the indios, but who were not white enough to qualify for social equality with the ruling caste. True 'sons of Spain' was how they proudly styled themselves.

And yet in the end the Chinese mestizo was to become an enemy of Spain, perhaps its worst in the Philippines. As we shall see, he more than anyone shaped the Filipino nationality. The ethnic and cultural interbreeding of the Philippines stood out from the admixtures of other Southeast Asian countries in the profound effect which it was to have on the emergence of the Filipinos as a nation.

In the story of the birth of Philippine nationhood, the families founded by Chinese immigrants played a role of durable prominence, as the begetters of a sizeable segment of the Filipino élite, intelligentsia and political leadership of later generations, and as the progenitor of José Rizal, the national hero whose writings inspired the Philippine Revolution, and who is widely recognized as having had a profounder influence on his people than any other man.

The order which the Spaniards imposed on Philippine society – with the Chinese forming one caste, the indio another, and the half-breed a third – was breaking down in the closing decades of the nineteenth century, and an inhabitant of the archipelago was beginning to call himself either Spanish, Chinese or Filipino. The term 'Filipino' had been narrowly applied to the creoles or the Spaniards born in the Philippines, but now it was infused with a wider, national meaning, one that was to embrace all the inhabitants of the Philippine archipelago. The adoption of a new system of taxation did away with the classification of people on racial lines, and there was now nothing to stop the Chinese mestizos and the moneyed indios from merging. They were all Hispanicized, they mixed on equal terms with the creoles and Spanish mestizos, their differences were watered down by wealth and education – and out of these interactions there were to crystallize the features of the modern Filipino identity.

The shift in pattern was also hastened by the new wave of Chinese immigration in the mid-1800s. Coming from what they assumed to be a superior civilization, these Chinese disparaged the cultural apostasy – as they saw it – of the Hispanicized half-caste descendants of their predecessors. Miscegenation there might still be – the Chinese community had only 4 females to every 1,000 males[20] – but parents who could afford to do so sent their sons to be educated in China and to be brought up as culturally Chinese. The old-stock Chinese mestizos, reacting to the challenge of the fresh Chinese immigration by becoming more devoutly Catholic, more Spanish, and ever more anti-Chinese, were at the same time spurred to forge their own identity, one that cut across the boundaries of earlier social groupings.

The most eloquent exponents of the emerging Filipino identity were the *ilustrados*, the 'enlightened ones'. The educated offspring of prosperous creoles, indios and Chinese mestizos, these men, their separate origins fused into a common set of values, were the beneficiaries of widened educational opportunities and the self-aware articulators of a swelling stream of political dissidence. The frustration of their aspirations for equal rights with the white man they channelled into a bitter mood of anger against the Spanish friars who held their people in thrall. In more idealistic moments they had aspired to be a proper province of Spain, but the exasperation of these hopes increasingly sharpened their assertion of a separate national identity; and in 1896, this sense of nation, the first to emerge in Asia, burst into the drama of the Philippine Revolution.[21]

The revolutionary movement was tinged with anti-Chinese sentiment, for it was the most thoroughly Westernized of the Filipinos who reacted the most strongly against the Chinese, culturally if not personally – and in those days the most Westernized Filipinos were probably the nationalists and patriots.[22] Behind the nationalist movement lay generations of resentment against Chinese cultural pride and commercial supremacy, and the revolution gave these feelings a chance to burst into the open. And yet, though the mestizo nationalists themselves had long forgotten that they were Chinese at all, there were still Spaniards who attributed their seditiousness and disloyalty to their Chinese antecedents.[23]

Indeed, the man who single-handedly awakened the Philippine people to national consciousness was a fifth-generation Chinese mestizo – José Rizal, the national hero. Rizal, recognized by most of his countrymen as the greatest Filipino who had ever lived, would in the ordinary course of events have borne a Hokkien-Chinese surname. His great-great-grandfather was a Chinese who came to the Philippines around 1690 from the southern Fukien city of Chang-chou, converted to Catholicism, and married a Chinese mestiza from a well-to-do Manila family. Known in the Philippines as Lamco, he was baptized at the age of thirty-five in the Parián church of San Gabriel on a Sunday in 1697, and given the name Domingo, the Spanish for 'Sunday'. His wife's father, a pure Chinese rice merchant called Agustin Chinco, was also from Chang-chou, and also converted. His son and grandson both married Chinese mestizas, but though the law defined all males of paternal Chinese ancestry as Chinese mestizos, Rizal's grandfather had the family classification changed from the mestizo tax-census register to that of the indio. To be classed as an indio was to pay less tax, but the alteration was not simply one of technical detail; it carried with it a change of psychological identity, and Rizal was to insist to the last that he was an *indio puro*.

The family name lost all trace of Chineseness when it was changed to Mercado, meaning 'market place'. The Spaniards, who allocated surnames as they pleased, refused the request of José's father, Francisco Mercado, to change the family name to Rizal; referring to the green of young growth, or the green of renewal, the name Rizal seemed more appropriate to Mercado's profession, which was that of a sugar planter and landowner. The name was adopted as a subsidiary, however, and in full José's name was José Rizal y Mercado.

On his mother's side, José Rizal had Spanish, Chinese, indio and even Japanese blood. The Spanish blood was thin, but it was in the culture of Spain that he was nurtured; if he was a poet, he was a Spanish poet, and if he was the first man to expound nationalism in Asia (Gandhi acknowledged him as a forerunner),[24] he did so with the ambivalence of one who, even as he questioned the idea of one race having the right to rule another, remained in his own mind a true son of Spain. To him the chief obstacle to the reform of his country was not Spain, but the Spanish friars' insidious oppression. Ultimately, he was a man above racial distinction, and though he did what he could to ensure the survival of the Philippine languages, and to publicize the islands' pre-Spanish history, there was nothing of the Gandhian in his thinking – no revivalism, no reversion to origins. Educated in Manila, Madrid, Paris, Heidelberg and Berlin, he conducted his correspondence in six languages – Spanish, Tagalog, German, French, English and Italian. In his responses to women he was very far from being trapped in his origins, and though the great love of his life was a cousin, a mestiza, he gave his heart at various times to a Japanese, an Englishwoman, an Anglo-Filipino and an Anglo-Chinese.

This last, Josephine Bracken, the illegitimate daughter of a British soldier in the Hong Kong garrison and an unknown Chinese woman, was the one he finally took as his wife. Like many another Hong Kong half-caste of the time, Josephine Bracken did her best to pass herself off as pure European, and this gave her a touch of phoniness which jarred on José's family, though not, it would seem, on José himself. They were an ill-matched pair, he so gifted, she so ordinary; and nothing was more suggestive of the pathos of their brief union, and its sense of waste, than the premature birth, about a year before his own death, of José Rizal's stillborn son. That night he buried the body of his dead son himself, alone, in a secluded spot where no one would ever find it.

When Josephine Bracken came into his life Rizal was in exile in a remote Jesuit town in the southern island of Mindanao. Through his writings, he had not only exposed the degenerate and oppressive system imposed by the friars, but he had sown the seeds of Filipino nationalism. Eight years before, he had written his novel, *Noli Me Tangere* (Touch Me Not), a book one day to be studied in all the colleges, as profound in its influence in the Philippines as Harriet Beecher Stowe's *Uncle Tom's Cabin* was in the United States. This had been followed by *El Filibusterismo*, a novel in which an unmistakable mood of insurrection impended, a feeling that the Filipino's hatred of his masters could only be vented in revolution. These feelings found their echoes all over the Philippines, and those who read the books found that they were never to look upon the Spanish friars in quite the same way again. All in all, then, the Church had every reason to fear and abhor Rizal.

All this was happening at a particularly eventful moment of Spanish and Philippine history. In 1896, when Spain was fighting to suppress the national war of independence in Cuba, a revolt led by a nationalist secret society, the Katipunan, broke out in the Philippines. Rizal thought the rising ridiculous and took no part in it, but the Spaniards made a martyr of him, trying him for sedition, finding him guilty of being 'the very soul' of the insurrection,[25] and publicly executing him before a firing squad – thereby doing the one thing likely to unite the nationalist movement, and to convince the Filipinos that there was no alternative to independence from Spain.

It has been said that the greatest Chinese contribution to the Philippines was the birth of Dr José Rizal.[26] And yet a high proportion of Chinese blood in an individual is no guarantee of his sympathy with the Chinese race. Rizal himself objected to being called a Chinese mestizo: when he was made to sign a document notifying him of his death sentence, he tried unsuccessfully to get the Spanish authorities, who had put him down as a Chinese mestizo in order to suggest that he was not even a real Filipino, to change the wording and to recognize him as an indio puro.

In the pages of his novels, being a briber is seen to be a Chinese forte, and he voiced the popular conception of the Chinese when he wrote of one of his Filipino characters in *El Filibusterismo* that 'For some time now he had been looking for an effective poison to smear on his fighting cock's spurs and the most deadly that he knew of was the blood of a Chinese who had died of a venereal disease.'[27] A character in *El Filibusterismo*, 'the Chinaman Quiroga' – at the mention of whose name another character cries, 'That pimp!' – is the very image of corruption. Quiroga is almost certainly modelled on Don Carlos Palanca Tan Chuey-liong, or Tan Chueco for short, a real-life Chinese grandee of the 1890s.

His smile 'wheedling' and 'deferential', 'his voice oily, his bows successive', Quiroga perfectly fitted the popular Filipino idea of what an unscrupulous, bootlicking Chinese businessman should be. He is a rich shopkeeper, the supplier of all that the friars and bureaucrats need, and at his party, held in a room hung with preposterously incongruous pictures – 'delicate blue landscapes painted in Canton and Hong Kong, loud chromos of odalisques and half-naked women, and lithographs of effeminate Christs produced by Jewish publishing houses in Germany for sale in Catholic countries'[28] – champagne corks pop, glasses clink, Spanish guests laugh, and cigar smoke fills the air.

Chinese businessmen will be Chinese businessmen, you feel, when you read of Quiroga's interest in diamond bracelets and discover that he has it in mind to give one, not to his wife, but to a certain beautiful lady, the friend of a powerful gentleman whose influence he needs in a profitable business transaction. Behind every Chinese business deal, you feel, gifts are always lurking. Rizal perfectly understood the place of the Chinese in Philippine life, and in *Noli Me Tangere* we read of the reaction of a Sister Rufa to the news that another one of those periodic massacres of the Chinese is in the offing: 'What a pity!' she cries; 'All the Chinese dead before Christmas, when they send us such nice gifts. They should have waited for New Year's Day.'

It is no wonder that the Chinese antagonized the Filipino nationalist – especially, it seemed, the nationalist who had Chinese blood in his veins. And yet, although Rizal felt anything but Chinese, it is quite impossible to deny or ignore genealogy if one is a hero, for historians will insist on taking one's life back to the beginning. To this day there are Filipino Chinese to remind you of the ethnic connection, and when they speak of him there still enters a suggestion of pride and proprietorial interest in their voice. In Manila's Chinatown in the autumn of 1987, I walked into a Filipino Chinese Heritage Exhibition in which almost the first thing one saw was a large board displaying the family tree of José Rizal.

The heritage was already cloudy in the nineteenth century; by the twentieth the Chinese streak in the Filipino mass would have become so mixed with other strains that all is inextricably confused in the bloodstream. Nevertheless, a very large number of modern Filipinos would still be identifiable as being of Chinese extraction by their family names, and a sizeable portion of the Filipino élite is made up of families founded by Chinese immigrants. One example is Manila's Archbishop, Cardinal Sin, whose father was a junk dealer from Amoy who emigrated to the Philippines and married a local woman.

A mixed pattern evolved in Java too. Initially, just as had happened in Thailand, the native rulers conferred titles on the most prominent Chinese and absorbed them into the hereditary Javanese nobility; there were ruling families in East Java, for instance, which were a cross-breed of Chinese and Javanese. But in Java the acculturation never proceeded as far it did in Siam, and the half-breed remained a hybrid, a member of an intermediate community which, for all its adaptation to native ways, was very far from being submerged in the human mainstream.

It makes sense to assume that how readily an immigrant integrates has something to do with the nature of the receiving society. What made nineteenth-century Siam different from contemporary Java? One answer, according to the scholar William Skinner, is its 'ethnic confidence' or 'cultural vigour'. Siam remained its own master even as its neighbours fell to foreign colonial domination; as a kingdom it had outlasted several less resilient; and the continuity of its independence and civilization had all gone to confirm it in its self-assurance. Java's experience had been quite different. Subjugation by the Dutch had shattered its confidence, narrowed its views, and burdened its élite with a crippling sense of inferiority. While their confidence made the Thais accepting, their lack of it made the Javanese rejecting; while the one nation counted as Thai anyone who took a Thai name and spoke the Thai language, the other counted as Javanese only those who were racially Javanese.

The Chinese migrants, a go-getting people, naturally opted for integration with the ruling class – the indigenous aristocracy in the case of Thailand, Dutch and Eurasians in the case of Java. In Thailand the most upwardly mobile Chinese sought titles bestowed by Thai nobles, but in Java it was decorations from the Dutch crown they coveted, not honours conferred by the moribund native rulers. The Thais were clever to ennoble the richest and most prominent of the Chinese settlers, for that way they creamed off the most respectable and thrusting part of Chinese society, and ensured that it was dynamic stock they were intermingling with and marrying. And whereas the ethnic groups in Java formed distinct legal categories – European, Foreign Oriental and Inlander – and were kept largely separate by divide-and-rule methods, nothing like as sharp a line divided Thai from Chinese. What was more, because the Chinese in Java were restricted in their movements by the Dutch requirement that they live in Chinese enclaves in the towns, and that they obtain a government pass whenever they travelled outside their own town, they could never get as close to local life as the Chinese in Thailand, who were allowed to roam everywhere.[29]

Religion made for another gap. The Thais were Theravada Buddhists, the Javanese Muslims. The Chinese, who practised a folk religion containing elements of Mahayana Buddhism, naturally found the gap easier to bridge in Thailand than in Java. Though the Chinese had their own temples (they still do), religiously they did not find themselves at odds with the locals. Economics played a part, too. The Thais kept to their rice-growing and their governing, leaving the Chinese unchallenged in trading, mining and all their other callings. In Java Chinese merchants did not enjoy the advantage of being all on their own; there were native traders to compete with them, and this made for rivalry and friction. The commercial drive which was said to characterize the Chinese came also to be disdained by the Thais in the twentieth century, but the Javanese's 'burning inferiority complex' made life harder for the Chinese in Java; in later years the intensity of Indonesian anti-sinicism would always suggest not confidence but insecurity, as well as, at times, an uglier sort of nationalism.

The descendants of the early Chinese immigrants in Java (who were almost all Hokkiens) evolved a recognizably mixed racial and cultural pattern called '*peranakan*'. Peranakans were not wholly Javan, nor exactly Hokkien. They saw themselves as Chinese, but they were Indies-born Chinese, different from the totoks, the pure-blooded, China-born newcomers. For one thing, they had almost all lost their ancestral tongue, and spoke to each other in Malay or the patois of their particular locality.

Before 1900, almost all the established Chinese communities in the Dutch Indies were peranakan in speech and culture. But by the first decade of the twentieth century the pattern had changed. For one thing, there were far more first-generation immigrants in the Indies; the rapid economic growth stimulating the immigration of both men and women had seen to that. For another, the overseas Chinese communities were infected by the nationalist mood of China; modern Chinese schools, inculcating a nationalism that provided a powerful focus of sentimental and political identification, were opening all over Southeast Asia. All this jolted the peranakan into wondering what he belonged to if not China. To say you were peranakan was one way of saying you were nothing in particular – a half-cock Chinese, out of touch with China; at least that was the way the totoks saw you. Like the Chinese mestizo, the peranakan was shamed into a quest for identity. Unlike the mestizo, he did not react by becoming anti-Chinese. He did one of two things: he went either to a Chinese school where he learnt Mandarin and became re-sinicized, or he went to a missionary school where he acquired not only Dutch and English but a modern European consciousness.

The label 'peranakan' is used also of the Chinese-Malay hybrid in the Straits Settlements of Malacca, Penang and Singapore, where it is interchangeable with 'Straits Chinese' and 'Baba'. The first Baba families were founded in Malacca (the earliest of the places in Malaya to be settled by the Chinese) by those voyaging Hokkien traders who bred outside the Chinese strain. Although nobody can be quite sure whether any intermarriage took place beyond that first generation – in later times the Babas were always to marry other Babas or new immigrants from China – it is certain that many of the earliest Babas were half-breeds, the offspring of Chinese-Malay unions. We can't be certain who the women were: if they were local Malay women, how could the Chinese, infidel almost to a soul, have married them without converting to Muhammadanism? One answer that has been given to this question is that Malaya was not so thoroughly Islamized as it is now;[30] another is that the women could have been slave-girls from neighbouring Sumatra.[31] Whoever they were, many of them must have been taken as concubines, their Chinese husbands perhaps having already married and sired children at home.

Marriage into a Baba family, inevitably more comfortably established than a first-generation immigrant one, was coveted by the mass of male sinkehs, the newcomers to the Straits Chinese community; for here was a quick and easy way to establishing a foothold in an alien society, quite apart from the fact that migrant women were extremely thin on the ground. Baba girls of marriageable age could therefore afford to

be very choosy, and for their hand only the most promising young
sinkehs, as it were, need apply. Once married, the son-in-law moved
in with the bride's parents, his freshness to his newly adopted country
binding him the more strongly to his wife's family. If he married into
Malacca money he could find himself living in the houses of the great
Dutch merchants in the celebrated Heeren Street, 'the fashionable and
aristocratic resort of the Chinese'.[32]

It was easy to overawe such a man into compliance with Baba ways.
Some of these ways, being fossilized forms of Chinese practices, would
be familiar enough, but unless the bridegroom had been in the Straits
Settlements for some time, others would seem a little strange to him.
Ancestors were worshipped just as much in Baba homes as in purely
Chinese families in the Straits Settlements, and the Baba's faith – a
hodgepodge of Confucianism, Buddhism and Taoism – would be
familiar to anyone acquainted with the folk religion of China. China
itself, though, no longer meant much to the Babas, and they had little
truck with the dialect associations and secret societies which formed
so much a part of the overseas Chinese scene.

The Babas had a language of their own, a sort of Malay laced
with Hokkien and even English words or phrases, and this the new
son-in-law now found himself using as his everyday vernacular in place
of his native Chinese tongue. With their strong sense of family, the
Babas went in greatly for kinship terms, and such were the ramifications
of their family bonds that their language has forms of address for up to
seven hundred degrees and categories of relationship. The son-in-law
probably converted to the food quickly enough, the cooking being a
very palatable mix of Chinese, Malay and Western elements, though
one would expect him to have some trouble adapting to the habit of
eating with his fingers (the traditional Malay way), abandoning his
chopsticks.

His wife, who would be called a Nonya (a female Baba), would be
dressed in Malay style, in a sarong topped by a long tunic pinned with
three gold or silver brooches, an attire differing from that of Malay
women in ways apparent only to the trained eye. Characteristically,
the Nonya wore her hair scraped back into a tall sleek chignon into
which were stuck curved, nail-like hairpins (three in the case of Malacca
Nonyas, six in the case of Penang ones). *Bijoux* usually abounded,
rings, bracelets, brooches and earrings. Her toilette and her manner
suggested a lady of leisure; and when one conjures up an image of
the Nonya, it is quite often of a woman comfortably indulging her

habit of betel-chewing. 'A revolting habit', the Victorian traveller Isabella Bird has called it, one which left a chewer's mouth looking as though it was full of blood.[33] Fruit of the areca palm, the betel nut has mildly stimulant properties and acts on the nervous system like nicotine. Natives of Malaya were accustomed to taking a slice of the nut with sireh (the leaf of the betel pepper), smearing it with moistened lime, folding the leaf into an oblong shape, and popping it into their mouths. Like chewing-gum, the sireh and its contents have to be spat out after they had done their job, and it was not uncommon to see Nonyas going about with their own little spittoons for the red expectorations. No Nonya bride went to her wedding without her own sireh set, the silver box handed down from mother to daughter in which were held the betel leaves neatly folded one on top of the other, the lime, the parings of betel nut and the pieces of gambier which some women like to add for extra bite.

Part Chinese and part Malay, in time the Babas were to become a touch English as well. Opportunities for copying British manners and for adopting British methods were open to them earlier than Dutch ones to the Indies peranakans. When schools run on British lines and using English as the medium of instruction were founded in Singapore, Penang and Malacca in the 1810s and 1820s, many Baba families sent their sons to them, convinced that to adopt the language of the colonial masters was a precondition for getting on in the world.

The English-educated Baba, drinking brandy and soda, playing billiards and bowls, despising the unacculturated Chinese for being impervious to improving Western influences, was an example of a type to be found everywhere in the British empire. Not for nothing was he called the 'King's Chinese'. Indeed he preferred not to be thought of as having Chinese tastes at all, doing his best to affect the predilections of the *orang putih*, 'white man'. And yet he had no exact equivalent in other subject societies, because although he would be offended indeed to be called a Chinaman – 'I am a British subject,' he would say, perhaps puffing up with self-importance, 'an *orang putih*' – in outward appearance he remained irredeemably Chinese. Not only was he dressed entirely in the Chinese manner, he still clung proudly and tenaciously to his queue.

And yet the important point about the Babas is that they were *not* like other Chinese. J. D. Vaughan, an English colonial officer who worked in Penang and Singapore in the mid-1800s, tells us that they even had their own social clubs, places to which they would admit no non-Straits Chinese. One of these clubs was visited by the Duke of Edinburgh in 1869; he bowled with the Babas there, and we have it from Vaughan that he 'expressed himself highly pleased with their pluck'. A true Chinaman, Vaughan adds correctly, would ridicule the idea of exercise in any shape.34

The Babas were eager to offer their loyalties to the British. The most notable of their organizations, the Straits Chinese British Association, established in Singapore in 1900 by, among others, the anti-opium campaigner Dr Lim Boon Keng, made it one of its aims 'to promote among the members an intelligent interest in the affairs of the British Empire, and to encourage and maintain their loyalty as subjects of the Queen'.35 They formed almost a comprador class, working for European firms as brokers, clerks and cashiers.

As a group, observed the English writer John Crawford, the 'Creole Chinese', as he called the Babas, were 'inferior in industry to the rest'36 (he has said the same of the peranakan in the Indies, judging them to have less 'energy and spirit' than the original settler).37 A later stereotype of the Baba man was that he was 'soft' and lazy, not a go-getter. It is a persistent feature of the history of migrant peoples that the immigrant drive seldom survives into the second or third generation; the commercial aggressiveness of the sinkeh or totok was partly owed to his having to reach success the hard way; and since he was the one who was truly determined to get ahead, he often did.

Baba culture and influence reached their apogee during the colonial period, between the closing years of the nineteenth century and the early part of the twentieth. Thereafter it waned, losing its distinctness and its *raison d'être* with the decline of the colonial milieu which nurtured and sustained it.

PART THREE

1920s–1960s

CHAPTER NINE

Three of the Men

Up a leafy road not far from the most fashionable shopping precinct in Singapore stands a very strange house indeed. It is white all over, and has classical columns, and in the very centre of its façade is set a large plaque depicting a tiger and leopard. It is approached through two sets of heavy iron gates, crowned at one end with a statue of a sitting tiger, and at the other with a leopard.

The gates are padlocked, the grounds are overgrown, weeds sprout from the cracks in the mansion's shapely cupola, and it is only too evident that the building, now dingy and deserted, has seen better days. It survives as a reminder of past grandeur, the days when, because it was designed by an American architect to resemble the residence of the American President in Washington, it was known far and wide as the White House.[1] Outside it was European; inside, the Italian marble sculptures apart, it was largely Chinese, the floors laid with Tientsin carpets, the rooms profusely adorned with Chinese works of art, vases, figures, plaques, screens, porcelain pots and fish-bowls. A collection of jade carvings was started in the early 1930s, and became so famous that the White House came also to be called the Jade House. Many of them superbly carved, with a richness of beasts, birds, flora and supernatural figures, these objects formed a valuable collection, goggled at by tourists when it was opened to public view.

The house, built in 1927, belonged to the elder of two well-known brothers, Aw Boon Haw, the Tiger Balm King, and his younger brother Aw Boon Par. Born in 1882 and 1886 in Rangoon, one was named for the tiger (*haw*), and the other for the leopard (*par*). Their father, a Hakka migrant from a small village in southern Fukien, was an apothecary who ran a Chinese herbal medicine shop, Yung-an T'ang (Forever Safe Drugstore), in Rangoon. Tiger Aw was sent back to school in the ancestral village when he was about sixteen, but he was no scholar, and survived only two years of China before coming home to Rangoon. Leopard Aw, in the mean time, had been studying at a local English school, Burma being a part of the British empire.[2]

Tiger and Leopard inherited the father's business when the old man breathed his last in 1907. Leopard, as the less outgoing of the two, would look after the business in Rangoon while his elder brother travelled to peddle their products in Malaya, Singapore, Thailand, Hong Kong, China and even Japan. It was clear from the start that the elder brother was the abler of the two, and that it was he who set the style and pace of the business, but Tiger Aw, who cherished his younger brother with a strong protective love, never left Leopard out of anything, and, when he moved himself and his family to Singapore in 1926, he moved his brother's too.

There he made his fabulous fortune with Tiger Balm, a brown ointment that became as ubiquitous in the Chinese world as Vicks vapour rub in the British one. It comes today in small glass jars or flat tins, with the colourful packet or wrapping paper picturing one or more energetic-looking tigers, and proclaiming it as a product of the Yung-an T'ang. The formula used to be a closely guarded secret, and it was popularly believed that the ointment, seen by many to be a cure-all embodying some of the tiger's legendary qualities, contained one or more parts of the animal's anatomy, ground up and mixed in with the rest of the ingredients. But today, anyone who takes the trouble to read the fine print on the package can see that it is little more than a mixture of menthol, camphor, clove oil, peppermint oil, cassia oil and cajuput oil, bound together by wax and petroleum. All the same, it is an effective muscle rub, and while it is not a household name in the West, it is by no means unknown there, finding favour with athletic Swiss and Dutch, and sold through chemists such as Boots in England (in which country it has also been spotted on the shelves of sex shops by visiting Singaporeans, billed as a stimulant).[3] Indeed, it was reported in 1986 that more than twenty million jars of Tiger Balm are sold in sixty-five countries annually.[4]

As to who invented this elixir, no two accounts agree. His daughter claimed that it was Tiger Aw himself;[5] his daughter-in-law said that it was Tiger's father; a third commentator named a doctor he met in the course of his travels in Singapore. The most plausible of the accounts seems to be that of the daughter-in-law, who has added that the ointment was not popular in the elder Aw's time, but that the sales took off only when the younger Aw was clever enough to market it properly.[6] As an early convert to the idea that branding was big business, and that a memorable trademark could turn a product into gold, Tiger was ahead of his time.

Other products added to the profits, nostrums such as the Tiger Headache Cure; the Eight Diagrams Remedy for sea-sickness, sore throat and nausea; and Chen K'uai (So Speedy), a laxative. As one who understood the value of publicity, Aw exploited the image of the leaping tiger for all it was worth. A massive tiger's head adorned the front of his custom-built car, with the animal's eyes for its lamps and a pre-recorded roar for a horn.[7] With its chassis painted in bold black stripes over orange and white, the car cut a dash and provoked curiosity wherever it went.

He gave generously to charity, supporting hospitals, orphanages, temples and old people's homes; but even his philanthropy redounded profitably to his business, for it made him even more of a celebrity, and his products still better known. He was perhaps at his splashiest in the building of the Tiger Balm Gardens, a Chinese Disneyland which, until it was closed to make way for a new theme park in 1988, had amused, delighted and appalled tourists for decades. An artist brought over from Swatow, Kwok Wan Shan, designed both it and the smaller version in Hong Kong, but Aw Boon Haw was anything but a passive bystander, and made sure the details conformed to his wishes. The greater part of the Singapore Tiger Balm Gardens was destroyed during the Japanese occupation, but it was rebuilt and repaired, and, until he died, Aw saw to it that new displays were added each year.

It was Chinese kitsch at its most exuberant, with grotto after grotto, panel after panel, clot after clot of gaudily coloured statuary arranged in scenes from folklore and mythology – the Monkey God clashing with Red Baby, white rabbits fighting black rats, men being cut into little pieces and boiled in a pot. An Italian Corner had a Greek discus thrower clothed in a Roman fig leaf, the Australian Corner its concrete kangaroos, the Spanish one its flamenco dancers, the American Corner its Statue of Liberty. Some of the tableaux were also meant to be edifying, affirming virtues like Filial Piety, Honesty and Discipline. Scenes of retribution warned the spectator against deviating from the straight and narrow, and it must have been the tableaux of Vices and Punishment that caused the writer John Masters to say, 'The villa is unspeakable, obscenely ugly . . . the enactment of legends and stories are usually sadistic . . . there are tortures, murders, assassinations, with pints of painted blood . . . there are flying skirts and lecherous women with chickens' heads.'[8] And yet one must be a killjoy indeed not to get some fun out of the Tiger Balm Gardens – the sheer bad taste was entertaining – or to object to the ones that plugged Tiger products, the papier mâché Chinese farmer leaping towards his fallen wife clutching a restorative bottle of Tiger Oil, or the Japanese sumo wrestlers vying for possession of Tiger remedies.

It worked. Tiger Balm was a household word; Forever Safe Drugstore, presently a wholly owned subsidiary of Haw Par Brothers Limited, had branches in Hong Kong, Canton, Amoy, Swatow, Batavia, Surabaya, Medan and Bangkok.9 But Aw was too good a publicity man to leave it at that. What better way to promote Tiger Balm, he now asked himself, than to start one's own newspaper, where the product could be advertised free of charge? Thus it was that, in 1929, the first of his newspapers, the *Sin Chiew Jit Poh* (Star Isle Daily), was launched in Singapore. This was to be followed by a dozen more periodicals, all carrying the character 'star' in their logo, but variously published in Hong Kong, Penang, Bangkok, Canton, Amoy, Shanghai and Swatow. Soon he was called not just the Tiger Balm King, but the Press King as well. In 1950 he started two English-language dailies, the *Hong Kong Standard* (which to this day calls itself *Tiger Paper* in Chinese) and the now defunct *Singapore Tiger Standard*.10 It has been said that as Aw's newspapers were primarily vehicles for promoting his pharmaceutical products, they were politically wishy-washy; but this is not entirely true, for though he carried a British passport all his life, Aw was not looked upon with particular favour by Singapore's British authorities, whose policies towards the Chinese he deplored in his papers, and who in turn suspected him of Communist sympathies.11

For staff, he used Hakkas as far as possible, and if they were called Aw, this was all the better, for Tiger Aw was clannish of habit, like most contemporary overseas Chinese. Many of the earliest employees of the Forever Safe factory were relatives, and it was generally accepted that fathers could bring sons into the company. He himself was father to a large brood, six boys and two girls, and for good measure there were the children of his brother, whom he considered part of his family. He had four wives in all, the daughters of overseas Chinese families settled in Burma and Penang, but it was whispered that all but two of his sons were adopted;12 indeed it is a matter of debate whether he fathered any children at all.

The family was separated when Singapore fell to the Japanese Army, with some members fleeing to Rangoon, some to China, and others remaining in Hong Kong. The brother, Leopard Aw, never made it back to Singapore, for he died in Burma in 1944. Two years later Tiger Aw returned to Singapore, where, miraculously, he recovered the bulk of his jade collection. (The family later donated the collection to the

National Museum of Singapore, and there, in the Haw Par Gallery, it may be viewed today.) His business interests expanded, but against the gains was to be balanced a huge loss, the takeover of his various enterprises in China by the Communists when they took power. At about the same time, pursuing the idea of setting up a plebeian bank for the low- to middling-income customer, he established the Chung Khiaw Bank, indicating by its name (which shared a character with the rubric of the Hakka Association in Singapore) that it was a Hakka concern.[13]

For the remainder of his life he made his home in Hong Kong, where lived his second and favourite wife, Chin-chih (Golden Bough), the mother of Sally, of whom more later. In 1954, on his way back to Hong Kong from Boston, where he underwent a serious operation, he was rushed into hospital in Honolulu and there died of a heart attack. It would not be quite true to say that his business empire died with him, but he had run it in a very patriarchal manner, and when a business of that nature lost its patriarch then its oneness was lost too. A cynic would expect dynastic squabbles, and sure enough, it was not long before lawsuits were brought by one branch of the family against another. As Sally Aw was later to say of it, '[it was] a tremendous empire. But there was no one to head it. Everyone wanted to, but no one was strong enough.'[14]

She herself was one of the chief contenders, but it was Tiger Aw's nephew Aw Cheng Chye, the eldest son of Leopard Aw, who took control of Haw Par Brothers. Born in Rangoon and educated at Singapore's St Andrew's School, Aw Cheng Chye had an honorary degree from an American university, the Farleigh Dickinson University in New Jersey.[15] He was well-intentioned, but he was no manager, and it was he who, in an ill-judged and regretted move in 1971, offered the family's forty-six per cent stake in Haw Par International (by then a public company embracing the various enterprises that Tiger Aw had started) for sale. The buyer was Slater Walker Securities, the British-Australian investment group headed by the infamous Jim Slater. With subsequent purchases in the market, Slater Walker took its forty-six per cent shareholding up to fifty-one per cent. The business that the Aw brothers built was the Aws' no longer.

Its majority shareholding of Haw Par gave Slater Walker a substantial share in the Star Press, the publisher of *Sin Chew Jit Poh* and the *Singapore Tiger Standard*. Very far from being persuaded that foreign ownership of a local newspaper was a good idea, the Singapore

government told Slater Walker to sell its shares in the Star Press back
to the Aw family. This it did, at great advantage to itself. Feeling as
shaken and as ashamed as any man who had just sold the family silver,
Aw Cheng Chye left Singapore for a long holiday abroad, accompanied
by his wife. He was never to return, for he died – many say by his
own hand – when they got to Brazil. (Jim Slater was also to come to a
sticky end, caught out four years later in a shady share deal involving
Haw Par. Like thunder upon his head came the ire of the Singapore
government and the crescendo of damaging publicity, making his life
so difficult that he had to resign as chairman of Slater Walker Securities
and retire from the City altogether.)[16]

You had to be rash indeed to cross swords with the Singapore
government, past master at making life uncomfortable for newspaper
publishers. This was brought home to Aw Kow, Tiger Aw's eldest
son and publisher of the Star newspapers, when he found himself the
hapless central figure in a *cause célèbre*, accused of allowing the *Eastern
Sun*, an English-language daily he launched in 1966, to be infiltrated
by the Communist intelligence network based in Hong Kong. He had,
so the allegations went, accepted a loan from the Communists at a
ridiculously low rate of interest, in return for which he would let them
dictate the editorial content of his newspaper.[17] Inevitably, the paper
folded. The pattern became hideously familiar. Not long after it started,
the *Singapore Herald*, a new English-language daily into which the Aws
(Sally included) had invested some of their money, had its licence
withdrawn by the government, which accused it of 'black operations',
a police term for activities directed against Singapore from outside the
country. The CIA was said to be behind the paper, and as proof the
government pointed to the loan which the Chase Manhattan Bank had
granted the paper to get it started. Sally Aw came from Hong Kong to
protest this, but described her interview with the Prime Minister Lee
Kuan Yew as 'a total waste of time'.

Sally Aw is seldom squashed, for she is a forceful personality, the
most forceful and, it so happens, the most successful of the Aw children.
As is so often the case with rich Chinese families, the daughter, being the
less pampered, turned out better than the sons. She inherited the *Sing
Tao Daily* from her father and turned it into the flagship of the largest
newspaper-publishing enterprise in Hong Kong, one which puts out
editions in Sydney, San Francisco, Vancouver, Toronto, New York
and London. She once expressed an interest in buying the *Observer*,
the London Sunday paper, but in course of time she would concentrate

most of her foreign investments in Sydney, to which city she would move her corporate base and where she would become a considerable property owner.[18] The first woman to be elected Chairman of the International Press Institute and an Officer of the Order of the British Empire, Sally Aw has remained single.

Much of what Tiger Aw did, he did in competition with Tan Kah Kee. Hardly an account of the overseas Chinese is complete without a reference to Tan Kah Kee. Like Aw Boon Haw, he was a household name in Singapore, and like Aw, he published a newspaper, the famous *Nanyang Siang Pau* (the *Chinese Journal of Commerce*), but there the similarities ended. For one thing, Tan was Hokkien-speaking, and the rivalry between the two for the leadership of the Singapore overseas Chinese was as much personal as communal. For another, while Aw liked to live in a kingly style, there was nothing Tan abhorred more than making a splash.

Tan Kah Kee was a native of Chi Mei (Gathered Beauty), one of those villages, almost exclusively inhabited by the Tan clan, which specialized in sending its men abroad. Chi Mei lies on the tip of a peninsula which extends some miles out to sea opposite Amoy, the island port from which so many emigrants had set sail for Nanyang. It was always to occupy a special place in Tan Kah Kee's heart, and when the time came it was there that he was buried.

His father had left Chi Mei to join two elder brothers in Singapore before Tan Kah Kee was born. When Tan Kah Kee emigrated to Singapore in 1890 as a young man of seventeen, the elder Tan's business interests had already branched out from rice to tinned pineapples, and the young Tan was able to make himself useful in the family firm immediately. Between 1890 and 1903 he revisited Chi Mei twice, the first time to marry, and the second time to bury his mother, whose death he mourned, as was proper, for three years.[19] The elder Tan had meanwhile relinquished his control of the business, and on his return to Singapore in 1903 Tan Kah Kee was appalled to find it on the verge of bankruptcy. A concubine of the elder Tan and her adopted son were chiefly to blame; she was an addict of gambling, and he a good-for-nothing, and by their mismanagement and embezzlement the two had saddled the company with staggering debts. It was years before the creditors agreed to a settlement.

But the collapse of the family firm was not without its brighter side, for it freed Tan Kah Kee to strike out on his own. Left some start-up money by what remained of his father's business, he went into pineapple-canning, rubber-planting, rice-milling, banking and shipping, and thrust himself into the company of millionaires in seven years flat.[20] His tyre and rubber-shoe factories were enterprises of great success, and when W. G. A. Ormsby-Gore, the Parliamentary Under-Secretary of State for the Colonies, came to visit in 1928 he pronounced Tan's business empire to be one of the most remarkable in Asia, 'if not of the world'.[21] Though the Great Depression blighted his success, he really was what people called him, the Henry Ford of Malaya.

What did he do with all his money? He was an enthusiastic and generous benefactor to schools in Chi Mei and Singapore, and he endowed a university, the University of Amoy. If there was one practice he thought worthy of his pursuit, it was philanthropy; he parted readily with his money, and in his will left all his savings to causes and charities. It is said that not a single penny went to his family – 'wealth would impair the ambition of the wise,' he had said, 'and increase the follies of the foolish.'

He had a large family: four wives and seventeen children. His polygamy was nothing remarkable in the Singapore of his time, but it is matter for wonder when set against the other elements of his character. Most of the time he seemed all super-ego, a great disciplinarian of the passions. The last word one would use of Tan Kah Kee was 'immoderate'. He was sober of taste and Spartan of habit, and his own self-denial was unremitting. He was as incapable of having fun as any puritan, and he was sixty before he saw his first movie. Hardship, he was convinced, was good for one; it was what made one strive a little harder. When his fifth son began work as a trainee manager in the family business, Tan Kah Kee would not hear of him travelling to the office by motor car, but insisted that he get there by bus, and that he walk half a mile each day from his home to catch it. Nor, when the time came for the young man to marry, would the father agree to the choice of fiancée, on the grounds that the girl was a socialite fond of Western dancing.

He was not much of a family man, and though he maintained two homes, he spent fewer of his after-office hours there than at his club, the Ee Ho Hean (Happy and Harmonious Studio) on Bukit Pasoh Road; indeed, at one point he took to sleeping there, so much did his life revolve around the place. The reason it did was that Ee Ho Hean, a rich businessmen's club, was a nest of Hokkien community leaders and a centre of political activity. More than this, it was the repository of overseas Chinese nationalism, a sentiment which Tan Kah Kee came supremely to personify.

It was no more than natural for Tan Kah Kee to identify politically with the Chinese homeland; he was caught up in the gathering emotions of the nationalist tide, and he was no Westernized Baba. Speaking no English and denied a place in the upper circles of colonial Singapore, Tan must have felt the pull of China all the more keenly. In 1937, China's Nationalist (Kuomintang) government found itself at war with Japan, and Chinese both at home and abroad were stirred to resistance. 'Unity!' they were heard to shout, 'National Salvation!' and 'Resist the Enemy!' Many overseas Chinese returned to China to offer their skills to the Nationalist government. Others raised funds for the war chest. There were mass rallies. There were boycotts of Japanese goods. And it was people like Tan Kah Kee who led these movements. He was Chairman of a pan-Southeast Asia fund-raising body, the Southseas China Relief Fund Union, and as such he spoke for some eight million overseas Chinese.

Chiang Kai-shek, as the leader of the war of resistance, rose to a climax of prestige among the expatriate Chinese. But in Southeast Asia the line between the far left of the Kuomintang and the Communists was fuzzy, and the war made many a young overseas Chinese receptive to the rival appeal of the Marxist message. Tan Kah Kee, too, had reason to be curious about the Communists, for he had read, a year into the war, the Chinese translation of Edgar Snow's classic *Red Star Over China*, a highly sympathetic portrait of the Chinese Communist Party and the Red Army. In 1940, under the auspices of the Southseas China Relief Fund Union, Tan went on a comfort mission to China; and he was interested enough in the Communists to want to visit them in their lair in Yenan.

Far up the loess plateau in northern China, Yenan was more than a place on the map; it was the symbolic core of the Communist movement, the terminus of the Long March and the place where Mao Tse-tung and his fellow revolutionaries laid the foundations of the new China. One day to become a revolutionary shrine, it was the headquarters of Mao's struggle against the Japanese and Nationalist armies. The Nationalists had retreated to Chungking, to the southwest, and it was at that city that Tan Kah Kee made the first of his several stops on his tour of China.

He was dismayed by what he saw. Why, there were women in

tight-fitting dresses, high-heeled shoes and painted fingernails, and bars and restaurants filled to capacity. Instead of wartime austerity, he found frivolity and cupidity. Chiang Kai-shek did quite the wrong thing by inviting Tan and the rest of the comfort mission to a lavish European-style banquet. It was to be very, very different in Yenan, where, taking a plain meal with Mao, he was told by his host, 'We normally can't afford to buy chicken, this one is a gift from an old lady who lives nearby.'[22]

Yenan must have seemed the very epitome of the lifestyle Tan favoured: simple, frugal, disciplined. Edgar Snow, he discovered, was right: the Nationalists were corrupt and unreliable, the Communists were austere and patriotic. Mao would be China's saviour, not Chiang Kai-shek.

Back in Singapore, his views, which he made little effort to hide, disconcerted the British, who were themselves headed for a clash with the Malayan Communist Party, and about to have a local Communist insurgency on their hands. What complicated matters was that Tan Kah Kee was a naturalized British subject – he became one in 1916, when he went into shipping, for unless he was a British subject he could not register his vessels. The colonial authorities were confirmed in their suspicions when, shortly before the Communist triumph, Mao sent Tan a telegram inviting him to take part in forming the new government – this set a bad example, they thought, 'for Chinese in Malaya who do not distinguish as clearly as he does between the China [Chinese] Communist Party and the Malayan Communist Party'.[23] So far as the colonial authorities were concerned he was clearly a fellow traveller, and when he left for Peking in 1949, they considered stripping him of his British citizenship and denying him re-entry into Singapore.

He came back to Singapore an elected official of the People's Republic of China. In April of the following year he took leave of his family and left Singapore, alone, for good; he was a British subject still, and would remain so until he renounced his citizenship in 1957, but by throwing in his lot with Peking he had burnt his bridges, and there would be no going back. In Peking he was made a great fuss of, but it was in a corner of his beloved Chi Mei that he chose to make his home. He lived another eleven years, dying of a stroke in 1961, when he was eighty-seven. It was just as well, for had he lived another five years he would have seen the bitter breaking of his dream in the convulsions of the Cultural Revolution.

In Chi Mei, the house he lived in may be visited by any tourist. It is an attractive two-storeyed building, European in style, with here and there a stucco sprig. The set of rooms he occupied on the upper floor are now a museum. The furnishings are almost monastic in their simplicity: an old bed, a writing-desk, a washbasin, a chipped tooth-mug, two old trunks he had brought with him from Singapore, a saucer he used as a candlestick, a much mended mosquito net. His personal belongings are displayed, carefully labelled, in glass-fronted cupboards. The captions draw attention to his worn quilted waistcoat, his frayed woollen coat, even the enema he used to relieve constipation. No sightseer can be left in any doubt that he lived frugally. For his lunch and supper, we are told, he ate potato porridge, vegetables, beans, a little fish and, now and then, fried oysters, an Amoy speciality.

Could anyone have fitted more exactly the Chinese idea of the model emigrant? To the Chinese at home, he was everything that an overseas Chinese should be: conspicuously successful, philanthropic, frugal, above all patriotic. If ever there was an embodiment of overseas Chinese nationalism, it was Tan Kah Kee. Today he arouses mixed emotions in the Chinese in Southeast Asia, who, in their anxiety to be accepted as full citizens of their adopted country and to establish their bona fides as genuine settlers, do not wish to be identified with one who remained a Chinese to the last, giving his all to the mother country.

Of an altogether different breed was Loke Wan Tho, the youngest son of Loke Yew, the tin magnate of Chapter Seven. Loke Yew, who died in 1917 at the age of seventy, had four wives, two of them born in China, two in Malaya. A teenager when she married him, the fourth wife was the niece of the third.[24] She had time to give him three children, Wan Tho and his two sisters, before he died. It would be wrong to say that the young widow was left to find her own solutions, for great wealth was bequeathed to her and her children; but you had to admire the purposeful way in which she rose to the challenge of being a single parent.

Born in 1915 in Kuala Lumpur, Loke Wan Tho was two when his father died. His childhood was as normal as the childhoods of fatherless children ever are, with holidays by the sea, where he and his sisters learnt to swim by having old coconuts placed under their arms, and on the hill stations.[25] He was a sickly child, and did not go to school until he was twelve. He went to the Victoria Institution, a school run to an English pattern in Kuala Lumpur, but he had not been there for much more than a year when his mother decided to move their home to Switzerland, where the climate would suit his lungs better. They settled in Montreux, taking a house by Lake Geneva, and there they lived for four years, with a Chinese amah to do their cooking and a Swiss maid to do the cleaning.

Loke Wan Tho thrived in Switzerland, playing soccer for his school, the Chillon College, and winning the college's best all-round record for athletics.[26] At eighteen he went to England, where, as a student at Cambridge University, he chose to read English. It was only to be expected perhaps that he should doubt the wisdom of his choice, for as a beneficiary of his father's vast estate he was destined to become a businessman, and a course of study like the law might have been more appropriate; and yet try as he might – and he did try for the length of a whole Long Vacation Term – he could not interest himself in that subject.

Leaving Cambridge with an Honours degree in English and History in 1936, he proceeded to the London School of Economics, but war broke out, and he returned to Malaya before he completed his studies. For a home he chose, not Kuala Lumpur, where he would feel himself encumbered by his father's shadow, but Singapore, where fewer people would compare him to Loke Yew.

It was from there that, escaping the Japanese, he took ship for India in February 1942. A five-hundred-pound bomb from a Japanese aircraft sank the ship before it got very far, and because Loke was standing at a spot near where the ship was hit, he was seriously wounded, his skin charred, his eyes very nearly blinded. He managed to get on to a lifeboat, a blanket thrown over his head, and there the Australian cruiser *Sydney* found him some hours later, and rescued him. He would certainly have gone blind if a surgeon hadn't treated his eyes there and then. When the *Sydney* arrived in Jakarta, he was admitted to the central hospital with the rest of the wounded. His condition improved remarkably quickly, and after three weeks he made ready to leave, anxious to get out of Jakarta ahead of the arrival of the Japanese.

It was in India that he truly came into his own – not as the business magnate that everyone expected him to be (though he would be that too), but as a passionate bird-watcher. While in India he met and made a lifelong friend of the great Indian explorer and ornithologist Salim Ali, who invited Loke to join him on an expedition to Kutch. Kutch, Loke later wrote in his book *A Company of Birds*, published by Michael Joseph in 1958, 'was my first classroom'. Under Salim

Ali's guidance, his interest in birds 'which hitherto had been but of a dilettante kind blossomed into a deeper passion'.[27] They shared an intense camaraderie, spending months in the desert, sleeping and living rough, with only rice and dal and a few vegetables for their lunch and supper, and going half-and-half in a small bucketful of bath water.

If there was a moment at which his bird-watching interest started, it was probably that summer he rented a cottage in Pembrokeshire, in a cliff-girt corner of South Wales that looks across a bay to the Atlantic. Though bare of trees, the rock-faces there were tumultuous with bird-life – buzzards, ravens, herons, peregrines, sea birds of many kinds. He was absolutely captivated, the more so when the black and white plumage of a flock of oyster-catchers streaked vividly across the sky above the sea's blue waters.

Afterwards he was often to be found immersed in the study of birds, photographing them with immense patience and increasing expertise. Here at last was the fulfilment of his several enthusiasms, a confluence, as he was later to observe, of the 'love of books and the desire to write, a deep interest in photography, the pleasures of living in the country and visiting strange and out-of-the-way places, the taste for mild adventure'.[28] Kutch was a beginning; now, casting his eyes beyond the valleys towards the still grander landscapes of the Himalayas, he made for Kashmir. He was enchanted with the place, relishing the mountain scenery and the staggering profusion of flowers. He would love Kashmir always, and would return to it after the war.

In 1952, in what was the most difficult expedition he had ever attempted, he went to photograph the birds of the moss forests of New Guinea. There he tried himself to the utmost; later he wrote that the trails took him over some of the worst country he had ever seen, and that the phrase of the Australian troops who fought in New Guinea in the war – 'Up on your hands and knees, down on your bellies' – was an exact description of his method of progression. He kept exhaustive notes, and came back from his field trip with photograph upon photograph of exotic birds, the fruit of incalculable patience and dedication. 'So far as I am aware,' he wrote of a picture he published from that expedition, 'no other photograph exists which shows a bird of paradise at its nest.'[29]

By now he was married, and his wife Christina shared his fascination with ornithology. As the wife of the heir to the Loke fortune, she was a glamorous society figure, but it would be wrong to suppose that she did nothing but throw dinner parties; for she was an enterprising traveller and a keen bird-watcher, and published two books of bird photography herself.

For a collaborator she had Malcolm MacDonald, the Commissioner-General for the United Kingdom in Southeast Asia and son of Ramsay MacDonald. A more charming person seldom lived. He and the Lokes became very close, and this is not surprising, since they had obvious affinities with each other. Malcolm MacDonald wrote the foreword to Loke's *A Company of Birds*, and the two worked together on a book about Angkor. Later, Christina Loke's name was romantically linked to Malcolm MacDonald's, and as rumours rustled their way through Singapore, she and Loke Wan Tho were divorced in 1962.

All the time, through all the ups and downs of his personal fortunes, his business interests were expanding, and he was finding, perhaps a little to his surprise, that the role of the rubber, tin and property magnate was not uncomfortably beyond his capacities. He worked tremendously hard – for years he would be at his desk by five o'clock in the morning. And, far from dissipating the great wealth he inherited from his father, he successfully added to it, branching out into hotels and film studios, and a chain of cinemas in Singapore and Malaysia. At one point he had a studio producing Chinese films in Hong Kong and a studio producing Malay films in Singapore, and some sixty cinemas spread far and wide the name of his organization, Cathay. Loke Wan Tho's mother, who was quite a businesswoman herself, would have been happier if he had gone into real estate, but his interest in the cinema was a natural enough consequence of his enthusiasm for photography.

But he was no dilettante, toying with his business. The immigrant drive and determination do not often survive into the second or third generation, and if Loke Wan Tho had turned out to be a ne'er-do-well, a squanderer of his enormous inheritance, no one would have been surprised. And yet, though he seemed on paper to be cut out for a playboy's life, he was a man of sober habits, who believed happiness to be a by-product of achievement, and not an achievement in itself. A half-brother of his had died an unhappy man, after a wasted life spent pursuing pleasure, and this had aroused in Loke Wan Tho an almost pathological distaste for gambling and drinking.[30]

In 1963 he remarried in London. His bride was a Mavis Chew, a third-generation Hokkien Chinese from a distinguished banking family in Singapore. In June of the following year he and his wife of nine months went to Taiwan to attend the Eleventh Asian Film Festival, and when they were there they were among the fifty-odd passengers killed in an air crash somewhere near the heart of the island. All the papers in Singapore carried the news, and at the funeral parlour in Taipei there was no missing the memorial tablet – inscribed with the words OUTSTANDING CONDUCT IS IMPERISHABLE – sent by President Chiang Kai-shek. A condolence cable was received from Earl Mountbatten, Admiral of the Fleet in Britain. The ashes were taken back to Kuala Lumpur and carried in a cortège up the slope of the family plot, there to be buried, in a spot overlooked by the grave of Loke Yew.

What a world away he was from the likes of Loke Yew, with his scholarly bent and his gentle manner. He was the very antithesis of the archetypal overseas Chinese, the philistine and opportunist that Singapore's immigrant society might have made of him. As it was, the crassness of the trader class only threw his refinement into greater relief. He was exceptionally cultivated, and temperamentally he belonged, if he belonged in any company, more to the society of scholars and artists than to that of the Chinese businessman. His achievements in ornithology and bird photography were outside the usual canons of immigrant success, and his were not the interests one expected of an overseas Chinese, whose concerns were likely to be material, and who could only think of a bird-watcher as a bit of a crank.

Of his hobby he once wrote: 'In my own humble fashion I follow in the footsteps of those great artists of China who made the countryside and the birds a vehicle for their self-expression.'[31] But he was really an explorer and naturalist of the English kind, not Chinese. He was a product of the English gentleman's culture, and he was a great lover of English literature. While travelling to India with damaged eyesight during the war, 'it was the sonnets of Shakespeare', he recalled, 'which gave me an inner clarity of vision almost totally lacking in my clouded physical sight'.[32] And on his ornithological expeditions he would often relax with a book of English prose or poetry.

He found it a great deal easier to express himself in English than in Cantonese, and this marked him as a member of the class of Anglicized Straits Chinese that British rule had brought into being. Only, he possessed the characteristics of that breed to a much finer degree; he was their epitome. If Tan Kah Kee represented one extreme of the overseas Chinese spectrum, Loke Wan Tho represented another. You would not find his exact counterpart in China, which never came under European rule, and where Westernization, where it genuinely occurred, would naturally not be accompanied by deracination. He was a type created by transplantation.

CHAPTER TEN

Some of the Women

There are of course as many ways of classifying the women of the immigrant Chinese communities as of any settlement of people. To begin with, money was a great divider, separating the wives and daughters of the rich from all the others. Often one or more generations removed from their family's immigrant roots, these well-to-do leisured women lived lives of great ease and luxury, were usually surrounded by servants, and were denied little in the way of material satisfaction. But, motherhood apart, they were not offered many chances of personal fulfilment. Their place was in the home, and their contribution to the world was in their reproductive capacity. Each would have had her husband chosen for her by her elders, was usually in her teens when she went to him, and it was generally only a matter of time before she stood by while he took a concubine. And yet, though the ideal of womanhood in immigrant Chinese societies was in most ways the same as that which prevailed in the ancestral homeland, the very fact of her exposure to other cultures, the contrasts of style and manners afforded by her adopted country, made the moneyed overseas Chinese woman a different creature from her sisters in China. Standards were bound to be less absolute overseas, and, for all the restrictions of the feminine status, she could stand outside convention more easily than could her contemporary in the home country.

If these women represented one extreme of society, the *mui tsai*, literally 'little sister', a Cantonese euphemism for bond maidservant, represented the other. These were girls who had been born to impoverished families, prostitutes or unmarried mothers, and sold off to rich families to be brought up as unpaid domestic servants or as future concubines for the household's male masters. If she was lucky a mui tsai was kindly treated, looked upon as an adopted daughter and married off to a man of her owner's choice on reaching maturity, but many mui tsai were utterly at the mercy of their callous employers, and lived no better than slaves.

There was scarcely a well-to-do household in Hong Kong, Macao, Singapore or Penang that did not possess one or more such children.

The first batches of mui tsai had been brought over from the coastal provinces of southern China, where the buying and selling of female children was conducted as openly as any traffic.¹ Brokers handled the business, which, with its cases of decoy and kidnapping, had obvious affinities with the coolie trade. Women emigrants were in such short supply that the trade could not help but become a thriving business. The distinction between women sold into domestic service on the one hand, and into prostitution on the other, was at best uncertain, and it was not uncommon for girls initially purchased as mui tsai to be brought up to be singsong girls and to end up in brothels. It was almost always as mui tsai that prostitutes, bought for US$70–150 and sold for five to ten times their purchase price, were imported into America in the gold-rush days.²

These were all matters to engage the conscience of humanitarians and social reformers. Allegations of slavery in the British colony of Hong Kong attracted the attention of the Anti-Slavery Society and the Society for the Protection of Aborigines in Britain, and the frequent cases of kidnapping impelled local Chinese merchants and dignitaries into founding the Po Leung Kuk, the Society for the Protection of Women and Girls. At its inception in 1878 the chief concern of the society was to catch kidnappers bringing women and children into Hong Kong; to do so it employed two full-time detectives to hang around the waterfront to eavesdrop on conversations and look over the new arrivals.³ Girls were taken into its care and sent home to their parents or, if unclaimed, put up for adoption or married off into respectable Chinese families. In later years the Po Leung Kuk grew into a prestigious charitable association with a general concern for the welfare of girls and women in need of care and protection (and this remains its commitment today). It was a benevolent society in the old Chinese mould, presided over by prominent Chinese men who aspired to social recognition by their acts of philanthropy; indeed it was not until 1937, well over half a century after its creation, that the first woman was elected to its committee.⁴

It was never the Po Leung Kuk's intention to work for the suppression of the mui tsai system, only the abuses that stemmed from it. Indeed it was not until the League of Nations took an interest in child slavery in the late 1920s, and questions were asked in Parliament about the practice in British colonies, that moves were seriously made to abolish it. Legislation was passed to make the registration of all mui tsai compulsory, but it was easy enough for an owner to present a mui tsai as an adopted daugher, and who was to say that she was not? So the system continued, and we hear of a case of two girls, aged six and eleven, being sold by their parents to a housewife as domestic servants even as late as the early 1970s.[5]

It was the same in Singapore and Malaya. There, the Mui Tsai Bill of 1933 made registration compulsory, but the number that complied with the ruling was only a fraction of the whole. Singapore and Malaya also had a Po Leung Kuk, offering a refuge to mui tsai who had been ill-treated by their mistresses. It had been set up by the Protector of Chinese William Pickering in the same year as its namesake in Hong Kong, and had subsequently evolved into the Centre for the Rehabilitation of Prostitutes.[6] It was more than a shelter for the homeless; it aimed to turn 'bad' girls into 'good', and to equip them for a measure of economic independence by teaching them skills and even to read. Male immigrants too poor to marry in the proper way often applied to the Po Leung Kuk for a wife, and it was by this means that many an ex-mui tsai or reformed prostitute found a respectable place in society.

The most curious women to enter domestic service in the British colonies were the groups of Cantonese emigrants from the counties of Shuntak, Namhoi and Punyu (the Three Districts) in the silk-producing area of the Canton delta. Shiploads of these women came to Malaya, Singapore and Hong Kong in the 1930s. Unlike mui tsai, these women were paid domestic servants, commonly known as 'amah' to their white colonial employers, and marked off from all other categories of womanhood by their distinctive pigtail and *samfoo*, virginal white tunic and black trousers.

They were unmarried women, and this, their single status, was far and away the most significant fact about them. They were members of a sisterhood, sworn to celibacy. Known to themselves and to others as *saw hei*, 'combed', these women had taken vows before a deity, and had undergone a hair-combing ceremony, such as was traditionally conducted before a wedding, to symbolize their eschewal of cohabitation and marriage. If, under the old system of arranged marriage, they found themselves betrothed against their will, they would make it difficult for the marriage to be consummated by wrapping themselves up like a mummy under their bridal gowns before they set off for their wedding, and taking herbal drugs to stop themselves from urinating. To ward off the bridegroom's advances, some women were rumoured to resort to charms.

How had these curious practices arisen? First of all it was a local custom for a bride to separate from her bridegroom after the wedding and return to live with her parents for a period, usually three years, before settling in the husband's home.[7] Many women discovered during this period of customary separation that they would rather go on living the way they did than take up their wifely duties. To redeem themselves, they would work to earn the money to buy the husband a mui tsai as a concubine, and then remit money to support her and any children that might transpire. (Such a saw hei worked for my family in North Borneo; however hard my mother tried, she could not persuade her against sending all her savings to the two good-for-nothing sons born to her husband and the concubine she had bought for him, for technically and psychologically these sons were hers.) Others might strike a bargain with their in-laws to go away for a few years and work to support the husband and his family, and upon their return to bear no more than two or three children before abstaining altogether from sexual relations.[8]

Later the women rejected marriage altogether, becoming sworn spinsters. If forced to marry some of them would kill themselves, and one sometimes heard tell of saw hei sisters resorting to mass suicide to safeguard their chastity: an illustrated story-book I remember reading as a child depicted half a dozen winsome women throwing themselves off a cliff tied together by rope around their waists. Some women were married off to men who were on the point of death, or who were already dead, so that they could become mothers to sons adopted posthumously to carry on the family line. Others were married to absent men, emigrants who had gone abroad to work, and who were represented at the wedding by a white cockerel.

Fear of sex had something to do with the women's aversion to marriage, as had the ancient belief that pregnancy and childbirth were 'unclean'. In any case it was not difficult to find reasons for resisting matrimony, so patently did women get the rougher deal in a Chinese marriage; and it was partly their aversion to concubinage, and partly because they did not want to end up as mere breeding machines, that many saw hei set themselves against marrying. What was more, there were ecological reasons for staying unwed, an economic basis for the single status: the sisterhoods were a phenomenon of an area exceptionally rich in silkworks, a great employer of unmarried women, whose labour was needed in almost every phase of silk production, from cultivating the mulberry bushes and picking the leaves to getting the silk threads off the cocoons and spinning. Elsewhere in China employment opportunities for unattached women did not extend much beyond matchmaking, prostitution and midwifery, but here there was no shortage of work for them; indeed employees preferred their independence to the family ties that entrammelled married women with children.

For the most part they lived away from home, in the *nu-wu* or Girls' House, a sort of hostel-cum-recreation centre organized entirely by women. Girls from these houses in Shuntak were often to be seen going out together in comradely groups, to enjoy themselves at theatrical performances put on during important religious festivals, or to offer their devotions in the places of worship in the surrounding hills. One place to which they were drawn was the Vegetarian Hall, which housed the adherents of certain semi-secret sects allied in some way to a religion called The Great Way of Former Heaven, and to the Buddhist faith. The subject of government suppression historically, these sects were obliged to pose as Buddhist establishments and to find a sanctuary in hilly out-of-the-way places. Women were especially drawn to them, for these institutions cherished sexual equality – at prayer men and women sat together, a custom that raised eyebrows elsewhere – and their loftiest diety was a mother goddess. To the goddess, it was popularly believed, were bonded many local children born with 'bad' fates – for 'bad', one could usually read 'non-marrying'. A 'non-marrying' fate is one in which one's predestined partner – the person one marries over and over again in different incarnations – happens not to be alive at the same time, or not to be of a marriageable age, or of the wrong sex.

There is no doubt that the saw hei's thinking was deeply coloured by these notions, expressed in tracts and other forms of religious literature. There were the Golden Treasuries of model women's biographies – which the women, taught reading by a tutor who regularly called at the Girls' House, would study together in groups. If they needed any reassurance that they were right to remain single, such books provided it powerfully; among other things they said that men could not be trusted, and that suicide was perfectly honourable if it was committed in the cause of one's purity. They tell of Kuan Yin, the goddess of mercy, becoming a nun over her parents' objections, deeming herself better off for not having a husband to demand her devotion, a mother-in-law to dominate her, and children to tie her down. It was impurity that they must guard against, the polluting effects of childbirth, a sin for which the mother was punished after death by being sent to a 'bloody pool' filled with birth fluids, and from which they could only be rescued by ritualistic observances. Women 'taint Heaven and Earth', declared one Golden Treasury, when they give birth to babies; 'When you are a man's wife . . . you cannot avoid the blood-stained water . . . and the sin of offending the Sun, Moon and Stars, the Three Brightnesses.'⁹ There is only one way of bringing about an improvement in one's destiny, of attaining the Buddhist paradise or achieving rebirth as a man in the next life, and that is by practising celibacy.

There were advantages to celibacy even in this existence; once you became a sect member, you could attain a position of responsibility, even of complete authority, in a Vegetarian Hall, and you could take up permanent residence there if you wished, without having to appear like a nun – without, that is, having to shave your head or don religious habit. You might even acquire a 'family', a line of disciples to honour your memory and to worship you as an 'ancestor' after your death. And you became privy to esoteric methods of self-protection, so useful to one who travelled freely about the countryside without the benefit of male company, risking hazards like rape.

There was a sense of fellowship in much of what the members did; the ones who reckoned they were born with 'bad' fates, for example, would make a point of worshipping the Mother Goddess together on ceremonial occasions, and it was common for pairs or groups of women to seal their friendship with an oath, becoming sworn sisters. They did not like to publicize these arrangements among people not of their persuasion; sisterhoods were private affairs, to be kept from the world as much as possible; it does not surprise us to learn that, among themselves, they had 'an emblematical, or enigmatical, method of communication'.¹⁰ If this seems self-defensive, it was probably because, with their unconventional intimacies, they came in for a certain amount of gossip; inevitably, some of the more passionate friendships were lesbian relationships (called *mo tofu*, 'grinding beancurd', after the two flat slabs of Chinese grindstones used in making beancurd). One hears tell also of dildos made of expandable raw silk.

Since, as unattached women, they only had themselves to look to for care and support, mutual assistance among 'sisters' was a habit early developed, and something greatly counted on in old age. Among themselves, they laid careful plans for their retirement, old age and death, setting up a death-benefit club to which they made monthly payments against future funeral expenses, for instance, or contributing to funds for emergency assistance to distressed sisters. Many of them saved up to build a retirement home together; others put money aside either to buy into a Vegetarian Hall or to pay for a place in a retirement home. This last, called a Spinsters' House, might come with a bit of farmland on which the retirees could cultivate some of their food.

Some women retired early to these homes in the 1930s, when the villages were plunged into the hardships and uncertainties of a slump, when filatures closed down and there was not enough work to go round. The young silk workers drifted into the cities to find work as domestic servants. Large numbers emigrated. To make matters worse there was the threat of war and the Japanese occupation of Canton. Colonial Malaya, though similarly hit by the Depression and widespread unemployment, soon found itself at the receiving end of a huge inflow of Cantonese women (from Shuntak particularly) – 190,000 female deck passengers between the ages of eighteen and forty landed in the five years between 1933 and 1938, it has been estimated.[11] An Aliens Ordinance passed by the colonial government in 1933 had imposed a quota on male immigration, but the door to female immigration remained open until 1938, when the strains of continuing unemployment obliged the government to stem the tide of female immigration as well. Until this happened, unattached women were encouraged to emigrate by their families, who frankly saw them as a source of remittances; and by ticket brokers who, to fill their ships, would sell the much sought-after quota tickets only if their customers bought three or four of the cheaper, non-quota passages.[12]

As unattached women, these immigrants had to find their own means of livelihood; they found it, naturally enough, in paid domestic service. Chinese women were few in Malaya and Singapore before the late 1920s and 1930s, and when wealthy Chinese ladies or colonial European masters rang for their 'cookboy' or 'houseboy', it was invariably a Hainanese man who appeared. But following the mass immigration of the women, the popularity of female Cantonese domestics, whether as 'house amahs' or 'baby amahs', became quickly apparent. There was no missing them in the parks, where they were often to be found in the afternoons pushing the prams of their blonde European charges. In some households the saw hei worked singly; in others they worked in pairs. To be an amah was for them not just a job but a calling, and the best of them commanded high salaries, better than what they would get if they worked as waitresses, cashiers or hairdressers.[13]

While working as live-in servants, they organized themselves, along sisterhood, dialect, occupational or village lines, into clubs and guilds and, by pooling wages, rented communal living quarters (called kongsi) rather as they did in their home province. These lodgings varied greatly in size, from mere cubicles to elaborate club-houses. In the 1930s a rash of Vegetarian Halls sprang up too, to offer support of one kind or another, including help with arranging funeral rites and burial. There was no worse fate than to find oneself destitute and alone in old age, with nowhere to end one's days but in those indescribably sad places called 'death houses', where one awaited one's death like the inmates of hospices in the West. The ones in Singapore excited enough morbid curiosity to become tourist attractions. It was to guard against such a fate that the amahs adopted children – girls rather than boys because daughters were thought more filial – obtaining them (at a price which ranged from a nominal US$5 to US$350 in 1954) from unmarried mothers, traffickers or impoverished families. In some instances it was the Vegetarian Hall, or the kongsi, which adopted the children, rather than the individual woman. But by no means did every adopted daughter live up to the hopes of the foster mother, or to the expectation that she would carry on the tradition of remaining unmarried. Even among the saw hei themselves there were those who broke their vows of celibacy once they found themselves in Singapore and Malaya, where men far outnumbered women; but for every 'sister' who succumbed to temptation, many more remained spinsters, firm in their view that 'if a woman marries and her husband becomes wealthy, he takes a concubine; if poor, he sends his wife out to work'.[14]

These women are cloaked in the anonymity of their kind, and we see them as a group, not as people with individual identities; if there were singular women among them, we do not hear of them. Immigrant Chinese communities in those days were not rich in female celebrities, and, of those who enjoyed some fame or notoriety in their own time, not very many are still remembered by name.

One who became known far outside her home town was Madame Wellington Koo, the second daughter of the fabulously wealthy Oei Tiong Ham, the Sugar King of Java. Thanks partly to her mother, Oei Hui-lan became a part of the international *haut monde* in the inter-war and post-war periods. Her mother, whose family had been ten generations in Java, was given to her father in marriage the moment she turned fifteen. While she bore him two daughters, she failed to give him a son, and her travails began and ended with that fact. What was more, the two were unsuited in many ways, he so sensual, she so frigid, and the casual ease with which Oei hopped from one concubine to the next certainly did not add to the domestic happiness. The daughters were a solace, and she was gratified to see them flower into beauties. One thing they must not be was ordinary. Hui-lan could not have been more than three years old when her mother hung a gold necklace with a chunky eighty-carat diamond around her neck. It was no wonder that she developed dizzyingly expensive tastes, and later the look of her – the glow and sparkle of her jewels, the stylishness of her couturier clothes, the unembarrassed opulence of her full-length mink coats and ermine capes, the tiny Pekinese worn like a fur on her arm – reflected those tastes. She was brought up in spectacular luxury, attended by countless servants and sheltered from every adversity. She grew up with the profligacy of the very wealthy, and she hardly thought first of cost or trouble when she demanded anything.

Living in Java, she learnt to speak several languages. Her family tongue was Hokkien, but as a child she spoke to her father in Malay, her nurse's language and the very first one she picked up. She learnt Javanese from the servants, Dutch from some of the girls she played with, Mandarin Chinese when she visited Peking, French from her sister's imported Parisian maid, and English from her British governess, a Miss Jones whose copies of *Tatler*, sent all the way to Java by surface mail from London, she regularly devoured. She never went to school, but her mother, who had ambitions for her, saw to it that by the time her tutors had finished with her Hui-lan possessed all the polish of a European sophisticate.

Travel added to her education. When she was fifteen or sixteen her mother decided to move to London, where she bought a mansion in Wimbledon filled with English antique furniture, and a house in Brooke Street, near the celebrated hotel Claridge's. They lived in considerable style, maintaining a Rolls-Royce and a Daimler, and when, every now and then, Mrs Oei sent her husband a telegram saying 'Send four', he would know to remit £4,000. No Chinese flapper had more fun than Hui-lan, finding her beaux and dancing partners among English earls and baronets. The mothers of her escorts did not approve of her, but then she did not admire them either – 'Their jewels were small and insignificant,' she recalled, and their husbands 'were often frightened pompous old bores – nothing, compared with Papa'.[15]

Her mother was absolutely determined that she should marry well. With very rich families it is not always easy to find a suitable partner

within the limited permutations of acceptability that their circumstances demand. Hui-lan's sister married a Chinese from a good family
in Indonesia, a young man who had been educated in Holland; but
Hui-lan, everyone thought, could do better. In 1919, a match presented
itself. A member of the Chinese delegation to the peace talks in
Versailles had seen Hui-lan's picture at her sister's flat in Paris and
asked to meet her. No sooner did her mother hear this than she was
packing her suitcases for Paris. On their arrival the sister gave a
dinner party, where the nineteen-year-old Hui-lan found herself seated
next to the thirty-two-year-old Wellington Koo. Born in Shanghai,
Koo had been a brilliant student at Columbia University and was
now a rising star in the Chinese diplomatic service. He is the one
of whom this well-known apocryphal story is told. At a banquet an
American gentleman seated next to him asked, by way of making
polite conversation, 'You likee soupee?' The perfect diplomat, Koo
merely smiled and nodded. Later in the evening he was introduced as
the chief speaker of the occasion and got up to deliver a brilliant talk on
international affairs. Returning to his seat to the sound of enthusiastic
applause, he turned to his neighbour and said, 'Likee speechee?'

A British newspaper was later to write of him that 'there is no
diplomat of the Western world who can surpass him in poise and
suavity',[16] but at their first meeting Hui-lan thought he lacked dash.
Yet he charmed her as the evening wore on, and, perhaps more importantly, Hui-lan's mother found him everything that she desired in a
son-in-law. His family in Shanghai was of middling means, neither
poor nor rich, but much could be forgiven a man who would become,
successively, Ambassador to the Court of St James, France, and the
United States. One could live grandly anywhere in the world, if one
was as rich as Oei Hui-lan, one could dress in the extreme of fashion and
finery and buy yet more expensive jewellery, but one had to be Madame
Wellington Koo to attend state functions at Buckingham Palace, the
White House and the Elysée Palace. Wealth could not wholly overcome
the taint of the provincial which overseas Chinese still bore in the eyes
of the metropolitans, who regarded their Nanyang cousins rather as
true-blue Englishmen regarded Australians and Canadians. It was only
as the wife of a high-placed Chinese official that Hui-lan could truly
come into her own.

She thrived in Peking, where her second son was born and where
they lived in a magnificent two-hundred-room palace lent to Koo by
a government official who had fallen out of favour. Not entirely happy

with the idea of living in a borrowed house, she made her father buy it for her, and pay for all the renovations at the same time. During their postings abroad she and her husband lived in a style which no civil servant's salary could have paid for, and it was patently clear that when there was not enough Chinese government money to cover their expenses, she used her own. She did so willingly, for she knew that appearances mattered, and, at a time when Western nations were all too eager to abase China, she was convinced that the attention she attracted by her gems and finery could only redound to the advantage of her country's image. She was proud of the fact that her bedroom in Washington was photographed in colour by *Life* magazine; it had green doors, mauve walls, a vivid blue ceiling and a Chinese bed whose pieces, taken apart for shipping, it took a man nine hours to reassemble.

Hers was a marriage in a truer sense than her mother's, in that each of the partners had something to give to the other, she her wealth, he his status; but it proved no less troubled in the end. In the end it came down to the same old Chinese pattern: her husband found himself another woman, a concubine – was there not always a concubine? Hui-lan had to come to terms with this, as with the toll that time, change and war took of her inheritance. In her apartment in New York, where she lived alone at last after a full life of running households with servants, she would cast many a backward glance to the days when life was more glamorous. It did not seem all trumpery, but she did not pass the shrinking years repining over vanished splendour either. In her memoirs she shows herself to be much interested in the occult. She had always been extremely fond of dogs, and it was with the hope that she would one day meet up with her reincarnated Pekinese puppies – 'my canine children' – that she ended one of her autobiographies.

Something else she held in concern was how the Chinese were perceived in the West: 'Does my husband shuffle along like a coolie? Am I a little doll with bound feet?' she once challenged a French diplomat at a dinner party in Paris just before the Second World War. The greatest honour we can confer on people is to see them as they are, but that is harder than one might imagine. There are such things as stereotypes, all the more pernicious for having some truth to them. The China Doll and the Dragon Lady never really existed as such, except in the imaginations of Western men and women; but once invented, they took on a life of their own. And when a Western man looked at a Chinese woman, all too often it was the image rather than the reality that he saw. Hollywood was a

powerful purveyor of such images. One who achieved early celebrity
by embodying the China Doll and the Dragon Lady was Oei Hui-lan's
contemporary, Anna May Wong. Not many people will have heard of
her today, but Anna May Wong was the first Chinese woman to project
the image of the Mysterious East on the American screen.

She was born Huang Liu-shuang in 1907 in Los Angeles, the daughter of a Chinese laundry man from Toishan, and the second of seven
children.[17] Growing up and coming to maturity with the first onrush
of Hollywood chinoiserie, she appeared in a succession of movies with
an oriental theme. She was discovered when she was about fifteen or
sixteen, and made her début in a silent movie starring the Japanese
actor Sessue Hayakawa. She was seen as a Chinese Madame Butterfly
in an early foray into Technicolor called *The Toll of the Sea*, and then,
from a part as a slave girl in *The Thief of Baghdad*, she rose to some
fame in the 1930s. But if she is remembered at all, it is for her role
as Hui Fei, a Chinese courtesan, in Josef von Sternberg's *Shanghai
Express*.[18]

Hui Fei shares a compartment on the Peking-Shanghai express with
Shanghai Lily, played by Marlene Dietrich. Shanghai Lily's one-time
lover, British officer Clive Brook, happens to be travelling on the same
train and the central drama of the film is the story of their reconciliation.
The journey is interrupted by a Chinese bandit who molests Hui Fei and
then makes a play for Shanghai Lily. To stop him harming her lover,
Shanghai Lily offers to be his mistress. But Hui Fei steps in as her
guardian angel and stabs the bandit to death. The lovers are reunited,
as the train resumes its journey.

Shanghai Express was a lavish production using a thousand Asian
extras. The sets, the opening credits with a hand brushing Chinese
characters, smoke curling round a dragon, a gong being struck, evoke
a China rooted less in reality than in von Sternberg's fantasies. Anna
May Wong was meant to contribute to that image of oriental mystique.
She speaks little, and presents the picture of Chinese inscrutability.
The early sequences show her descending silently from a palanquin
carried through the throng of Peking's railway station, then settling
into a compartment by herself to smoke and play patience. Until her
hands are seen in close-up drawing a heavily bejewelled dagger out of
her bag, she seems so impassive that one suspects her of a total lack of
feeling. The full range of her hidden emotions is only discovered when
she creeps up behind the bandit and murders him. When Shanghai Lily
says to her, 'I don't know if I ought to be grateful to you or not,' she

answers coolly, 'It's of no consequence, I didn't do it for you. Death cancelled his debt to me.' And goes on smoking and playing patience, ever the inscrutable oriental.

The film was an enormous success, and is still something of a cult movie today. But Anna May Wong was to become a prisoner of her star personality, and what she had started simply could not be kept up for long without the audience tiring of it. The fad passed, and she was forgotten. In 1936 she made a trip to China, but it did not give her career the boost that she had hoped for. Many Chinese felt insulted by the racialist overtones of her films, and in Hong Kong she had to call a press conference to mollify their sense of outrage. Among left-wing Chinese the reaction to *Shanghai Express* was particularly hostile, and on its opening night in Shanghai itself, a well-known actor and director went up to the screen to stop it in mid-run, a dramatic protest followed by a student demonstration outside the theatre.[19]

Toughness was a quality displayed by many immigrant women, rising to the challenge and burdens of their expatriation. One of the toughest of all was a New World frontierswoman, remembered today as China Mary, who arrived as a fifteen-year-old in Sitka, Alaska, in 1895, and died a citizen of the United States in 1958. Sitka was a pioneer settlement peopled by Tlinglit Indians, Russians, Swedes, Norwegians, Finns, English and Chinese. Mary was its (and perhaps Alaska's) first Chinese woman. She had set about things with a down-to-earth Chinese calculation, deciding that she was going to have one Ah Bong for a husband, and then, having contrived this, taking over the running of his bakery and restaurant. But she was far more than a mere restaurant manager. Not only did she pick up the language of the Tlingit Indians, but, having had two daughters of her own, she helped their women to deliver their babies, and learnt from them the art of making silver trinkets.

Ah Bong died in 1902 and for five years Mary supported herself and her children, then six and one, by doing housework; for reasons we will not now know she no longer had the restaurant. When she remarried it was to Fred Johnson, a miner of Swedish-Finnish descent. For a time she joined him in the mines, shovelling gold ore and handling blasting powder. Nothing seemed to faze her; when she broke a finger so that the bone stuck out through the skin, she simply drew the skin over the bone and sewed up the wound. Later she and her new husband earned their living variously, sometimes precariously, as dairymen, prospectors, trappers, trollers and fox farmers. Every venture was a struggle, life was bitterly hard in Alaska, but for doggedness and resilience nobody could beat China Mary. She was the first woman troller in Sitka, and she trolled alone, little daunted by rough wind or water. Even when the weather kept everybody in, Mary would be out there in her boat; she would be 'all smiles' when she returned with her catch, 'but were the faces of the other trollers red!' During her fox-farming days she wielded a gun to keep poachers at bay, and we find her still working at seventy – as the Matron of the federal jail in Sitka.[20] From her portrait she looks out, very steady of eye, with a gentle yet unmistakable air of determination, wearing a Manchu dress of embroidered brocade, and deceptively appearing, with her dainty hands and ladylike pose, as though she would not be adept at the rougher kinds of work.

She never did prosper. But what else might she have done? One fate she escaped when she bought a passage for Vancouver was that of the wives left behind, those grass widows who could see off their husbands and then not set eyes on them again for a decade. They had remittances and letters to solace them, it was true, but upheavals like war and changes in immigration law could cut these off too. How many forlorn hours these wives must have endured, even as heartsickness receded with new worries and distractions, the tyrannies of mothers-in-law and the burdens of motherhood. 'Don't marry your daughter to a Gold Hills boy,' said a folk rhyme still heard in the village today:

> He will not be in bed one full year out of ten.
> Spiders spin webs on top of her bed,
> While dust covers fully one side.[21]

CHAPTER ELEVEN

Trojan Horse?

By the early to mid-1950s the wife left behind in China was one of about eight and a half million souls – six and a half in Kwangtung, two in Fukien – dependent on money sent home by emigrants to their relatives in China.[1] Remittances came for the support of parents, wives or children; for importing Chinese products for sale in the adopted country; for investment in enterprises at home; and very often, if the emigrant had made good abroad, for the express purpose of building himself a monument – a new house, an ancestral hall, a grave, a school or a bridge – to inspire the admiration of his fellow villagers. *Yang-lou*, foreign-style homes, were inescapable in the sending villages, displaying such features of their Western prototype as swimming-pools (water for which had none the less to be pumped from a nearby fish-pond where buffaloes took their baths) and sofas, and quickly elevating their owners into public esteem.[2] Foreign influence came in the guise of radios, coffee, orange squash, Siamese turbans, Malay velvet caps and Western hats.[3]

Added up, overseas Chinese remittances amounted to a considerable sum, averaging US$80–100 million a year between 1929 and 1941, and providing, during some years before the war, enough foreign exchange to offset China's massive balance of payments deficits.[4]

A century before, the enormous asset represented by the overseas Chinese had gone unrecognized. The Manchu government had been dismissive of their remittance, as is apparent from this conversation between a Chinese viceroy and a Captain Dupont, the representative of the American plenipotentiary, in 1858:

'Your people on the farther shore of the Pacific', observed Dupont, 'are very numerous, numbering several tens of thousands.'

'When the emperor rules over so many millions,' the Viceroy answered, 'what does he care for the few waifs that have drifted away to a foreign land?'

'Those people are, many of them, rich, having gathered gold in our mines. They might be worth looking after on that account.'

To this the Viceroy replied, 'The emperor's wealth is beyond com-
putation; why should he care for those of his subjects who have left
their home, or for the sands they have scraped together?'[5]

The Son of Heaven was wrong about his overseas subjects, of course;
for within one short generation just the part they sent home from
the sands they had scraped together was running each year to tens
of millions of Spanish dollars. Now the remittances were a kind of
foreign aid to the government – staunch the flow, and the economies of
Kwangtung and Fukien would feel the ill-effects almost immediately.

How to keep the funds flowing was a matter of concern to the
successive Chinese governments, Manchu, Nationalist (Kuomintang)
and Communist. As the Manchus saw it, Chinese wherever born
and wherever resident were Chinese subjects. Their allegiance to the
Emperor of China was held to be indissoluble, and to keep them from
falling under foreign dominion a nationality law, based on the principle
of *jus sanguinis*, was passed in 1909 making a Chinese citizen of anyone
born of a Chinese father or a Chinese mother.[6] The Kuomintang
regime, which inherited this law, and which was to continue to apply
it in Taiwan after it was driven off the Chinese mainland by the
Communist forces in 1949, was the keenest of the three governments
to retain its expatriate following, and this is not surprising, since in
many ways it was itself a creation of the overseas Chinese, ushered
into being by the diaspora's patriotic donations.

The Nationalists had made it a cornerstone of their overseas Chinese
policy to promote the Chinese language (specifically the Mandarin
dialect) and Chinese education in the immigrant communities – 'Without Chinese education,' it had declared, 'there can be no overseas
Chinese.'[7] The animosity felt by one dialect group against another did
not disappear with the introduction of Mandarin as the *lingua franca*
of all emigrants, but just to be able to talk to each other was a big
step forward. And it was in the classroom that the expatriate's political
loyalties to China and the Kuomintang were engendered and nurtured.
From about 1920 large numbers of teachers arrived from China to teach
the children of Chinese immigrants in the countries of Southeast Asia, to
indoctrinate them, and to mobilize their nationalism. The schools were
what kept the overseas Chinese communities Chinese, generation after
generation, and narrowed the political vision of the residents abroad
to what was happening at home, in metropolitan China.

There a nationalist revolution had brought the Kuomintang Party into
power, but the regime, lacking cohesion to begin with, was to be

increasingly challenged by Japanese militarism and by domestic Communism. Set against the sweep of the social revolution that was eventually to overtake China, the Nationalists seem in retrospect to be a power out of its historical depth. Yet in the late 1920s the country's future seemed to belong to the Kuomintang; the Chinese Communist Party, once a left-wing appendage, had been excised from it and consigned, or so it would seem, to the dustbin of history. In 1937, the eight-year war of resistance against the invading Japanese forces began. That year the Kuomintang and the Communists agreed on a united front alliance against the common enemy, but all the time Mao Tse-tung was advancing his own cause, riding the fervent wave of national resistance to expand his bases of popular support. On the surface it was a united front; underneath the Kuomintang and the Communists fought on two fronts: against the Japanese invader, and against each other.

The political life of the overseas Chinese communities was animated by the same concerns, by identical rivalries. Until the inter-war period, when the world Depression staunched the torrent of Chinese emigration, the expatriate communities in Southeast Asia were continually refreshed by the flow of newcomers, and it would be strange if these communities, made up as they were of a large proportion of first-generation immigrants, were indifferent to the goings-on in China. Nationalism transplanted successfully among such people, and when the war of resistance began, few answered the call to 'save the mother country' with greater alacrity than the overseas Chinese, or gave more generously to the war chest. And when the Japanese invaded Southeast Asia, the overseas Chinese were, with the Filipinos, the only people (until late in the war) to offer real resistance.[8] The outstanding example was Malaya, which of all the adoptive territories had the highest proportion of Chinese immigrants: about forty per cent of the population in 1931, surpassing the Indians (the other big immigrant community) by as much as eighteen per cent, and even the indigenous Malays by about five.[9] Not many thought they were in Malaya for life, and yet if the mass of Chinese were transients, an active minority was forging a Malayan Chinese nationalism of its own.

When the Japanese Army invaded Malaya, it was to the Chinese, whose contributions to the war effort in the Chinese homeland it much resented, that it showed its most brutal side; neither the Malays nor the Indians were as harshly treated. Under the Japanese the Malays came off best, many of them were offered the chance to fill senior posts in government service, something the British had denied them. The

Chinese, on the other hand were the ones who most fiercely resisted Japanese rule, organizing an active guerrilla campaign and meting out summary justice to those suspected of collaborating with the enemy, mostly Malays.[10] This the Chinese remembered, when in the chaotic aftermath of war old scores were settled. It is perhaps digressive though instructive to observe, in view of all that was to follow, that the two races could not have demonstrated their animosities more explicitly. Blood flowed in rounds of communal killings; in one instance, Malays attacked and massacred forty Chinese villagers, mostly women and children; nor were the Chinese slow to exact their vengeance.[11] The ill-feeling between the two communities, already strong, was to harden two decades later into racial antipathy.

The struggle against the occupying army, then, was largely a Chinese struggle; it was carried out by the Malayan People's Anti-Japanese Army, an almost entirely Chinese body of which the Malayan Communist Party (MCP) formed the nucleus. Communism had been introduced to Malaya by the radicals of the Kuomintang Party, and had found its most enthusiastic adherents among the Hainanese, one of the lesser dialect groups, whose members earned their livings as rubber tappers, domestic servants, cobblers, carpenters, seamen and mechanics.[12] As a people down at the bottom of the social heap, the Hainanese understandably harboured a strong sense of grievance; among them the Communist organizers of labour successfully exerted their influence. No one, it seemed, had a mind to mobilize the Malay or Indian workers, so that, for all its ideological emphasis on proletarian solidarity across ethnic lines, the Communist movement was by and large a Chinese – even a chauvinist – affair.

The white man's defences having crumbled before the invading army, it was the Communists who continued the struggle against the Japanese. That they should work with the British officers who remained in the jungle to harass the enemy, or who were parachuted into Malaya or secretly landed by submarine, seemed natural enough. That the British should train them in jungle warfare and supply them with modern weapons was equally unremarked; the irony only struck one some years later, when, with the Japanese gone and the British restored to power, the Communists used those very weapons to try and free Malaya of its white colonial masters.

For their food and other provisions, for local intelligence and sometimes recruits, the Communist guerrillas depended on the squatter population, Chinese peasants living off the land on the fringes of the jungle. Some of these had been driven there by mass unemployment in the tin mines and plantations during the Depression of the early 1930s, others by the brutalities of the Japanese military. In the power vacuum left by the Japanese surrender, the only local authority of any kind was the MCP and the Malayan Races Liberation Army it shortly set up; and it proved fairly easy for the Communists to enlist the support of the squatters when they turned their energies from anti-Japanese resistance to anti-British insurgency. Some squatters were genuinely sympathetic to the cause and gave their support voluntarily; others were bullied or coerced into it.

The protracted armed struggle, which began in mid-1948 with a series of seemingly random murders and attacks, came to be known as the Malayan Emergency, and its perpetrators as CTs, short for Communist Terrorists. Though the back of it was broken by the mid-1950s, it was to drag on for twelve long years; and there were times when the British could never really be sure whether their Chinese grocer, or indeed the houseboy serving them an after-dinner cigar, was a Communist sympathizer or not. But bit by bit the guerrillas were cut off from their supply lines, a process set in train by a vast operation – the Briggs Plan – involving the forcible regrouping of the squatter settlements into fenced-in camps guarded night and day by the police. Subjected to constant and often harsh military surveillance, the evacuees were prevented from giving help to the Communists. The Briggs Plan dealt the Communist guerrillas a blow from which they would never recover, and in time drove their cause to the brink of extermination. Surrounded by rotting vegetation in their jungle hide-outs, the guerrillas were driven to live on bananas, tapioca, snake and elephant meat. Cheroots made of papaya leaves took the place of cigarettes. Dysentery and malaria ravaged bodies already debilitated by hunger. Gradually, the Communist ranks were thinned out by offers of amnesty and outright bribery; many top-ranking cadres surrendered or defected. The last six hundred men found a sanctuary in the jungle on the Thai side of the border, and there they lurked until November 1989, when the guiding genius of the MCP, Chin Peng, emerged from his hiding-place in Peking to negotiate an end to the guerrilla campaign.[13]

Chin Peng, alias Ong Boon Hwa, is a hero figure whom in earlier, friendlier days a British colonel had described as 'Britain's most trusted guerrilla'.[14] For his help to British guerrillas during the war, he was awarded the Burma Star by Lord Louis Mountbatten, and sent to

represent the Malayan guerrillas in the Victory Parade past King
George VI.[15] Photographs of the man show him dressed in a white
shirt and khaki shorts, his face split by a melon-slice of a grin, his
demeanour gentle. He had visited China in 1945 and 1946, and one
might suppose from this that he was a Peking lackey.[16] But not a bit
of it; he was his own man, and it was Malaya he identified with, not
China.

The Chinese revolution no doubt inspired him, and it could not have
been mere coincidence that the overseas Chinese Communist bid for
power through armed insurrection in Southeast Asia was at its most
ambitious in the early years of Communist rule in China; and yet there
is no hard and fast evidence for the popular theory that the MCP was
a creature of Peking, or that the revolutionary outbreaks in Southeast
Asia were part of a revolutionary conspiracy directed by the People's
Republic of China. The British government did not, apparently, see
the overseas communities in Malaya and Singapore as 'potential arms of
Peking', or as 'part of a generalized Chinese threat in the area',[17] but the
proposition that China was 'exporting' its revolution to Southeast Asia
through the medium of the immigrant Chinese nevertheless enjoyed
a currency beyond the circles of Red Scare alarmists. The Malayan
insurgency was a gift to these alarmists, for it allowed them to represent
the overseas Chinese as potentially or in fact a Fifth Column, a Trojan
Horse insinuated into the countries where they had settled to bring
about those countries' downfall. It seemed to confirm suspicions that
the Yellow Peril was also a Red Peril, that race and ideology, Chinese
and Communist, were one and the same.

It was to China that captured diehard Communists were deported –
between 1950 and 1952 nearly ten thousand Chinese were repatriated.[18]
In his book on the Emergency, *The War of the Running Dogs*, Noël
Barber gives a description of one boatload of deportees to Swatow:
'2,000 CTs – men, women, even some children, festooned with a few
worldly possessions they had been able to bring with them: pots and
pans, bicycles, parcels, tattered suitcases, prams – and something else,
unseen until each deportee had crossed the gangplank . . . one after
another [they pulled out] hidden paper flags – of the kind children
wave on royal occasions – bearing in blazing red the hammer and
sickle . . . [then they] started crying slogans . . .'[19]

China received a massive infusion of Malayan returnees in the first
half of the 1950s, not just deported Communists, but draft dodgers and
enthusiasts for the new regime.[20] Something had happened towards the

end of 1950 to occasion a mass exodus of Chinese youths to Singapore, Hong Kong and mainland China: much to the horror of the Chinese in Malaya, conscription of young men between the ages of eighteen and twenty-four for military or paramilitary service was introduced. At its height the outflow averaged about one thousand Chinese a month. It only went to show, sceptical Malays were quick to point out, that they were right to question the loyalties of the overseas Chinese.

They were seen to be people of doubtful loyalty, ever susceptible to metropolitan Chinese calls for everyone to 'join together in patriotic unity'. This made them inherently untrustworthy, for loyalty to China could so easily mean, in those days, disloyalty to the adoptive country. What was to stop them from becoming a tool of expansionism by Peking? So long as they were seen to be 'the enemy within', no country with an overseas Chinese minority was going to recognize Peking. These Southeast Asian fears made Chinese diplomacy very tough going. Peking well understood the usefulness of having the overseas Chinese on its side, but this is not to say that, when it proved expedient to dissociate itself from them, it would hesitate to do so. To gain the trust of the host countries, Peking had to keep its fingers out of their politics and, in effect, to disown the overseas Chinese. This it did after a fashion in 1954, when it formally repudiated the principle of *sui sanguinis*.

But it continued to offer China as a place of refuge – though not a particularly comfortable one – to expellees and voluntary repatriates. The first of the dozens of colonies it established for receiving these was a place on Hainan Island for resettling the Malayan deportees. Such places, officially called Overseas Chinese Farms, proliferated as the number of repatriates increased: as many as five hundred thousand of these arrived between 1949, when the New China was inaugurated, and 1966, when the horrendous Cultural Revolution started. Many returnees had homes and relatives to go to; others, with money to invest or special expertise to offer, were housed in special overseas Chinese apartment blocks in 'villages' in the cities; it was the ones who had nothing going for them that were housed in the Overseas Chinese Farms.[21]

I visited one in the autumn of 1987. Called T'ien-ma, Heavenly Horse, it was less than a hour's drive from Amoy. Overseas Chinese Farms are supposed to be self-supporting, but it was difficult to see how the inhabitants of T'ien-ma managed even to keep themselves in food, the land looked so barren and unyielding. Later I learnt that the returnees had been pioneers, and had reclaimed the land themselves; now they raised pigs and poultry on it, and also grew some ground-nuts. I was told that extra income came from factories producing fermented rice wine and soft drinks, and saw for myself a cardboard-making workshop financed by a grant of US$110,000 from the United Nations High Commissioner for Refugees (UNHCR). There was a shop of sorts, dusty and poorly stocked, with no one about but a gentle Cantonese-speaking woman who said here you could count your blessings: you were in China not Vietnam.

There was nothing to suggest a flow of remittances from abroad, though I thought there must be some, judging from the two banks (looking utterly out of place in the rural setting) I saw as I entered T'ien-ma. The place nevertheless looked as though it had little to hope for, tomorrow, next year, or in ten, twenty years.

My guide was a repatriate from Malaya. He was a high-up at the farm, and wherever we went people greeted him respectfully. He was courteous and gentle, and did his best to give me a rounded picture of life on the farm. He looked to be a man in his forties, but was probably much older, to go by the biographical details that came out little by little. I did not ask him point-blank if he was a CT during the Emergency; but I suspected he was. We spoke in Mandarin, but I was quite convinced – and this to me was extraordinary – that he was not Chinese. I have lived in Malaysia, and I know a Malay when I see one: his facial features, his eyes, his hair, his complexion, the way he moved – every sign pointed to his being racially Malay. I finally asked him where in the Malay peninsula he came from, and when he said Pahang, I knew that I was right.

The Malayan Races Liberation Army was, its name notwithstanding, almost entirely Chinese, but the one place where it succeeded in raising a Malay regiment was in Pahang, of all the states in the peninsula the most Malay. When the British deported their Communist captives, my guide must have been deported with them, and at that time it must have seemed as if there were worse places to be expelled to than an Overseas Chinese Farm in Fukien province. He could not have known what he was in for, but he no doubt made the best of things, settling down and becoming to all intents and purposes Chinese. There was a kind of pathos in the thought that, if he were to be repatriated to Pahang, he'd feel as uprooted as any Chinese.

I met a handful of young men who had arrived at T'ien-ma from Burma as children, and who had but the dimmest understanding of why they had left that country. They had left in 1967, the year Red Guards arrived in Rangoon from Peking to enact an overseas version of the Cultural Revolution. Among other things, the overseas Chinese students there were called upon to show their patriotism and revolutionary ardour by wearing Mao badges to school. The teachers objected, invoking a law which prohibited the wearing of political insignia in public; but when they tried to take the badges off they found themselves resisted. The matter then built up into an absurdity. Fighting broke out, at this and other schools. Across the city emotions gathered, the Chinese shouting slogans and staging demonstrations, swayed to a man by the passions of the Cultural Revolution, and the Burmese retaliating, attacking Chinese homes, shops, schools and the Chinese embassy.

After 1967 Chinese business in Burma was severely curtailed. To the parents of these youngsters in T'ien-ma, it doubtless seemed wiser to leave for China. Was it the right thing to do? It was hard to say. Their children, now come almost to adulthood, had the loitering air of out-of-work people, and the sad look of refugees, pale bored faces disclosing endless vacancy.

I met repatriates from Cambodia. There, too, Red Guards had fomented incidents in 1967, resuscitating fears of the export of the Chinese revolution, but it was not in that year that these people left Phnom Penh, but in 1975, when Pol Pot's men seized control of the capital. (Of those that stayed, about two hundred thousand, or half of Cambodia's Chinese population, perished, a death toll twice as high proportionally as that of indigenous urban Cambodians during the same period.)[22] Like the Burmese Chinese, the repatriates from Cambodia had the sad look of a people cut adrift from their natural milieu without arriving upon a more congenial shore. They said that they yearned to go to Paris, the metropolis of colonial Cambodia; many fellow Cambodian emigrants have thrived there, and so might they, given half a chance.

China's foreign relations added to the difficulties of the overseas Chinese; to the suspicion they aroused in being Eastern Jews and revolutionary subversives was sometimes added the fear that they might be traitors to their adopted country. When the border disputes China had with India broke out into a short war in the Himalayan Mountains in the autumn of 1962, China had to send its own ships to transport Chinese repatriates from that country.[23] In Vietnam, too, their position deteriorated to a point where the Chinese residents could no longer feel safe in their adopted country. In the cardboard-making workshop I spoke to one of the 250,000 Hoa, or Vietnamese Chinese, who left Vietnam for China between March 1978 and mid-1979, a casualty of Sino-Vietnamese hostility.

One could have pitied the man, if he had not seemed so numb to his misfortune. His gentle vulnerability, his withdrawal, was disturbing. He said he had a small business in Haiphong, but, a laconic man, he did not elaborate. His wife and three daughters, and a younger son, were with him in T'ien-ma, but his oldest boy had made his own way – to England, he believed, though he couldn't tell me anything about him, where he was, how he might be found, what he was doing. I left him my card, and asked him to tell his son to get in touch should they re-establish contact. I did not, in all honesty, believe that I would hear from him, but eight months after my encounter with his father, and two months after my return to London, the son telephoned me. It was his twelfth attempt. After leaving T'ien-ma I had spent six months in Southeast Asia, and all that time he had been trying to reach me; it was a measure of how much he craved news of his family. It turned out he was working as a kitchen hand at – of all places – a Chinese restaurant in Upper Street, about a fifteen-minute drive from where I lived. When I went to see him at the restaurant I had to make it very clear that, though yes, I would indeed eat there, he was not to pay for my meal. We fought over this, as Chinese do. I left him with the photographs I'd taken of his father, and encouraged him to save up for a visit to T'ien-ma.

T'ien-ma had been set up, not for Vietnamese Chinese refugees, but for the wave of repatriates, 102,196-strong by one reckoning, deported from Indonesia in 1960.[24] No country harbouring a Chinese minority possesses a blacker record of persecution and racial violence than Indonesia. Nowhere, wrote the doyen of overseas Chinese studies Wang Gungwu in the 1970s, had more expatriate Chinese 'been killed or wounded, run away or been chased away, and been so insecure' than in Indonesia.[25] The pogroms there had been more horrendous, the mob violence more hysterical.

Their enterprise put the Chinese ahead of the indigenes everywhere in Southeast Asia, but it was in Indonesia that this sowed the bitterest harvest of hatred. Why was this so? It is not as though the Chinese were more venal there than elsewhere, more exploitative, more perverse or more doggedly 'chauvinist'. What was unusual about Indonesia was perhaps not its Chinese minority, but its *pribumi*, or indigenous Indonesian, majority. Perhaps there was more friction between the Chinese and the *pribumi* because there was more commercial competition; in the writing on the Chinese in Indonesia much has been made of the fact that Sarekat Islam, the first mass movement to appear in Indies history, founded in 1912 by indigenous Muslim traders, had as its initial purpose the breaking of the Chinese hold on the economic life of the country. The Chinese were seen to stand in the way of indigenous commercial ambitions, which were perhaps larger here than elsewhere; in the Chinese presence native aspirations repeatedly shrivelled. But that is by no means the whole story. It was in the years after the Dutch left, years of economic chaos, inflation and material shortages, that the Chinese excited the intensest hatred and envy, and, paradoxically, saw some of the biggest upturns in their fortunes – they were not the first people to discover that disorder could be very conducive to business. And yet, as Jews and Indians have also learnt, racial minorities are almost always the first victims of instability. Worse even than a racially antagonistic leader is a mercurial one; and Sukarno, the charismatic demagogue who created the new nation of Indonesia and ruled it from 1949 to 1965, was extremely mercurial.

One of the things he did was to flirt with Peking. China was eager to support Sukarno, in whom it thought it had a powerful friend and ally against American and Western imperialism. Because of the warmth of the relationship between the two countries, it proved easy for Peking to exert a strong influence over the Chinese minority, and over those stalwarts of expatriate Chinese communities: schools, guilds, newspapers, native-place associations, and so on – those sponsored by Taiwan were in any case all closed down in 1958, in reprisal for the help Taiwan gave to some Indonesian rebels.[26] (It always astonishes me, when I meet Indonesian Chinese settled in Europe, how conversant they are with mainland Chinese politics and vocabulary, how at home with Marxist theory, and I could just picture them in their Jakarta classrooms, those nurseries of Chinese identity, imbibing Communist doctrine along with their Chinese History and Geography.)

But consistency or steadiness was not the quality one should expect of a relationship with Sukarno, as Peking was to learn to its cost. For one thing, Sukarno's policies – based on a dubious revolutionary formula which reconciled, or so he told his susceptible people, nationalism, Islam and socialism – were setting the country on a disaster course. For another, his way of avoiding a crash, which was to balance the Army and the Communist Party (the Partai Komunis Indonesia, or PKI) against one another, made for wild political volatility. The Chinese residents in Indonesia were to become the first casualties of this precariousness, and Peking's attempts to protect them only made things worse, reinforcing in many Indonesians the tendency to lump all Chinese together as Communists.

Peking's courtship of Jakarta was to prove to be one of the most terrible of all diplomatic miscalculations. This was demonstrated in 1959, when, giving in to the demands of indigenous Indonesian merchants, the government issued a decree banning 'alien' (read 'Chinese') retail trade in rural areas and requiring alien owners to transfer their businesses to Indonesian citizens; in some parts of Indonesia, local military commanders went beyond the ban on trade to impose a ban on residence by Chinese in the rural areas as well. Already operating in a political climate made extremely unfavourable by the socialist and fervidly nationalist tenor of Sukarno's policies, Chinese shopkeepers now found themselves done out of their livelihood.

The Chinese minority found a great many supporters in the Indonesian Communist Party, but both the Chinese and PKI were the *bêtes noires* of the increasingly powerful Army. The Army happened to have benefited enormously from the government's nationalization policy – all the largest enterprises appropriated by the government fell under its management – and the takeover of Chinese assets would make complete the generals' plunder of confiscated assets and properties.[27]

Peking was caught in a bind: was it to defend the Chinese traders, capitalist to a man, against the Indonesians, allies in the united front against the imperialist West?[28] It could not abandon the Chinese to the mounting racialist forces, but neither could it, by too vigorous a defence of their interests, jeopardize their position still further, giving the Army a pretext for demanding the proscription of the PKI on the grounds of Chinese Communist subversion. Matters were brought to a head when the Chinese embassy tried to obstruct the eviction of the resident Chinese in the villages where they were being snatched from their homes by the military police. Peking did what it could to get Sukarno to intervene, but to no avail; Sukarno was not going to risk an open split with the generals over an issue that had so much popular support.

What happened next gave to the annals of the overseas Chinese one of their most poignant chapters. On 10 December 1959, Peking launched a campaign to call the overseas Chinese home. 'We want none of our dear ones to suffer in foreign lands,' a statement by a well-known Chinese official declared, 'and it is our hope that they will all come back to the arms of the motherland.'[29] Whether they were half a million, a million or several million, he said, overseas Chinese would find a warm reception in China. Within months, China was sending its ships, four vessels from its tiny merchant fleet, to bring home the hundred thousand and more Chinese who answered its call. At the ports passers-by could glimpse them stumbling through the exit formalities and crowding the decks, stripped of everything but such clothing and personal belongings as they could carry by hand, and leaving behind them an economy badly shaken by their departure.

They were by no means the only Chinese in Southeast Asia to find themselves the target of discriminatory measures designed to better the lot of the indigenous majority. In those post-war years there was scarcely a country where the Chinese could pursue their callings or their commercial preferences without disapproval or interference. In Thailand Chinese aliens were excluded from twenty-seven occupations, in Cambodia from eighteen[30] and it was a lucky, or cunning, Chinese who managed to elude the Filipinization of alien retail enterprises in the Philippines.[31] Indeed, to suffer harsh economic discrimination of one kind or another was part of being Southeast Asian Chinese.

Yet only in Indonesia did this result in large-scale repatriation, and part of the reason for this must lie in the very special interest which Peking took in the Chinese there, the designs which it had for them. It was partly to get them out of harm's way that Peking sent for them, but it was also to punish Indonesia, whose economy, Peking well knew, could only be hurt by the withdrawal of the immigrant Chinese. I met a number of the returned Chinese in T'ien-ma. There was an elderly Hakka-speaking couple who had a son killed in the Cultural Revolution, but who seemed in every other way to be quite reconciled to their hard lives in China. But there was another repatriate, a middle-aged man only too clearly soured by the realization that he was but a pawn in a game beyond his understanding. 'Do you know why I'm here?' he asked in a voice shot through with regret and resentment. 'Because I loved the Communist Party,' he said with bitter irony, pronouncing the word 'loved' in a cynical parody of the Chinese Communist propaganda style.

The events leading to the repatriation naturally created a rift in the relations between Jakarta and Peking, but the friendship did not crumble. Later moves were made to mend fences. Communists in Indonesia were delighted at the course of events as the two powers moved ever closer together and as the PKI increased its power. Among the overseas Chinese there, Peking's influence was unexampled. And yet, paradoxically, Peking's influence in Indonesia in fact greatly increased the vulnerability of the Indonesian Chinese, since it made them seem ever more like Fifth Columnists. On balance, and considering what was to come to pass in 1965, they might have been better off without it.

This was the year of the fateful coup attempt – the so-called September 30 Movement – that brought about the political demise of Sukarno, the collapse of Peking's policy in Indonesia, and the rise to power of General Suharto. The true facts surrounding this abortive attempt, which entailed the murder of six anti-Communist generals by junior officers, will keep historians and political scientists speculating for years to come. No one can say for sure who or what was behind it, but for the Chinese minority the unfortunate thing was that, in what became the officially accepted version of the story, the attempt was said to have been planned by the PKI with the backing of money and arms from Peking.

The collapse of Sukarno's power was followed by a fierce backlash of hostility towards the Communists and their erstwhile allies. The triumph of the Army meant the doom of the PKI. Indonesian Communists were massacred in their thousands, and the local Chinese, long viewed with distrust and hatred, became invitingly easy marks for mob violence, extortion and harassment. All over the country, the bubble of old resentment burst out in waves of destruction. The degree of violence varied from place to place and from month to month. In 1966 anti-Chinese sentiment was at its most intense in northern Sumatra, where slogans – DRIVE OUT THE CHINESE NOW, YOU WILL BE BEHEADED IF YOU DON'T LEAVE – were scrawled on walls and shops and houses were looted. There hundreds of Chinese were killed and thousands terrorized.[32] The most fearful of the stories came out of West Kalimantan, or Indonesian West Borneo, where Chinese were horribly murdered by the native Dyaks. It was widely believed that the local Indonesian military command condoned these killings, because they had been fighting a campaign against a band of Communist guerrillas, mostly young Chinese from Sarawak, who had been attacking Dyak villages and receiving food and shelter from the Chinese villagers and shopkeepers of the interior, and they were happy enough to have the Dyaks do their work for them. If many of the Chinese killed were innocent villagers, well, they probably deserved to

die, for weren't the Chinese all Communist subversives, 'hand in glove
with Mao Tse-tung,' as the West Kalimantan Governor put it, 'and a
part of his plan to take over Asia'?[33]

The military command, upon receiving news of the killings, ordered
the Chinese to evacuate the jungle villages and make for the coastal
towns. This had the effect of cutting off the guerrillas' supply lines
– and perhaps this, rather than the safety of the evacuees, had been
the main purpose of the exodus. If any of the tens of thousands of
Chinese who left the interior thought that the worst was behind him,
he could not have been more mistaken. The conditions of the camps
were appalling. Food ran short, typhoid and cholera were rife, and
within ten weeks of the evacuation order some four thousand Chinese
had died. An English journalist who visited one of the camps in 1968
learnt that relief workers were removing between fifteen and twenty
corpses a day.[34]

There was, in contrast to 1959–60, no mass exodus of Chinese to
China. Peking announced that ships would be sent to repatriate those
who wished to leave Indonesia, but only ten thousand seem to have
plumped for the option.[35] To a China about to be turned topsy-turvy
by the Cultural Revolution, more would have meant a terrible burden,
and this time Peking knew better than to encourage mass repatriation.
But there can be no overlooking the fact that the Peking-Jakarta axis
was in tatters.

'The main obstacle to the finding of a *modus vivendi* between the
overseas Chinese and the other races', wrote the late scholar Victor
Purcell in 1965, 'was the continuance of the Cold War. If the artificial
alignment of humanity consequent upon this could be removed, it
was likely that the presence of Overseas Chinese in Southeast Asia
would become increasingly less a "problem".'[36] There is no doubt
that anti-Communism blurred into anti-sinicism (and vice-versa), and
not just in Southeast Asia. In the wave of anti-Communist hysteria
that swept the United States during the Cold War of the 1950s, many
American Chinese were persecuted for being sympathetic to Peking.
The effect of the Korean War, recalled Betty Lee Sung, the author of
a book on Chinese Americans, was to make people 'look at you in the
street and think, Well, you're one of the enemy'.[37]

One of the reasons given for America's refusal to recognize the
Peking government was that if it did so the Chinese abroad would
turn Communist overnight. All through the 1950s the American policy

towards the Chinese disapora had as its aim the preservation of overseas Chinese loyalty to the Nationalist government on Taiwan. At home, the anxieties of the Red scare set the tone of Chinatown society, and it was a foolhardy Chinese who professed any sympathy for Peking. Federal agents swooped through the Chinatowns repeatedly, to sniff out 'un-American activities', and it is said that the FBI kept a close watch on the Chinese Democratic Youth League of San Francisco, an anti-Kuomintang organization, taking photographs of everyone who entered its office on Stockton Street.[38]

To prove themselves loyal Americans, the Chinese had to style themselves Nationalist supporters. Out of their anxiousness to allay American suspicion they formed pro-Kuomintang organizations. One, the All-America Overseas Chinese Anti-Communist League, inaugurated in September 1954 in New York City, declared in its charter that its purpose was to 'let the American people know that the Chinese are not Communists, and to rally all overseas Chinese people against Communism and to the support of the Republic of China'.[39] The actions of this organization were not without their global implications, for it lobbied American Congressmen against recognizing Peking.

Chinese-American apprehensions were heightened when, in 1955, the US Consul in Hong Kong, Everett Drumwright, charged that Peking was insinuating its spies and agents into the United States, using false or fraudulently obtained American passports. The Chinese communities could scarcely shrug off the federal investigations that ensued, since so many of their members had indeed entered the US with false papers – think of all those 'paper sons'. When news reached it of Chinese being prosecuted and deported for passport fraud, the Six Companies held a meeting. What, it decided to put to the federal authorities, if all those who had entered the country illegally came forward and confessed their guilt to the immigration authorities? If they satisfied the authorities that they were innocent of Communist complicity, might they be allowed to assume their true identities and be assured a place in American society? The authorities agreed to the deal, and under the Confession Programme, as it was called, the immigration status of tens of thousands of Chinese Americans was clarified.

It would have been odd if, given the political mood of the time, the Six Companies did not side with Taiwan. Besides, faced with the unpleasant prospect of an increasingly Americanized – and indifferent – constituency, the old-style community leaders could only gain from an alliance with those tireless keepers of the traditionalist Chinese flame, the Nationalists. Taiwan, for its part, was keen to bolster the prestige of the Six Companies, through which, in a cosy symbiosis, it could work its purpose of courting the overseas Chinese. It does not surprise us in the least to learn that a number of Six Companies leaders were appointed National Policy Advisers to Chiang Kai-shek. It was all in the family, so to speak.

Outside the United States, the Kuomintang was pre-eminent in the Philippines, the ex-American colony. There was hardly a major city there that did not have a chapter or a cultural organization controlled by the party. Large numbers of the settlers, even if they were born in the Philippines, remained citizens of the Republic of China (Taiwan), for the naturalization laws of the Philippines made it virtually impossible for a Chinese of less than exceptional means to acquire Philippine nationality. How much influence Taiwan enjoyed in that country was dramatically demonstrated in 1962, when the brothers Quintin and Rizal Yuyitung, publishers of the largest Chinese-language newspaper (the *Chinese Commercial News*), were arrested with the paper's editorial staff and accused of propagating 'anti-Filipino and pro-communist sentiments'.

The paper was in fact very far from being anti-Filipino, for it had been started in 1919 by the brothers' father, himself an immigrant from China, to urge the integration of the overseas Chinese into Philippine life. It did, however, publish news of mainland China, items it had picked up from Reuters and other Western wire services. What was more, it was also highly critical of the Kuomintang government. There was no question, so far as the Kuomintang authorities were concerned, that the brothers had to be silenced, and to do so they secured the cooperation of the government of President Marcos. In a farcical trial in which a key witness, a certain professor from Taipei, turned out to have been Editor of a rival local paper, the Yuyitungs were accused of being secret agents of the Communist government in Peking.

The case dragged on for seven years. To buy their freedom the brothers had to publish an apology in the *Chinese Commercial News*. But this was not the end of the story, for in 1970, in an even more dramatic re-enactment of history, the brothers were kidnapped one weekend and deported to Taipei. They spent some years in gaol, and were it not for the protests of the International Press Institute they might, as Quintin Yuyitung was later to recall, have been left to die. Later, helped by the Institute, the brothers found their way to North

America, and it was not until the Marcos government fell in 1986 that they returned to Manila to revive their paper.⁴⁰

Forlorn on its small island retreat, curtailed of its sovereignty, the Kuomintang worked all the harder for the allegiance of the overseas Chinese. To rally the millions of expatriate Chinese to its flag was to enlarge its fief; to relax its grip upon them was perhaps to allow them to drift into the arms of the Communists. In Manila, in Washington, in whichever capital the Kuomintang government was diplomatically represented, it vied with the Communists for the hearts and minds of the expatriate Chinese, turning every Chinatown into an arena of Nationalist-Communist rivalry, lavishing upon it money to start a newspaper or to establish a club, and teachers and teaching materials to keep Chinese language and culture alive among the overseas Chinese. To win them over to Chinese culture was, it was hoped, to win them over to Taiwan, for it was the boast of the Nationalists that they, rather than the Marxist iconoclasts of the Chinese mainland, were the orthodox guardians of the Chinese cultural tradition. The desinicization of emigrant Chinese did not worry Peking quite so much; it was all right for the overseas Chinese to cut their ancestral ties so long as they transferred their attachments to their adopted countries and not to Taiwan.

In the long run, the contest between the two harmed the reputation of the overseas Chinese, for it encouraged the image of an unassimilable and chauvinistic minority, one which the indigenous nationalists and politicians of the host societies were all too ready to exploit, to keep alive the overseas Chinese scapegoat. There is no reason to suppose that the overseas Chinese, left to themelves, would not have conformed to the classic immigrant pattern, the first generation resolutely resisting change, the third generation becoming totally assimilated, to the dismay of their grandparents.

PART FOUR

1960s–1980s

CHAPTER TWELVE

Crooks or Capitalists?

The Chinese make up a disproportionate share of the commercial class of every Southeast Asian country where they have built up a community, and some of them are big players in the national economies. Their business success is all the more remarkable when you consider the odds against which it has been achieved. They might have had the will, energy, flair and capital to do well, but the governments of their adopted countries have allowed these qualities to flourish only grudgingly. Like the world's other commercial migrants, whether Jews or Lebanese or Indians, the Chinese in Southeast Asia have always been disliked for having profited from the indigenous reluctance to make money.

Even their thrift has been made, as in this Thai joke, the butt of ridicule: a Chinese family hang a salted fish over their dinner table, and look at it as they eat their rice; 'Don't stare too hard at the fish,' the mother cautions, 'or you'll be thirsty all night.'[1] The Thai was the first of the Southeast Asian governments to try and reduce their economic dominance, taking over large numbers of Chinese private enterprises between the late 1930s and mid-1950s. Had the government not set up the Thai Rice Company, for example, the country's chief industry would have remained in Chinese hands.[2]

Other countries locked the Chinese out of certain sectors of the economy as part of an effort to foster and promote indigenous business. The Philippines did this with Chinese who were not citizens of the country – and that meant, as we have seen, the majority of the Chinese residents, since it was only in the mid-1970s, when the establishment of diplomatic relations between the Philippines and the People's Republic of China impended, that Marcos agreed to relax the laws to allow the mass naturalization of the Chinese.

In Indonesia, too, the government discriminated in favour of the indigenous people. We have seen how hard life became for the Chinese trader in the 1960s; and though matters greatly improved after Suharto came to power, a policy of preferment prevails and the Chinese capitalist remains wary.

The last country to act was Malaysia, and it is there that the problem of economic and racial rivalry seems at its most intractable. The country's racial composition – with Malays making up over half the population, the Chinese a third, and the Indians a tenth – destined it for trouble when it became independent in 1957. After the British left, a new country came into being in which political power was in the hands of one race, the Malays, and economic power in the hands of another, the Chinese. The latter were fewer but richer, and that was a recipe for a racial trouble. Sure enough, on 13 May 1969, when it was learnt that opposition parties dominated by the Chinese did better than was expected in a general election, and their members celebrated their gains with a victory parade, violent fighting broke out in Kuala Lumpur between the Chinese and the Malays. By a conservative official count, 196 died and 440 were wounded, while scores of cars were burnt and hundreds of houses gutted.

The race riots hastened the recognition that unless something was done to redress the economic balance between the haves (who happened to be mostly Chinese) and the have-nots (who happened to be mostly Malays), the racial divide would widen. The answer the politicians came up with was the New Economic Policy (NEP), launched in 1970 to raise the Malay share of the country's corporate cake, standing then at 2.3%, to 30% by 1990. To achieve its aim, the NEP gave advantages of all kinds to *bumiputras*, 'sons of the soil', practising what in America would be called Affirmative Action, with the difference that the action discriminated in favour of not an ethnic minority, but an ethnic majority, who also happened to be the power-holders of the country.

With privileged access to education, jobs, government subsidies and company shares, a large and well-to-do Malay middle class was ushered into being. By the mid-1980s, highly educated Malay civil servants, professionals or company directors were no longer as thin on the ground as they used to be; but there are those who argue, as the Japanese economics professor Yoshihara Kunio does, that most of the newly rich capitalists are merely 'rent-seekers', beneficiaries of government favours and handouts rather than true entrepreneurs. Countless politicians line their own pockets, awarding contracts to businesses secretly owned by themselves or by their families. If anything, the gap between rich and poor has grown since the policy was put into effect, and large numbers of Malays live below the poverty line. By 1988, if the government statistics are to be trusted (many Chinese say not), the Malay stake in the country's corporate equity had risen to twenty per cent, ten points short of the original target. This is grounds enough for prolonging the life of the NEP, say some Malays, while others worry that continual government favouritism would create in the Malay an ultimately detrimental habit of over-dependency.

The Chinese did not take at all kindly to the NEP, as the famous case of the mandarin oranges may serve to illustrate. In 1985, Pernas, the national corporation set up with the backing of the top Malay politicians, established its own company to buy 410,000 crates of mandarin oranges, which are to Chinese New Year festivities what turkey and mince pies are to English Christmases. It then outraged the Chinese by denying permits to the traditional Chinese wholesalers. When strong protests were voiced, Pernas at the last minute issued thirty-three permits to the Chinese wholesalers and reduced its own order by 270,000 crates, paying a hefty cancellation penalty. By this time it was already too late for the Chinese wholesalers to do any importing, for Chinese New Year was upon them, but instead of buying the remaining shipments of mandarin oranges from Pernas, the fruiterers sold California Sunkist oranges instead. Though Sunkist oranges are a poor substitute for mandarin oranges, since the name for them is not *kum*, an auspicious homonym of the Cantonese word for 'gold', the Chinese made do with them anyway, happy in the thought that they had done the Malays out of a profitable deal.[3]

Small and medium-sized Chinese businesses were badly hit by the NEP,[4] and today one detects in the Chinese attitude towards the newly rich Malays some of the feelings, from envy to diminished self-confidence, once harboured by the Malays. Their equanimity much disturbed, it is small wonder that the Chinese have chosen to advance their interests by takeovers and acquisitions rather than by starting new businesses, putting their money in enterprises which promise quick profits, such as finance and property. Their feelings of insecurity, says Yoshihara Kunio, have turned them into 'rent-seekers, speculators, or predators'.[5] Instead of applying their skills to the manufacturing industry, they become owners of hotel chains, developers of property, bankers, stockbrokers and insurance men, gravitating towards businesses that hold out the promise of a fast buck, that present opportunities for amassing capital in a fairly liquid form which can later be exported. If they can, the Chinese transfer their assets abroad, and of course they emigrate. If capitalism in Malaysia is not as dynamic as it could be, it is partly because, people like Yoshihara have argued, in discriminating against the Chinese the Malays have been cutting off their nose to spite their face.

The Chinese have always found ways of getting round economic restrictions; for example, when they were prevented from opening shops in Papua New Guinea in the 1930s they paid Europeans to obtain licences on their behalf and to act as their dummies.[6] In Malaysia, too, the purposes of the NEP are frequently subverted by such practices. One of the many racial jokes current in Kuala Lumpur encapsulates this Chinese propensity: 'What's two and two?' asks a Malay politician of a Malay. 'Two and two are four,' the Malay answers. 'What's two and two?' the Malay politician asks an Indian. 'Sometimes three, sometimes four, sometimes five,' answers the Indian. 'What's two and two?' the Malay politician asks a Jew. 'Buying or selling?' the Jew replies. The same question is then put to a Chinese. Leaning forward, the Chinese asks the Malay politician, 'What figure do you have in mind?'

As in much of the developing world, it suits many people in Southeast Asia that corruption can oil the wheels of bureaucracy, making it that much easier for them to win fat contracts over the heads of those more deserving. If, say, the imports and foreign exchange they need for the expansion of their company are subject to licensing – and they usually are in these countries – it suits some people, the ones with privileged access to the right circles, that a cheque made payable to a relative of a certain politician or government functionary would see to it that the necessary permits are issued.

But the near-impossibility in these countries of knowing where politics ends and business begins can also mean that, unless he is good at cultivating friendships with politicians and civil servants, an aspiring businessman will find it hard to cut a dash on the economic stage. It isn't enough to be shrewd, adaptable, daring, credit-worthy and all the rest of it; in such a climate it is necessary to be politically canny.

The Chinese businessman is no stranger to the world of bribes and back-room deal-making. He has learnt, over the years, that a government policy favouring the indigenous businessman need not always be a bar to his own activities; for it is certainly not beyond his ingenuity to find himself a native sleeping partner, a front man who gets the licence, takes a cut, and leaves him to run the actual business. Very often a native suitor for a government concession is without the means or ambition to work it, and would have to pass it on to a Chinese to make it operable. In much of Southeast Asia, it is well known that it takes two to get an 'Ali Baba' business off the ground – Ali the Indonesian or Malay who qualifies for government handouts, Baba the Chinese with the capital and the skill. Consider the 1950 Benteng Programme, by which certain categories of import were reserved for native Indonesians. The way it worked out was a far cry from the intention of the government, which was to foster indigenous business; for, excepting only a handful of bona fide Indonesian importers, the programme merely gave rise to 'briefcase importers' or Ali Baba companies.[7] The native importers had simply sold their licences to Chinese businessmen (at twice or two and a half times the nominal value), and even the genuine native importers turned out to be people with powerful political connections rather than true entrepreneurs. When it might have paved the way for the emergence of a home-grown business class, the Benteng system merely created a group of brokers and fixers.

Better times came to the Chinese capitalist with the rise of President Suharto, beneath whose hand the Ali Baba alliance flowered into the *cukong* system. Cukong is a Hokkien Chinese word meaning 'master', but in Indonesia the term is used of an arrangement whereby Chinese businessmen act as financiers and corporate managers to powerful political figures, in particular the military, in return for access to government contracts, funds, favours and protection.[8] The government wanted economic growth, injections of private capital and expansion of business activities; and if they could not have these from native entrepreneurs, Chinese and foreign it would have to be. With entrepreneurial qualifications beyond the capacities of their indigenous rivals, Chinese businessmen provided the leaven in the Indonesian economy. There was a wide range of money-making opportunities, and into nearly all of them, from shipping and import-export to banking, rice-milling and forestry, Chinese cash, experience and energy went. It was understood that the benefits thus assured the Chinese would be shared between them and their political protectors.

Every now and then disgruntled voices, some anti-government, some anti-Chinese, some both, are raised against the cukong system, which has been judged irregular by even the grand standards of Indonesian corruption. The thought of all those Chinese making their pile particularly outraged people who found themselves relegated to a back seat. There were critics who publicly inveighed against the system, awkward questions asked in Parliament, exposés published by newspapers and student periodicals. But the government was not quite ready to hear their message, and, lest they made things hot for business, took steps to silence the critics (by closing down newspapers and arresting student leaders, among other classic methods).

Outside events conspired to help the Chinese, and it wasn't only the generals who preferred Chinese partners over their native competitors, it was the foreign companies too. As the people with the experience, connections and capital, the Chinese were the ones invited to enter into joint ventures with Japanese and Western firms.

As business conglomerates the cukong families – one count in 1984 put their number at over forty – are very big-time indeed. But of all the thriving empires governed from downtown Jakarta, none is as well known as the Liem Group. If it is possible to conceive of a London family owning controlling stakes in B.A.T., British Steel, Trusthouse Forte, Jaguar, Barclays Bank, Wates, and dozens of other companies, it may just be possible to grasp the position of the Liem group in the Indonesian scheme of things and its significance in the national economy.

The head of it all, Liem Sioe Liong (or Sudono Salim in Indonesian), was born a Hockchia in 1916 in Fukien province, the second son of a peasant. His business life began when, aged sixteen, he set up a noodle stall in his home village. About a year before war broke out between China and Japan, he arrived in the central Javanese town of Kudus to join his elder brother, Liem Sioe Hie, who was helping to run his uncle's small peanut-oil trading business, having arrived in the Dutch East Indies some twelve years before. The first couple of years, the younger Liem was later to recall, were very hard indeed; he was hardly more than an apprentice, doing his best to cope with the local customs and language. In those days Hockchias (a people who, the reader may recall, were vocationally concentrated in rickshaw-pulling in Singapore) didn't have much going for them. The poorest and most despised of the Chinese petty traders in Indonesia, the Hockchias mostly earned a peripatetic living in the rural areas, engaged in something between hire-purchase and money-lending, a line of business few other people found attractive, involving as it did high risks and minute profit margins. But for Liem this moving about was all to the good in the end, because it allowed him to build up some useful contacts, and to discover where goods in short supply could be had.

Kudus, it so happened, was the centre of the *kretek* industry, kreteks being cigarettes made from a blend of tobacco and cloves. They are a great favourite with Indonesians, and whoever is on to a good supply of cloves in Indonesia is on to the golden goose. All commodity trading fell into the hands of the Japanese when the invading army arrived in Java in 1942, but as Japan faded from the scene with its defeat in 1945, so the likes of Liem stepped in. As well as resuming the peanut-oil business and expanding into coffee-milling, Liem now eyed the clove trade with increasing interest. It was a time of change and confusion, when people felt their lives to be on the turn; long-established Chinese firms were collapsing, and those small-time Hockchia traders who never got a look-in before found in the aftermath of war the chance to make their mark. Sukarno's independence movement was fighting to inherit the archipelago from the Japanese, and the country divided between the Dutch and the Republicans. It was the sort of time when, provided you were alert and supple enough, you could earn a pretty penny smuggling goods from one side of the battle lines to the other. Traditional trading routes were disrupted, and Liem, his nose for profit as sharp as anyone else's, saw how he could exploit the situation for his own benefit. By smuggling cloves from the Moluccas, Sumatra and North Sulawesi through Singapore to supply the kretek factories in Kudus, he acquired the makings of his fabulous fortune.

Sugar was another thing he smuggled, and also, according to British intelligence, arms and munitions. Asked about that part of his career many years later, Liem unabashedly denied it – he himself likes to lay more stress on the medical supplies with which he furnished the independence fighters – but there are people who remember his reputation for gun-running through Singapore, then still a British colony. What is not in any doubt, though, is that much of his smuggling business in the years between 1945 and 1949 was conducted on behalf of the Republican Army. The friendships forged with the military in those years were to become, together with his interests in the clove trade, the basis for his ever expanding business empire, for these were the very people who came to power in post-colonial Indonesia.

It was Liem's good luck that the headquarters of the paramount military division, the Diponegoro or Seventh Military District, came to be stationed in the city of Semarang – which is not only very close to Kudus but is thickly settled with Chinese. Liem was conveniently placed to do business with the Diponegoro, and to get to know its officers. One of these officers was Soedjono Hoemardani, the future general, personal presidential adviser, and political linchpin of a complex web of Chinese and Japanese business interests. Another was the young Suharto, one day to become the President of Indonesia.

It was the character of the Indonesian Army that gave Liem his opportunity. Since the early 1950s, when it routinely raised money by going into business for itself, privately making the most of its public opportunities, the Indonesian military had been deeply entangled in the business life of the country. The various regiments could always use some extra money – as could the individual officers and political factions. Initially the means chosen were the obvious strong-arm ones: smuggling, protection rackets, extortion, the forced purchase of crops at below market prices, and so on. Later the Army took over most of the nationalized Dutch concerns. Still later it took it upon itself to manage the incalculable wealth of such state-owned enterprises as the oil giant Pertamina, making sure that much of it flowed into their own pockets, and the pockets of their relatives and favourites.

Liem Sioe Liong's early links with Suharto paid off in several directions. There was already a bond of some fourteen years' standing between the two men when Suharto became President in 1965. When the government decided to restrict the import of cloves (chiefly from Madagascar and Zanzibar) to only two companies, Liem's firm was one, that of Suharto's brother was another. And nobody thinks it fortuitous that some of Liem's companies had Suharto's stepbrother Sudwikatmono for a partner, or that Suharto's son Sigit and daughter Siti were big shareholders in Bank Central Asia, the pride of Liem's financial interests. Liem's business was to expand spectacularly into manufacturing, finance, property and construction, but it was on the back of his trading activities that it rode to its first success. Here, where political bestowals like monopolies and licences are so important, his links to the ruling families stood him in very good stead indeed. He did enormously well out of the export trade in rubber and coffee, and though he took out more than the proper quota of export licences, the government simply winked at the transgression. His name did come up in a presidential commission of enquiry into corruption, but, although his case cried out for investigation, nothing more was heard of it publicly.[9]

Where Indonesian business is concerned, some truths are best left undiscovered. The embarrassment of what came to light when Mrs Kartika Ratner's millions were enquired into is ample proof of that. The lady was the widow of Haji Thahir, the personal assistant to the Director of Pertamina. Upon her husband's death she had withdrawn a cool US$45 million from the deceased's personal accounts in the Hongkong and Shanghai Bank and the Chase Manhattan. She was on the point of withdrawing another US$35 million from the Sumitomo Bank when she was served with a writ from the Indonesian government, pointing out that the money was rightfully Pertamina's – her husband had simply, and altogether illegally, helped himself to it – and that she must give it back. She was also reminded by the government's lawyers of the bribes her husband had accepted from the German firms Siemens A.G. and Klochner Industrie-Anlagen, suitors for contracts worth US$500 million for a mammoth state-owned steel mill.

It was generous of the government to offer her the $1.5 million interest on the deposit in the Sumitomo, but Mrs Kartika Ratna sniffed at the figure; not one to take defeat lying down, she insisted on fighting the case in the courts of Singapore. In the scandalized uproar accompanying the widow's courtroom revelations, it emerged that in accepting gifts from successful contractors Thahir was merely following customary practice. He was doing nothing out of the ordinary, his widow asserted, and his boss, the Director of Pertamina, knew what he was up to all along. Indeed, the Director had a hand in it himself – and not just him but President Suharto, Mrs Suharto and Liem Sioe Liong. Just look, the widow insisted, at the ownership of the P.T. First Reality Corporation, a beneficiary of Pertamina contracts: the names of some of its shareholders – Liem Sioe Liong, two of his sons, Thahir's son – are no more than a reminder that to deplore Thahir's conduct was, in the context of Indonesian business, sheer hypocrisy. Those who live in glass houses, the widow was saying, though not in so many words, shouldn't throw stones.[10]

In Indonesia, every car, motor cycle, truck or minibus made by Hino, Mazda, Suzuki, Ford or Volvo has been either imported, assembled or distributed by one of Liem's agencies. But Liem's enterprises make things as well as import them, and thanks to government loans and contracts, their manufacturing activities greatly developed in the late 1960s and early 1970s. Liem started off in textiles as an importer of cheap fabrics from the mills of Shanghai, but it was not long before he became a manufacturer himself, establishing looms in Kudus and Bandung. He went into flour-milling, where he enjoys a virtual monopoly in the market thanks to government licensing. He went into cement-manufacturing, an industry which has benefited from government protection and hefty public-works spending. He went into steel, joining forces with state enterprises and French and Spanish consortia. He chalked up properties, one of them the swanky Jakarta Mandarin Hotel. He acquired interests in construction, logging and tin-mining. And like many a great overseas Chinese magnate, he has a sizeable stake in a bank – the Bank Central Asia, the largest local private bank in the country. Hardly an area of Indonesian economic life escapes penetration by the tentacles of the Liem group of companies, and it has been said by Chinese commentators that, like it or not, in Indonesia Liem Sioe Liong affects your *i-shih-chu-hsing*, the four basic needs of everyday life – clothing, food, shelter and transportation.

Nor does he lack weight in the wider world. Liem has been active internationally, buying up European and US companies, and building up an offshore empire in trade and finance and related activities. Charts of the structure of his overseas operations, of the kind beloved of business magazines, show corporate appendages registered in Liberia, Hong Kong, Singapore, California, Delaware, Holland and the Netherlands Antilles.[11]

Going international is a move one expects of an enterprise of the breadth and sophistication of the Liem group, but given the uncertainties of Indonesian politics, the impression that Liem is exporting capital to safer havens is unavoidable. Of course there is no reason why any businessman should put all his eggs in one basket, whether or not political risks are involved, and the Liem conglomerate might simply have based its offshore move on business calculations, responding to some corporate imperative to stretch its wings. But those who subscribe to the view of the overseas Chinese as 'bloodsuckers', people who milk their host countries for all they are worth and then take their money and run, will say that Liem's was not an uncharacteristic Chinese move. But then who can blame the Chinese businessman for diversifying abroad when there seems so little certainty of racial tolerance at home, and when political favours matter so much to success? Next year one's political connections could count for as little as the influence of one's patrons.

Liem's success doubtless owes much to his friendship with the Suharto family and with military officers close to the Palace, but it was partly his personality too, and his way of doing business, that gained him the trust and confidence of his patrons. They knew where they stood with him. He has always kept his part of the bargain. It is hard to say of him, as it is so often said of the Chinese in Southeast Asia, that he has a short-term view, that he eschews investment in manufacturing and industry for the promise of easier money in trading.

As a successful Chinese, the target of so much popular antagonism, he has to tread lightly, avoiding ostentation and any public accentuation of his racial origins. For somebody who has been listed by America's *Fortune* magazine as one of the richest men in the world,[12] he lives surprisingly modestly, in the same bungalow that he and his family have occupied since 1951. Of course it has been renovated and extended, augmented with a swimming-pool and all the rest of it, but it stands in a lane off Kota, a far from fashionable neighbourhood in Jakarta's Chinese quarter. With his Chinese faith in geomancy, Liem believes the house to have brought him luck, and rather than move to a better part of town he has bought up the other properties along the street and got his children to live there.

Keeping a low profile at home is not so hard when you can let your hair down abroad. A luxurious home in the Katong area of Singapore and a Rolls-Royce in Hong Kong are only two of the many symbols of the Liem family's cosmopolitan lifestyle. In Singapore and Hong Kong, you can be as Chinese as you like without exciting comment; and it is in these places too that Liem Sioe Liong hobnobs with visiting dignitaries from the People's Republic of China. Utter pragmatism governs his relations with China, and he would go for a hard-nosed deal with Peking with as much sang-froid as he would one with Taipei. When, in the 1970s, Peking found itself burdened with large quantities of unwanted Zanzibar cloves, part of the payment in kind which China received for building the Tanzam Railway in Africa, it was Liem Sioe Liong who took them off its hands.[13]

In Thailand, the symbiosis of Chinese capital and indigenous ruling power is so inescapable, and seems to date so far back, that it has become a fact of life, something normal to the country. Chinese businessmen and Thai upper classes have become particularly close over the last two or three decades, but their relations had been intimate from the very beginning, and their present-day collaboration may be seen as the continuation of an older pattern. The Chinese merchants who came to trade in Thailand in earlier centuries served a purpose for which the mass of the Thai populace, mostly slaves and corvée labourers, was largely unfitted, namely that of the middleman, handling the commerce from which the court derived so much of its revenue. With the opening of Thailand to international trade by the Bowring Treaty, the Chinese found an even greater arena for their trading talents, quickly becoming the essential link between foreign interests and the local economy.

Yet for all their wealth and economic influence, the Chinese felt themselves to be less than masters of their own fates, for it was the

Siamese, the aristocrats and the government bureaucrats, who held ultimate power. The only way they could be sure of political protection was by offering to share their wealth with the power-holders; and this was what the Chinese merchants did, giving to the Thai nobility not only their daughters' hands in marriage but also generous shares in their companies. With the Thai governing classes engaging in business by way of the Chinese, and the Chinese gaining protection and privilege thereby, a profitable, not to say cosy, relationship was struck between the people at the top of the political and economic hierarchies.

But even Thailand, where the Chinese have suffered less racial antagonism than in other Southeast Asian countries, was not without its anti-Chinese phase. To keep their capital safe from Thai economic nationalism, Chinese businessmen fell back on the old practice of giving a share of it to the ruling élite. By the early 1950s, the boards of directors of Chinese companies were like a roll-call of the blue-blooded and mighty in indigenous society. Many observers would probably have described these Thais as no more than paper chairmen or directors, but still the Chinese businesses could not have done without them.

The cukong relationships of Indonesia find a parallel in the alliances of Chinese businessmen and Thai generals of the 1960s. Twenty-five years later the highest reaches of Bangkok business still seem a world of strong Thai and Chinese alliances, and scholars of progressive orientation love to draw charts to show how close and complex are the corporate and family links between certain Chinese businessmen and notables in the civil or military bureaucracy. Often their relationship is far more than a *modus vivendi*, for it has come to be based upon personal friendships as well, and even intermarriage between their families.[14]

Much the best known of such Chinese families is the Sophonpanich, a byword for high finance and banking. The founder, who died at the age of seventy-seven in January 1988, was Chin Sophonpanich, or Ch'en Pi-ch'en to the Chinese. Though born in the outskirts of Bangkok, in Thonburi, Chin's education was entirely Chinese. This was because his parents did what was customary and sent him back to school in their ancestral homeland when he was five. Home was Ch'ao-yang, the provenance of so many of the Teochiu immigrants to Thailand.

Chin was there until he was seventeen, when his father lost his job as a sawmill clerk and the money which paid for his schooling suddenly dried up. He returned to Bangkok and, while studying to speak Thai at night-school, held his head above water by working, first as a dogsbody, then as a coolie, and finally as the Assistant Manager of a construction company. When fire destroyed the construction company in 1931, Chin's fortunes might have gone down with his employer's, but his aptitudes had caught the eye of a successful Chinese in the insurance business, and Chin was given a chance to run another construction company. His experience and confidence growing, Chin presently went into business for himself, pursuing interests in timber, paper, hardware, pharmaceuticals, canned goods and insurance, and making his reputation as a rice exporter. A stint as a comprador to a foreign commercial bank got him interested in banking, and in 1944, two years into the Japanese occupation, he acquired the Bangkok Bank, which was to become supreme among the country's private institutions.

He played an honourable part in the Japanese war, lending his support to the Free Thai resistance movement, and winning a medal for his courage and daring. But the story of his rise to pre-eminence in the business community is not without its seamier side. The growth of the Bangkok Bank in the post-war period was nothing short of spectacular, and while it is true that the closure of foreign banks during the Japanese occupation, coupled with wartime inflation, helped to create domestic banks and boost their business, it has nevertheless been noted by many observers that the breathtaking expansion of the Bangkok Bank in the early and mid-1950s coincided with Chin's alliances with Thailand's political-military figures.[15]

Indeed, his case seems a classic illustration of the truism that in those days no businessman could hope to grow rich without cultivating a military patron. Chin found a political protector in a most unsavoury character, a man who has been described as a 'superlative crook': Pao Sriyanont was a criminal of the old familiar kind, the gangster and opium racketeer underneath his police-general's uniform.[16] As an anti-Communist, he enjoyed the sponsorship of the CIA, but who was to say to which of Pao's chief interests the police resources were largely devoted, the witch-hunting or the drug-smuggling? An intemperate man, he was said to chew glasses when drunk, leaving blood all over the place; it did not surprise those who knew him that in Switzerland, where he ended his days (penniless, Chin was later to claim), he was found to have drunk himself to death. Those Chinese businessmen who enjoyed his protection greatly prospered; and it is perhaps a measure of how intimate was their relationship that when Pao was ousted in a coup by the military dictator Sarit Thanarat in the late 1950s, Chin Sophonpanich decamped swiftly to Hong Kong, and stayed away from Thailand for more than five years.

He was lucky to be able to entrust the running of the bank's affairs to Boonchu Rojanastien, a young auditor he had brought into the company some years earlier, and who was later to become the country's Finance Minister and still later its Deputy Prime Minister. Since 1953, when the government bought up a share of the bank, the Bangkok Bank has been deeply involved in the politics of the nation, and counted among its board directors a number of deputy prime ministers and speakers of Parliament.[17] For sixteen years, the Chairman of the bank just happened to be Field Marshal Prapass Charusathiara, the military strongman who (as Deputy Prime Minister) ruled Thailand with Premier Thanom Kittikachorn until they were toppled by a mass uprising in 1973. And one of the country's most influential men, General Arthit Kamlang-ek, Commander-in-Chief of the Thai Army, just happens to be a close personal friend of Chin's son and heir, the bank's President Chatri Sophonpanich.

It is the same wherever one looks; the political patronage is only too apparent. A family which runs absolutely true to type is that of Cheng Wu-lou, a second-generation Chinese who goes by the Thai name of Udane Techapaibul. Techapaibul was born in 1914 in Thailand, the son of a Teochiu who made his money selling rice liquor and running an opium-house. The second generation is rather more respectable, choosing to prosper through banking, insurance, real estate, sugar-milling and brewing. In all the towns in Thailand, in every corner of Bangkok, one would find a branch of the Bangkok Metropolitan Bank, the largest of the three banks controlled by the Techapaibul family. One count put the number of the family's enterprises at ninety-two, and there is no doubt that in any reckoning of Thai big business, the Techapaibul group would appear somewhere near the apex, amongst the top two or three.

There has probably not been a time since 1939, the inaugural year of the Bank of Asia, another of the banks now controlled by Techapaibul, when there was not somebody politically well connected sitting on the board. During the time of Sarit Thanarat, the military dictator who ran Thailand from 1958 to 1963, and who died leaving millions for his family and mistresses to fight over, the bank had Sarit's half-brother for a manager and an assured stake in the gold industry and in the handling of the state lottery, a large contributor to Sarit's riches. Later, the company's board members found themselves working side by side in partnership with Thanom Kittikachorn's son Narong, whose cupidity left the most venal mobster far behind; when not wearing his banker's hat, and before his exile in 1973, he could be discovered running a drugs racket and amassing a fortune from a host of criminal activities.[18]

Other business families have had members of the royal family as board members or shareholders, and, until the Prapass-Thanom regime fell, the boards of directors of successful companies were rife with high-ranking officers and generals. The age of political protection, though, is said to be almost over, and those Chinese businessmen whose dependence on Thai patronage earned them the unflattering name of 'pariah entrepreneurs' in the 1960s have become more their own men, though this is not to say that it doesn't still help to have friends in high places.

Chin Sophonpanich typifies his kind in a number of other ways. One of the old sort, he returned to China when he was twenty to marry the girl his parents had chosen for him, taking a second wife in 1936, a Thai-born Chinese called Boonsri. He had two sons by his first wife, Rabin and Chatri; and four sons and a daughter by Boonsri. He died leaving a large portion of his business empire in family hands, and every one of his six sons can be discovered managing a part of it. No Chinese entrepreneur dies without having given a great deal of thought to the question of who runs the company after he is gone. 'Keep it in the family' is said to be a Chinese business motto, though one has only to think of Italian business families to realize that it isn't just the Chinese who are dynastic.

Chin Sophonpanich's eldest son Rabin has always lived in Hong Kong (where he is known as Robin Chan), looking after the family interests there. The Sophonpanich empire is typical of big overseas Chinese enterprises in having an overseas nexus. The international expansion of the Bangkok Bank had its start in the branch which Chin had the foresight to open in Hong Kong in 1954, to service the growing trade between the British colony and Thailand. One branch led to another, each market to the next, until the bank had reached out east and west, north and south, across the seas to Singapore, Kuala Lumpur, Saigon, Jakarta, Tokyo, Osaka, Taipei, London, Hamburg, New York and Los Angeles. It is a matter of pride to the family that Chin was one of the first bankers to underwrite the expansion of post-war business in the region, lending money to Chinese businessmen – complete unknowns with nothing to offer save ideas and ambition – at a time when none of the Western banks would. Out of the personal web of customers he spun would emerge world-class tycoons like Liem Sioe Liong.

Besides personal links, kith and kin were important to the business's overseas expansion. One son, Chote, headed the London branch of the bank in the early 1980s, and another, Charn, helped to computerize it in the 1970s.[19] A son in Singapore, a brother in Hong Kong, an uncle in Manila, a cousin in New York, and various relations all over the globe – this is supposed to be the overseas Chinese scheme of things, the means by which Chinese commerce gains access to markets, agents and information. It is certainly true that contacts and commercial advantages can arise out of the diaspora, facilitated and strengthened by blood-bonds and comradeships based on family name, dialect and village of origin. This has made for trade specialization and monopolies, with a particular line of business becoming the sole preserve of a particular dialect group, conducted almost exclusively by Hokkiens, say, or Cantonese. It comes as no surprise to learn that the bank headed by Rabin Sophonpanich in Hong Kong, for example, specializes in trade finance for Teochiu customers.

Such a style of business can never be entirely rational – the clansman you have working for you may not be the best man for the job; the supplies you get from your fellow Teochiu may not be as competitively priced as those from his Cantonese rival. And in an organization where the family head's authority is absolute, nepotism, favouritism and feuding will thrive. All in all, the family-dominated Chinese firm would find little favour with management pundits from American business schools. But if it has too strong a personal emphasis – and certainly who you know is more important than what you know in the Chinese scheme – that is partly because it represents an immature stage of business development. General Motors-style organization has yet to triumph over family.

In wanting firms to remain family fiefs, Chinese tycoons have something in common with people like Giovanni Agnelli, the Chairman of Fiat, and Chung Ju Yung, the founder of Hyundai, the South Korean industrial conglomerate that grew from a garage to a legend in less than a single generation. But this is not to say that big Chinese firms are not broadening their ownership base with share sales on stock exchanges, or that family authority is not being diluted and diffused as, with the organizations growing in size and complexity, close family control becomes an inefficient and impractical proposition and more and more top executive positions are filled by professional managers with no blood or tribal ties to the owner. A modern manufacturing firm will be claimed by the international context of its operations, the highly competitive nature of its market, the need for foreign industrial technology and far more capital than can be raised from traditional sources, for a style of doing business that is both less personal and more recognizably Western. Nevertheless, it would still be difficult to imagine the head of a Chinese family-owned corporation turning power over to a Lee Iacocca.

The optimist will say that as Chinese enterprises get increasingly absorbed into the international capitalist pattern, they will lose their distinctness, their tribal loyalties will no longer remain primitively uppermost, and the us-them demarcations that so bedevil race relations will blur. By his membership in the worldwide society of capitalists, the modern Chinese magnate will feel happier in the company of those who operate on the same urbane, cosmopolitan scale, whether they are Chinese or not, than among those who earn a living selling Hainanese Chicken Rice or hawking ice-cream. His social circle, overlapping with his business one, is more likely to be built up from contacts made through membership of the Rotary and Golf Clubs than through those of clan halls and dialect associations. At this end of the business scale, it is not so much being Hokkien or Cantonese that matters as class.

Numerous academics, learned papers and Ph.D. dissertations have advanced theories to account for the economic success of the Chinese in Southeast Asia.[20] Some have sought an explanation in Chinese business style and practice, others in Chinese culture.

The reader may remember that the Chinese predilection for low-margin, high-turnover business impressed an observer, Bishop Salazar of Manila, as far back as the sixteenth century. Four hundred years later, this characteristically Chinese *modus operandi* is still noticeable. A study worth citing is that of George Hicks and Gordon Redding, which looks at the largest enterprises in the Philippines and compares the ones owned by ethnic Chinese with the ones owned by Filipinos, Spaniards and Americans. The authors are interested to know how a people representing only two per cent of the population have managed to control fifty-eight per cent of the commerce, and they find, using measures such as income to sales ratio and days of accounts receivable, that, in the commercial sector especially, Chinese firms are more efficient, maintaining tougher financial control, and that they make do with lower margins, suggesting an 'ability to persevere on the basis of a steady accumulation of small returns'.[21]

Does their way of doing business have anything to do with their being

Chinese? In other words, is it a question of culture? It is certainly true that Chinese commerce is inconceivable without Chinese kin and social networks. But Linda Lim of Michigan University, herself an overseas Chinese, is one of those scholars who eschew an excessively culturalist approach to the explanation of Chinese business success. 'Chinese social organization', she writes, 'is neither necessary nor sufficient as an explanation of Chinese dominance . . .'[22] On the basis of her own research in the electronics manufacturing industry in Singapore and Malaysia in 1976, and of the work of a number of other scholars, she concludes that ethnic factors do not matter much if you are a multinational, nor do they matter at the level of petty trading and low-wage labour, but they do have a part to play in the middle reaches of business life, the level where Chinese business is concentrated, and where the old relationships can be an advantage.[23]

Simple and definitive explanations for overseas Chinese business success are not to be found. Illumination of a kind comes from an unexpected source, the passage in Anthony Burgess's *Malayan Trilogy* where a young Chinese student, a musical prodigy who by eighteen has produced what look to be works of genius, tells his English teacher, who proposes to get him a scholarship to England, why he can't go abroad to study music. 'We'll get that symphony performed,' the teacher has said to the pupil. 'We'll get you to Europe.'

In reply, the boy says only: 'I don't think my father will let me go to Europe. There is the business, you see, and I am the eldest son. He wants me to take a course in accountancy.'[24]

In the same work Burgess describes the attitude of a Malay: 'He had few illusions about his own people: amiable, well-favoured, courteous, they loved rest better than industry; through them the peninsula would never advance – rather their function was to remind the toiling Chinese, Indians and British of the ultimate vanity of labour.'[25]

So the question of why the Chinese have done so well is perhaps a politer way of asking why the natives have done so badly. There is many a bigoted Chinese who has a ready answer to this: the native is lazy, or dumb, or backward, or easily satisfied with little. Their part, the most racist Chinese say, is to fetch and carry. The riposte to that is that the Chinese are acquisitive, greedy, devious and calculating. Much nonsense has been uttered about the Chinese's Midas touch and the native's lack of it, and there is a rampant fiction that if you are a Chinese you are sprung from a mercantile tradition. The Chinese, it is popularly believed, are natural capitalists, and the natives, who are not, simply cannot match them.

Contrary to such belief, though, the passion for business is by no means a general Chinese trait, and in China itself, the merchant has been disparaged as the lowest of people. In a society ordered by Confucian values, the ability to profit from trading was never admired, and this put rather a damper on a universal flowering of Chinese entrepreneurship. If the Thais believed that entering the civil service was the surest way of getting on in the world, so did the majority of the Chinese; and for every Chinese who prospered from trading, there were hundreds who held themselves aloof from commerce. If there is such a thing as a tradition of enterprise among the Chinese, it is only to be found among the coastal Chinese and the diaspora. Those enthusiastic Hokkien traders who sailed to Nanyang were not heirs to a mercantile tradition; if anything, they were people who, by emigrating, were able to leave their inherited cultural inhibitions behind.

The careers of Liem Sioe Liong and Chin Sophonpanich show that the chances of history, and the character of the country in which each found himself (including the monumental scale of its corruption), were factors in their rise to riches, but the success of the Chinese as a group is not adequately explained by these. After all, why is it that these same factors have not thrown up an Indonesian Liem Sioe Liong, or a Siamese Chin Sophonpanich?

Success has come for the overseas Chinese as it does for any emigrant, from what social scientists would call a 'high achievement drive'. It can certainly be argued that the desperate circumstances which have impelled immigration have ultimately benefited those who at first sight were their chief victims, because they have produced in those people who had to find their own solutions a burst of energy fuelled by the need to survive. Immigrants are highly motivated people, powered by dispossession and the wish to make a fresh start. And in the Chinese case there was the added factor that, when they had had to leave their homeland, they had done so to make enough money quickly so that they could return to live comfortably in China.

So when the Chinese say that the native is happy to sit under a tree and wait for the coconuts and the durians to fall into his lap, they are stating a fact in a way: the native was the one with the land, the one with the self-sufficiency and economic security to live a life of tropical idyll in preference to the rough and tumble of the market-place. It was left to the immigrant Chinese to corner every market from crop-dealing to ironmongery; and once established, the monopolies perpetuated themselves, to be broken only by the actions of governments bent on righting the economic balance.

Among the overseas Chinese themselves, a very complimentary self-image is upheld; they see themselves as nothing less than the very embodiment of Diligence and Thrift, and they claim that these are Chinese qualities. Their confidence in the superiority of their own culture reinforced at every turn by the visible evidence of their wealth, they have no doubt at all that it is hereditary flair that does it. To their way of thinking, to be Chinese is to be business-minded, and it is a combination of genetics and upbringing that makes them the dedicated entrepreneurs they are. The further one moves from the core of tradition, they think, the less business-minded one becomes – which is why, to their mind, peranakans and Babas do not take so readily to trade. A Western education is well enough in its way, and very helpful to one's advance in a colonial or modern society, but sending one's son to an English public school is asking for trouble, because the experience could do irreparable damage to the child's aptitude for business, and turn him into a wishy-washy liberal or worse. (My own father, a gifted entrepreneur, never ceased to regret that his children all received English education – which he said had a lot to answer for, as he sighed over our deplorable lack of business fervour.)

In the past decade, those determined to find the roots of overseas Chinese economic success in Chinese culture have been abetted in their views by a fashionable theory. This is the theory that the economic miracles they call the Four Little Dragons of Asia – Taiwan, South Korea, Hong Kong and Singapore – have been helped in their breath-taking development of modern industrial capitalism by their Confucian tradition. What the Protestant ethic has done for Europe, it is posited, Confucianism has done for these Asian societies. The irony of this is that in the 1950s a number of analysts saw Confucianism, particularly its conservatism and its antagonism to commercial activity, as one of the *obstacles* to the modernization of East Asia. Certainly the very fount of that tradition, China itself, doesn't make a very convincing case for the notion that Confucianism is a help rather than a hindrance to capitalist development. But there's Confucianism and Confucianism, today's exponents say; the Confucianism we're talking about, they explain, is not that of old imperial China, but a set of values and attitudes common to all the national cultures falling within the orbit of Chinese civilization and Confucian influence. They further explain that these attributes – a developed capacity for discipline and delayed gratification, an emphasis on harmony in social relations, and respect for superiors – have given the Little Dragons a comparative advantage in modern capitalist development.

Of course the Chinese do not have a monopoly of the values so glibly ascribed to Confucianism; such values would be just as familiar to a Samuel Smiles or a Victorian, and on a scientific plane it is well-nigh impossible to prove that the Chinese are more richly imbued with these virtues than the other races in Southeast Asia. But many Chinese have taken the idea of a 'Chinese spirit of capitalism' to imply ethnic and cultural superiority. There are plenty of Chinese in Singapore, for example, who believe that the place would not be the economic success that it is if it were populated, not by a majority of Chinese, but by a majority of Malays. Racial explanations of ability, while discredited scientifically, sadly still go down very well in uninformed quarters.

In actual fact, Chinese culture is inhibiting in many ways. Like other traditional societies, China appears to be acting out an ancient historical curse, which, delivered centuries ago, still seems to keep the nation in an enfeebled condition. Overseas Chinese have escaped that curse by emigrating. All human beings are burdened by their cultural inheritance, but people on the move have a less rooted feeling for the permanency of their country's institutions than people who stay put. The sins of the father cannot be visited on a son who has emigrated.

CHAPTER THIRTEEN

Cultural and National Identities

Like much of Africa, most of the Southeast Asian countries where the Chinese are settled are newly defined nations within old colonial boundaries, many of which have ethnically varied populations whose members have little in common beyond the fact that they happen to live in the same country. The definition of a group of people as constituting a nation is always an act of political and social creation; it is always artificial. This is as true of Malaysia, say, as it is of Italy. The difference is that Italy has been a national unit longer, and its people have had more time to evolve a national identity.

The post-Second World War years in Southeast Asia were years of 'nation building', when newly independent states struggled to preserve their unity and to give expression to their own particular identity, as yet not quite confident as to what that might be. For the ethnically mixed countries, the omens for nationhood were not good. It had been a policy of the colonial masters to keep immigrant and native apart; but though the days of deliberate ethnic segregation were now over, elements of the old relationship – with the Europeans above, the Chinese in the middle, and the indigenes below – remained. Yet in an independent Southeast Asia, Chinese separateness was no longer acceptable. The Chinese must integrate; they must, in a sense, relinquish their Chinese identity, or at least grow indifferent to it. The Chinese propensity for forming exclusive communities was proverbial; and nothing short of force, it has been said, could ever break the back of Chinese racial pride and intransigence.

But integration is a two-way process; you can't become one with people who make you feel you don't belong. If made welcome the Chinese could and did acculturate to their host society. It had been done, and without people making much of a song and dance about it. Until the Khmer Rouge took over in 1975, the Chinese settler mixed easily with the Cambodian indigene, and it has been said that in all Southeast Asia his was probably the most successful of the cases of smooth Chinese merger with native society.[1] An even better-known example of successful integration is Thailand, where, unusually for a country with a large ethnic minority, politicians do not play on the ethnic issue. The Thais are touchingly pleased about this; rightly so perhaps, since they seem to have succeeded where others have failed. Does it not represent a reproach to those countries where inhospitality and stigmatization have marked the Chinese off and kept him apart? It is said with pride by Chinese and Thai alike that the two races are fused into a common culture, and that their country is free from the clashes of race and religion that bedevil the communal relations of nations like Malaysia, its immediate southern neighbour. The Chinese have taken Thai nationality and adopted Thai names, with the Kho family becoming the Khotrakuls, for instance, and the Ma family the Mingwatanabuls.

On the other hand, while one should not begrudge the Thais their satisfaction at this happy state of affairs, one would be right to wonder if they sometimes do not over-congratulate themselves. Reading one of Bangkok's Chinese newspapers (its front page splashed with news from Taiwan or the People's Republic of China), or wandering into the headquarters of the dialect associations, where the Teochius seem to be unmistakably Teochiu, and the Hokkiens Hokkien, you would never guess that any intermingling had taken place.

Clearly the Chinese, like any ethnic minority, lead lives that are balanced on an invisible see-saw between two or more identities. Circumstances, the nature of their audience, and calculations of risk and benefit dictate whether their 'backstage' or 'frontstage' identity is to the fore in any particular situation. Sometimes it pays to appear more Chinese, sometimes more Thai, say, or Malay. One cannot pretend that the Chinese are not selective, manipulative even, in their acculturation. Peter Gosling, who studied this process in Malaysia, reports on the behaviour of an apparently Malayanized Chinese shopkeeper who, when it suited him to appear Chinese, did so without the slightest hesitation or difficulty.[2] Normally he was scarcely to be distinguished from the indigenes – he wore a sarong, spoke a quiet and polite Malay, and was self-effacing and affable in manner – but come harvest-time, when he had to go to the fields to collect from the Malay farmers the crops on which he had advanced them credit, and he would put on his shorts and vest, and assume an altogether brusquer manner. You have to be Chinese to drive a hard bargain; a Malay would be expected to be gentle and more easygoing. One can almost see our shopkeeper stiffened into a Chinese attitude, living up to the legend of the grasping Asian Jew. Something similar has been observed to be at work in Sri Racha, a small town in southern Thailand, probably because the Chinese have been typecast there by their mercantile role. At the uppermost end of income and business prosperity, as at the very bottom, Chinese readily admit themselves to be Thai – wealth is a great equalizer, as is poverty – but merchants and entrepreneurs in the lower and middle strata of the middle class find it useful to claim Chinese identity.[3]

If materialism and a way with money are seen, rightly or wrongly, to be facets of Chinese identity, the doggedness with which the Chinese have hung on to their language is seen to be another. The possession of the ancestral language is the supreme mark of being Chinese, imparting as it does a sense of unbroken continuity with the earliest years of Chinese history. Any account of Chinese acculturation to other societies must deal with the way in which they have maintained their own schools and, above all, their own words. Though their settlements do not depend entirely upon Chinese-language schools and Chinese newspapers for their continued existence as distinct communities, any more than an overseas Chinese depends on knowledge of his ancestral language for his consciousness of Chinese identity, nevertheless there is nothing like Chinese education for fostering a pride in, if not a love of, the homeland. No one who has studied the Chinese classics and Chinese poetry can remain indifferent to China. Indeed, a well-regarded study into the integration of young Chinese into Filipino society in 1970 found the Chinese language to be the most important criterion of ethnic identity.[4]

Chinese education in the Philippines exemplifies overseas Chinese education in general. The classic pattern was for one or more sons of immigrant fathers to be sent back to the home village to be educated in a Chinese school and to be brought up as proper Chinese. (The split that this often created in the second generation is illustrated by a young Chinese I met in Bangkok. He could not converse with his two elder brothers without an interpreter because he had gone to a local school and spoke no Chinese, while they had attended a school in Swatow and spoke no Thai; their having been educated in China had left the brothers feeling more Chinese than Thai, and they had gone on to work in Taiwan, widening the gap between them and the rest of the family.) As the overseas communities grew big enough, the Chinese established their own schools; these, depending on one's point of view, were either vehicles of Chinese humanism and tradition or incubators of Chinese nationalism. The first such school to be founded in the Philippines was the Anglo-Chinese School, set up in 1899 in the grounds of the

Chinese embassy in Manila. By 1963, when enrolment reached a peak, there were 162 such schools, with a student population of no less than 67,800, financed and run entirely by the Chinese themselves.[5]

A visitor newly arrived from Taiwan, when he entered the portals of any of these institutions, would not think himself abroad at all. The teachers had been imported from Taiwan, the textbooks too; the medium of instruction was Mandarin; the portraits on the walls were of Dr Sun Yat-sen. The pupils recited the Confucian classics, and celebrated Chinese holidays by marching to Chinese music down the streets in brightly coloured and orderly processions. Most remarkable of all, the schools were administered by the Overseas Chinese Affairs Commission of the Kuomintang government, which made it its business to dictate the curriculum, the teaching methods and standards, and regularly sent its own inspectors to the schools to see that they conformed to pattern. When the schools issued diplomas, they were signed and sealed by the Taiwan embassy. When the pupils graduated, they were assured places at Taiwan's universities. You had to be blind not to see that the schools were aimed at turning out good Chinese citizens, not good Philippine ones.

So long as it denied them Philippine citizenship, the government could not prohibit Chinese education, but in 1973, not long before the Chinese were naturalized *en masse*, the inevitable happened: a presidential decree issued by Marcos ordered all alien schools to be phased out within four years. Permits previously granted to Chinese schools were revoked, and only two hours of Chinese a day were allowed on top of the standard English curriculum. This was a battering from which Chinese education in the Philippines would never recover. Prophets of doom have pronounced its demise ever since, and many have said that it would die a natural death anyway, as Chineseness wore off in the second and third generations.

With the change of syllabus, the schools have indeed lost part of their point; and yet, fourteen years on, the three I visited in Manila still seemed unmistakably Chinese places. The first was closed for the day, it being Confucius's birthday. In the entrance hall of the second, the former Overseas Chinese Secondary School, the notice-board was pinned with exhortatory posters proclaiming September to be Thrift and Industriousness Month, and October to be Helpfulness and Cooperation Month. To judge by a new wing, built and equipped entirely by alumni's donations, the Chinese tradition of self-help remained strong. A scroll inscribed with a single Chinese character on a wall in the headmaster's office enjoined an immemorial Chinese virtue: *jen*, 'forbearance'. For the pupils, Chinese has become a second language; and yet the parents had successfully pleaded for mathematics to be taught in Mandarin instead of English, experience having shown that the children advance to a higher standard that way. Nobody knew why this should be so, but I was reminded of my own experience in North Borneo, where ethnic Chinese students who had started off in a Chinese-medium primary school were almost always better at maths than those from an English-medium one.

The other school was named for Chiang Kai-shek. To call it a school is perhaps to do it an injustice, since it is an institution that encompasses every stage of education from kindergarten to university. Talking to its bespectacled teachers in Mandarin, breathing its air of industry and prudence, one is strongly reminded of educational establishments in Taiwan. In the grounds, an obelisk commemorates the thirteen alumni martyred in the war of resistance against Japan. It was a place which inspired confidence; it did not have the haphazardness of the rest of Manila. Clearly there was a good deal of discipline. The children in the kindergarten sat compactly on stools, neat and well cared-for, doing as they were told. The whole scene was one of bright and easy discipline, and adding a reassuring touch to the whole were the young, sensible-looking teachers, every one of them in a pretty, sensible uniform.

Chinese schools had a harder time of it in Thailand. Again and again the authorities tried to suppress them, threatening their sponsors with penalties of one kind or another. The first attempt, in 1938, failed to stamp them out once and for all, and another drive was mounted ten years later. This was a relentless exercise, given added ferocity by its anti-Communist thrust. Seen to be springs of Communism, the schools were subjected to police raids and inspection. Many were forced to close, or else became Chinese in name only, with their management and curriculum brought under Thai authority. Out went the Chinese teaching materials, Chinese usages; in came Thai textbooks, Thai teachers, the Thai flag and the Thai national anthem.[6] Looking back, Thai and Chinese alike are now agreed that these measures, harsh as they were, were not all bad in their effect: they did much to make the Chinese identify with Thai ways, and hastened their integration into Thai society.

The language is now little heard among the Chinese young. But their parents have not given up. Chinese classes there still are – like the ones

I came upon in the southern towns of Hat Yai and Pattani, where the children, some with their minds on their lesson, some not, are made to recite their proverbs and maxims in exactly the same way as children in China have done throughout the ages. The survival of the language is astonishing, but seems less so when it is remembered that it is but a short hop from southern Thailand to Malaysia, where Chinese education has never ceased. Many of the Chinese in their fifties had circumvented the Thai ban by going to Penang for their Chinese education, and speak warmly still of their classmates there, and of school reunions which they continue enthusiastically to attend.

How long the language will survive in Malaysia itself is anyone's guess. A dead issue in the rest of Nanyang, the matter of Chinese education still raises hackles and sparks quarrels in Malaysia. The uneasy awareness of the need to defend it haunts the Malaysian Chinese, who has seen Mandarin retreat before Malay and English. Nobody can be casual about it, since it is entangled in racial antipathies and questions of ethnic and national identities. Like that of many another new country, the Malaysian search for a national identity has assumed a linguistic complexion.

Education has long been a sensitive issue and not even the British had known what to do about it. After the war, when they gave it some thought, one committee suggested starting all primary school children off on English and Malay, and then letting the best ones go on to English-medium secondary schools. Another proposed the opposite, finding virtue in the sense of belonging that could be fostered by maintaining the Malays, Chinese and Tamils in their different cultures and separate schools. The dithering ended with independence, which signalled the official ascendancy of Malay (or Bahasa Malaysia, as it came to be called) over the other languages, accompanied by vigorous but fruitless protest on the part of the Chinese community. English was allowed as an alternative official language, but only until 1967.

All along, the British had been specially solicitous of the interests of the Malays, recognizing the Malays and not the Chinese as their wards. A British Resident summed up a common enough British attitude when he reported that 'whatever may be the supposed advantages resulting from the introduction of Chinese or other foreign adventurers', the Governor was satisfied that these were 'dearly purchased by the exclusion, depression and degradation of the Original Malay Inhabitants of the Peninsula, who are in the first instance entitled to our protection and encouragement'.[7] The reasons for the British protectiveness of the

Malays are not hard to find: the Malays are gentler people, easier to govern than the Chinese, and Malay was the language the British learnt to speak. There was also the special affinity of the English ruling class for Islam, an affinity which expressed itself in the generations of British favouritism to Muslims in India at the expense of Hindus, and in the preference for Arabs against Jews in the Middle East. At any rate, ever mindful of the need to safeguard the 'special position' of the native, British policy was by and large pro-Malay and anti-Chinese. The need to guarantee the Malays' 'special position' or privileges was eventually to be written into the constitution of the newly sovereign country. And the new nation was to be Malay of identity: among other things the designation of Malay as the national language would see to that.

Many Chinese spoke demotic Malay, carrying their bilingualism lightly; but now they had to acquire a reading and writing knowledge of it. Not a few did so with a feeling of resentment, believing the sway of Malay to have had no roots of literary or cultural superiority. Linguistic specialists say that, just as no language is either beautiful or ugly, so no language is intrinsically either superior or inferior to another; but you will not find many Malaysian Chinese believing this. To them Malay (a language cognate with Fijian and Maori, and spoken in Indonesia, the southern Philippines, southern Thailand and Singapore) is a tongue whose vocabulary is fundamentally fitted to the concerns of a primitive society – concerns such as fishing, begetting children, lying under coconut trees. They do not see its acquisition as gaining them *entrée* into the beauties of classical literature or philosophy, or giving them an aesthetic thrill. The fact that, to be adequate to the needs now to be served by it, Bahasa Malaysia has had to forge a new vocabulary by borrowing massively from English, does not increase its appeal to the Chinese, who find it hard to take Bahasa Malaysia neologisms like *universiti* and *teknologi* seriously.

The government's national language policy only goes to feed their fervour for Chinese education. Chinese parents can still send their children to Mandarin-medium primary schools (roughly a third of them fully financed by the government, the rest partially assisted), but upon reaching secondary school about nine out of ten such children switch to national institutions where the teaching is in Bahasa Malaysia, with the rest either going on to independent Chinese secondary schools or dropping out altogether. This is too little Chinese, mutter the Mandarin speakers, the hopefuls among whom had gone as far as calling for a Chinese university in the late 1970s and early 1980s. It

15. Shantung men at a camp in France during the First World War

16. A twelve-year-old Chinese boy being interrogated
at the San Francisco Immigration Station, 1923

17. The opening of the Kuomin Chinese School, Locke, California, 1926

18. Single women (*saw hei*)
arriving in Singapore from Kwangtung, 1930s

19. A Chinese funeral in England, 1922

20. Madame Wellington Koo

21. Tan Kah Kee, 1938   22. Chin Sophonpanich, aged twenty-two

23. Anna May Wong in *Shanghai Express*

24. Lee Kuan Yew with Margaret Thatcher, 1982

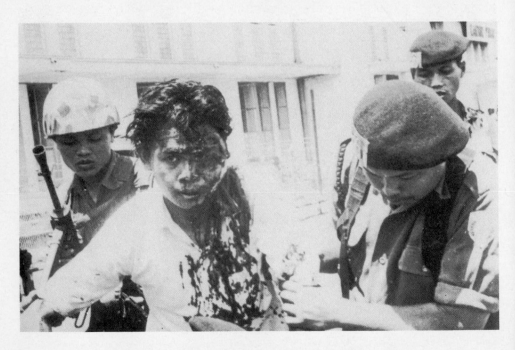

25. An Indonesian soldier props up a Chinese youth
wounded in a mob attack in Jakarta's Chinatown, 1967

26. Screen kung fu star Bruce Lee, 1972

27. Li Ka-shing with
Her Royal Highness Princess Alexandra
in London, 1987

28. Chinese students and residents demonstrate their support of the Tiananmen protestors, Gerrard Street, London's Chinatown, 1989

is already too much, counter some Malay politicians, who think that they have been more than generous in their concessions to linguistic diversity.

That feelings run high on this issue is well demonstrated by an incident in the autumn of 1987, when an apparently trivial matter, the promotion of a hundred-odd Chinese-teachers by the Education Ministry to senior administrative posts in the Chinese primary schools, all but flared into racial rioting. The teachers, though of Chinese descent, were not themselves graduates of Mandarin-medium schools; their appointment, in the opinion of the Chinese community leaders who came forward to threaten a boycott of classes if the government didn't retract it, would change the character of Chinese schools. It would not do to give in because, unless they bucked the trend, they might, before they knew it, find their schools administered by Malays or Indians. The threat opened the door to political and racial dissension, for it pitted the chief Chinese political party, the Malaysian Chinese Association, which came out in support of it, against the chief Malay party, the United Malays National Organization (Umno), its partner in the National Front coalition. Outraged by the Chinese stand, the youth wing of Umno summoned Malays to a giant rally, urging firmness upon the government and digging their own heels in with cries of 'Long live the Malays' and 'Allah is great'. Memories of the race riots of May 1969 were rekindled, as both sides squared up for a fight, and as rumours of imagined or impending clashes swept through the country. Overwrought parents ordered their children indoors, jittery shops put up shutters, nervous people rushed to supermarkets to stock up on food. Racial animosities worsened as the weeks passed, and might have degenerated into rioting if a potentially explosive political rally of Malays had not been called off.

The Chinese may seem to have over-reacted in their opposition to the school appointments, but, after so many years of economic and cultural attrition, they are simply bristling with defensive reflexes, and regard each small concession as a battle lost to the Malays, and worse, as the thin edge of the wedge, an invitation to further incursions into their rights. Their reaction is understandable when seen for what it was: a defence of constantly threatened ethnic turf. Besides, a knowledge of Mandarin is important to their concept of themselves as a unity, for they are a diverse people, forming Cantonese groups, Hakka groups, class groups, city groups, rural groups, locally born groups, foreign-born groups, and so on. It is not a property of any one group but something held in common. It is thus an important symbol of ethnic consciousness and solidarity.

Far more than most people in Southeast Asia, certainly far more than the Malays, the Chinese are confident of their cultural identity. Such certainty is bound to be disconcerting to the Malays, a people who have had less time to accustom themselves to their self-identification and their nationality. Malaysian nationhood still feels like a design of man, and that feeling is enhanced by the fact that, though Chinese and Indians make up a large part of the population, the gauges by which a man could claim himself to be fully Malaysian are almost always Malay – this gives it a contrived feeling. Identities are formed by the sum of inherited beliefs and historical experience, not by government fiat, but in Malaysia part of the pursuit of 'national integration' (a catchword of Malaysian politics) relates to the fostering of a new collective identity and an identity for the individual citizen. In effect, this means a Malay identity. If the Malays can deny the Chinese contribution to the country's cultural heritage, they will; in 1987 a visiting European delegation shown the sights of Malacca was driven to see the Portuguese cathedral and Dutch civic buildings, but the tour deliberately bypassed the old and architecturally distinct Straits Chinese streets.

But what does Malayness consist of? The Malay language certainly, but Malay identity needs more than a language to keep it strong and distinctive. By constitutional and legal definition, a Malay is and must be a Muslim. To be Malay, therefore, is to speak Malay and to practise Islam. But this does not mean that the many Malay-speaking Chinese converts to Islam are regarded as Malay. In contrast to Thailand, which pursues a policy of tolerant, active assimilation that insists on the importance of Thainess but does not use this notion as an instrument of exclusion, Malaysia demands standards of assimilation which, in effect, will debar the mass of the Chinese from Malay identity and from the rights and privileges that go with it. It is not even much good converting to Islam, because Chinese converts are only too clearly seen for the ingratiating opportunists and social climbers that some of them undoubtedly are; and so far from gaining acceptance into Malay society, they find themselves out on a limb, with neither their status nor their prospects bettered by the step they have taken.

Indeed, as the Chinese move ever closer towards integration, they find, to quote a Chinese politician, the 'goal post' shifting 'further and further back'.[8] The Chinese surmount one barrier, that of language, only to find themselves faced with another, a resurgent Islam.

Deposited uninformed in Malaysia in the 1970s, you would not easily guess yourself to be in a Muslim country. Now you would. New forces have urged the country to a closer identification with Muhammedanism and its people to a greater devoutness; today Malaysia feels what it was not meant to be: an Islamic state. Under Mahathir, the Prime Minister, Islam has been promoted at a pace that disturbs the undevout of all races.9 Urged by Malay chauvinists like the activists of the Muslim Youth Movement, the Islamization can be made to bear a racial interpretation, and it is partly because it does not want to be considered 'soft' on race by the parties which challenge its power that Umno has taken a more strongly Muslim attitude itself. Politicians do not shrink from exploiting racial rivalries for their own ends, and in the factional feuding into which Malaysian party politics has degenerated, Malay chauvinism is an obvious weapon.

The reflowering of Islam in Malaysia, which is an aspect of Malay chauvinism, cannot be understood by looking for internal causes in the Malay community alone. Of course Islam has always been prone to movements of reforming zeal, but its resurgence in Malaysia, while riding a global tide, is in part a consequence of inter-ethnic relations, a symbol of separatism aimed at distinguishing Us from Them. It gives Malayness an extra dimension, and raises its stature by linking it with a world culture, one shared by Indonesia, Egypt, Iran, Libya, Pakistan and Saudi Arabia. It helps the Malay define his position in the world. The Chinese has no such problem; he may feel cut off from Chinese culture, but for him to have a sense of his place in the world it is enough to know that that culture exists and that its glories are universally acknowledged.

Through contacts with fellow students from the Middle East in the 1970s, young Malays studying in Australia, England and North America were made suddenly aware of the weakness of their religious identity, and they reacted to their feelings of insecurity by becoming Muslim to the hilt. Back in Malaysia, there sprouted a host of fundamentalist groups preaching a return to untainted Islamic ways. Fired by Ayatollah Khomeini's revolution, many of these organizations cheerfully accepted the largesse of Libya and Saudi Arabia. Their members wear Arab dress, advocate sex segregation, and practise what they believe to be Arabic customs. Their repudiation of the West and all its works finds expression in their rejection of such 'Western' artefacts as tables, chairs and television sets, and their pursuit of strict dietary purity in their abhorrence of anything of possible Chinese origin.

Called *dakwah*, an Arabic term commonly rendered as 'missionary', these groups find their most enthusiastic recruits among Malay university students. They certainly seem to be at their more concentrated and visible on the campuses; at the national university in Kuala Lumpur, for example, they are instantly recognizable, the men in their white turbans, the women in their dark veils and neck-to-ankle robes. Costume has its meaningful place in identity, and one should no more disparage the new apparel as faked than one should dismiss Scottish kilts and tartans as bogus folkloristic trappings. If their dress seems inappropriate to the setting and climate, their religious ardour (of which the dress is a symbol) is what braces them for life in the unfamiliar, competitive environment in which they find themselves – an environment in which they, the newly urbanized Malays, are confronted by the entrenched, town-dwelling Chinese.

They are people caught in the anxieties of change in the modern city. An anthropologist who has studied them, Judith Nagata, relates their movement to 'a Malay identity crisis' and sees reflected in dakwah the wider unresolved ethnic conflicts of 'language, youth, education, rural-urban imbalances and Malay identity and rights'.[10] Is there something familiar about these people? There is a similarity to the born-again Christian who suddenly comes into his own at a Bible meeting, the American youth who joins the Hari Krishna consciousness movement, the black who seeks fulfilment in the Rastafarian cult.

They feel overwhelmed, perhaps, by the tide of modernity flooding heedless all around them, and by the proximity of non-Muslims. To them, all that is new seems to be alien, and often thoroughly undesirable. They will have no truck with the 'coffee-shop and blue jeans routine'.[11] Their attitude is the opposite of 'cultural cringe', the belief that everything from the West must be better; they resist Western modernity's universal appeal. This bodes ill for ethnic relations, for the irony is that, on some levels the coffee-shop and blue jeans routine is the only form of culture that can be shared by a population divided into exclusive cliques of race and religion: it is ethnically neutral. A 'modern' identity can submerge an ethnic one. A Malay engineer educated at a Western university would have more in common with an Indian or Chinese engineer than with a Malay peasant, even though, because of cultural conditioning, he would feel more at ease with the peasant on some level of his being. In educated and professional circles, Chinese and Malay alike find it easier to communicate their thoughts in English. This is often the case with immigrant, once-colonial societies, where an English education could rob the native of his ethnic singularity. As V. S. Naipaul has said of Trinidad: 'It was only our Britishness, our belonging to the British Empire, which gave us any identity.'[12]

The race problem in Malaysia is one of Malay-Chinese antipathy, not of white prejudices or East-West rivalry. But the dakwah movement's repugnance against Western culture complicates the scene. Malaysia is a tangle of racialist emotions, one kind of racialism reacting on the other. It takes two to make a problem, and I have dealt with the Malays at some length because it will be easier for them to come to terms with the Chinese in their midst once they have come to terms with themselves.

What are the categories and tests of national identity? Race, language, religion. By the first test Singapore's should be Chinese; if the national identity of Malaysia, with a population fifty-nine per cent Malay, is Malay, then that of Singapore, with a population two-thirds Chinese, should surely be Chinese.

But it is not, at least not officially. While it is the only country in the world where overseas Chinese predominate not only numerically but politically, Singapore considers itself a multiracial society – that is to say, it subscribes officially to the ideal of equal rights for all before the law and in the market-place, while at the same time respecting the languages, religions and customs of its ethnic minorities. None of the cultural patterns has been singled out as an official pet. With a population fifteen per cent Malay and over six per cent Indian, Singapore has four official languages: Malay, Chinese, Tamil and English.

'Instant Asia', its tourist board says of Singapore, and it is certainly true that nearly all of the diversity of the wider region can be found concentrated in the 224 square miles of the tiny republic. Yet the place does not have a confused or patchwork feeling to it, and the sort of tourist who goes round the world packaged in successively indistinguishable environments will feel instantly at home in it. The street signs are in only one script, English; and everyone of importance appears to speak English as his first language.

The writer Paul Theroux says that when he was teaching in Singapore he was asked by a student if he was going to write a novel about Singapore.

'No thanks,' he replied. 'But you've lived here your whole life – why don't you write one?'

'Can't,' the student said, then added, 'There's nothing to write about.'[13]

He had a point. The Prime Minister Lee Kuan Yew himself has said, 'Every time anybody starts anything which will unwind or unravel this orderly, organized, sensible, rational society, and make it irrational and emotional, I put a stop to it and without hesitation.'[14] Elsewhere they would think you were being disparaging if you likened a place to a computer or a machine, but not in Singapore, or at least not among its leading politicians – one of them once invoked the image of a jet fighter, automated to the hilt but needing a trained pilot to demonstrate its full potential.[15] Here they are immensely proud of the house they have built, of its reputation as the Switzerland of Asia. Detractors say they have created a robotic and boring people, and it is true that there is a swaddled and synthetic feel to Singapore, that no romantic, no eccentric, could really enjoy the city; but still it would be hypocritical of these critics to deny that when one enters Singapore out of another Southeast Asian city, one enters it with a sense of relief. Here things work. Here no fearful tropical sickness will befall you. Here no odious Marcos enriches himself from the public funds of a society of grinding poverty. Here almost nobody will irritate you with their inefficiency, or displease you by leaving litter about and scrawling graffiti on walls. Arriving from England, I never fail to take heart at the thought that no stagnant seediness of the kind inescapable in run-down British cities will greet me, that the restaurants will be reliable, the trains will not be cancelled. You have to hand it to these politicians: just think, twenty-five years ago, the island was a run-down newly independent ex-British colony; yet by 1988 it had become as rich as Spain, with a higher gross domestic product per head than New Zealand.

The tidiness bears the imprint of a social engineer, himself obsessional about cleanliness (on his first voyage to England in 1946, it has been reported, Lee Kuan Yew would selfishly use up more than six passengers' rations of fresh water each day to wash himself).[16] If it was Stamford Raffles who brought the island to life, it was Lee Kuan Yew who gave it its present persona.

He did so by a mixture of paternalism and paranoia. Talking to or observing its citizens, one often has the feeling in Singapore of a people cajoled and cowed into obedience, turned into children the better to follow the leader's instructions. Lee's unwillingness to brook dissent is well known. The island republic is a democracy, in so far as the word has any meaning; but in Lee Kuan Yew's Singapore one will discern many of the indices of autocracy. Opposition figures are apt to find themselves in trouble; dissenters are branded subversives or Marxist conspirators and jailed; the press reflects and flatters the prejudices of the ruling party, the PAP or People's Action Party; foreign periodicals critical of the government's actions will find their correspondents expelled or their circulation cut on the grounds that they are 'interfering with domestic affairs'; nobody says no to Lee Kuan Yew. And with it all goes a knee-jerk defensiveness, an obscurantism that at first sight seems puzzling. Lee Kuan Yew's country is enviably stable, the majority of the citizens are with him in putting prosperity before political and civil liberties: against what, then, is he on guard?

One concern is racial disharmony. There is little apparent sign of racial tension, but this is not to say that ethnically insensitive policies won't kindle it. Besides, at its narrowest a strait of only about a quarter of a mile divides the island from Malaysia, which is not difficult to imagine given over once more to racial riot; and Indonesia, where anti-Chinese feeling was tinder until recently, is not far away. Situated in a Malay archipelago, Singapore thinks itself another Israel, another migrant enclave surrounded by Islamic nations and vulnerable to tensions generated from within by Muslim disaffection.

Geopolitical realities, then, have greatly determined the face which Singapore has presented to the world. Another factor, of which more later, has been the Prime Minister's personal convictions and political aspirations. As these changed, so Singapore's persona changed. All this is reflected in the twists and turns of the language policy.

As a fighter against British colonialism in the 1950s, Lee Kuan Yew was a ready enough champion of the local languages, disparaging Anglicization and the study of English as an exercise in which people learnt 'about Francis Drake and his bowls, and Sir Walter Raleigh and his cloak, and daffodils and buttercups, which they have never seen'.[17] He and his party the PAP were helped to power by the activism of the Chinese stream, for colonialism's chief opponents were Chinese-educated students, Communists and trade unions – as we saw, it would be unusual to go through the Chinese school system without becoming imbued with Chinese nationalism, whereas students schooled in the language of the colonial master for jobs in the middle reaches of the civil service were by and large politically apathetic. 'The English-educated do not riot,' Lee Kuan Yew has said,[18] and he should know, since he is one of them himself. It was at about this time that he started applying himself to learning Hokkien and Mandarin.

But he did not doubt that what was directed against the British today, the immense emotive power of Chineseness, could be directed against the PAP tomorrow; and he was astute enough, perhaps even Machiavellian enough, to make it his first business, once he was sure of his authority, to hobble it. Chinese education, accused of being a vehicle of dangerous Chinese chauvinism, was laid low by the PAP; his biographer and confidant Alex Josey told us in 1974 that 'Within ten or 15 years, Lee Kuan Yew expects the Chinese language to be unimportant.'[19] Singaporeans still remember the time he cracked down on Nanyang, the Chinese-medium university and the pride of the Chinese community, to rid it of Communist influence and 'extreme racialist sentiment', arresting and expelling its students, and depriving its Chinese founder of his citizenship rights. It was dangerous, he said, to make the university a symbol of Chinese superiority.

By the late 1960s the years had swallowed the Communist impetus, but during the days when Southeast Asia's racial fear was bound up with the Communist scare, the Yellow Peril with the Red Peril, Singapore had to be on guard against any suggestion that it was a 'third China'. Speaking in America in 1967, Lee Kuan Yew said,

> I am no more a Chinese than President Kennedy was an Irishman. Slowly the world will learn that the Lees, the Tohs, the Gohs, the Ongs, the Yongs, the Lims in Singapore, though they may look Chinese and speak Chinese, they are different. They are of Chinese stock and not apologetic about it. But most important, they think in terms of Singapore and Singapore's interests, not of China and China's interests.[20]

As part of the government's effort to turn Singapore into a commercial hub with the global importance of a London or a Tokyo, English, characterized as 'the language of commerce, science and technology', was urged upon the populace. English was already the primary language of a section of the population, the 'King's Chinese', but it presently became *the* language of Singapore, in a creolization which Lee Kuan Yew's biographer James Minchin describes as 'the single most dramatic index of the changes that the island's people have experienced' since the Second World War.[21] In Singapore it pays to be fluent in English, such are the political and social criteria for career advancement and upward mobility, and Chinese schools died what seemed to be a natural death as 'parents voted with their children's feet'. Chinese schools were decidedly second best. 'The switch to

English happened,' Minchin observes, 'surreptitiously almost, as part of the logic of Singapore's position, colonial to begin with, then global.' When one thinks of Hong Kong, where neither British colonial rule nor internationalization has done much to erode the supremacy of Cantonese, one guesses that the switch was also helped by the diversity of Chinese speech in Singapore, and the need for speakers of Hokkien, Cantonese, Hakka and other mutually unintelligible dialects to communicate with each other through a second language – which might as well be English. The cleavage that separates those educated with English as their first language from those educated in Chinese cuts across the dialect subdivisions, and the affinities of English-educated Hokkiens, say, are with other English-educated Singaporeans, whether they are speakers of Hokkien, Cantonese or any other Chinese dialect. You can almost tell from his appearance whether a person studied at Chung Cheng High School or at Raffles Institution – one is apt to look a little square if one went to a Chinese-medium school.

The Singaporeans learnt their English, but in no deep sense learnt English habits of thought or culture; even the most casual visitor will discern a lack of 'inwardness' with the language. What did transpire, however, was an estrangement from Chinese culture. Perhaps it would have happened anyway, as part of the assimilation to the culture of a modern economy. A Singaporean Hokkien who speaks English as his first language does not seem exactly Chinese to someone fresh from Amoy, so little does he know (or even care) about his heritage, so different is he of mentality, but how far the unfamiliarity is simply an aspect of the general disparity between modern and traditional identities, and how far it comes of the Singaporean losing his ancestral language, nobody can really say.

In 1979, after years of encouraging Chinese education to die on its feet, Lee Kuan Yew launched a campaign to promote the use of Mandarin. This was something new. 'In ten years,' a bemused population was told by Lee Kuan Yew, 'we should be able to get Mandarin established as the language of the coffee shop, of the hawker centre, of the shops, of course, together with English. And I think unavoidably also Malay, because Indonesian customers come in speaking Malay.'[22] It was to be the lingua franca of the Singapore Chinese, bridging the gulf between Hokkiens and Cantonese, Cantonese and Teochius, Teochius and Hakkas, and so on, and therefore augmenting their sense of community. The dialects, the Prime Minister observed, were in any case degenerating into 'limited, pidgin-type patois',[23] and for someone who will only have speakers of BBC English as news readers in Singapore broadcasting, this was a situation which cried out for immediate remedy.

No sooner was the campaign started than popular Cantonese films and television programmes from Hong Kong were dubbed into Mandarin; even the video-cassettes brought in for private viewing were subject to censorship. The government's message was hammered home in slogans and downright hectoring. Those who could speak Mandarin did, or were persuaded to go through the motions. Ring up a government department in Hokkien and you would find yourself spoken to in Mandarin. Summon a hospital nurse in Cantonese and she would answer you in Mandarin. But family rows or private conversations are another matter, and it would indeed be a miracle if Mandarin were adopted with a complete naturalness in the home.

Eight years into the campaign, the government claimed that eighty-seven per cent of the population could now speak Mandarin; but there is Mandarin and Mandarin, and just as Singaporean English is usually a localized 'Singlish', so Singapore Mandarin is not easily recognizable to a native of Peking. Worse, children are growing up without speaking any language properly, their Mandarin adulterated by English, their English by Malay, unable to use their own dialects in anything other than very limited contexts, and failing to achieve first-language proficiency in any tongue. A purist would squirm to hear the Singaporean schoolboy speak, the way he has to resort to the vocabulary of two or more languages to utter the simplest sentence.

The most curious of the reasons for which the policy of bilingualism is pursued is the belief among the politicians that while English was conducive to purposes of business and technology, Chinese was the transmitter of 'traditional values'. Traditional values were Asian values, superior to, and infinitely more desirable than, 'Western values', a byword for all that was bad about modern society, associated with individualism and the counter-culture, 'hippism, permissiveness, student radicalism, ideologies of the welfare state and anti-establishment and anti-multinational company attitudes'.[24] To hear these politicans is to believe that bilingualism was one's weapon against all that, a corrective serving 'to inoculate our young people against the epidemic of unwholesome fads and fetishes and make them understand that they are they and we are ourselves'.[25]

As for 'Asian values', the ones to be inculcated by the study of

Chinese, these turn out on closer examination to be the good old-fashioned virtues of obedience, thrift, diligence, self-discipline, respect for family, and so on. These are of course universal attributes, hardly peculiar to the East, but it is largely by their contrast with their supposed opposites, 'Western values', that they are defined in Singapore. And even if it is conceded that some Western societies – America in its youth, England in its moments of Victorian vigour – possessed these virtues too, it is with the implication that there they have now decayed.

Is there not something familiar about this wish to have it both ways, to produce a society that would be modern and traditional at once? Of course there is. It may remind you perhaps of that refrain of Third World intellectuals, 'modernization without Westernization', or of all those countries, China included, which have tried to draw a line between foreign techniques and foreign philosophies, the one to be pragmatically welcomed, the other to be kept at bay. It is a recurring theme in the assertions of young nations, ex-European colonies many of them, which feel themselves wronged by history (or by what is more often called cultural imperialism), and which set out, in a protestation of nationalism, to harness indigenous traditions – usually this is religion – to the business of economic evolution. On an individual level, what once was reason for pride – one's Europeanization – was now reason for shame and anger.

There has been enough of a public debate on Asian values in Singapore to suggest a determined if hazy recognition by the PAP of the notion that man does not live by bread alone. Asian or traditional values were characterized as the mortar of Singapore society, the 'cultural ballast' – a term much favoured by the government and by the academics and journalists who parrot it – needed to keep Singapore together and to give it solidity. All this touches on the question of what it is to be a Singaporean, and in what sense the country has a cultural identity. Cultural identity is of course a multi-faceted, sometimes treacherous, idea, all the more so in a country where its definition has had to be deliberately fuzzy (hence 'Asian' rather than 'Chinese' values) so as to be simultaneously inoffensive to Malays, to Chinese, to Eurasians, to Muslims, to Hindus, to Christians, to Buddhists. 'This desiderated culture', D. J. Enright called it (in his book about his time in Singapore, *Memoirs of a Mendicant Professor*), and it is certainly true that at the heart of Singapore one comes across a kind of emptiness.

What was missing, the country's leaders decided, was a 'national ideology'; unless they found it quickly, Singaporeans would 'decul-turalize'; deculturalized, they would grow ever more Westernized, and Westernization could come in so many sneaking shapes: individualism, an attitude of opposition, a desire for true democracy.

A true national identity will presumably come to Singapore in time, but its minders want to hurry it, since, left to itself, it may not turn out to be the one they wanted. One way of creating a cultural identity is to attach oneself to an older civilization or tradition. This Singapore has done: once upon a time Chinese culture had to fight for its life in the city state; now the government has arrogated Confucianism to itself.

The day the Chinese lose their Confucianness, Lee Kuan Yew told university students in 1986, 'their Confucian tendencies to coalesce around the middle ground, that day we become just another Third World society'. That they were possessors of Confucian characteristics was probably news to the Chinese students in the audience, many of them educated in English, and speaking at best a fractured Chinese. After all, to be Chinese by descent is one thing, to be Confucian of culture is quite another. What has been confused in the official definition of identity are two overlapping, but not necessarily congruent, things: race and culture. As John Clammer, a one-time sociology lecturer at the National University of Singapore, puts it, it is assumed 'that people of Chinese descent "have" Chinese culture by virtue of their race. Culture and ethnicity in other words are believed to be definable in terms of each other.'

One is bound to ask what exactly is meant by 'Chinese' culture in Singapore; according to Clammer, the answer is that 'it is an amal-gam of many bits of tradition, many utterly transformed by their transplantation to Southeast Asia, some more Malayan than Chinese, and very few any longer practised in China, the whole thing held together by a rather vague ideological model of what Chinese culture *should* be.'[26] The 'many bits of tradition' may include a cleaving to Confucian values, but in Singapore these values come mixed with elements of popular religion, Taoist and Buddhist superstitions, and folk cults and beliefs which, so far from being Confucian, would make a true-blue Confucian wince. To say that the Chinese of Singapore are Confucian is thus to give them a contrived, even bogus, identity; and ironically enough it is precisely the people who are most remote from their Chinese heritage – the English-educated – who have been urging it.

Singapore's embrace of Confucianism happens to chime with the theory, already summarized in the last chapter, that explains the capitalist upsurge of the economies of Taiwan, South Korea, Hong Kong and Singapore by linking it with certain features of Confucian culture, such as a sense of hierarchy and an emphasis on harmony in social relations. There are those who scorn this fashionable argument, but Singapore's top leaders are not among them. People who remember the PAP's anti-Chinese-chauvinism phase could scarcely believe their ears when they heard the top leaders styling themselves as 'Confucian gentlemen'. To those suspicious of the PAP's motives, this identification with Confucianism was ominous indeed. For a Confucian-style government, as history abundantly shows, is an authoritarian government which demands as a first principle that people know their place. It would indeed serve the PAP's purpose well if Singaporeans were to accept the notion that nation came before individual, that good government rested on a natural harmony of interest between the ruler and the people, and that contentiousness against authority was, besides being unChinese, fundamentally immoral.

Many are not waiting to have their suspicions confirmed. Educated Singaporeans, wearied by the PAP's bland assumption that it always knows better than they what's good for them, are emigrating. Young Singaporeans have been going abroad to study for years, but instead of returning home, more are staying. In 1987 more than two thousand Singaporeans emigrated to Australia alone, a fifty per cent increase on the previous year[27] – not, it must be admitted, a large figure, but large enough for a country of just 2.6 million whose only resources, everybody is fond of saying, are human.

'There's no way but Lee's way', goes an informal slogan in Singapore. To write about Singapore is indeed to write about Lee Kuan Yew, and to write about its evolving identity is to write about the changes in Lee Kuan Yew's attitudes towards his Chinese ancestry. The remaking of Singapore in the Confucian image is in some ways a larger embodiment of a personal *enracinement*.

I once asked an English-educated Singaporean Chinese, 'What is Chinese about Singapore?' and was told, without a moment's hesitation, 'The Prime Minister – that's what's Chinese about it.' I thought I knew what she meant; she meant the authoritarianism, the paternalistic style of governing so reminiscent of the emperors of old. And I could tell from the way she said it that she was one of those people who believed that one had only to be born a Chinese to exhibit Chinese cultural behaviour – that Chinese traits, in other words, were somehow intrinsic to Chinese racial descent. It made no odds that Lee Kuan Yew was several generations removed from his Chinese roots, or that he had been brought up outside Chinese tradition; he was a natural autocrat because he was Chinese. It was clear that she was also one of those people who believed that there was an intrinsic affinity between Chineseness and autocracy. A variation on this belief is the cliché that Chinese traditionally prefer order and conformity to individual liberty and so are unsuited to democracy. To extrapolate from this line of reasoning, one would have to conclude that the thousands of courageous men and women who have risen up to fight political oppression across the length of Chinese history have been somehow unChinese.

My friend's remark made me think at once of something the anthropologist Barbara Ward had written:

> Anyone who has ever asked unsophisticated Chinese informants why they follow such and such a custom knows the maddeningly reiterated answer: 'Because we are Chinese.' At first one assumes that this is simply a stock response to the uncultured foreigner or a way of fobbing off an impertinent outsider; after a time one realizes that most of one's informants do themselves see it as a correct explanation of almost all their own cultural behaviour and social organization.[28]

They carry something in their minds labelled 'Chinese', a model they use 'to explain, predict and justify their actual behaviour'. To put it in another way, the Chinese have stereotypes of Chineseness, the details of which vary from person to person and from group to group. I am told, for example, that it is unChinese of me to spurn traditional Chinese medicine, by a Chinese friend whose stereotype of Chineseness clearly includes a faith in Chinese medicine, whereas mine does not. To give another example, whereas I would consider knowledge of the Chinese language to be an essential criterion of Chinese identity, there are plenty of Chinese who would not. As Barbara Ward has observed, 'What the people of one locality or time in the vast territory and history of the Chinese people think of as "Chinese" may not necessarily be recognized as such by Chinese people elsewhere.' This is certainly true of all those Babas who are considered Chinese in Singapore but who will not be easily recognized as such by anybody from China. There are considerable numbers of Singaporean Chinese who, if they were to be repatriated to their countries of origin, would feel less at home in China than in England; yet they consider themselves ineradicably Chinese.

So in what sense are they Chinese? To talk to Singaporeans is to realize that what qualifies one as Chinese in Singapore is not so much language, or religion, or any of the other markers of ethnicity, but some primordial core or unalterable essence of Chineseness which one has by virtue of one's Chinese genes – so that, as Clammer puts it, 'one cannot become a Chinese unless one is born as such and nor strictly speaking can one cease to be a Chinese either, however much one deviates from the desired or expected cultural pattern'.[29] By this token, you would (to draw an analogy) still regard as French a man of French stock who speaks no French; a Frenchman who speaks, say, Russian as his first language; a Creole; or a Quebecker of French ancestry but Anglo-Saxon upbringing.

It is a view which Lee Kuan Yew appears to share, to go by what he once said about his own ingrained values:

> A person who gets deculturalized – and I nearly was, so I
> know this danger – loses his self-confidence. He suffers from
> a sense of deprivation. For optimum performance a man
> must know himself and the world. He must know where
> he stands. I may speak the English language better than the
> Chinese language because I learnt English early in life. But
> I will never be an Englishman in a thousand generations and
> I have not got the Western value system inside; mine is an
> Eastern value system. Nevertheless I use Western concepts,
> Western words because I understand them. But I also have
> a different system in my mind.[30]

On another occasion he said, 'I understand the Englishman. He knows deep in his heart that he is superior to the Welshman and the Scotsman. Deep [down], I am a Chinaman. Yes, an uprooted Chinaman, transformed into a Singaporean.'[31]

As a matter of fact Lee Kuan Yew's cultural affiliations have shifted over the years, and he has not always been so keen to claim his Chinese patrimony. Who could have predicted that he would advocate Confucianism? That a schoolboy who refused to have Chinese tuition would champion the study of Mandarin? All this would appear puzzling until one takes a closer look at his personal history.

He was born Harry Lee Kuan Yew (the Harry was dropped after he became a politician) on 16 September 1923. The official records say he was born in Singapore, but there are people who believe that he was in fact born in Kudus, Java. In Singapore, the Lees already went back a century; Harry's paternal great-grandfather arrived in Singapore shortly after Stamford Raffles. Harry is thus trebly removed from his origins on his father's side. His grandfather, born in 1873, was educated in the English stream, thereby establishing a pattern in which son and grandson were to follow. Starting out as a sub-agent with one shipping line, he worked his way up to become the Managing Director of another. The company traded largely with Indonesia, so it was natural enough that he should marry into the Indonesian Chinese community.

His son, Lee Chin Koon, became a clerk in a ship chandler's company after finishing secondary school, but he played safe and left the job for a post in the Shell Company. He was with Shell for some thirty years, and seemed to have been posted by the company to Indonesia for a while. Upon retirement from the company, he became a salesman with a Ceylonese jewellery firm.[32] His remaining with Shell for so long proved characteristic, for he was a man modest in his aspirations, who was happy not to have to strive or compete. Son and father were thus poles apart. The elder Lee was no man a Lee Kuan Yew could measure himself by.

There is no doubt that Harry's mother, Lee Jim Neo, was the stronger personality. The elder Lee was often away on business, and during his absence it was as if he didn't count. The marriage was unhappy, there were frequent rows between husband and wife, and it didn't help that the straitened circumstances in which she found herself during the Depression of the 1930s obliged Lee Jim Neo to make money however she could. It was no easy matter to grow up in a house where a 'special friend' of one's mother, a wealthy Chinese contractor, came sometimes to stay[33] – one can imagine the speculation. 'Whatever hurts came – ' writes James Minchin, 'from perceived marital infidelity (which is surely not unconnected with Lee's tendency to be both prudish and prurient) or nagging . . . Harry lashed out in retaliation, sought the upper ground or withdrew.'[34] It did not escape Minchin that in the eulogy Lee gave at his mother's funeral in 1980 he pointedly made no reference to his father's presence or grief.

Lee Jim Neo was one of twelve girls from a well-to-do Baba family. The Malay strain in her family was more than merely cultural, for it is said that Jim Neo's great-grandmother had been Malay. At home the Lees spoke to each other in Malay and English. The standards they aspired to were the standards of the British, the colonial presence having seen to that. When Harry was born, the grandfather is said to have looked proudly at the baby and declared that the child should be educated to be the equal of any Englishman. He was sent to a Chinese kindergarten, yes, but it was to make her sons 'professional gentlemen in the best English tradition'[35] that Jim Neo put aside the money she earned from giving cookery lessons and saved from housekeeping. The example of so many Baba families producing only small shopkeepers or lesser government officers seemed to have convinced her that to get on in the world, her sons had to be as English as possible.

When Harry began school, his grandmother thought it a good idea that he take Chinese tuition outside his normal classes. But to study a language that had to be 'learnt parrot-fashion', as he was later to put it,[36] was not at all to his taste, and he put his foot down and refused. Nor would he succumb to Singlish: it was 'proper English' he was going to speak. 'For my last two years at Raffles Institution [RI],' he said in 1980, 'I had native English teachers to teach me English: an Englishman in Junior Cambridge, two, an Australian and a Scotsman, in Senior Cambridge. For the four years I was in RI, the principal was a Scotsman. He addressed the school every Monday. I have little doubt that my spoken English improved immeasurably because of their attention and example, especially in accent, diction and rhythm.'[37]

He was thus as near perfect an example as it was possible to be of that breed for whom the generic term in India has been 'Macaulay's bastards' – 'brown Englishmen', as Lord Macaulay would have called its Indian exemplars, 'a class of persons Indian in blood and colour, but English in taste, in opinion, in morals, and in intellect'.

It was his parents' intention that Harry should go on to England from Raffles Institution, but war intervened and he entered Raffles College, one day to become the University of Singapore, instead. He read Economics, Mathematics and English Literature. It was a trauma for him to see the Japanese Army march into Singapore, an event he was later to describe as the single most important in his life, and to see the British cut down to size. Nevertheless he made himself study Japanese, and became a stenographer and then a translator with Domei, the Japanese news agency. In 1946 he left at last for England. Just one term at the London School of Economics was enough for him – not 'my idea of university life', he later said of the 'buses, fumes, tubes'[38] – and he got himself admitted to Cambridge to read Law. There he met up with his future wife, a scholastically brilliant Chinese girl he had known at Raffles, now studying Law on a Queen's scholarship at Girton College. He graduated with a double first, of course, and also a star for special distinction.

In England he had already begun to respond to his political destiny, and no sooner was he back in Singapore than he was working to expel the British. 'We were latecomers,' he was to discover, 'trying to tap the same oil fields' as the Communists.39 As a returned student from Britain and a member of the English-educated élite, he was head of no mass following, with no experience 'either of the hurly-burly of politics or the conspiracies of revolution'.40 But, good at going straight to the mark like an arrow, he knew to throw himself into the popular politics of the day, to ally himself with the students and the trade unions. Later he was to dedicate himself to obliterating the Communists, but just then he needed them, for he took their measure exactly, and recognized that they, and only they, had the strength and the organization to rally the Chinese masses. By championing popular causes, by professing radical politics, he became a nationalist hero even to the Chinese-educated. Lee had, and still has, the common touch. When the British agreed to a measure of popular representation in Singapore, the Chinese gave their hearts to him, thrusting him and the PAP to power.

It had been an eye-opener, his initiation into the world of the Chinese speakers, 'a world teeming', he was to recall, 'with vitality, dynamism and revolution, a world in which the communists had been working for over the last 30 years with considerable success'.41 Compared to them, the returned students and the English-educated seemed to him a 'devitalized' people, lacking the charge of tribal pride, 'speaking and thinking in a language which was not part of their being'.42 British patronage, and a secure middle-of-the-road existence, were fulfilment enough for such people. He couldn't quite identify with them, though he had come from among them, and he doubted that it had been such a good idea of his parents' to make him over into an Englishman, for at the end of it all he had sensed 'the whole set of values' to be 'wrong, fundamentally and radically wrong',43 and he had felt something of Jawaharlal Nehru's pathos when that 'un-English English gentleman', as André Malraux has called him, lamented, 'I cry when I think that I cannot speak my own mother tongue as well as I can speak the English language.'

He has claimed not to be an Anglophile,44 but it would be unusual if, even as he sneered at the British decline, he didn't think that his 'long education in the British tradition', as he himself has put it, were cause for satisfaction, the more so as he enjoys displaying it – it was as a result of that education, he has said, that 'I am rather choosy about the form of words one puts ideas in and dresses one's ideas in.'[45] His sons have followed him to Cambridge, and he has bought a house near the city.

As for his Chineseness, it has been an instrument of policy, to be exploited this way or that as circumstances demand. There were times when he preferred not to be thought of as Chinese, but more recently observers have detected 'an emergent chauvinism' in him.[46] It would indeed be strange if this highly competitive man were to be utterly aloof to the reputation for economic success that the Chinese enjoy in the region. He has been heard to say that, quarantined elsewhere in Southeast Asia, the overseas Chinese have found in Singapore the one place where they could still hold their heads high,[47] and that 'innate ethnic qualities', combined with climate and diet, gave to the East Asians – the Chinese, the Japanese and the Koreans – a cultural edge over the Indians and Southeast Asians.[48]

It turns out that he has fairly decided opinions on race and culture, and his mind is inclined to cultural explanations for how well a people performs economically – 'It's not excellence that drove Singapore on,' he has declared. 'It is the cultural drive, something deep and fundamental.'[49] He sees the world's people as divided into two breeds: the soft, intuitive, pleasure-loving kind, easygoing on all but matters of custom and religion; and the intense, calculating, disciplined, achievement-oriented and sceptical kind. Very broadly speaking the first kind has its geographical origins in the tropics; the second in cooler, more bracing climes. These breeds differ in their genetic endowment, and the first kind, 'low-compression' people as he has termed them, are less capable of the sustained endeavour necessary for material and social progress than the second. Give an 'unintense' people 'a sophisticated surface-to-air missile', he once said contemptuously of the Thais, and 'you will have to have the instructor there till the end of time'.[50]

Others have noted the correspondence between temperature and poverty – so striking that a naive observer may be forgiven for taking one look at an atlas and declaring that a hot climate was the cause of underdevelopment – without arriving at a view of heredity. But Lee Kuan Yew is a man much concerned with genetic legacy. As a Hakka, with the Hakkas' touching pride in their remote northern antecedents, he clearly counts himself among the non-equatorial peoples. In 1972, in the course of an interview on Australian television, he said that he was 'extremely sensitive to changes in temperature, humidity, mainly because I think after four generations here I'm still not acclimatized'. 'You come from northern China?' asked the interviewer. 'Northern China,' Lee replied,[51] with presumably his Hakka forebears, the ones who migrated to South China between six to ten centuries ago, in mind. He is like all southern Chinese in regarding northern Chinese norms as 'best'.

Yet to another half of him the fact of the overseas Chinese's uprooting is also the source of their energy, for, unlike their cousins in the motherland, they are not continually dragged back by a past that refuses to die. Freed of the dead hand of inherited baggage, 'immigrants or their children', he observed, 'are keener or emotionally more ready to try out new ideas for better results'; and he added, 'this is the main reason for the progress we have made'.[52] But the strengths do not obscure the weaknesses that lie, to Lee's mind, in the pedigree of the immigrants, few of whom can look back far without finding a labourer or a peasant; so that, as he put it during the opening of a new polytechnic in 1979, 'It is prudent to assume that our talent pyramid, as a society descended of immigrants of peasant stock, will not be as rich and creamy as that of Germans and Japanese.'[53]

Still, whatever may be the weaknesses of the breed, Singapore could do with more, not less of it. The city state's Chinese have probably the world's lowest birth rate, and equally worrying to the PAP has been the finding that well-educated women were failing to get married and breed – this because male graduates want to marry their educational inferiors, while female graduates are not willing to do the same. How is the human stock of Singapore to be improved, runs the Prime Minister's unabashedly eugenic reasoning, if graduate men and women don't marry? In 1986, the number of births per woman was 2.05 for Malays, 1.89 for Indians, and a mere 1.26 for the Chinese.[54] Clearly, the ethnic composition of the country will change if the Chinese population goes on under-reproducing itself. To put Lee's question in another way, how was Singapore to maintain its competitive edge if its most successful community went on dwindling? Singapore wouldn't mind an infusion of educated Chinese – from Hong Kong, say – but such people prefer Canada, Australia, and the United States. One answer Lee came up with was the setting-up of an official matchmaking agency, the Social Development Unit;[55] another was polygamy. Here is how he argued it: in the old society, whether you're a scholar, a Mandarin or a successful businessman or successful farmer, you had more than one wife . . . In other words, the unsuccessful are like the weak lions or bucks in a herd. They were neutralized. So, over the generations, you must have the physically and the mentally more vibrant and vital reproduce. We are doing just the opposite. We introduced monogamy. It seems so manifestly correct. The West was successful, superior. Why? Because they are monogamous [we thought]. It was wrong; it was stupid.[56]

He went on to note that Mr Tanaka, the Japanese Prime Minister, was quite open about the children he had by his mistresses, and said that 'the more Tanakas there are in Japan, I have no doubt the more dynamic will be Japanese society'.

His conception of breeding and heritage are intimately bound up with his élitism. He is leery of all but the best. 'Best' is often defined by academic distinction. 'I speak to Harold Macmillan and Duncan Sandys as equals,' he once said; 'At Cambridge I got two firsts and a star for distinction. Harold Macmillan did not.' (Lee failed to add that Macmillan went to Oxford, which unlike Cambridge does not award 'starred firsts'.)[57] He declared without blushing that his wife was the only woman intellectually worthy of him; and one is glad, for their sakes, that the three children were all academic over-achievers.[58]

His sense of superiority makes him a man of childish conceit, a bully incapable of apology. For Lee it is of the essence that he win, and that everyone know he has won. His feuds with his opponents or critics tend to have, on his side, a macho quality to them, as though his very manhood were at stake. Often he seems to have the naiveté of a man on a pedestal, a man who must dominate all – and who therefore can so easily despise all. And whoever tangles with him finds out sooner or later how vengeful he can be. The spines of subordinates shiver at his snarling sarcasm. This is how Professor C. Northcote Parkinson, who taught history at Singapore University, has written of him: 'Utterly without charm, his expression is one of barely concealed contempt; for his opponents, for his followers, perhaps for himself . . . One cannot imagine that he is even capable of friendship.'[59]

No one thing explains him, but the journalist T. J. S. George thinks he detected in Lee the insecurity of a man alienated from his Chinese moorings, a man who, because he does not quite belong anywhere, has had to remake Singapore in his own image to compensate for his own alienation.⁶⁰ It has certainly been said of him by Singaporean Chinese affronted by his Anglicization policy that he was a man who did not know in himself what it was to be Chinese. And yet if he had started out as a Singaporean version of the 'brown Englishman', he now places himself within the Confucian tradition. But there are many Chinese to question his presumption, and to think of him still as a barbarian. The late Chinese statesman Chou En-lai is said to have used the none-too-complimentary epithet 'banana' of him – meaning by it that he was yellow on the outside, white inside.

CHAPTER FOURTEEN

Melting Pot

In his novel *Time for a Tiger*, Anthony Burgess writes of a school in Malaya where 'the occidental bias in the curriculum has made many of the alumni despise their own cultures, leading them, deracinated, to a yearning for the furthest west of all'. What unites the diverse races are 'the myths of the cinema and the syndicated cartoon'.[1] The attractions of American popular culture, globalized by communications technology, are certainly strong, and Singapore is not the only new nation to feel that Americanization will have to be actively resisted if it is to arrive at a cultural identity that suits its own needs.

America is not just the fount of a culture whose marks are adopted, if only superficially, worldwide; it is also the world's ultimate immigrant destination. At a time when most Western countries are slamming their doors on foreigners from poorer countries, the United States is experiencing the highest tide of immigration since the early decades of this century, taking in more legal newcomers than the rest of the world combined.[2] What is more, the composition of that immigration is different from what it was a century ago, when more than nine-tenths of the newcomers originated from Germany, Britain, Ireland, Italy, central Europe and Russia. Between 1960 and 1969 twelve per cent came from Asia, thirty-six per cent from Latin America and thirty-nine from Europe, but after 1980 nearly half the immigrants were Asian, thirty-five per cent Latin American and only twelve per cent European.[3]

The 1980 census showed the Chinese to be the largest single group of Asians in America (though today they are exceeded by the Filipinos); four out of ten were settled in California, two out of ten in New York.[4] To get rid of a few more statistics, by 1985 the Chinese population in America was more than four times its size in 1960, numbering over a million.[5] This came of America changing its immigration rules in 1965. In the years following the passage of the 1965 Immigration Act, which replaced a twenty-one-year-old exclusionary system of immigration aimed at freezing the country's ethnic balance with one in which a flat annual quota of twenty thousand immigrant visas was assigned to every country outside the Western Hemisphere, the Chinese inflow reached its high-water mark. The families of Chinese already resident in the United States were the chief beneficiaries of the new laws, though under a 'professional preference' provision people with skills also found it easier to come to America.

Before 1979, when the US established diplomatic relations with China and switched its recognition of the Nationalist government of Taiwan to that of the People's Republic, it was mostly Taiwan nationals who made use of the twenty-thousand-a-year quota. They did not lose the quota when Washington normalized its relations with Peking, for the Chinese mainland was given its own quota of twenty thousand. On top of this, there was an additional quota of six hundred (increased to five thousand on 1 October 1987) set aside for immigrants from Hong Kong, so that a total of 40,600 Chinese could come to the US each year. The number of Chinese who ended up in America was of course larger than this, because many of the immigrants from countries in Southeast Asia (Malaysia, Singapore, Indonesia, and so on) will also have been of Chinese descent, as were many of the refugees from Vietnam and Cambodia. If immigration continues at the current rate, the Chinese population in America will double every ten years.

Since American immigration policy favours the reuniting of families, the Chinese population remains predominantly Cantonese. The days when the people of the Four Districts fought the people of the Three Districts to death are over, but speech differences, overlapping with class differences, continue to divide the Chinese community. A gulf exists between the descendants of the earlier immigrants and the newcomers from Taiwan, who, even if their first dialect is Hokkien, will all be speakers of Mandarin, the language of education back home. Unlike the Four Districts immigrants of humble rural origin, many of the Taiwan arrivals will have come from well-to-do or well-educated families, and not a few will have been students who, upon their graduation from an American university, have stayed on to work in the United States.

The student-immigrant has long been a special category. It was not only the Exclusion laws which set him apart, but the attitudes of the host country. Chinese coolies were a despised group, but students were regarded differently. In 1949, when China went Communist, the US government offered asylum and aid to some five thousand Chinese pursuing higher education or professional careers in the United States, calling them 'stranded students' and defining their status in such a way as to enable them to stay on and work. It was out of this group that many of the most distinguished Chinese Americans were to emerge; and there is no doubt that many white Americans thought better of the Chinese immigrant for the accomplishments of people like these. If, very broadly speaking, wealth has been the gauge of social worth among Southeast Asia's Chinese immigrants, in America it has been academic success; not to be a student, after all, was to be a coolie. People talk glibly of the Chinese reverence for learning, but the pronounced emphasis on scholastic achievement among Chinese Americans has to be set against the heavily working-class character of early Chinese immigration into the United States; the emphasis seems to the visiting foreigner, if not to the resident, to reflect an intense concern to show how far removed one is from cooliedom. 'If a group's first representatives were cultured and educated,' Nathan Glazer and Daniel Patrick Moynihan have written of immigrants, 'those who came after them might benefit, unless they were so numerous as to destroy the first image.'6 Middle-class Chinese immigrants were up against the fact that because the first Chinese to enter America had been labourers, in the ordering of minorities ethnic Chinese had been assigned a low place in American minds. It therefore became all the more important for the Chinese to dignify themselves with university degrees. Only a Chinese-American woman, getting up to make a speech at her birthday party, could have given such a description of her family:

> We have six children . . . Our eldest daughter, Anlin, got her MA from Wellesley, and her husband is an assistant professor at MIT. Our second daughter, Anchen, received her MA from Smith in sociology, and is working at New York Hospital. Our eldest son, Kung-ping, received his Ph.D. from Columbia University, and is now chief of the Far Eastern Mineral Section of the Bureau of Mines. Our second son, Kung-chih, received his BS from Brown, and MS from MIT, and is an instructor in Mechanical Engineering at Brown University. Our third son, Kung-lee, has his MS from Brown, and MBA from Columbia, and is an assistant in the Department of Economics at Brown. Our youngest son, Kung-yeh, is a sophomore in the school of engineering at Brown.

Clearly education is for the Chinese what it has been for generations of other migrants, the vehicle of upward mobility. If the image of the Chinese has greatly improved in recent years, it is because they had become by 1980 the best-educated ethnic group in the United States.[7] Along with other 'Asian Americans' (a category made up chiefly of Chinese, Japanese, Koreans and Indochinese), the Chinese are represented by the media as super-achievers, the latest success story of the American Dream. They certainly cut a dazzling figure in the schools and universities, where people have come to expect a larger than average proportion of the best brains to be Chinese. There is some truth to the flood of hyperbole let loose by newspaper reports. In San Francisco's James Russell Lowell High, the famous stepping-stone to a coveted place at Berkeley, Harvard, Yale and other prestigious universities, forty-five per cent of the pupils are of Chinese ancestry. Heavily Jewish until the 1950s, Lowell High graduated eighteen Chans, seven Fongs, six Laus and forty-nine Wongs in 1987.[8]

Many at Stanford University will have heard the story of the white American engineering student who, told by his professor that he could have done better in his exams, retorted, 'What do you think I am, Chinese?' To judge by the surnames, more than ten thousand Chinese engineers were working in the Silicon Valley in the late 1980s.[9] To counter the stereotype of Chinese as narrow engineering prodigies, first-year students have been known to wear buttons proclaiming I AM NOT A CHINESE AMERICAN ELECTRICAL ENGINEER. Explanations for why the Chinese do so extraordinarily well range from the absurd ('They have higher IQs and there are genetic differences in the rate at which Asians and whites mature mentally')[10] to the commonsensical ('They work harder than white American students'). At all events, theories and investigations abound. Some academics say that the bias towards science and maths is to be explained by the fact that these are subjects in which the immigrant's unfamiliarity with the English language is not such a handicap. Others think that the Chinese are born mathematicians, noting the findings of a study by Michigan University which shows schoolchildren in Peking to be higher scorers on maths tests than those in Chicago and Sendai in Japan.[11] What is perhaps even more intriguing is that the Chinese mathematical bent seems to have something to do with language; I mentioned in the last chapter that when I was at school in Malaysia it was a matter of conventional wisdom that you were better at maths if you attended a Chinese-medium school than if you attended an English-medium one, and that Philippine Chinese schoolchildren, even if they were more at home in English or Tagalog, made faster progress in maths when the language of instruction was switched from English to Mandarin (not a first language for the pupils, who are mostly Hokkien speakers).

But the image of Chinese children as high academic achievers is by no means universal. In striking contrast to their cousins in America, many of the three hundred thousand Chinese children in British schools lag behind their English peers. Educational reseachers in Britain find that Asians do better at school than whites and West Indians,[12] but by Asian they mean chiefly Indians and Pakistanis. Looking into the poor performance of Chinese children in British schools, an enquiry undertaken by the House of Commons Home Affairs Committee in 1984–85 found that, of the factors which lay at the root of their problems, the most important appeared to be their difficulty with the English language.[13] Similar observations had been made by the Swann Committee of Inquiry into the Education of Children from Ethnic Minority Groups in 1983; among other things, its report said that Chinese children were 'under-achieving in relation to their true potential because of a lack of necessary language support'.[14] Various people have pondered this and come up with theories. Some invoke Chinese reserve; others say that the dispersed nature of Chinese settlement results in children being placed in schools with little or no experience of dealing with ethnic minorities. Yet others say that it is because the children are confused, alienated and unhappy, or they have to help out in the family catering business, or because they are so withdrawn that their difficulties are overlooked by their teachers. This last is the reason they are seen to be self-reliant model pupils – 'You wouldn't know they were in the room' is a comment all too frequently made of Chinese children by their British teachers. To be passive and unassertive, to think of learning as a one-way process in which one waits to be dictated to and bidden – these habitual Chinese responses, so different from those of their more extroverted and ebullient English and West Indian peers, impose a handicap not easily overcome.[15]

But to arrive at a satisfactory explanation, one must see the lack of fluency in English as a carry-over from Hong Kong (the migrants' place of origin), where students' peculiar difficulty with the language has been an imponderable for years. Hong Kong Chinese have a block where English is concerned; their whole mental set is against learning it. The happily relaxed way in which Malaysian, Singaporean and Filipino Chinese acquire fluency in English and other languages seems to elude the Hong Kong Chinese, and they go on being monolingual after emigration to England. Furthermore, though it makes sense of a kind to assume that, because Chinese traditionally place great stress on academic achievement, the parents of immigrant children must value good education, the truth is that many of the ones in England, little educated themselves, find it hard to see the relevance of university degrees to the running of the family business. Their attitudes to education are frankly utilitarian; these attitudes were brought to England and then amplified by the immigrant struggle, which tends to reduce everything to pecuniary standards.

Their ambitions modestly pitched, Chinese immigrants in Britain are a different class from the high achievers in the United States. While the bulk of the Chinese in Britain came from rural or working-class backgrounds, many of the high achievers on the other side of the Atlantic arrived with the advantages that material well-being and education bestow, and did not have to start from scratch to 'make it' in America.

Many of the latter group have risen to international prominence in academic life and business, and have become 'role models' for other Chinese Americans. Well-known exemplars of this group are Tsung-dao Lee, the Nobel Prize winner; An Wang, the computer entrepreneur; I. M. Pei, the architect who designed, among other of the world's landmarks, the controversial glass pyramid in the courtyard of the Louvre in Paris; Dr Paul Ching-wu Chu, the scientist who, with his colleagues at the University of Houston, discovered a novel type of superconductor, one which researchers have described as the basis of a technological revolution; Yo-yo Ma, the renowned cellist; and Gerry Chih-yung Tsai, the Wall Street star performer.

The most colourful of these is Gerry Tsai, one of 'the wildest, and most successful, gun-slingers on Wall Street', as the *Financial Times* has described him.[16] Born the son of a Ford district manager in Shanghai, Tsai moved to America, aged seventeen, a little before Shanghai fell to the Communists. In 1952 he began working as an analyst for the Fidelity Fund, and quickly proved himself to be a 'hot-shot' portfolio manager.[17] He saw, before other speculators did, the promise in Polaroid, Xerox, Texas Instruments, Avon, IBM – all to become blue-chip stocks one day. 'What grace, what timing – glorious,' his boss at Fidelity told John Brooks, a *New Yorker* writer and the author of a book about the early 1960s on Wall Street, the 'go-go years' when the market was taking off and people were making colossal sums of money.[18] In those days, writes David Halberstam of Tsai:

he was like a man on a roll at a gambling table. He loved speculating. He bought in huge blocks, ten thousand shares at a
time, and the turnover of his portfolio was incredible. Where
in the past a stockbroker might have turned over a family's
portfolio some 5 or, at the most, 10 percent in a year, Tsai was
turning over his portfolio more than 100 percent annually.
Everyone wanted to know what he was buying. Tipsters used
his name to push their pet stock: 'Tsai is buying it.' In some
ways there was an advantage to his fame, he mused, because
the moment it came out that he had bought, others jumped in
and the stock surged . . . He was the action . . . On February
9, 1966, the Dow hit 1000 for the first time, just as Tsai had
predicted, and that made him all the more a prophet.[19]

Being Chinese was no hindrance, because, as he said, 'If you buy
General Motors at 40 and it goes to 50, whether you are an Oriental
or a Buddhist or an Italian doesn't make a difference.' In fact, if
anything it helped to be different: 'Thousands of portfolio managers
went around the country to talk to brokers about selling funds . . .
I was the only one that did not look Irish.'[20] His star slipped in 1968,
but ten years later he began a comeback so dramatic that it verged, a
business magazine said, 'on reincarnation'. Today, whenever his name
crops up, fantastic sums are mentioned too.

There is obviously more to his success than having come from an
educated urban family – his father was himself a graduate of Michigan
University – but pre-migration background does matter, as will be clear
when we consider the other role models. Tellingly, except for George
Chu, who was born in China's Hunan province in 1941 and who went
on to study at a university in Taiwan, all the other successful Chinese
named a few paragraphs back have had some ties to Shanghai, of all
Chinese cities the most urbane and Westernized. Tsung-dao Lee was
born in Shanghai. An Wang, whose father taught English in a private
primary school, was born in Shanghai in 1920 and studied electrical
engineering at the Communications University in that city. The family
of I. M. Pei, the first foreigner to design for the Louvre since Bernini
in the 1660s, had its seat in Soochow, a satellite town to Shanghai,
from which it is but three hours by car. Yo-yo Ma, the most gifted
of musicians, was born in Paris of Shanghainese parentage.

In the list of Chinese who have become famous in America, the
Shanghainese enjoy a prominence out of proportion to their actual
numbers. (The term 'Shanghainese', incidentally, refers not only to

an indigene of that city but any speaker of the Shanghainese dialect and its variants; and this means a community embracing not just the city dwellers, but the populace of the neighbouring regions.) Bette Bao Lord, the author of the bestselling novel *Spring Moon*, was born in Shanghai in 1938, the daughter of a graduate of Communications University, An Wang's Alma Mater. S. B. Woo, who as Lieutenant Governor of Delaware became the highest ranking immigrant Chinese state official in American history, was born in Shanghai in 1937. Joan Chen, the actress who played the empress in Bernardo Bertolucci's film *The Last Emperor*, was a celebrated movie star in Shanghai, her birthplace, before she moved to America in 1981. The young playwright David Hwang, whose play *M. Butterfly* was a huge hit on Broadway, was born the son of a Shanghainese banker who studied at the University of Southern California.

The mother of Wayne Wang, the film director who made the highly successful *Dim Sum*, was pregnant with him when she and her husband fled Shanghai for Hong Kong in 1949. (What Chinese but a Shanghainese would name his son for a Hollywood movie star – John Wayne, whose *Red River* the elder Wang had enjoyed watching in Shanghai?) The idea of 1940s Shanghai as a sort of Casablanca appeals to Wayne Wang's imagination, and he has spoken of his dream of making a film of it, a *Last Tango in Shanghai*.

Pre-Communist Shanghai was indeed a metropolis as much in the mind as on the map. It was a magnet for Dick Whittingtons from the provinces, as good a place as any to test your adequacy to that universal challenge: trying to make it in the big city. It was a place of in-migration, not a fount of emigration, and he who left it for other shores was more émigré than emigrant. When the Shanghainese had to leave, they left to escape not want but political circumstance – 'White Chinese' is the name by which they are sometimes called. They are people whose exposure to Western ways and thinking had begun before their departure from China, and who were thus better fitted to adapt to life abroad than the average villager from Kwangtung or Fukien. An Wang has said, 'It was exciting to meet America, but not strange. Frankly the United States seemed a lot like China to me.'[21] The Shanghainese immigrant to an American city had come from a place not much less advanced, so perhaps it is not surprising that of the internationally renowned Chinese Americans a disproportionately high number are Shanghainese. You will find no community of Shanghainese settlers in Mauritius or the

Solomon Islands, but small groups of them might be discovered here and there in the world's big cities.

China, Taiwan, Hong Kong and other Chinese communities in Asia sent many more of their brightest and best when America opened its doors in 1965. Of a quality to do well, they and other Asian immigrants have been named a 'model minority', the new leaven in America. But they don't all take kindly to this description, because it makes them out to be embodiments of the American Dream, starting from nothing and getting to the top through hard work, when the truth is that there are plenty of Asians who have yet to rise from the bottom of the heap, who give the lie to the notion that anyone can get to the top by working hard, and who have still to share in the Dream. The promise of deserved rewards for merit or work is false, they say; Asians get so far but no further because of what they call the 'glass ceiling', the barrier of white discrimination that prevents them from graduating from the back room or the laboratory into senior management.

Their attitudes are self-contradictory, though, for while on one level they decry the label, on another they take pride in it – their own magazines, for example, are full of success stories and profiles of famous Asians who have 'contributed' to American society as scientists, millionaires, writers, artists, actors, and so on. In this they are like all immigrant groups in America, for whom it is somehow not enough simply to have their success; everyone has to see it if it is to be real. The need for the approval of the white majority is an old thread in immigrant history, and Irving Howe has noticed its manifestations – 'a mode of apologia' he calls it – among the East European Jewish immigrants. Behind the apologia, he says, 'lies an unspoken assumption that a court of native American opinion has the right to pass final judgement, deciding whether or not immigrant cultures merit acceptance and respect. While the East European immigrant Jews can claim an abundant share of [contributions], their very readiness to indulge such claims may be a kind of self-denigration, a failure of dignity.'[22] The world of white America, the mainstream, is the heap whose summit all immigrants want ultimately to reach.

Chinese Americans, then, are a heterogeneous lot, sharing neither language nor class. They also differ by their emotional distance from China. Many look back to the homeland from a safe distance, seeing it as a place they might visit occasionally, or even do business with; but by and large the vicissitudes of Chinese politics, the twists and turns of the Party line, the fortunes of the Chinese intelligentsia and of dissent, are not intense or absorbing concerns for these people. In this they differ from certain recent arrivals from the People's Republic of China, students who have made themselves political refugees by their opposition to the home government.

The number of students from China, more than seventy thousand in 1989,[23] has surged ahead of that from any other nation. Many of them had arrived in America fresh from the momentous experience of the Peking Spring in 1978 and of the democracy protests culminating in the Tiananmen demonstrations of 1989, and the freedom of the United States, a country long idealized in their imaginations, seemed just what they had craved. Ten to one they will not go back if they can find a way of staying on when they finish their studies. Some can't go back, because they have become campaigners for human rights and democracy, and face imprisonment or worse if they return to China. The case of Yang Wei as good as warned them. Within eight months of his return to Shanghai with a master's degree in Molecular Biology from the University of Arizona, Yang Wei was arrested for his involvement in the student demonstrations of 1986–87. Out of this large expatriate community has emerged a number of organizations, the Chinese Alliance for Democracy, and latterly the All-America Chinese Students and Scholars Union and the Federation for a Democratic China, to continue in exile the fight for democracy in China.

The Chairman of the Chinese Alliance for Democracy, the earliest of the bodies to be established, is a bespectacled, frailly built student named Hu Ping, a graduate in Philosophy from Peking University. The first time his name was heard abroad was in 1980, when he caused a sensation by being elected the university's delegate to the District People's Assembly on a platform calling for freedom of speech and democracy. Seven years later, he was awarded a government scholarship and left China to study for a doctorate in Political Science at Harvard University. He had been in America just over a year when, because of his political activities, his scholarship was withdrawn and his passport invalidated by the Chinese consulate in New York.

Psychologically he remains a citizen of the country left behind; and except in a practical, workaday sense, China remains closer to him than the country in which he lives. That he does not enjoy the best of both worlds marks him off from those of his compatriots who, either because they have been in America longer or because they were more cosmopolitan to start with (having originated, as many of them have, from Taiwan or Hong Kong), can comfortably live in two worlds at once. These people feel a greater sense of distance than does Hu Ping, though still tugged in some part of them into participation in the affairs of China, studying and writing about them as sinologists or political pundits, or expressing their views as concerned critics when, say, the Chinese Communist Party cracks down hard on dissenting intellectuals or students. They keep alive the connection between Chinese at home and abroad, arranging for beleaguered writers in China to come to America, writing commentaries on Chinese matters in journals published in Hong Kong, and periodically putting their names to open letters addressed to the Party leaders.

One of the best known of these names is Chen Jo-hsi, whose writing is known to millions of Chinese across the world. Chen Jo-hsi was born the daughter of a carpenter in Taiwan in 1938. She read Literature at Taiwan National University and then went on to pursue postgraduate studies in America. And it was while she was there that she and her husband decided to go and 'serve the people' in the People's Republic of China. Their decision may seem naive to us now, but it is hard for a younger generation of overseas Chinese to realize how compelling was the nationalist passion among the group of educated Chinese abroad in those early years of revolutionary endeavour, before the scales fell from their eyes. With her husband and two children, Chen Jo-hsi stayed seven years, living through almost the entire span of the Cultural Revolution, leaving in 1973. For a while she and her family lived in Hong Kong, but eventually they migrated to America.

She wrote not a single line in all the years she was in China, but once out, the burden of her experience – the life she had not only observed but had been part of, the impressions and insights she had accumulated – demanded to be delivered, to be transferred on to the pages of fiction without distortion. Making reality real was not just a self-assignment but a compulsion; and the works of fiction she published bore witness to Chinese life in a way that no writing had previously done. Much of the writing on China makes too much noise for us to hear what the people are trying to say, but Chen Jo-hsi's voice is calm and quiet. In good fiction there is absolutely everything but an unequivocal answer, and because her work shows that, for all the harshness of life in a Communist state, there is kindness and happiness too, ironically the first impulse of the Kuomintang government in Taiwan, which would have preferred the picture to have been all black, was to ban her work.

Chen Jo-hsi, though American by residence, writes in Chinese and publishes in Hong Kong and Taiwan. A world of difference lies between her and Maxine Hong Kingston, a writer who is Chinese by race but American of speech and sensibility. The author of two highly successful memoirs, *The Woman Warrior: Memoirs of a Girlhood among Ghosts* (1976) and *China Men* (1980); and a work of fiction, *Tripmaster Monkey: His Fake Book* (1989), Maxine Hong Kingston (her Chinese name is T'ang T'ing-t'ing) has made it her business to portray, through mixing Chinese legends with family memories, what it is to be an acculturated Chinese American – or, to put it in another way, to be the kind of Chinese she is, a kind people like Chen Jo-hsi or Hu Ping would scarcely recognize as being of the same breed as themselves. Indeed, when I saw Hu Ping in New York and asked him, 'How do you see the Chinese here?' he answered, almost dismissively, 'Well, they're American, aren't they?'

Maxine Hong Kingston, married to an American of Russian Jewish and Irish Portuguese descent, was born in Stockton, California. Her father, a villager from the Four Districts, emigrated to California in the 1920s, followed by his wife in 1939, a year before Maxine was born. They lived humbly, operating a laundry, and after years in America still spoke only Sze Yap, the dialect of the Four Districts. What Chinese culture Maxine imbibed was the folk culture of the peasantry, a culture judged unworthy of loyalty by the thousands of English-speaking, American-born Chinese who deserted it for Americanness. Four Districts of origin, Californian of upbringing, her father a laundry man, Maxine Hong Kingston is the archetypal Chinese American.

Many Chinese find it hard to read Maxine Hong Kingston, because as they read her they are constantly nagged by a feeling of inauthenticity. Could her mother really have said, 'The emperors used to eat the peaked hump of purple dromedaries'?[24] One has only to try translating these words back into the homely speech of Sze Yap – which wouldn't have that sort of vocabulary to begin with – to realize how implausible it is for any speaker of that dialect to have uttered them. And you could see that she had lifted many of the details of the legends she retells from English translations of Chinese stories, and not from having been told them as a child.

Maxine Hong Kingston says that Chinese reviewers miss the point when they complain that she gets her Chinese mythology all wrong, because what they don't realize is that it is American mythology she is writing – the Chinese stories, taken to America by immigrants, are changed in the retelling.[25] What she is saying is that she is not trying to be true to Chinese culture but to immigrant Chinese-American culture, a different matter. But some critics say she is not true to that either; Frank Chin, a Chinese-American writer every bit as Americanized as she, for example, accuses her of pandering to 'white, racist stereotypes' in her writing.

If Chinese Americans find her less than wholly satisfying, it is perhaps because being an acculturated Chinese American is unsatisfying. Kingston suggests this in her novel *Tripmaster Monkey*, the hero of which, Wittman Ah Sing, is 'as American as Jack Kerouac or James Baldwin or Allen Ginsberg, as American as Walt Whitman, the poet that his father tried to name him after, as American as five generations in California and a Berkeley education in the 1960s can make him'.[26] The trouble is, American as he is, people still take him for a Chinese, still insist upon his exoticism and inscrutability. Now this would be perfectly all right if he was still culturally Chinese, but the likes of Wittman Ah Sing can't be Chinese even if they tried, because they have already lost all cultural markers of their ethnicity, above all language, the very core of the Chinese identity. Only 'backscratcher swizzle sticks, pointed chopsticks for the hair, Jade East aftershave in a Buddha-shaped bottle'[27] are left to him. Nor does it help, one might add, that what his immigrant forebears brought with them was not the urbane high culture of China, but the vulgar culture of the villages; it is not only his assimilation to American society that locked him out of the splendours of the Chinese heritage, but the fact that the splendours were never there for him to inherit in the first place.

The identity that *is* available to him is 'Chinese American' or 'Asian American', but what are the cultural markers of this nebulous entity? Those Chinese Americans to whom cultural identification matters feel an unease in their condition – anxieties, resentments, defensiveness, self-hate, even at times a kind of snobbery. They feel something of what the Philippine Chinese mestizo and the Indies peranakan felt when they suddenly found themselves overwhelmed by a large influx of new Chinese immigrants who looked down upon them as so many Chinese *manqués*; 'what they see', as Frank Chin put it, 'is that the English speaking American born don't know shit [about Chinese culture] and are faking it.'[28] But their shame is mixed with snobbery, a disdain of the greenhorn, the raw innocent who speaks the wrong language, wears the

wrong clothes, and exhibits the wrong habits. 'Spitting seeds,' Wittman
Ah Sing observes of a family of newcomers; 'So uncool. You wouldn't
mislike them on sight if their pants weren't so highwater, gym socks
white and noticeable. FOB fashions – highwaters or puddlecuffs. Can't
get it right. Uncool. Uncool.'[29] Yet many American-born English-
speaking Chinese can't help but feel that they have lost something
of their true selves in their embrace of American culture; they can't
help but wonder if they may not have given up too much of their own
identity, paid too high a price, to achieve their fusion with the rest
of American society. When an ABC (American-born Chinese) looks
around him, he becomes aware that the new arrivals, even if they
are nothing else, can tell themselves that they are Chinese and draw
comfort from the fact; he has no such recourse. And it certainly doesn't
help that the league table of Chinese academic and business celebrities
in America is top-heavy with the names of foreign-born immigrants; it
is the greenhorn who is most obviously 'making it' in America.

'It takes one generation to lose China. How many does it take to gain
America?'[30] Robbed of his singularity as Chinese, the ABC is yet denied
his Americanness by what he calls, too frequently to non-American
ears, 'white racist stereotypes'. Like the black, he is stamped with a
permanent racial visibility. Having aspired to Americanness and failed,
or rather having succeeded and still harbouring feelings of failure, he
hates himself all the more because deep down he knows that while it
takes more than ordinary determination to keep one's identity intact
in the United States, so powerful are the Americanizing influences of
that country, he has become detribalized partly from choice: he has
renounced his Chineseness, not wanting to be identified with what was
for many years a despised community.

His Americanization attests to the powerful pull of the American
Dream, the compelling metaphor of which was the Melting Pot, the
image of a fusion of different nationalities into a new race of men.
When first coined, the phrase was 'seized upon as a concise evocation
of a profoundly significant American fact'.[31]

But did the fusion occur? In their enormously influential book
Beyond the Melting Pot, Nathan Glazer and Daniel Patrick Moynihan
observe that 'The point about the melting pot is that it did not happen.'
It had once been supposed that, except where colour was concerned,
immigrants would be assimilated by the Anglo-Saxon core into a seam-
less pattern by the third generation; but immigrants did not become as
fully American as had been expected; they remained distinctive even

after they had become successfully integrated into their host country as full members and loyal citizens. In the mid-1960s, the notion of cultural pluralism came to rival the notion of a fusion. A more accurate image, it was thought, would be a 'stew' or 'salad bowl', a mosaic of different groups co-existing in a multiracial, multicultural or pluralistic society, the tomatoes remaining tomatoes, distinguishable from the lettuce and the chicory.

We all know what happened in the 1960s: the civil rights movement, the student struggle, whites linking hands with blacks to sing 'We Shall Overcome', Martin Luther King sounding the beginning of a new age with the words 'I have a dream that my four little children will one day live in a nation where they will not be judged by the color of their skin but by the content of their character.'

Out of the social transformations of the 1960s and 1970s has emerged an obsessive preoccupation with ethnicity. The erstwhile badge of shame has become a badge of pride. Antecedents are sought, ethnic immigrant histories are recovered. One no longer feels apologetic for being a minority; one is prouder than ever of being an 'ethnic' – KISS ME, I'M POLISH, declared the lapel button of an immigrant descendant. With pride came dignified nomenclature. Of so much emotional moment was the struggle over the proper label for Mexican Americans, for example – some thought it should be Americano, some Hispano, others preferred Chicano – that it has been called 'the battle of the name'. There have even been debates over whether or not one should use a hyphen, and some immigrants would be offended indeed if you call them hyphenated Americans, Asian-Americans, say, instead of Asian Americans.

Even Belgian Americans stressed their immigrant heritage and their separate origins. The fillip to all this came from the federal government's campaign to help disadvantaged minorities get a firmer social and economic foothold in American societies through Affirmative Action, the use of ethnic quotas and preferences. Blacks, Puerto Ricans, Native Americans (American Indians), Mexicans and Asians benefited from this redistribution of opportunity, but not, obviously, immigrant Europeans and Caucasians. To make sure that they were not left out, immigrants from India, until 1977 categorized as Caucasians, quickly formed an ethnic association to protest against their classification and to press for minority status. A similar opportunism gave birth to Chinese organizations.

It says much for the potency of ethnic politics in the United States that over the years such organizations have become growth industries. A visitor with an interest in Chinese affairs does not have to be in California long before hearing of the National Coalition of Americans of Pacific-Asian Ancestry, the Organization of Chinese American Women, the Organization of Chinese-Americans, Chinese for Affirmative Action, and so on. Hardly a day goes by without some Asian American group busying itself to hold a meeting, sponsor an event, organize an exhibition or host a party. Take a week in May 1988: the Asian American Drug Abuse Programme is celebrating its fifteenth anniversary; Asian Americans for Jesse Jackson is sponsoring a 'fundraiser' at Berkeley; the Asian American Friends of Dukakis Committee is doing the same at the Golden Dragon Restaurant in Los Angeles; the Chinese American Political Association of Contra Costa County is hosting a dinner and dance at the Round Hill Country Club; while Asian Americans for Community Involvement is urging the prosecution of a case of racial assault in Santa Clara County.

What has been called the 'ethnic preservation movement' has been carried into the groves of Academe. Recognizing the change in the cultural composition of the population, many Americans are asking in what sense the sources of their national culture remain European. Shouldn't the study of non-European cultures, these people ask, be made a requirement of graduation from university? Shouldn't courses on civilization be reshaped to reflect the increasing diversity of racial origins among America's students – by 1989, more than half of Berkeley's students will be members of ethnic minorities? Courses in black, Asian and Amerindian cultures are already offered by some universities, but these are not compulsory. Instead of dismissing the undergraduates who pressed for this as student militants, some academics spoke in favour of broadening the curriculum, but others argued that students should be exposed, as Matthew Arnold put it, to 'the best which has been thought and said in the world', regardless of whether it was thought or said by a white, black, Asian or Hispanic. In a letter to *The Economist*, one who gave his address as the City University of New York was no doubt speaking for many when he wrote, 'We should not replace physics by witchcraft, economics by astrology, nor the landmarks of history, philosophy and literature with what is less good because it would placate objectors.'[32]

Sooner or later all societies except the culturally homogeneous have to face the question of whether they should have one culture, or several. Even Britain, hardly a multicultural country, has been faced with this problem. This is because, while the country as a whole is not multiracial (its non-white population was only 4.4 per cent of the total in 1985), some cities are. It has taken a long time for British statistics to reflect this, and the census of 1991 will be the first to include questions about the respondent's ethnic origin. (Such questions had been resisted by the black community, who fear that the information thus obtained may be passed on to the Immigration Department and used against them.) The ethnic categories listed will be: white, three black groups (Caribbean, African and Other), four Asian groups (Indian, Pakistani, Bangladeshi and Chinese) and Other.

In Britain public attitudes to the idea of a many-cultured society can roughly be sorted into three categories: the racist, the anti-racist and the neutral. The racist, if he doesn't actually hold them in contempt, is unable to take minority cultures altogether seriously. To the Little Englander in him, Urdu or Cantonese is so much native jibberish, and the idea that such barbarous tongues should be taught in the English classroom seems to him utterly misconceived, if not downright dangerous, leading to a dilution of English culture.

He is opposed by the anti-racist, who may be white or coloured, a member of any ethnic category, and who works as likely as not in what its detractors call the Race Relations Industry. Positive discrimination, mother-tongue schooling, anti-racist education, minority arts centres – these are the things for which he presses, while railing at British xenophobia, denouncing dissenters as fascists, raising the spectre of the National Front, and stressing victimization as the cause of educational and social failure among the minorities. It is not only multicultural schooling that he likes to see instituted, but also a policy of active 'anti-racist education'; this includes, among other things, combing children's books for matter which can be deemed racialist.

In an exercise reported in 1988, reading schemes in nearly two hundred primary schools in Sheffield were examined to see if the portrayal of Japanese or Chinese characters was racially or culturally offensive. Only eight, out of a total of more than eight hundred, were found to feature Chinese and Japanese characters at all, and none showed them living or working side by side with white people, or playing together with them. In one, a slit-eyed mandarin figure with a drooping moustache is depicted wearing a quilted jacket and wooden platform shoes. In another, a story set 'long ago' in China, the accoutrements of the villagers are strictly stereotypical, down to rice-straw hats and pigtails. 'One can only guess', said the teacher who conducted the study, 'at the bewilderment and indignation of an ethnic Chinese/Japanese child in a British school faced with such a patronizing and ignorant portrayal of his ethnic culture.'33 To take the exercise to its crazy and logical conclusion, school-books showing Chinese wearing platform shoes and pigtails would have to be banned. This, to a neutral, is to trivialize the race question. Even supposing that what is or is not racialist can be unequivocally known, it is only too clear that a vivid imagination (or hypocrisy, as the case may be) can present perfectly harmless or even commendatory matter as an affront to, say, blacks, Chinese or the female sex.

Fighting stereotypes has gone a good deal further in the United States, where many Chinese have become walking conditioned reflexes, hotly resenting any action that could be construed as having a racial dimension. This is illustrated by the outcry over a new film about Charlie Chan in 1980. Charlie Chan, the famous Chinese sleuth, is a fictional figure, introduced by Earl Derr Biggers in 1925 and familiar to almost every American above a certain age. One met him in column after column of the *Saturday Evening Post*, book after book, feature film after feature film, and it was always as the epitome of the 'damned clever Chinese' that he appeared to us, the detective who confounded his scornful white detractors by solving every mystery and tracking down every villain. He came across as not only wise but genial, and this was deliberate, for it had been the intention of the producer of the original Chan movies at Fox Studios to counter with a sympathetic portrayal the characterization of Chinese as Fu Manchus. Yet when plans were laid to revive Charlie Chan in a new film – with Peter Sellers playing the part of the detective – Chinese protestors in San Francisco threatened demonstrations. 'Racist stereotypes . . . Chinese don't talk like that,' they complained, objecting at the same time to a white actor playing the part of a Chinese. They had behind them a pressure group, Chinese for Affirmative Action. Some years before, an organization which called itself Asian-Americans for Fair Media had prevented a cinema in New York from screening Charlie Chan and Fu Manchu films.34

But what if Chinese were portrayed as all-American successes, would those who object to the label of 'model minority' cry 'Racist!' too? The anti-racist can be as intolerant as the racist. On the other hand, while it is true that discrimination is sometimes in the eye of the beholder, and people do have a point when they say that the highest compliment one can pay a minority is to hold it up to exactly the same standards to which one subjects the white race, the fact remains that white Americans haven't inherited a Fu Manchu image to make them sensitive to how others portray them. To be colour-blind is to see men as simply men, while there is plenty of evidence to suggest that the American public is as yet incapable of looking at a black, say, as an individual rather than as a symbol.

When Chinese Americans accuse white Americans of racism, they often invoke the case of Vincent Chin. Vincent Chin was a twenty-seven-year-old Chinese who, on the night of his bachelor party in the summer of 1982, had his brains beaten out with a baseball bat by Ronald Ebens, a forty-three-year-old laid-off Chrysler foreman in East Detroit, a city with an unemployment rate of almost eleven per cent. In the topless bar where the two had met, Ebens had taken Vincent Chin for a Japanese, one of those people whose car exports had put so many Americans out of work, and a quarrel had ensued. In a parking lot later that evening, Ebens swung his bat while his stepson held Vincent Chin in a bear hug. When the court handed down its sentence it outraged the Chinese community: for killing Vincent Chin, Ebens and his stepson were merely placed on three years' probation and fined $3,780 each.[35]

It is difficult, however, to generalize about racial attitudes in America. To a casual overseas Chinese visitor from Malaysia or Indonesia, America will seem wonderfully unracist. An immigrant in America will not accept being a second-class citizen there even if he would take that condition for granted at home, expecting nothing better from his own government. Elsewhere in the world – in Indonesia, say, or Malaysia – any thought on the part of the Chinese of taking up the cudgels for minority rights would be undercut by an inhibiting pessimism as to even the possibility of Chinese redress and equality. The Chinese in America are not so inhibited, and this, perhaps, is what chiefly identifies them as American. When he despairs of a better deal the Malaysian Chinese will simply go away and start life in Australia. But the American Chinese will stand intransigent upon his rights, backed as he is by the crusades and racial sensitivities of American society, Affirmative Action, ticket-balancing, the whole grand idea of American equality.

In America it is not threat of force or persecution which makes an immigrant succumb to cultural conformity, but 'a trap or lure of the most pleasant kind',[36] a kind of bribery. He can feel himself to be an American without presumption or ingratiation, not a feeling he would get in an old established European society. The readiness of Chinese

Americans to salute the flag, take the oath, express all-American sentiments or think themselves American astonishes a traveller from England like myself. But then each country absorbs its foreigners in its own way. In their colonial possessions the British liked to keep the races apart – and themselves aloof. They produced a class of Anglicized Asians and Africans, the Babas of the Straits Settlements and English-speaking Indians yearning for metropolitan sophistications being prime examples. But though 'niggers began at Calais' for many an Englishman, on the whole the English did not have much respect for those of their subject peoples who, in their eagerness to acquire second-hand English manners, turned their backs on their own culture. Such people were seen to demean themselves, taking on the veneer of a culture they did not fully understand. Not the native villagers but the Westernized social climbers had been the most despised; not the cherishing of indigenous ways but the crude devotion to things English. These were confused attitudes, for deep down not many imperialists really thought the indigenous cultures worth preserving. Back home the colonial pattern has been repeated, and an ambivalence continues to colour English attitudes to assimilation; there is nothing in England to match the strong Americanizing influence of American society. Here one can remain oneself longer, if one wants to; here it is easier to resist the threats and blandishments of cultural conformity. (I am sure that if I had lived in America for as long as I have in England, I would have become far more Americanized than British.)

Foreigners have looked at this in two ways: favourably, as signalling the proverbial British sympathy for eccentricity; and unfavourably, as reflecting a deep unadmitted British need to keep foreigners in their place. However one looks at it, there is no doubting the complexity of British society and the difficulty the foreigner has in grasping its norms and nuances. A Chinese academic may manage a tweed jacket, leather patches, and perhaps even a Dunhill pipe more readily than a Khomeini-style turban, but this in no way suggests that he fits better into an English university than a Malaysian one. A foreigner may become British, but he can never become English. Speaking of the West Indian, V. S. Naipaul observes: 'In the French territories he aimed at Frenchness, in the Dutch territories at Dutchness; in the English territories he aimed at simple whiteness and modernity, Englishness being impossible.'

By contrast, because American culture is still not quite set, in the way that English or French culture is set, the immigrant to America arrives upon a world that he feels is going to be partly of his own making. To be in a state of flux, to be refuelled by new blood, and to have the ethnic patchwork continually added to, is part of the American experience. The immigrant comes upon a society that still takes the business of self-definition seriously. We are told by historians that rootlessness and the search for identity have always been features of American life, and we are not surprised that, of all Chinese settlers abroad, it is the ones in America who feel most keenly what Simone Weil, in her tormented wartime exile among the English, called 'perhaps the most important and least recognized need of the human soul' – the need to be rooted.

Among migrants, as among new nations, there are few causes more fashionable today than the quest for identity. The phenomenal success of the television serial *Roots*; the popularity of Irving Howe's book *World of Our Fathers*, a reconstruction of the life of East European Jewish immigrants in America; the rediscovery of Isaac Bashevis Singer – all these express the interest in ancestry. To the villagers in Toishan, the Chinese American who returns to rediscover his origins is doing a very American thing, for the last thing *they* feel is the need for roots. Toishan, like other sending societies, has not been slow to tap what the Irish and Scottish holiday trade calls the 'roots business' in the United States, offering tours to ancestral villages and wooing investments by local sons made good.

In their hurry and anxiety to win acceptance in white American society, immigrants had forgotten, ignored, or discarded without a backward glance the habits which had set them apart. Only now, when it is all but irretrievable, has the past acquired value for America's immigrants. Now they are at pains to recover their distinctiveness, and to re-invent their identity. And yet their need to do this is itself an expression of their Americanness. How American it is, after all, to protest one's ethnicity. A Chinese American is never more American than when he tells me, 'I'm proud of my Chinese heritage.' Amy Tan, the Chinese-American author of the bestselling novel *The Joy Luck Club*, could not have made a more American remark than when she said, 'As soon as my feet touched China, I felt Chinese.' Only a Chinese lost to Chineseness, whether through renunciation or unconscious drift, could feel like this.

What Irving Howe says of the Jews may equally be said of the Chinese immigrants, that 'in bearing the troubles of an unfixed identity, they had finally entered the American condition'.[37]

CHAPTER FIFTEEN

Chinatowns

A core of Chinese concentration may be found in many of the world's big cities where the Chinese are settled. In London it is the broad corridor traversed by Lisle Street, Gerrard Street and Newport Place. In Manila it is the huddle of shops and office buildings approached along Ongpin Street in Binondo. In Yokohama it is the mesh of streets running behind the seafront, between Yamashita Park and Yokohama Stadium. In Calcutta, before the Chinese were dispersed by the border war between China and India in 1962, it was the area between the start of Lower Chitpore Road and Chittaranjan Avenue.

Living in separate enclaves was not always of their own choosing, however much immigrants may like to cluster around their own kind. In the ports early traders lived in wards according to place of origin, and racial separation was employed by the imperial powers as an instrument of government. On founding Singapore, for example, Stamford Raffles concentrated the different classes and ethnic groups of the population in their separate quarters, allotting the Chinese their own kampong (neighbourhood) to the southwest of the Singapore river.[1] In Spanish Manila the Chinese were confined to the Parián; and under the system of pass and residential restrictions practised by the Dutch in Batavia, the Chinese were segregated in a ghetto.

Chinese migrants have also conjured new towns where none had existed before – Phuket (in southern Thailand), Taiping and Seremban in the Malay states, and even Kuala Lumpur, which began life as a huddle of Chinese huts, were all called into being by Chinese miners. Perhaps the most remarkable of the towns the Chinese built abroad was Locke, in the Sacramento-San Joaquin Delta in California. A ghost town listed in the National Register of Historic Places and visited by tourists and souvenir hunters, this was built by a group of Cantonese farm workers in 1915. It was a colony like no other in America, a western town that looked like something out of Hollywood, but inhabited exclusively by Chinese who lived all on their own and who kept their way of life complete, down to the gambling-houses.[2]

The more typical Chinatown, though, is a neighbourhood or district in a city that others have developed. Two or more could sprout in a single city. Paris, for example, has three Chinese quarters. The largest of these is the Porte d'Ivry quarter to the southeast of the city, where, the more you wander, the more likely you are to be reminded of the Chinese neighbourhoods in Indochina. You know yourself to be among Southeast Asians when, approaching Tang Frères, arguably the largest Chinese supermarket in Europe, the foetid odour of the durian, the king of tropical fruits, pungently assails your nostrils.

Large numbers of Laotian and Cambodian Chinese are also to be found in the Belleville quarter, in the nineteenth and twentieth *arrondissements*, fulfilling their traditional immigrant role by running shops and reviving the commercial life of the neighbourhood. Their miniature teacups, a speciality of the Swatow area to be seen in many a shop or home in Belleville, show that they are, like the majority of Chinese in Bangkok, Teochiu speakers. They are the latest wave of newcomers to have colonized Belleville, once the very heart of the Jewish ghetto, sheltering immigrants from first Eastern Europe and then the Maghreb.

Finally, there is the Chinese concentration along Rue des Gravilliers in the third *arrondissement*, between Rue Beaubourg and Rue du Temple. What is chiefly remarkable about this tiny community is that its members are heavily concentrated in the leather wholesale trade – shop after shop on the street offers belts, handbags and suitcases – and have originated from a place which few will have heard of. This is Ch'ing-t'ien (Blue Fields) County in Chekiang province, whose emigrants have traditionally found their way to continental Europe rather than to Southeast Asia or America, sailing from the eastern port of Wenchow and winding up in France, Italy, Belgium and Holland, where they earned a meagre living as pedlars.[3] In Holland so many of them took to hawking peanuts and peanut brittle that the Dutch called them *pinda* ('peanut') Chinese.[4] In Paris between the wars, they formed a small colony near the Gare de Lyon – a plaque on an obscure street behind the station was unveiled in 1988 to mark its site – and took over much of the leather industry from the Jews the Germans deported.

As in Paris, more than one Chinatown has arisen in Los Angeles and New York City. As a hub of Chinese life and commerce, the old downtown Los Angeles Chinatown has been challenged by Monterey Park, a community five miles to the east of LA. Downtown Chinatown still feels like an immigrant funnel, one lot of newcomers replacing another, in an evolutionary way; it received waves of French, Croatians and Italians, and now the Vietnamese are increasingly replacing the Toishan Chinese, giving the place a Saigon flavour. Monterey Park, by contrast, does not feel like a Chinatown at all, but more like a corner of middle-class suburbia. In fact it is the first suburban Chinatown to appear in America. Something similar has happened in New York City, where secondary areas of Chinese concentration have sprung up in the southern part of Brooklyn and in the Jackson Heights, Flushing and Elmhurst sections of Queens.

Urban Chinatowns are much what you would expect, and the perennial sights – the Chinese restaurants, the Chinese grocery shops and the Chinese gateways – are familiar enough to us all. But though there is a certain sameness to them, they are by no means exact equivalents of each other. Some induce a sensation of menace, like the one in Amsterdam; others exude an almost Parisian chic, like the one in Yokohama. But though there is no generic Chinatown to be offered as an example for them all, you will never see the type more completely than in Bangkok.

To get the feel of it, it is best to head for Sampeng, to where the oldest part of the city stands soggy and steamy upon the Chao Phraya River, and to start sidestepping your way down Yaowarat and Charoen Krung Roads, past hawkers and lottery-ticket sellers. Together with the river itself, Sampeng was where, 150 years ago, the busiest markets for imported merchandise in Bangkok, an Eastern Venice with the river and canals as its drains and its thoroughfares, were located. In those days a shopper coming by boat or canoe could stop to examine the wares of any one of about seventy Chinese junks and over four miles of floating shops moored to the shore.5 Bangkok had a Chinese pocket built into it from the very start. By the early 1800s, over half of its population was Chinese,6 and even today there are as many people of Chinese descent in Bangkok as there are Siamese.

Sampeng, decried by a Western writer in 1898 as 'Chinese Bangkok, malodorous and ill-mannered',7 is a narrow, cluttered bazaar about a mile and a quarter in length, roofed over by sheets of cloth and plastic. These lie like a cloak upon the huddles of goods and humanity, keeping the terrible sun out but the furnace heat in. Gone are the Chinese craftsmen who used to ply their trade here, the blacksmiths and the weavers, the lapidaries and the workers in gold and silver. Today the pedestrian barges his way between food hawkers through piles of flowery bath caps, trayfuls of buttons, streams of PVC belts, and any amount of synthetic textiles. For fabrics are the speciality of this bazaar, and up and down the alley stand the drapers with their bolts of cotton and polyester.

There are Thai tradeswomen about, there is the odd blond backpacker from Australia or Scandinavia, there is a sprinkling of turbanned Sikh drapers and watchmen, but most of the people you bump into along Sampeng are Chinese. The shop-girl that you see in the doorway, the one spooning rice into her mouth – she may never eat with chopsticks, she may have difficulty forcing her thoughts into Mandarin, but she is pure Chinese, with not a jot of Thai blood in her.

Bangkok's Chinatown is not a neatly identifiable little enclave within the confines of Sampeng. It proliferates beyond, pushing against the cars, the motor bikes, the motorized trishaws and the coating of dust and exhaust fumes that is like a condensation of the heat-haze itself. An unlovely splurge of concrete housing and pounding traffic, it has whole sequences of open-fronted shops whose cluttered interiors look like warehouses and the backs of removal vans, where sweating torsos may be glimpsed bending over tyres, mudguards, carburettors, and bits of chassis and motor bike. And near the western end of Yaowarat Road, beside a canal holding puddles of greasy and smelly water, flimsy and shanty-like constructions haphazardly spill their contents – bits of broken furniture, parts of kitchens, piles of refuse – on to the edge of the water beneath rags and plastic awnings.

And yet, unlikely as it may seem at first glance, some of the dearest real estate in Bangkok lies just around the corner,[8] for it is instantly evident in the feel of the place that it is an Eastern emporium at its most untrammelled, pulsing irrepressibly with the energies of money-making. Under a jumble of Chinese and Thai lettering on shopfronts ablaze with neon lighting, you can see shelves packed tight with anything from cassette tapes to plastic dildos; canisters of tea-leaves from the hillsides of Wu-i Mountains in Fukien province; gunny sacks fragrant with dried herbs and spices; stalls vivid with mounds of vegetables and tropical fruits; stacks of yellow lacquered coffins looking like flat-bottomed, square-nosed boats; restaurants with air-conditioning and a spittoon placed statutorily beneath every table.

But it is the preponderance of gold jewellery shops, flashing and scintillating on Yaowarat Road, that gives Bangkok's Chinatown its distinctive character. The Chinese are popularly supposed to be extremely fond of gold (the yellower the metal, the better), and shopkeepers in

Bangkok cannot go wrong with gold jewellery, which is looked upon by many as their own personal savings bank.

This is a great place too for those stock characters of Chinese commerce: the pawnbroker, half-hidden from view by the partition that traditionally screens counter from doorway; the seller of cooked snacks from a wheeled cart, pursuing his skills over a bubbling wok and displaying in a neon-lit glass showcase his collection of pendant or heaped ingredients, piscine, crustacean or intestinal; the fortune-teller behind his booth, cashing in on the belief in the immutability of one's horoscope; the dealer in dry goods; the bookseller offering Chinese-Thai dictionaries and Taiwan editions of *The Three Kingdoms*; the travel agent arranging tours to Swatow and Canton and other home towns in the motherland.

Of course there are herb shops and pharmacies too, for the Chinese are great hypochondriacs, and people who have been brought up with food myths and astrology surrender themselves readily to folk medicines. To judge by the ads in the seven Chinese-language newspapers in Bangkok, the great preoccupation here, as in all the Chinese world, is the search for an efficacious remedy for piles. Drugstores with décors reminiscent of old China are a commonplace in Bangkok's Chinatown. Here you will find pigeonholes of bezoar and powdered deer horns and Chinese wolfberry. Here are tins of Hacks lozenges made under licence from White Hudson & Co. Ltd of Southport, England. Here are boxes of nursing mothers' 'milk suckers' or breast pumps. Here their consciences do not prick them when they sell you as much Valium and Librium as you want without a prescription.

The dim inner recesses of many a shop in Chinatown are like images from an old print, frozen in time for ever; and there are side lanes which look as if they have strayed from an earlier era in rural China, an era long since gone in China itself, but surviving hauntingly here in Bangkok. The spindly old men that you sometimes glimpse through the dark mouth of an alley doorway, the ones with faces like shrivelled brown nuts – these seem indeed to have wandered straight out of some turn-of-the-century lorcha from Swatow, and to have cut off their pigtails only yesterday.

No less suggestive of Chinese continuity is the joss-house that one may stumble upon at the end of a cul-de-sac, usually a brick and stucco place of incense and murmured prayers, and scarlet hangings and garish fairground decoration which only age and soot have made beautiful. There are many temples, since each dialect group likes to have its own.

When it comes to number and influence, no dialect group in Thailand can hold a candle to the Teochius; and in Bangkok even the most rabid Cantonese chauvinst has been ready to learn to speak Teochiu. The grand building which houses the Teochiu Association in Bangkok, though it has about it an echoing, mausoleum sterility, is an unequivocal statement of Teochiu supremacy. Teochius thronged Thailand in three successive waves over the centuries, more than a million and a half of them arriving between 1782 and 1868, three hundred thousand of them between 1900 and 1906, and two hundred thousand of them between 1946 and 1949.[9] Teochius are heavily represented in the country's established ascendancy of merchants and bankers, and the Teochiu Association's annual report, replete with the colour photographs and hagiographies of its officers and benefactors, is tellingly studded with the names of wealthy families and business bigwigs.

Take the report for 1987, which shows the association's two honorary life presidents to be Chin Sophonpanich and Udane Techapaibul, the giants of business we met in Chapter Twelve. These two Teochius may be ciphers to the world at large, but at home they are household names, their business interests ramifying into every corner of Thai life, making the consumer feel, if he stops to think about it, that whatever he is doing, whether he is cashing a cheque or drinking a bottle of Kloster beer, he is making these rich families richer still. Their photographs in the report show them resplendently sashed and bemedalled, for Chinese tycoons conventionally clothe their natural cupidity in public-spiritedness and chairmanships of charitable organizations, and the well-publicized philanthropy of these two gentlemen had earned them decorations by the King.

To observe that gambling is an essential of the expatriate Chinese scene is to be guilty of tedious repetition, but it must nevertheless be said that a good many games of dice and cards take place out of sight of policemen in Bangkok's Chinatown. On the day I was there, a special task force of the Central Investigation Bureau raided a four-storey wooden house behind the Texas Theatre on Charoen Krung Road and caught about thirty of the fifty people gambling there, the rest having eluded arrest through a secret exit.

In the first decades of this century the gambling-houses stood cheek by jowl with the brothels, in a corner of Chinatown called Samyod.[10] Girls were abducted to Thailand from China for immoral purposes right up to the 1930s. In the late nineteenth century, during the reign of Rama V, a famous brothel keeper, a millionaire in her day called

Mrs Fang, even had a lane in Sampeng and a Buddhist temple (one she built herself, in a bid for merit) named after her. The last people to give up regular whoring were the poor Hainanese, the least well-off of the Chinese settlers and the last immigrants to be joined by their women. Once the women started coming, the numbers of brothels and their denizens were halved.

Even so, today there are few places to rival Thailand for the sheer ebullience of its sex industry; the willingness of Thai girls to offer good times to American GIs resting from the Vietnam war, and the growth of mass tourism, have seen to that. Parts of the capital are speckled with massage parlours (where the masseuses are picked from behind a one-way mirror), go-go bars (where the visiting Japanese or Europeans enjoy the fondling of bar-girls at the same time as they are treated to the spectacle of a copulating couple at fairly close range on stage), and VD clinics (which somehow seem a little anachronistic in the age of Aids). The girls are Thai rather than Chinese, but, however muffled may be the actual business arrangements, you can be certain of Chinese money behind the industry.

But although advertisements with pictures of girls in dishabille abound in the Chinese press, the mass of Chinese indulge in pastimes of a tamer sort. The surprise of Bangkok's Chinatown, which has its complement of theatres and cinemas, is that Chinese local opera, the variety popular among Teochiu speakers, should still be performed there, when so few traditional forms of entertainment have succeeded in holding their own against the onslaught of Hollywood-style spectaculars. The opera has miraculously survived the intrusions of the Western world – but only just. The Hsin-hua Theatre on Yaowarat Road, for example, began life as a forum for Chinese opera, then turned itself into a cinema screening imported Hong Kong films – Cantonese soap operas which had to be dubbed into Teochiu – in the 1950s. Now tastes have changed again, and the advertising stills in the cinema on a November day in 1987 show scenes from a James Bond movie and *The Year of the Dragon*.

The Chinese couple who own the theatre live in a flat approached by an outside staircase above the cinema. They told me much about what it is to be a Chinese in Thailand. Mr Ch'en, tall, large and dark-skinned enough to be Thai, was born in a provincial town in Thailand to second-generation Teochiu immigrants. Unusually for a Chinese of his background – neither his father nor his mother spoke Chinese at home – he has taken the trouble to learn Mandarin and is quite fluent in the language, although he firmly believes, and reiterates this opinion several times in the course of an evening, that it is scarcely possible to tell Thais and Chinese apart these days. His relative remoteness from his Chinese origins has clearly affected his manners and perceptions, making him at once more easygoing and less divided in his loyalties than first or second-generation immigrant Chinese. To the question of whom he would side with in a ping-pong match between China and Thailand, he unhesitatingly answers, 'Thailand.'

In his wife, whose very fair skin would instantly set her apart from Thais, the process of acculturation has clearly not gone as far. Her father came from China, leaving a wife and children at home. As was customary, he took a Thai wife in Bangkok; but she died before she could give him any children, and he married again, this time to a pure Chinese, Mrs Ch'en's mother. It was he who started the Hsin-hua Theatre, so unlike her husband Mrs Ch'en has lived in Chinatown practically all her life. In the ordinary course of events, she says, she would have supported the Chinese ping-pong team, but China, or more specifically the Chinese government, has disappointed her in many ways, and now she thinks she might simply want the best side to win.

The couple have three children, two daughters and a son. The daughters, one a vet, the other a doctor, were educated in France and the United States, and upon their return to Bangkok have moved out of Chinatown, like so many of their generation, to live in a style which identifies them as the modern professionals they are. They no longer speak any Chinese, and on many levels of their being they no doubt feel that they have more in common with Thai professionals than with Chinese shopkeepers.

Very different is their brother, who read English Literature at one of Bangkok's universities and who announced one day, to the astonishment and secret delight of his mother, that he was going to study modern Chinese Literature at Peking University. He is there now, and he has become so thoroughly Chinese, his mother reports, that you would never guess he wasn't a Swatow boy who had never left China. Mrs Ch'en speaks of all this wonderingly, but surely her son's resinicization is only extraordinary in the Thai context: in Europe and North America, plenty of deracinated Chinese have gone back to China to find their roots, seeking to recover their lost identities. It is true that other Chinese in Thailand have gone happily native, but they have not studied English Literature, have not, perhaps, been brought by their acquaintance with a great literary tradition, and the sensibilities to which it provides a window, to the disconcerting realization of their own dispossession.

Bangkok's Chinese quarter traces its history back to a grand bazaar. New York's traces its origin to just one shop, but today it is the Western Hemisphere's largest Chinatown. The Chinese were among the waves and waves of immigrants – Britons, Germans, Finns, Jews, Swedes, Africans, Italians, Irish – who beat upon the shores of Manhattan and helped to turn it into the city of cities. All the world is in New York, and the Chinese, who are in all the world, are in New York in force. A survey by the US immigration authorities shows New York to be the first choice of Chinese immigrants to America,[11] and a count in 1988 put their number at three hundred thousand.[12]

New York is particularly favoured by Chinese of working-class origin, who know that manual and semi-skilled work can be found in the garment factories, restaurants and sweatshops of the booming downtown Chinatown. In New York, as in any big city, class divisions have detectable geographical centres, overlapping or coinciding with ethnic quarters. To dare a simplification, New York's Chinese are divided into two broad groups, the working-class Chinese who live inside Chinatown, and the middle-class Chinese who live outside it; and if it weren't for the fact that they sometimes shop there, the latter need never set foot in Chinatown from one year to the next.

The heart of Chinatown is the eight blocks bounded by Canal Street to the north, Baxter Street to the west, Bowery Street to the east, and Worth Street and Park Row to the south, but the geographical limits have become more and more indeterminate as Chinatown eats into the ethnic enclaves that run into it – Chinese signs now overlook what used to be Little Italy; roast duck and beef in oyster sauce have taken the place of blintzes and bortsch in the old, famous Garden Cafeteria, haunt of Jewish intellectuals on East Broadway; the old offices of that most Jewish of institutions, the socialist paper *Jewish Daily Forward*, have been taken over by a Chinese church and are emblazoned with the Chinese characters for the Confucian virtues of filial piety, righteousness, loyalty and trustworthiness, as well as some words by Jesus. Bursting the bounds of the old quarter, the Chinese have spread into Center Street, Broome Street, Allen Street and Pike Street up to the East River, and theirs now looks to be the most vigorous of the city's ethnic neighbourhoods.

One imagines those little neighbourhoods separately evolving, each on its well-beaten immigrant path of Ellis Island-Lower East Side-Midtown success or failure. Of these neighbourhoods Chinatown has stuck to its own ways the longest, a classic, self-contained ghetto that was haunted by the Exclusion Acts and little freshened by new blood. The residents huddled together for comfort and let the rest of the world go by, a world which merely seemed a place apart in the eyes of some and loomed up to frightening heights in the eyes of others. It did not help that the Jews across the way were looked upon with suspicion and prejudiced dislike too, for victims can all too easily become victimizers, and in 1905, for example, the *Daily Forward* bewailed the fact that 'hooting Jewish boys' had been seen to throw stones at a Chinese man.[13]

To the world outside, converging upon it in tourist buses, it was picturesquely sinister, the sort of place where it was best not to walk singly and to keep away from the dark passageways, those 'hatchet alleys', for you had heard of Chinese torture and Chinese white-slave traders, and you knew from films and magazines that the Chinese sliced their victims to death by inches. It was thrilling, though, to be walking through a place whose sin and mystery had been impressed upon you by a whole array of titillating screen images – 'the ominous shadow of an Oriental figure thrown against a wall, secret panels which slide back to reveal an inscrutable Oriental face, the huge shadow of a hand with tapering fingers and long pointed fingernails poised menacingly, the raised dagger appearing suddenly and unexpectedly from between closed curtains'.[14]

As time passed the aura of danger wore off; Chinese grocers, it turned out, did not all keep cleavers under their counters. The white *habitués* of Chinatown's eating-places felt as safe there as anywhere in New York. Though the blacks would complain that the Chinese followed the whites in imposing Jim Crow restrictions on their restaurants' clienteles, when New Yorkers or out-of-towners wanted a good cheap meal they often found what they wished for in Chinatown.

Since the end of the last war Chinatown has experienced two waves of immigration: the first in the late 1940s, when large numbers of women, the wives of veterans and Chinese with American citizenship, came to join their husbands; the second with the lifting of entry restrictions in 1965. The effect of so many people gravitating here, 1,400 each month,[15] many of them young and uneducated, was explosive. There was suddenly more of everything: more overcrowding, more social problems, more money, too, for the tongs to fight over. Until 1960 more than half the inhabitants were from Toishan, but the influx of immigrants from Hong Kong, Taiwan, Vietnam and the People's Republic of China shifted the linguistic and tribal balance.

Those who gravitated towards Chinatown found an enclave clad in the whole paraphernalia of immigrant Chinese communities, from secret societies to clan associations, each group looking after its own, the whole presided over by the Chinese Consolidated Benevolent Association (CCBA), a staunch supporter of the Kuomintang. The heads of the CCBA, elderly, self-made men of a traditional cast of mind, were all-powerful, but powerless too, for it would have been beyond their range to urge the interests of their people outside the confines of Chinatown. The last thing they wanted was to engage with the larger world, the world of city politics and administration – for so long as the Chinese community kept itself to itself, so long as the Chinese looked to the traditional associations for all their needs, these men ruled the roost in Chinatown.

In this as in much else, the mid-1960s was a time of change. This was when young, better-educated Chinese began to take up the cause of the disadvantaged in Chinatown, setting up institutions to match – the Basement Workshop, the Free Health Clinic, the Food Co-op, and so on. The establishment of the Anti-Poverty Programme of the mid-1960s gave these people their chance.[16] This was a fateful event for Chinatown, for suddenly money was available for the creation of new service agencies which not only challenged the authority of the old associations but involved the Chinese in the life of the larger society. Old moulds were broken, as people began to look beyond Chinatown. There were now alternatives to the clan and native-place associations; there was the Chinatown Planning Council, for example, which was set up with funds from the Anti-Poverty Programme to provide social services to the community. And the Chinese leaders of these new organizations were sitting with Jews, blacks, Italians and Puerto Ricans on the committees of community associations sprouting up all over the Lower East Side. This was not exactly a breaking of ethnic barriers but it nevertheless symbolized the ending of a century of Chinese isolation. The neighbourhood programmes were forcing outwards the frontiers of Chinatown at the same time as they were incorporating it into the wider community. The Chinese were not used to seeing themselves as one of many minorities who should get their due from an even-handed distribution of opportunity, but now they realized that if they wanted better schools, housing, health and status, they had to make themselves heard.

One of those affected by the political mood of the late 1960s and early 1970s was Jack Tchen, an American-born Chinese student of History from Wisconsin. In 1978, in the course of working with the Basement Workshop, a cultural organization in Chinatown, he conceived the idea of launching what came to be called the Chinatown History Project, an attempt to salvage the historical legacy of the neighbourhood before it disappears with the passing of the older generation of immigrants, before memories and lore fade beyond recall, and before old letters, photographs, shop signs, newspapers and other relics are lost for ever. The project's co-founder is Charlie Lai, a Hong Kong immigrant who has a cook for a father and a seamstress for a mother, and who grew up in the very streets whose history he now works to preserve. The project does more than draw out the life of old Chinatown, for by organizing the material it has collected into exhibitions and radio programmes it retells what it has reclaimed, giving to the community what it has so far lacked, a sense of how it began, and how far it has come.

Bangkok's Chinatown is as old as Bangkok itself, New York's dates from 1844; London's is new, going back no further than 1965. This was the year five Chinese restaurants opened in rapid succession on a little-known street in the heart of the metropolis's theatreland in Soho.[17] Lined with largely eighteenth-century buildings, Gerrard Street was where Dryden and Burke once lived, and Chesterton and Belloc had met; but when the Chinese started their restaurants there the literary flavour had long gone.

The point about these restaurants was that they catered almost entirely to the Chinese, so that the street on which they stood became the nearest thing the growing Chinese population had to a gathering-place of its own. In time restaurants spread to the surrounding areas, springing up on Lisle Street, Macclesfield Street, a stretch of Wardour Street and Shaftesbury Avenue. Together the streets formed a Chinese neighbourhood, one they called Tong Yan Gai, Cantonese for 'the street of the people of T'ang', a universal Chinese synonym for 'Chinatown'. It is a small Chinatown, but it represents a focal point, with a centrality in the life of the Chinese that is well expressed in the name they give the London Borough of Westminster to which it belongs: Wong Sing, or Imperial City.

The birth of Chinatown coincided with a new phase of Chinese immigration into Britain. Between 1962 and 1966 the number of Chinese dependants and relatives arriving from Hong Kong – wives, children, elderly parents – rose almost tenfold. Before 1962, Hong Kong immigrants could freely enter Britain and work there, but the Commonwealth Immigrants Act passed in the summer of that year introduced restrictions, requiring each Commonwealth immigrant to have a job waiting for him upon arrival and for his prospective employer to have applied for a labour voucher on his behalf. The act was aimed at discouraging immigration from the Commonwealth, but it had the opposite effect, precipitating a 'beat-the-ban' rush of immigrants from India, Pakistan, the West Indies and Hong Kong into Britain in the six months before the restrictions were introduced. Later a limit was set on the number of vouchers a Hong Kong restaurant employer could take out for new employees; still later that quota was further reduced. If the Chinese needed any urging to send for their families, these changes persuaded ever larger numbers of Chinese to do so and to put down roots before further restrictions stopped them.

The immigrants were from a handful of villages in Hong Kong's New Territories, the rural hinterland bordering Kwangtung province leased to the British under a ninety-nine-year agreement with China that expires in 1997. As in Kwangtung province, the New Territories village was the family writ large, the lineage that traced its ancestry to a common patriarch. If every other person on Gerrard Street seemed to bear the surname Man, it was because that was the surname shared by almost all the inhabitants of San Tin, a village which specialized in sending males to Britain. (Chain migration was at work, too, in the movement of people from the island of Ap Chau to Edinburgh.)

The early immigrants were rice growers, driven out of business by the cheap Thai rice that flooded the Hong Kong market. Lacking skills, they turned their hand to cooking, serving the fry-ups that passed for Chinese food before British palates grew more discriminating. In time no British town was without its Chinese restaurant or takeaway. Meanwhile, like water overflowing from a brimming basin, restaurants spilt across the Channel to continental Europe. Cities there became the next resort of villagers from the New Territories, a new Promised Land; and Holland, Belgium and West Germany all saw an increase in Chinese immigrants, many of them sons and nephews of those who had settled in Britain. These immigrants were taking advantage of the fact that, under the rules of the European Economic Community, holders of British passports granted the right of abode in Britain could eventually be admitted without restrictions to member countries.[18] The communities that sprouted on the Continent may be seen as extensions of the British settlements; certainly Gerrard Street became a nucleus of not just the Chinese in Britain, but of Western Europe as a whole.

At about the same time, another category of immigrants found work in Britain: Chinese who had arrived in Hong Kong as refugees from Kwangtung province – 'stateless aliens', as they were called, who were not British subjects and who did not enter Britain under the voucher system. Work permits had to be obtained for them, but their entry was not subject to the quotas restricting the numbers of Hong Kong citizens in Britain, and so the ten years between 1963 and 1973 saw an influx of some ten thousand of them. By 1977, however, the immigration loophole was closed, and a single system of work permits governed the admission of all unskilled or semi-skilled workers from Hong Kong.[19] Culturally these aliens were no different from the Hong Kongers – they were as Cantonese as the next New Territories immigrant – but socially they were seen to be inferior, lacking kinsmen among the established families, and almost entirely dependent for their livelihood upon their sponsors. One cannot pretend that they were not exploited, given the more menial jobs in the kitchens and working almost always for lower pay.

They found they had to share their niche with newcomers when Vietnamese refugees began arriving in England in the mid-1970s. About eighty per cent of these refugees, whose numbers reached sixteen thousand by 1981, were ethnic Chinese from North Vietnam, with a background which ill fitted them for life in Britain, most of them having earned their livings before as farmers, fishermen, artisans, hawkers and semi-skilled workers.[20] Just as Chinese coolies were seen to be undercutters by resentful white workers, so these newcomers, willing to work for a song, were regarded as unfair competition by the more established Chinese. Indeed it would be surprising if the latter did not feel what all established minorities feel at being joined by larger numbers of more recent immigrants – at once superior and invaded. If some of them felt sorry for the newcomers, others thought them coarse and unfamiliarly 'Vietnamese'. The new arrivals were Cantonese-speaking and by and large thought of themselves as Chinese; but as Chinese cast in a Vietnamese mould, they were bound to seem different to the Chinese from Hong Kong and Kwangtung province.

Though some of them found their way into the kitchens of Chinatown, the Vietnamese Chinese in London are chiefly concentrated in the East End, more specifically in Tower Hamlets, the borough incorporating the docklands and the old Limehouse. It had not been intended that these people should cluster in a ghetto; indeed the resettlement policy of the British government had been to disperse the refugees, so as not to put too much pressure on any one community or local authority, quite apart from the practical difficulty of providing mass housing. Inevitably, though, secondary migration occurred, as Vietnamese refugees moved from their initial place of settlement to live near their friends and relatives, forsaking their tenancies in other parts of the country to live in the cities (particularly London), if necessary squatting in empty property. Not only were they seeking to be with their own kind, these migrants were also gravitating to where there was a better chance of work.

They are not the only people to add diversity to the Chinese population in Britain. The 167,000 foreign-born Chinese in Britain[21] can be divided by place of origin into Hong Kong, China, Vietnam, Singapore and Malaysia. Many of the latter two groups came to England as students and then stayed on, becoming adoptive Britons. The population is widely dispersed, with London as the biggest centre and Manchester as the next biggest, and with Birmingham, Glasgow, Liverpool, Edinburgh and Cardiff all hosting largish enclaves. There is a certain amount of rivalry between London's Chinatown and Manchester's but Gerrard Street remains pre-eminent as a focus for the scattered groups of Chinese, and Sundays see many out-of-town families converging upon the Imperial City.

It is a comfortable repository of Chineseness: social centre, bazaar, town forum, recreation hub all rolled into one. There was a time, not so long ago, when England itself seemed to be an intruder here, and Western diners venturing into the restaurants did not feel themselves welcome. This has changed and, like Chinatowns the world over, Gerrard Street has evolved as a tourist attraction, bracketed with a pair of archways and turned into a pedestrian precinct. In the early 1970s Chinatown nearly faced extinction when, as part of a plan to redevelop Soho and build an extension to the Telephone Exchange, the City of Westminster considered demolishing the buildings in Gerrard Street.[22] Lobbying by the Chinese Chamber of Commerce successfully prevented this, and since that time Chinatown has seen its frontiers expand around the corner into Gerrard Place, where redevelopment has yielded shop space for Chinese grocers and fishmongers, and room for a pavilion where Chinese passers-by and European tourists go to take shelter from Britain's frequent showers.

It is a kind of package culture that you find here, one that smacks distinctly of Hong Kong and that is supported by a range of goods and services which do not, on the whole, diffuse more widely into the larger economy. Hong Kong is duplicated down to the buns and the cakes in the tea-shops and bakeries, for just as an Englishman can sometimes prefer the curries he gets at home to the curries he finds in India, so the Chinese prefer their pastries with a Hong Kong rather than an authentic European flavour. The businesses in Chinatown constitute what specialist writers on minorities would call an ethnic economic niche or internal economy. It is possible for a Chinese to consult a doctor in traditional medicine, an accountant, a lawyer, a banker and a travel agent without going beyond the confines of Chinatown. Observe, as you enter Little Newport Street, the queue of people, including many Westerners, Indians, Pakistanis and Arabs, that has formed outside the clinic of the Chinese herbalist, whose treatment of eczema has proved so effective that a London hospital specializing in skin diseases refers its patients to her. It is reassuring to the Chinese, who tend to give you a medical bulletin if you ask them how they are, to know that she is there to attend to their ailments, just as it is handy for those who regularly remit money to their home villages to have the Hongkong and Shanghai Bank on Gerrard Street and the Bank of China on Shaftesbury Avenue. And if, like many another *habitué* of Chinatown, you are a frequent traveller to your homeland, several travel agencies will handle your flights to Hong Kong and beyond. One that bulks large in the story of Chinese emigration to Britain is the charter-flight business begun by an enterprising member of the Man family from San Tin. Starting life in a restaurant, the company based its fortunes on the emigrant traffic and now has offices in London, Manchester, Birmingham, Liverpool, Brussels, Amsterdam, Utrecht, downtown Hong Kong and the New Territories. Every British Airways scheduled flight on the Hong Kong run came to have a portion of the seats given over to the charter service.

Of the services Chinatown provides, not the least is recreation. Surely a description of Chinatowns has never been written without a mention of the eager Chinese appetite for gambling. This passion is well served here. There are three licensed betting offices within a minute's walk from each other, and in addition there are five or six exclusively Chinese gambling clubs in and around Gerrard Street alone. The customers are chiefly people who lead unadventurous existences enclosed within their own familiar networks. The clubs are illegal, lacking gaming licences, but the police tolerate them up to a point, much of the time leaving the gamblers to pursue their particular pleasures, but raiding the clubs every now and then to remind them that they are only there on sufferance. Fines are extracted after each raid, but once these have been paid the clubs return to business as usual. Nor are the police the only nuisances to be placated by the payment of money; rumours, freak accidents and bombing incidents speak of criminal gangs and protection rackets. It is widely assumed that the clubs find their bouncers, men schooled in the martial arts, in the street gangs.

The clubs are supposed to be at their fullest during the quiet end of the afternoon, from three o'clock to five, when the restaurant workers are off duty after lunch and before dinner. The clubs then become leisure centres, used in default of other diverting alternatives. But the two I looked into one Saturday afternoon turned out to be far less busy than I had been led to expect. Called Hap On (Joined in Peace) and Tung Lok (Happy Together), these clubs have their premises in the dingy basements of two old buildings in Gerrard Street. In the first, harsh overhead strip-lighting illuminated two tables; a small, elderly fridge; a counter where five or six women were making tea and eating instant noodles; a sheet of paper with the betting rules spelt out in Chinese pinned to the wall; and a picture of Kuan Ti (the god of war), the favourite deity of the overseas Chinese, set in a little roofed shrine against a far wall. Men and women with sheaves of ten- and twenty-pound notes in their hands were crowded around a table where a game of fan-tan was being played. At the other table, on a high stool, a thin, stooped man sat with a newspaper in front of him. Nothing was happening at that table, but had there been a game it would have been *pai kau*, Chinese dominoes played to rules resembling those of Russian poker.

The other club gave me no sense of novelty. It was smaller and lacked a counter, but it was otherwise exactly like the one I had just left, with the same bare, poky look about it, the same betting limit of £600. And as in the other club, a plate of the plumpest root ginger I had ever seen stood on a ledge behind the croupier, piled in a pyramid and pierced by an upstanding fruit knife. The croupier, also a woman (and a housewife by the look of her), had a plate of freshly sliced ginger beside her; and every now and then she would take a few slivers and rub her hands with them. That way any *hsieh-ch'i*, perverse or evil influences, would be kept at bay. One end of the fan-tan table was completely surrounded by women: housewives, grandmothers, waitresses and shop assistants. They spoke little, each engrossed in her private dream or anxiety, but when they did they showed themselves to be either Hakka or Cantonese. These women, with their ordinariness and homeliness, refute the idea of Chinese gambling dens as sinister and dangerous places into which one ventures at one's peril.

The habits of home do not stop at fan-tan and pai kau. Immigrants have a way of defining themselves against those they have left behind rather than those they have joined. Expatriation does not preclude a continuing interest in China or Hong Kong; indeed, it can increase it. Keeping abreast of events at home is never a problem, since no Chinatown is without its Chinese newspapers. The European edition of *Sing Tao Daily News*, the paper published by the Star heiress Sally Aw, is on sale at the bookshops, as are a host of weekly and monthly Chinese magazines, from the po-faced *Peking Review* to the cellophane-wrapped editions of the Hong Kong *Playboy*. The biggest bookshop is devoted to literature from the People's Republic, theoretical treatises on Socialism with Chinese Characteristics, apologias of China's apparent deviation from Marxist principles, the latest novels from Peking or Shanghai, reprints of classics, editions of dynastic histories, picture books on bronzes or ceramics, travel guides, yearbooks and handbooks, hagiographies of revolutionary figures, propaganda of one sort or another. There is even something about the look and feel of the publications, the poor quality of the colour printing, the thinness of the paper, the sobriety of the covers, the very smell of the books, which speaks of a socialist Chinese provenance.

And yet whether or not one patronizes the bookstore has nothing to do with one's political affiliations; you could be a Kuomintang sympathizer and still shop there. But this is not to say that the rivalry between the Communists and the Nationalists has not been carried over to Britain's Chinese community. The influence of Taiwan is slight in Soho, and this is as one would expect; the strong bonds which link Hong Kong with the People's Republic have travelled to England without changing a great deal, and the British government itself has associated more closely with China than with Taiwan. In the 1960s, when the ideological factor was more pronounced than it is today, and there were twice-monthly screenings of mainland Chinese films at the Hammer Theatre in Wardour Street, the audiences rose to stand respectfully at the playing of the Communist national anthem.[23]

Soho is where Chinese mothers take their children for Sunday mother-tongue teaching, that tried and true vehicle for transmitting Chinese values and cultural identity to the second generation. Weekend Chinese schools have proliferated across the country, increasing dramatically in number from a handful in the 1970s to eighty-three in 1984, with pupils totalling some nine thousand.[24] The classes have different sponsors – some come under the Chinese Chamber of Commerce and other Chinese organizations (including the Cheung Clan Association); others grew under the wing of Christian church groups and government-funded community centres – but they are hardly different in style or intention. Sadly, the parents' enthusiasm is not always shared by the children, who reckon they have quite enough on their hands without having to go to school at the weekends.

Up to a point many of the *habitués* of Chinatown can live within their own familiar world, cut off from the people whose language they do not speak; but when it comes to matters such as housing, health, taxation, immigration regulations, welfare entitlements and their children's education, some engagement with the alien environment is necessary. In July 1980 a Chinese Community Centre was set up on Gerrard Street to provide a free consulting service, run by Chinese- and English-speaking staff who can advise on these matters and also help with translating or decoding English officialese.

As has happened in New York, it took groups from 'outside' Chinatown, middle-class professionals or ex-students, to organize the Chinese community in Britain and to mediate between it and the larger society. On the whole the Chinese in Britain do not have a keen sense of their rights and are hazy about the state benefits for which they and their families are eligible; like Indian and Pakistani immigrants, they show what is called a 'low take-up' of social services. It was the Home Affairs Committee and the arrival of needy Vietnamese Chinese refugees which drew public attention to this; and now there are people, social workers and race relations officers, who get steamed up about this and demand that the government do more for the Chinese minority. According to these people, to regard the Chinese as self-reliant people who happily paddle their own canoe is to be conveniently provided with an excuse for ignoring their needs. A paper demanding more state aid by the Chinese Association of Tower Hamlets in 1985 put it this way: 'To those who cling to the myth that the Chinese community prefers self-help and does not need social services intervention, I could only say: stop treating us like super human beings . . .'²⁵ Unhappily, those Chinese who have woken to the realization of their rights have done so at a time when the thrust of government social policies is to wean people off 'dependency'.

The Chinese in Britain are behind their American counterparts in discovering their identity as an 'ethnic minority'. If a Chinese-American champion of minority rights from the 1960s were to survey the condition of the Chinese in Britain in the 1980s, it is not unlikely that he would think to himself: 'We have gone beyond all that business, and you have it still to go through.'

CHAPTER SIXTEEN

Food

For much of the Western world, Chinese food is the first channel through which an interest in Chinese culture develops, and even if one does not actually know any Chinese, one is sure to have been to a Chinese restaurant, or heard of Peking Duck or Chow Mein. Immigrant Chinese communities are bracketed in most Western minds with the sights and sounds and above all the smells of eating-places in Chinatown, and the one without the other almost does not exist.

The Chinese take their cuisine with them wherever they go, and much trade in the ingredients needed to produce it has arisen out of the diaspora. But while food and cookery were among the Chinese's chief cultural exports, the traffic was by no means one-way; many of the foodstuffs that the Chinese now think of as being native to China are in fact of foreign origin, and since medieval times the Chinese table has been wonderfully enriched by Persian and Indian importations. The quest for new and strange edibles played a part of some prominence in the story of overseas Chinese travel and settlement; the reader may recall that it was for the purpose of harvesting and exporting *bêche-de-mer* that Chinese migrants were lured to the western coasts of Africa, to Madagascar and Zanzibar; and in the eighteenth and nineteenth centuries, fleets of Chinese junks would sail each year to Borneo, not only to deal in the pepper cherished by European traders, but to buy bird's nests, *bêche-de-mer*, shark's fins and other items of exotic gourmandise for their own tables.

The so-called Southern Ocean was rich hunting-ground for things which, if one must put them under headings, would be called spices, foods, drugs and aromatics, though the boundaries between the classes are never very distinct in the Chinese scheme. Some foods were extravagantly prized because of their supposed medicinal properties, and an aromatic substance could enjoy enormous popularity as both a perfume and a treatment for 'blood congestion'. The camphor which the Chinese sought in Borneo and Sumatra, for example, was profitably much in demand as a perfume, as a food, and as a cure for, among other ailments, cataract and evil vapours in the heart.[1]

The most extraordinary of the many remarkable foods sought by the Chinese in Southeast Asia was bird's nest, the product of a species of swiftlet (*Collocalia*) and the basis of the famous bird's-nest soup. Living mostly in caves, these swiftlets build nests of leaves, moss, hair and feathers glued together and stuck to the cave walls with a sticky secretion of the bird's very large salivary glands. It is the saliva that the Chinese go for. The nests of one species, the edible-nest swiftlet (*C. fuciphaga*), are cups of almost pure spittle.[2] Whitish, translucent and brittle, the nests are tiny, barely large enough to hold a single egg. To these the Chinese have ascribed so many wonder-working properties that they are sold more often by herbalists than by grocers, though a cool modern analyst would simply say that they are just very rich in protein.

Caves in Java, the Moluccas, Borneo, Burma and Thailand have all been sources of this valuable gunk, and over the centuries Chinese bird's-nest merchants have been drawn to them in a more or less uninterrupted stream. The operative end of the business, the actual gathering of the nests, has remained much as it was five to six centuries ago, and it is still the locals, whether Dyak tribesmen or Moluccan aborigines, who clamber up to the cave roofs to pluck them.[3] One can see how it is done in the Niah caves of Sarawak, which lie in massive limestone outcrops reached by a none-too-comfortable trek through steamy jungles. The caverns, some of them half a mile deep, have been sculpted out of the limestone by millennia of rain water. Their roofs soar to a great height, about a hundred yards in some places; and local tribesmen scamper up to them by scaling firemen's poles, flimsy-looking bamboo ladders with thread-like footholds. In earlier times the collectors would have inherited the rights to gather the nests from their forefathers, and the more enterprising of them would have sailed up to the trading stations to barter the nests for Chinese stoneware and porcelains, iron, brass, gold, glass beads and textiles.

Some swiftlets nest in buildings, and lucky the man whose house they choose for this. You could see this down in the southern Thai port of Pattani, last glimpsed in these pages as the anchorage of the sixteenth-century Chinese pirate Lin Tao-ch'ien. Along a dusty street, amid a row of slowly crumbling Chinese terraced buildings, there stands a derelict house which echoes at nesting-time with the clicking call of thickly swarming swiftlets. The nests left there have greatly enriched the owner of the house, an old Chinese woman long settled in Pattani. For some inexplicable reason, the birds do not nest in the house next door, which seems in every respect to be an exact replica of its neighbour. The explanation offered by local lore for this anomaly is that the old woman's house has been blessed by Lin Ku-niang, Maiden Lin, the townsfolk's favourite deity.

The story goes that Maiden Lin had come to Pattani from Swatow to persuade her brother Lin Tao-ch'ien to forsake Islam (to which he had converted) and return home to China. Married to the daughter of the local Malay ruler, and headed for bigger things, Lin Tao-ch'ien refused to do so – whereupon, in one version of the story, Maiden Lin killed herself, putting a curse on the mosque that was being built near the scene of her martyrdom. The events that took place four centuries ago are still very real to the Chinese community in Pattani, and as well as the fervent devotions offered at her temple, the incense-burning and the praying, the rituals celebrating her birthday, the pageantry and the fire-walking, can still be witnessed in Pattani today.

Whether blessed by Maiden Lin or not, the bird's-nest trade flourishes wherever the Chinese are settled. Large and costly quantities of bird's nests, for example, were imported from Java and the Sulu Archipelago by the Chinese in the Straits Settlements, of whose exports to China the delicacy was one of the most valuable – trade statistics for one year in the 1830s show it to amount to no less than 162,852 Spanish dollars.[4] Today overseas Chinese believe that the finest bird's nests come from islands off the southern coastlines of Thailand, and enormous cachet attaches to the brand-name of Laem Thong, the Thai company that holds the country's bird's-nest monopoly. The undistinguished premises of this company's head office are embedded in Bangkok's Chinatown, at 454 Yaowarat Road, but you get a better idea of the extent of the enterprise in a restaurant in the Causeway Bay area of Hong Kong. There, at the Siamese Teochiu Bird's Nest Restaurant, only a stone's throw from Food Street, you will find a counter well-stocked with Laem Thong's products, packed in small boxes of assorted sizes and colours, some square, some round, all emblazoned with Thai letters and Chinese characters, and the silhouette of a swiftlet with its wings spread in flight. A casual glance at the counter instantly reveals that very high prices are paid for these products: the tags show each box to sell for the equivalent of between £100 and £200. The restaurant is the hub of an extensive distribution network that not only supplies all the Chinese drugstores in Hong Kong and all the restaurants which offer bird's nest on their menus, but despatches Laem Thong's bird's nests to all of the Greater Chinese world.

Overlooking the counter is a framed photograph of a rock humping out of an unpicturesque sea – the source, the shop assistant will tell you with little exaggeration, of the best swiftlet's nests in the world. The rock is one of several offshore islands lying beyond the southern Thai province of Songkhla, between the Songkhla Lake and the Gulf of Thailand. 'It's ours,' the Hong Kong shop assistant says of the pictured island, but what she means is that her employer in Bangkok holds the concession for all the bird's nests found in its caves, and has done so for three decades. The concessionaire is said to be Dilok Mahadamrongkul, or Wu Tuo-lu to his compatriots, one of those very successful Chinese businessmen whose interests are intertwined with those of the Thai plutocracy. The bird's-nest monopoly is not something to be sniffed at, and one of the ways in which the Chinese were made to suffer during Thailand's anti-sinitic era was to have the concession taken out of their hands.

The first Chinese bird's-nest concessionaire was the founder of a remarkable family, a Hokkien immigrant who arrived in Songkhla by junk from Fukien in 1750. Aged thirty-four at the time, Wu Jang worked as a vegetable gardener and fisherman and sired five sons by a Thai woman he married. When King Taksin came on a visit to Songkhla Wu Jang did the right thing by presenting him with fifty cases of tobacco, a list of his estates, and a pledge to put all he had at the disposal of the King. Much pleased by this unambiguous demonstration of fealty, and anxious, no doubt, to keep him that way, King Taksin buttered Wu Jang up by conferring a noble title on him, by adopting one of Wu's boys as a royal aide, and by making a bird's-nest concessionaire of him. Always regular with his payments to the capital, Wu Jang was to be further honoured, and made a governor of Songkhla, the first of nine Songkhla governors to arise from this very upwardly mobile family. Adopting the Thai name of Na Songkhla in 1916 ('Na' being the Thai equivalent of the German 'von' or the French 'de'), the family descendants, no longer thought of as Chinese, are to be found filling high ranks in Thai government and business today.[5]

The place to watch the Chinese at their bird's-nest soup is Hat Yai, which is one of those brash, coarse-grained cities for which the Chinese-tradesman-made-good harbours such an inexplicable preference. The overall appearance of the place is that of any provincial boom town in Southeast Asia, but actually there is no place quite like

Hat Yai anywhere in the world. Southwest from Songkhla Lake, it
calls itself southern Thailand's major tourist centre, and the brochure
issued by the Tourist Authority lists sites like the Southern Culture
Village and the Elephant Tusks Waterfall among its chief attractions.
But the busloads of Chinese tourists who come over the border from
Malaysia – only thirty-six miles away from the city centre – do not all
come for the sightseeing. Nor do they all come for the shopping. The
two magnets which the tourist brochures do not mention are massage
parlours and bird's-nest restaurants, and it is these that explain the
preponderance of males in those group tours from Malaysia.

Hat Yai is the bird's-nest city *par excellence*, the place with surely
the world's highest concentration of bird's-nest retail outlets and restaurants. Here, in any one of dozens of restaurants, you can have bird's
nest in a sweet soup, or in a savoury one; served hot, or served cold;
braised with shark's fin, or simmered with shredded chicken; flavoured
with almond and coconut, or mixed with pigeon's eggs and honey.

What is so extraordinary about this peculiarly Chinese cult is that
the bird's nest itself does not actually taste of anything. But this is of
no concern to the millions of Chinese who pay through the nose for it;
hypochondriac to a man, these people could only think of all the good
that it is doing them, and all the afflictions that it is keeping at bay –
the digestive troubles it is preventing, the phlegm it is dissolving, the
ageing process it is retarding, the loss of vigour its tonic qualities are
remedying. While not exactly an aphrodisiac, the delicacy is thought
to have a bracing effect on masculine vigour, and it seems only right
that massage parlours should be interspersed among the bird's-nest
restaurants in the streets of Hat Yai.

As an expensive delicacy, bird's nest is at one extreme of the Chinese
diet; rice, the everyday staple of southern Chinese, is at another.
Here Thailand also enjoys pre-eminence, for it is the world's biggest
exporter of the grain, with overseas Chinese communities as some of
its most steadfast customers. Rice-milling in Thailand started off as a
Chinese business, and it was not so long ago that the management of
a Siamese rice business was Teochiu through and through.[6] Walk into
a supermarket in any of the world's larger Chinatowns, and there is no
getting away from the packets of Siamese rice amid the Japanese and
Basmati varieties.

Advancing up the aisle with your trolley, you will also discover
several brands offering you *lau-ch'ou* (dark soy sauce) and *sheng-ch'ou*
(light soy sauce) in large bottles and small. Some come from Taiwan,

others from the People's Republic of China, but for many an overseas Chinese customer perhaps no label has quite the resonance of Amoy. Amoy Food Limited is now an international concern with its main base in Hong Kong, but it was in Amoy, in the last years of the Manchu dynasty, that it started life.

Its founder was a Yang Ko-fei, a native, like the rubber and pineapple magnate Tan Kah Kee, of Chi Mei, and a so-called Returned Overseas Chinese with a stint in British Malaya behind him. Amoy being one of those places to which Christian civilization was introduced along with treaty-port status, European merchants and houses in the English colonial manner, Yang Ko-fei at sixteen was a keen Protestant church-goer, as well as a useful helper in his father's modest cake-making business. His father died when he was twenty-six and Yang went to work for a time in a cake-shop in Taiwan. Later he went on to cake-shops in Penang and Kuala Lumpur, where he did better and rose to the position of supervisor.

His family remained at home, and was one of the reasons he decided to return to Amoy; the other being the possibility of working in his brother's pharmacy, where it fell to him to help wean opium smokers from their addiction. From this it was but a short step to a bookkeeper's job at a local hospital, where he made many friends among the physicians, and used his time too to see to the extension of Christianity among staff and patients. It was with these people, some of them Christian like himself, that he began to discuss the idea that was taking shape in his mind, the idea that he could make a go of a soy sauce and canning factory. Bottled soy sauce, tinned lychee and other fruits would go down well in Nanyang's Chinese communities, he thought – where, as he had seen for himself, such things could not be had very easily.

In 1908, T'ao-hua-ta-t'ung, or Amoy Canning to its English-speaking customers, was duly established, with ten people, doctors among them, each putting in some money. For its premises it bought over the factory of a British-run creamery, and it additionally invested in a few hand-operated canning machines. The company had its ups and downs, and three years into its operation clashes between Yang Ko-fei and the other shareholders resulted in a break-up of the company, with one party going it alone as T'ao-hua, and the other as Ta-t'ung. For its chief shareholder, the latter company, set up by Yang, could not have had a brighter luminary, for he was none other than Tan Kah Kee.

It became increasingly apparent, however, that T'ao-hua and Ta-t'ung would be better off operating as a single unit, and when a new rival appeared on the scene in 1928, the two companies were spurred to merge. Thereafter the story of T'ao-hua-ta-t'ung became one of steady expansion – in assets, in range of products, in reputation and in the geographical spread of its markets. In time the branch in Hong Kong came to eclipse the parent company in size, importance and profitability; for as a free port and a trading hub, Hong Kong had many advantages which Amoy lacked. When war broke out with the Japanese invasion of China in 1937, almost the entire canning plant was moved from Amoy to Hong Kong, and when the company went public in 1951, the ownership passed mainly into the hands of expatriate Chinese.[7]

Today the products of Amoy Food end up on the shelves of shops and supermarkets in thirty-seven countries. At the time of writing, the American food giant Pillsbury, the owner of Häagen Dags Ice-cream and the Burger King hamburger chain, holds half of the shares, and Hang Lung, a Hong Kong property group, holds the other half. In addition to its line of thirty-four sauces (such as chilli purée, black bean sauce, sweet and sour sauce, barbecue sauce, ginger topping, and so on), Amoy produces a range of convenience foods which find their biggest markets in the United States, Britain and Japan. Within a few years it found itself selling more abroad than it did at home. Never has there been so little need to cook; a housewife in America can simply unwrap one of Amoy's Dim Sum Combination Boxes or Sichuan Prawns, heat in a microwave or conventional oven – no need even to add salt or pepper – and hey presto! there's a meal. In Britain the shopper finds Amoy's prepared meals – Prawn and Vegetable Dumplings or Crispy Wontons filled with Prawns and Bamboo Shoots – among Marks and Spencer's chilled fresh foods (bearing the retailer's name rather than the manufacturer's). When the line proved more popular than anyone had expected, and the British retailer greatly increased its order, Amoy was nimble enough to expand its production capacity to supply it.

Even a casual visit to the Amoy factory makes it plain that, for all its modernity, its American management style, the manufacturing process is not one that can be easily duplicated in the West. Part of the method for making soy sauce remains unchanged from the days when the factory was an adapted creamery furnished with hand-operated machines. There is no bypassing the old-fashioned process which takes place on the roof of the main building. What the visitor sees there is dramatic and unexpected. Elsewhere the sauce is pasteurized in laboratory-like conditions; here, an old man with sleeves rolled up goes from earthen vat to earthen vat plunging his arm into its thick brew of black and yellow soy beans to give it a gentle, almost loving, stir. He works rhythmically, with deep concentration. A Soy Master with thirty to forty years of experience behind him, he stands in a line which goes back to the fifth century, from when dates the earliest surviving soy sauce recipe.

It is companies like Amoy which have made Chinese foods more widely available in the West. One remembers a time when Chinese cookery books published in Britain said you could use Worcester sauce, the bottled English standby, as a substitute for soy sauce, because the latter was not to be obtained except at delicatessens or specialist shops in London, instead of every other Waitrose or Sainsbury. People who shopped in Chinatown only five or six years ago would be surprised at how much the range of foods has grown. The small number of Shanghainese living in England used to envy their compatriots in America for being able to indulge the Shanghainese passion for hairy crabs every autumn, because these were flown to New York and San Francisco the minute they came into season in Shanghai; but a few years ago these crabs started making their appearance in London too, and one could get hold of a few if one was quick enough off the mark. Both the diversity and the rate of East and Southeast Asian immigration to Britain are reflected in the merchandise of Chinatown's grocers, so that you could tell at a glance, merely from the appearance of such things as *nam plah* (fish sauce), lemon grass and coriander leaf on the shelves, that a community of Thai or Thai Chinese has been added to the Hong Kong mainstream.

Most expatriate Chinese, pining for the vegetables of home, grow them wherever it is physically feasible or profitable to do so. To be a food merchant is an old Chinese calling, but in their adopted countries the emigrant Chinese have also been vegetable growers, pepper planters, fishermen and agricultural labourers. It was a Chinese, Lue Gim Gong of De Land, Florida, who developed the famous frost-resistant orange of Florida in the late nineteenth century, launching in that state its great citrus fruit industry;[8] and it was also the Chinese who helped establish celery as a commerical crop and introduced abalone to the market in America. Many nineteenth-century Chinese settlers on the West Coast of America caught fish and shellfish for a living – salmon, sturgeon, crab, squid and shark (this last partly for its fins, the basis of that other great Chinese delicacy, shark's-fin soup, and partly for its liver, the source of a lubricating oil).9

The first person to manufacture cakes of tofu, Chinese beancurd, and to make it more widely available in Europe was Li Shih-tseng, a renowned Chinese intellectual and educationalist. Li was in France at the turn of the century, a young student of biochemistry who was to be much influenced by the writings of Nietzsche and Bergson. A Francophile, Li Shih-tseng was one of the founders of the Work and Study Scheme, a programme for sending Chinese students abroad for part-time work and part-time study. (One of the best known of these students was the young Deng Xiaoping.) As well as founding the Université Franco-Chinoise at Lyons, a sort of accommodation and placement agency, Li established a beancurd factory in France, drawing upon his knowledge of biochemistry and providing jobs for many of the students on the Work and Study Scheme.

A vegetarian himself, Li could not have been a firmer believer in tofu's nutritional properties. Offering also bean flour, fermented beancurd, soy-bean milk and soy-bean jam, his company fed not just Chinese but Westerners, providing nourishment to American soldiers who fought in France during the First World War.10 All this was before the faddish demand for tofu by health food enthusiasts, and before it became widely known as an unbeatable source of protein. The company closed after the war, but among certain Chinese *émigrés* France was never to lose its reputation for beancurd. In Europe up to the 1980s *tofu kan*, a particular variety of fermented beancurd much demanded by eastern Chinese palates, could only be had in Paris, and the handful of Shanghainese émigrés in London had to send over to Paris for it.

If there have been eager food traders and manufacturers among the Chinese abroad, there has been as great a number of adept cooks, bartenders and waiters. When, at the height of the anti-Chinese frenzy in the United States, no white American would dream of admitting a Chinese to his home, an American housewife could think of giving a Chinese cook the run of her kitchen. Where else but in the kitchen would a Chinese work if he worked in a white milieu? Consider Fong Sec, a graduate of the University of California at Berkeley who, upon his return to China in 1906, became the chief English-language editor of the prestigious Commercial Press in Peking. What did he do when he came back to the United States? He became cook to a white family.

He later joined the Salvation Army, and, after working as a cook in one of its chapters, eventually rose to the post of Secretary.[11]

In the tropical Far East an essential figure behind the bar at any oil-lamp-lit drinking-shop or luxurious hotel was an overseas Chinese. Here is one described by Anthony Burgess in his *Malayan Trilogy*: 'Ah Hun was the richest man in Cooler Huntu. He ran a sort of auxiliary Club for his friends at the back of the real Club. That was pure profit, for all the drink came out of the real Club. The gin and whisky were watered and always short-measured.'[12] For generations, a large part of the catering trade in Southeast Asia has lain in the hands of the Hainanese. Just as the Chinese cooks in the tiny nineteenth-century Limehouse community, it may be recalled, came from Hainan, so the man who poured you your Tiger beer at the Club in British Singapore or Malaya, or the soft-footed houseboy who served you your sherry and bitters at an English planter's private dinner party, was likely to be a Hainanese. The mulligatawny soup, the joint of Bengal mutton, the rice and curry, the apple crumble and caramel custard offered at the party might be served by liveried native servants, but they would have all issued from a kitchen presided over by a Hainanese. The equation between Hainanese and cooking remains to this day, and for a cheap and delicious lunch in Singapore or Malaysia, there are still few dishes to beat Hainanese Chicken Rice, their celebrated speciality.

An earlier generation of Hainanese cooks passed on what they learnt from memsahib, and thanks to these cooks the English kitchen has survived the departure of the British. Intensely English cooking, as opposed to the buffet luncheon kind served at poolside hotel restaurants, can still be found in Malaysia, and to sample it at its most evocatively colonial, you need spend only a day at one of the country's two most popular hill stations, Fraser's Hill or the Cameron Highlands. These places abound in Hainanese, the men still to be seen spotlessly liveried in white, and still beginning their careers as houseboys before becoming cooks and caretakers. The traditional bill of fare is honoured here, and your tiffin will be roast beef and Yorkshire pudding, your tea cup-cakes and cucumber sandwiches, and your dinner roast lamb with mint sauce. The curry is the way the English like it, with mango chutney; and it would take a connoisseur indeed to find the hill station's own marmalade inferior to Fortnum and Mason's.

Elsewhere in the world it is the Cantonese who have done most for the export of Chinese tastes and cookery to new habitats. In the Philippines, for example, they are the ones who can make a restaurant pay, not the Hokkiens by whom they are greatly outnumbered. In much of the present-day Western world Cantonese immigrants are vocationally concentrated in the catering business. The Chinese in Britain are perhaps the prime example of a community which has mushroomed in response to a restaurant boom; had there not been the expansion of opportunities in the catering business in the 1960s and early 1970s, there would not have been the impetus for so much migration from Hong Kong to Britain during that period. It was at a moment of Britain's culinary history when people were becoming more adventurous and 'ethnic' cuisines were spreading. Although by 1955 the British diet had more or less achieved its post-war recovery, the taste for exotic cuisines would take quite a bit longer to evolve. Outside London the idea of a restaurant serving exclusively non-European food was altogether novel, and *The Good Food Guide 1955* listed only single examples of Chinese eating-places in Brighton, Liverpool and Manchester, and a single Indian place in Manchester; for diners in London the guide recommended two Chinese eateries and seven Indian (including one Burmese). The Chinese successfully broke down the intolerance of foreign food by offering the one thing that the masses find difficult to resist: cheapness. Ten years later a national catering enquiry found that, of those who ate out regularly or occasionally, as many as thirty-one per cent had visited Chinese restaurants, whereas only five per cent had eaten at Italian and French ones.[13] By 1970 there were four thousand Chinese eating establishments in Britain – twice the number of Indian/Pakistani places, and eight times the number of French ones.[14] By the mid-1980s, the number of Chinese restaurants and takeaways is estimated to have risen to seven thousand. By then the restaurant boom had already slackened off, and market saturation combined with stiffer immigration laws made it harder for the Chinese catering trade to expand in Britain. The Chinese continued to extend themselves, but now they did so across the English Channel, as we saw, in Holland, Germany, Denmark and France.

The takeaway market was one the Chinese had to share with the Cypriots. It was not a market universally receptive to foreign food, and many a Chinese takeaway owner runs what is more appropriately called a 'Chinese chippy', which is merely the old English fish and chips shop brought under Chinese ownership and management. In any case, because of the kind of customers they get, even takeaways offering Chinese food have chips and English meat pies on their menus. Most takeaways would have some thirty to forty items on their menu, dishes of pork, beef, chicken and prawn combined with vegetables of one kind or another. Then there would be rice, plain or fried; and noodles, fried rather than soupy. You go in. There is a counter. If the husband is in the kitchen at the back the wife takes your order. The premises are not inviting, and there is usually too much Formica. A couple of chairs stand against one wall, and a TV set, permanently switched on, beams colour images from another. Smells of oil and onion escape through the open door from a cramped, steamy kitchen full of hiss and clatter. Your order arrives on the counter packed in covered tin-foil containers. The establishment is open from midday to midnight, every day of the week including public holidays. No life of drudgery can be more unremitting than that of a takeaway couple, a life now burdened further by the charging of Value Added Tax on hot takeaway food, and the vandalism and harassment of rough or rowdy customers. The wife is as bone-weary as she looks, and what is more, she is isolated, with no social life beyond her immediate family.

In Manchester in the autumn of 1988, I met what is called a BBC, a British-born Chinese, in a takeaway on the London Road near Stockport. She writes poetry and was going up to Oxford to read English, but in the mean time she was helping her widowed mother run the family takeaway. Here is how she describes a typical evening:

> It must be approaching eleven p.m. now; I am collecting
> my thoughts in the dining-room where Burt Lancaster has
> just gunned down half the labour force at some secret base.
> Lawrence [a brother] sits mesmerized by the TV but is
> still fairly conscious as he increases the volume. Mother is
> mopping the floor with Domestos and blustering with the
> two-day Vietnamese worker. The topic is some dramatic
> social event – gossip – and mother raises her voice a further
> thirty decibels for emphasis on the key words . . . This is
> the Silver River Takeaway.
>   Meal for one: steamed fish, vegetables and rice . . . The
> prime food is money. The recipe includes the following
> ingredients: forty grams effort or slavery; thirty grams
> cerebral power; the both seasoned ad lib with tolerance
> and other virtues. Method: work.

And yet her mother probably counts herself lucky when she remembers that her husband was his own boss, and not a waiter or a meat chopper in somebody else's restaurant. For every Chinese who succeeds in graduating from one to the other, countless failures languish in restaurant kitchens. But never be sorry for a waiter, George Orwell has written percipiently in *Down and Out in Paris and London*: 'Sometimes when you sit in a restaurant, still stuffing yourself half an hour after closing time, you feel that the tired waiter at your side must surely be despising you. But he is not. He is not thinking as he looks at you, "What an overfed lout"; he is thinking, "One day, when I have saved enough money, I shall be able to imitate that man".'[15] He might have been writing about the Chinese waiter. By no means all Chinese waiters are savers, but many are incipient capitalists, conjuring visions of accumulating enough money to start their own establishments one day.

On top of his basic wage the waiter receives a share of the tips, the amount usually varying with seniority; he is provided with free meals by his employer, and is usually housed by him too, in rooms above the restaurant if it is not in a high-rent area. He works ten to twelve hours a day six days a week, and he is lucky if he is home by one o'clock in the morning. No fool he, to be doing all this if there were better prospects elsewhere; for many Chinese, catering is a question less of vocation than of necessity. They are called to the kitchen or restaurant because, as unskilled workers with little or no English, they are not called to much else.

Western diners are lured into Chinese restaurants by the food; rarely are they lured there by the service. The range of meanings expressed by the word 'service' is wide; in a transport café it can mean no more than passing you the bottle of tomato ketchup; in a top-class restaurant it may mean being fed without being made to feel ignorant by the head waiter. In Chinese restaurants the customer is often served with the brusque and nonchalant manners of a cheap eatery. The Chinese waiter has a particular reputation, as the food writer Christopher Driver puts it patronizingly, for being 'rude, offhand, and deliberately uncomprehending until they have been shown reason – by patience and curiosity rather than abuse – to behave differently'. The rudeness of the Chinese waiter has become such a cliché, in fact, that when English diners do indeed find themselves curtly treated, by waiters who move among the tables with their faces set in what look like masks to foreigners (almost as if they are deliberately living up to their stereotype), they are positively delighted, as one is when one's beliefs prove true. Jeffrey Bernard, who writes a column in the *Spectator*, is making a cultural reference which a non-English reader would not necessarily share when, in an article in which he lists his day's expenses, he includes 'Chicken in lemon sauce, beef with spring onions and ginger, mixed vegetables in Jubilee Dragon . . . £6.50. Iodine, sticking plaster and bandages for wounds inflicted by Chinese waiters £1.75.'[16]

It is not, as many English customers assume, that the Chinese think themselves superior to foreign barbarians; it is just that these waiters are only the children of their culture, which happens to be that of working-class Hong Kong, a place as little noted for its public *politesse* as New York. (One can tell by his manners, almost as easily as one can by his speech and accent, whether a Chinese waiter is from Hong Kong, China or Malaysia.) And to balance the Chinese sullenness, there is the fact that, of the loutish bilkers by whom they are continually and inescapably troubled, they find the British ones to be the worst. This fact finds its reflection in fiction: discussing the idiosyncrasies of their English patrons, a group of waiters in Timothy Mo's novel *Sour Sweet* agreed that one of these 'was the strange and widespread habit of not paying bills, a practice so prevalent as to arouse suspicions it was a national sport and which involved even the most respectable-looking of customers'.[17] They formed the theory that the defaulters were saboteurs sent by rival restaurateurs, but this still did not explain why there were no absconding Indian customers.

Over the years Chinese waiters have had to suffer countless such cases, but until they were dramatized by the trial of the so-called Diamond Four, they received little publicity. The case, reported by the *Guardian* under the headline 'Foreign Office Man Clubbed By Waiters', involved the sentencing of four Chinese, waiters at the Diamond Restaurant in London's Chinatown, to two years in prison after being found guilty of causing an affray on 29 June 1986. What happened was this. Late one Saturday night, after the pubs had closed, a party of five, one of them an employee of the British diplomatic service called Steve Richards, walked into the Diamond Restaurant. They had each had about six pints of beer to drink. In the Diamond they were refused more drinks on the grounds that it was after licensing hours. They ordered a dish; on being told that there were no spare ribs, Richards is reported to have said, 'Fucking hell, is this a restaurant?' They ordered another dish and some soft drinks. Presently they got up to leave. 'Bilkers,' thought a waiter, as he barred their way. A fight ensued in which a broken chair-leg was used and blood was drawn. One of the waiters called the police, whose first move was to take statements from the white customers, asking them to identify their 'assailants' before taking them to hospital. It having been assumed that the attack was started by the Chinese, five waiters were taken to Bow Street police station, where they were interrogated and charged without benefit of solicitors or interpreters. Four were then jailed. As people are viewed, so they will be treated: and the conventional view of Chinese waiters is that they are belligerent. At the trial, it was their word against that of their customers – sober and well behaved people, the prosecution argued, violently set upon by the Chinese when they asked for the bill. The defence, on the other hand, claimed that they were drunk and abusive, and that it was after having been struck on the face that the waiter who tried to stop them leaving began hitting back. The judges, though, had swallowed the stereotype whole.

The sentences, judged excessively harsh by all who knew the waiters, drew cries of injustice, even of racism, from the normally phlegmatic Chinese community, and a campaign was started in Chinatown to collect money for an appeal and to raise questions about police partiality. People came forward to protest the unjustness of the sentences, and unjust they seemed to have been. When the case presently came up before the Court of Appeal, it was found that no specific act of violence could be pinned on the waiters with any certainty, and that their previous good record had not been taken sufficiently into account. Their sentences were then reduced to nine months each.[18] Between the trial and the appeal much had come to light to bring the conventional view of the Chinese waiter up to date; it turned out that the case of the Diamond Four had behind it a background of Chinese grievances and frustrations. Of the long litany of stories other waiters now came forward to tell, we will relate just one.

A party of diners at the Wong Kei Restaurant in Soho decides to pay its bill in coins, stacking them up in tall piles on the table. As the diners get up to leave, one of them knocks the piles over, sending the coins flying. When a waiter tries to stop them leaving before the money has been counted, a woman in the party hits him over the head. The waiter, his hands full of dishes, pushes back. The woman's reaction to this is to produce her police identification and to declare that she is going to charge him with assault. A bystander protests, and offers to act as witness for the waiter. He is told to shut up and mind his own business. He reveals that he is a journalist, whereupon the group apologizes and departs.[19]

The Chinese, by tradition a people who put guild before government, are not encouraged to turn to the police by incidents such as this. Cases also go unreported because of the language difficulties. Instead, you hear of takeaway owners taking the law into their own hands, such as the ones in Merseyside who defended themselves against harassment by pouring boiling oil out of their windows and festooning their window-frames with high-voltage wires.[20]

Chinese eating-places are naturally not uniformly vulnerable. Clienteles differ with class and location. In London Chinese restaurants can roughly be sorted by location into inside and outside Chinatown, by class into upmarket and downmarket, and by menu into Cantonese and Peking. Until the 1960s a Chinese restaurateur would think twice about opening a high-class establishment in a fashionable part of town or a suburb. With the arrival of the Swinging Sixties, however, there appeared something new, Chinese restaurants in the smart European mode. The opening of Mr Chow in Knightsbridge was a sign that change was on the way. Decorated in a style that was then fashionable, Mr Chow had stark, white interiors and Italian waiters. (Mr Chow himself is something of a society figure, often to be seen with his European wife Tina at the sort of parties that one finds featured in *Harper's and Queen*.) None of these restaurants is a typical immigrant place, if by 'typical immigrant' is meant the working-class or rural family from the New Territories. Indeed, not a few are owned by European restaurateurs working with Chinese partners.

Another category of restaurateurs consists of Chinese who are more properly émigrés than immigrants. When China went Communist, diplomats who worked in the Nationalist Chinese embassy and consulate in London and Liverpool found it expedient to remain in Britain, and, for want of something better to do, to turn their hand to the restaurant business. They were not proud of this, and I know one such person who retired just as soon as he could to devote himself to more scholarly pursuits. An ex-diplomat who has made a full career out of Chinese food is Kenneth Lo, the owner of a couple of Chinese restaurants and a cookery school, the writer of many Chinese cookery books, and the organizer of periodic gastronomical tours to China. In his time he has been a student at Cambridge University, a professional tennis player and the Industrial Relations Officer of the Chinese consulate in Liverpool.

But it was a chef from the diplomatic service of the People's Republic of China, rather than anyone attached to the Kuomintang government, who exerted the larger influence on British eating habits. In 1966, Mr

Kuo, the northern Chinese chef of the Chinese chargé d'affaires in London, decided that a capitalist style of life in a restaurant in Willesden High Road would suit him better, and made a move that the *Good Food Guide* was to describe as 'the most important cultural defection since Nureyev'. The happy effect of this was a greater awareness on the part of the British public of the diversity of the Chinese kitchen, for apart from being a gifted cook Mr Kuo kept a Pekinese table.

Peking food is mistakenly taken by the English to be the *haute cuisine* of China,[21] perhaps because the restaurants which purportedly serve it tend to be the more stylish ones catering to European diners. The most refined of the Chinese provincial cuisines is in fact the Cantonese, and in any case much that goes under the name of Peking – a cuisine with a small repertoire, extending little beyond the famous Peking Duck – is actually a blurry assortment of Szechuan and Cantonese dishes. The differentiation of Chinese restaurants by provincial styles of cooking, however spurious, was part of a growing consciousness of regional difference in the British public, a consciousness which cookery books and food writers have done much to encourage. It was paralleled by the appearance of a similar diversity in Indian-Pakistani restaurants, and followed by the establishment of other oriental cuisines, cuisines influenced in one way or another by the Chinese – Indonesian, Thai, Japanese, Singapore-Malaysian and Vietnamese. All this was intimately linked with the evolution of British tastes, with the growth in international tourism and with the advances made among the moneyed classes by the modish idea of gastronomy as part of the art of the good life.

In the 1980s the Chinese waiter finds himself having to put up increasingly with foodies, food snobbism, and customers who, on being presented with the menu, keep him waiting while they flaunt their ignorance or their pretensions to knowledge. Such people do not blurt some stock order. They are after authenticity; they do not want menus to be angled to British palates, nor flavours amended to British taste-buds. They mind very much the fact that many of the more 'ethnic' dishes, dishes which the restaurant assumes will not appeal to foreign palates, are listed in a separate menu accessible only to those who read Chinese. They will not on any account order sweet and sour pork and chop suey. They will not be fobbed off with naturalized Chinese food.

Actually they've got hold of the wrong end of the stick, insisting upon authenticity when they should simply have demanded quality. Sweet and sour pork and chop suey are perfectly authentic Chinese dishes. Just as French onion soup can be superb or ghastly, depending on the art and care which go into making it, without ceasing to be French, so sweet and sour pork and chop suey remain Chinese dishes whether they are cooked well or badly. And yet chop suey, surely the best known of the Chinese dishes among foreigners, is widely supposed to be an American invention. How it acquired that reputation is part of Chinese-American immigrant lore and worth considering in some detail.

The basic recipe for chop suey is chicken's livers and gizzards fried with sliced fungi, bamboo shoots, pig's tripe and bean sprouts. It did not spring virgin from anyone's brain in America, but was a dish taken there from China by the immigrants. When offered to white customers in Chinatown restaurants in the nineteenth century, it had the usual giblets and innards, but these became less obtrusive with time, no doubt because of the general American aversion to what was thought of as offal. But however much it might have been modified, there is no doubt that the dish had been on offer in restaurants in New York long before the story got about that it had its origin in America.

There are at least two versions of this anecdote. In one version, Li Hung-chang, the greatest of the Chinese Emperor's ministers in the late nineteenth century, was served this dish when he came on a visit to the United States in 1896. The Mayor of San Francisco had laid on a banquet to welcome him, but Li could not bring himself to eat anything, his doctor having warned him to steer clear of rich food for the sake of his weak stomach. It was not the happiest of occasions, but the cook saved the day. A clever soul, he went back into the kitchen, made a palatable concoction of all the leftovers, and presented it as a special dish to the Chinese minister. It was just what Li Hung-chang needed, a plain dish, but with a little bit of everything. Afterwards the delighted Mayor asked the chef for the name of the masterpiece: 'Chop suey,' the man replied. It was an inspired answer, for though chop suey, or *tsa-sui* in its Mandarin rendering, means the chopped entrails of ox or sheep, it could also be made to stand for 'miscellaneous bits and pieces' – a hash, in other words.

The other version of the story has a group of white Californian miners arriving late one night in the 1860s at a Chinese restaurant, the only place still open, and demanding to be fed. The cook is getting ready to close up, but not wishing to offend the customers, men twice his size and hungry enough to be insensible to niceties, he throws together what he finds in the kitchen, scraps of this and leftovers of that, and produces a dish. Inevitably, he is asked for the name of the dish, and just as inevitably, he comes up with the Cantonese word for 'hash', plucking it out of the air. There are variations on this story and the previous one, but the theme that they all share is that of deft, hurried improvisation. They also express something true about Chinese cooking, which is that it is without waste. And in the stories the name is always one the Chinese cooks make up on the spur of the moment, to pass it off as a real dish or to satisfy American curiosity. But the stories are apocryphal, given extra touches that are never the same each time they are retold.

Nevertheless, they were good for trade; they put chop suey on America's culinary map. Li Hung-chang was never in San Francisco, but his visits to New York, Philadelphia and Washington DC attracted enormous publicity, and the story that he ate chop suey in America naturally gave the dish a special cachet. Li Hung-chang was received like royalty, the representative of the Chinese Emperor and 'the greatest man', hyperbolized the *New York Times*, 'the Chinese race has produced since Confucius'. The rumour that he ate chop suey was enough to send thousands of Americans to Chinatown in pursuit of the same dish. For this was America, quick to embrace fads and easily flamed into fervour for celebrities. Chinese restaurants were canny enough to cash in on this; what better way to advertise the dish than to say that it was Li Hung-chang's favourite? The heady publicity surrounding the mandarin could only have helped the Chinese catering business; and so a legend was created, Americanizing the origins of chop suey. If it was a ploy on the part of the Chinese restaurateurs, it could not have been more successful, for while there were only about a dozen Chinese restaurants in New York's Chinatown at around the time of Li's visit, there were three to four hundred seven or eight years later.²² Chinese restaurants themselves came to be called chop suey houses, and the word went into the American language – Webster's Dictionary defines it as 'odds and ends: a dish prepared chiefly from bean sprouts, bamboo shoots, water chestnuts, onions, mushrooms, and meat or fish and served with rice and soy sauce'. So inseparable became its link to America that we even hear of a neon sign proclaiming GENUINE AMERICAN CHOP SUEY SERVED HERE in a main street in 1940s Shanghai.

What America did beget was the fortune cookie, the confection that comes free with every Chinese meal, and with a slip of paper inside inscribed with a gnomic prophecy. The most interesting story about the fortune cookie is a true one, related as it happens to the immigrant theme.²³ An Immigration Act of 1986 gave illegal aliens until May 1988 to apply for amnesty. As is perhaps to be expected, many such immigrants preferred to stay in the shadows, afraid that they could be deported, or that their coming out into the light would split their families, with some members accepted and some not. In fact nearly all those who came forward were given legal status, but more would do so, the Immigration and Naturalization Service (INS) thought, if it could somehow get its message across to them. But how to reach them? The officials came up with an idea: why not communicate with the Hispanics and the Chinese by putting appropriate messages in tortillas and fortune cookies? Unhappily, this did not work out as well as they had hoped. After printing eighty thousand messages in Spanish, they found only one tortilla manufacturer to package them. As for the fortune cookies, which were to be distributed at the Chinese New Year festival, the INS officials could persuade no cookie maker at all to cooperate with them. Worse still, it was pointed out to them that Chinese did not eat fortune cookies, only tourists did.²³

All the same the INS was right when it looked to reach the Chinese immigrants through food. In America the Chinese lead the field for immigrant cuisines in equality with the Italians. There the demand for more jobs for the growing population of Chinese immigrants has been satisfied in no small measure by the increase in Chinese eating-places. American interest in Chinese cookery boomed in the early 1970s. As in Britain, the specialization of restaurants in regional styles of cooking reflects not just the sharpening of collective American palates but also the diversity of Chinese immigration: there would have been fewer good Hunanese restaurants if there had been fewer immigrants from Taiwan, and there would certainly have been no Cuban-Chinese restaurants at all if there hadn't been a wave of migration of Chinese from Cuba.

One would suppose Chinese restaurants evolving on American soil to be naturalized to some extent, and so they were, though not always in the ways expected – in New York some establishments provided jazz entertainment, and it was in a Chinese restaurant in Pell Street that Irving Berlin began his career as a singing waiter. And just as there are Islamically *halal* Chinese restaurants in Kuala Lumpur, so there are kosher Chinese restaurants in New York (where Romanian pastrami, for example, is substituted for pork, and sea bass or other white fish for shellfish). Many restaurants are hardly Chinese at all, offering Combination Platters and Choice of Soup or Juice before the main course – the menu of a Chinese restaurant in a small town in the late 1960s listed Barbecued Spare Ribs and Pork Chow Mein along with Roast Maryland Turkey with Dressing and Broiled Live Maine Lobster.[24]

Indigenous modification is no bad thing in itself; quite often it speaks of pliancy in adapting cuisines to the supplies locally available. What a Chinese-American chef does to the original recipe for a dish invented years ago in a village in Kwangtung is not necessarily a stunting but an enrichment, imaginative and unusual. A famous exponent of what is called East-West cooking is Ken Hom, a gifted Chinese-American chef and writer who would happily serve cannelloni stuffed with Chinese sausages, or mayonnaise flavoured with Szechuan peppercorns. His enormously successful book, *East Meets West Cuisine*, is full of recipes that would horrify a purist, but they are creations of true originality, besides being fresh and seductive to the taste. Because Ken Hom is that rare being, somebody who knows not just Chinese cooking but also French and Italian, he can make Chinese cuisine blossom in new colours.

Another success to have come out of the cross-fertilization of Chinese and other food cultures is the Nonya cooking of Singapore and Malaya. Like much else in Baba culture, this is an amalgam, part Chinese and part Malayan, but with a character and lustiness of its own. What sets it instantly apart from Malay cooking is its use of pork, a meat shunned by Muslims but much favoured by the Chinese. What also distinguishes it from the Chinese is its flavours and seasonings; the standard make-up of a Nonya dish is seldom without something hot and tart, whether it is chilli, or tamarind, or *langkuas* (galangal, a ginger-like root). To go by an authoritative cookbook, that written by Mrs Lee Chin Koon of Singapore, the mother of the Prime Minister himself, other needed ingredients include the familiar Southeast Asian ones of lime leaf, turmeric, green mangoes, candlenuts, shallots, *pandan* leaf (a fragrant leaf much used in cakes) and, of course, *blachan*, a pungent condiment derived, much like the Roman *garum*, from shellfish that has been salted, dried, pounded and allowed to go completely putrid.

A recipe that a cook knows in Amoy quite often turns up on a table in Singapore curried and more generously sweetened, Malayanized out of shape but still recognizable and still delicious. Some Nonya dishes go by their Hokkien names, others by Malay ones or by a mixture of the two. The sacrificial food with which the Babas and Nonyas worshipped their ancestors (a practice that was a normal part of domestic life, now largely nostalgic) included plates of Nonya dishes, not all of which, one would have thought, the remoter Chinese forefathers would have recognized. The Nonya festival foods are fundamentally Chinese, but given an indigenous twist. A good example is the leaf-wrapped glutinous rice cake eaten by Chinese on the fifth day of the fifth lunar month, during the Dragon Boat Festival. In China these cakes, called *tsung* in Mandarin, come in different shapes, oblong in some regions, pyramid in others; and one unwraps the leaves to find anything from sweetened mashed red bean and nuts to pork or ham and egg, their casing of glutinous rice steamed to a sticky softness and scented by the jacket of leaves. The Babas, who have a sweet tooth, have a *tsung* which they eat with spoonfuls of *gula melaka*, the coconut-palm sugar one knows from Malay and Indonesian puddings. They also like to give their *tsung* the iridescent look of certain Malay cakes, using a particular local flower to impart blue streaks to the rice, and a colouring agent derived from dried and ground durian skin to dye the cakes a glistening yellow.

One cannot eat a Chinese dish in its virgin state in Singapore or Malaysia, and quite often one does not want to, so much have one's taste-buds changed. In Singapore and Malaysia little side-plates of chilli sauce or fresh sliced chillis are not much less inevitable than the routine salt and pepper cellars on the English table; and to add lashings of these to a delicately flavoured Chinese dish, completely masking its subtleties, is not judged unwise or inappropriate. We eat what our bodies tell us to eat. The changes undergone by food on being transferred from home ground to adoptive country are part of that complex process by which migrants themselves acquire new tastes, new habits and even new physiques.

CHAPTER SEVENTEEN

Triads

If Chinese restaurants are one feature of Chinatown, Chinese secret societies are another. Secret societies have always been endemic to overseas Chinese communities, and although their nature has changed, a mysterious Chinatown murder or a gang war may still remind one of the days when secret brotherhoods fought each other in the tin mines of Malaya. All over the world these gangs survive on fear and corruption, are engaged in the same kind of business, are likely to have a figurative language in common, and very probably share contacts in Hong Kong. Liaison might be tenuous between city and city, or even gang and gang, but set almost any two secret society men side by side, whatever their affiliations, from East or West, speaking Cantonese or Teochiu, and they would not feel altogether strangers to each other. To outsiders, this makes them seem like members of a huge worldwide conspiracy, and yet they may not be linked at all in their operations; may, indeed, be split by deadly rivalry.

If there is a capital in the Chinese criminal diaspora, that capital is Hong Kong. In 1997 the British colony reverts to the People's Republic of China; if the executive rich of Hong Kong, fearful of a future under the five-star flag, are leaving for Canada, Australia and America in droves, should these countries expect an influx of triad magnates too? The Australian authorities, for one, have been told by Hong Kong police that ninety thousand criminals with links to the triads will leave the colony before 1997.[1]

The 1986 report of the Hong Kong government Fight Crime Committee's working group on gangs and organized crime reckons there are about fifty triad societies in Hong Kong; their sizes vary, with membership ranging from as little as a hundred or so to as large as several thousand. The line between the legal and illegal blurs in most societies, since nearly all of them form associations registered either under the Societies Ordinance or the Companies Ordinance, so that they are not only able to hold meetings and elect office-bearers, but to bring some of their activities within the law. Some societies are more loosely organized than others, consisting of a number of separate street gangs taking orders from a few office-bearers who work together only now and then, when it suits them to do so. The better-organized societies, on the other hand, are presided over by a strong central leadership which sees to it that money is regularly collected from the members to be used for the legal defence of an arrested gang official, say, or the burial of a gang-war casualty, or even for such self-aggrandizing displays as processions, lion dances and dinner parties on auspicious occasions. The initiation ceremony continues to be conducted by some societies, albeit simplified or altogether curtailed in others – partly because police raids surprising them in the act make the ceremony impractical and dangerous.

The triad societies remain highly hierarchical, structured in the traditional pyramid fashion with the ranks denoted by the old sobriquets and coded numbers. The supreme authority is the Dragon Head, or 489, a truly exalted rank which in Hong Kong is filled in only one or two societies. Next in rank comes the Second Marshal, alias 438; followed by the Red Pole, or 426; the White Paper Fan, 415; and the Straw Sandals, 432. The rank and file, the members at the lowest rung of the triad pecking order, are called 49 Boys. The numbers have mystical connotations, but they acquired their meaning such a long time ago that none of the explanations offered for them is historically verifiable. The triad liking for the numeral 4, it is generally supposed, has its source in the idea of universal fraternity, expressed in the familiar Chinese saying 'Within four seas, all men are brothers'. The figure 489 is meaningful, but is it meaningful because the three digits add up to twenty-one, which is the multiple of 3 (signifying the triad of heaven, earth and man) and 7 (the symbol of death); or is it because the Chinese characters for 21 form the top part of the character for Hung – and Hung Men, or Vast Gate, as we saw, is another name for the triads? It is impossible to know, but there is no doubting the arcane symbolism of the numerals, or their connection with Chinese numerology.[2] It has been noted, for example, that all the numbers have been taken from an ancient Chinese riddle in which the digits add up to fifteen no matter which way you count them, across or from top to bottom:

$$4\ 3\ 8$$
$$9\ 5\ 1$$
$$2\ 7\ 6$$

The jobs that go with the ranks are well known; Red Poles are fight fixers, the ones who oversee gang warfare, choosing the location, the weapons and the strategy, and who mete out punishment to those who break triad codes; White Paper Fans are administrators, counsellors and planners; while Straw Sandals are liaison officers, concerned with protection and debt collection. The names and the numbers, together with the passwords and hand signs peculiar to the triads, give a suggestion of cabalistic ritual to quite ordinary matters, very attractive to the susceptible youngsters who are recruited into the gangs.

Recruitment into a triad gang, an event preceded by a probationary period known in triad jargon as 'hanging the blue lantern', gives the new member, often a street-wise schoolboy who is frequently to be found loitering about fast-food shops, video-machine parlours, roller-skating rinks and football pitches, a certain amount of cachet and a chance to demonstrate his manhood. It also assures him of the protection, and often the care, of his Elder Brother, the one he undertakes to 'follow' with unquestioning loyalty as he tries to earn his spurs. Often enough, it comes as a surprise to the parents to discover their son is a triad member, because there is usually nothing at all in his behaviour at home to suggest it, and it is only when he is among his fellows that the hoodlum and delinquent in him are revealed.

In his subsequent progression into organized crime, one might see the classic pattern of the triad career. A triad member might begin as an underling, doing the bidding of his elders in gang wars and settlement talks with rival societies. But once he has proved himself, he may become Elder Brother to aspiring triad recruits himself. While involved in the larger business of the society, he may be running his own small rackets, such as street-level drug-dealing, minor protection rackets and debt collection. With a following of his own to support, these businesses may widen into larger activities. Promotion to the rank of office-bearer may follow, accompanied by progression to typical mob businesses like prostitution, gambling, loan-sharking, drug distribution and criminal monopolies. It is then time to set up front companies to act as a screen behind which to pursue the syndicate's criminal activities, and to go partly legitimate by investing some of the illegal income in above-board businesses. At this stage, the syndicate's profits – of which the tax authorities will of course have seen very little – will have become quite colossal, and the mobster himself will have acquired a thoroughly respectable persona to mask his nefarious activities, one he is eager to maintain as he hobnobs with the swells at the racecourses, and donates generous sums to the local charities.

In the West, the best known of the triad societies is the 14K. This is a relative newcomer to Hong Kong, its history going back only as far as 1949, to a secret meeting at 14 Pao Wa Street in Canton.3 The instigators were the secret police chiefs of the Kuomintang, and the object was to create a force supporting the Nationalist cause in its struggle with the Communists. The cause lost, many of the conspirators followed the Kuomintang to Taiwan; the ones that did not went on to form the core of the 14K in Hong Kong. For a long time this triad society retained its Nationalist sympathies, but today it cares little for politics and is nothing but a collection of crime syndicates. Its interests in drugs has made it reach out to the world; and now, with the spectre of 1997 looming, there is all the more reason for it to put down international roots. It has been caught on the prowl in Japan, where it would be glad of a tie-up with the yakuza, the Japanese mob.4 It is not as strong as it used to be, despite the fact that there are many people in the world who have heard of the triads only because of the 14K: though it is still influential enough in Chinatowns in America and Australia, for example, its command of the Amsterdam drug market, a highly lucrative arena of triad competition, was usurped by the Wo network in the 1970s.

The loose-knit Wo network is so called because the groups which comprise it bear names which start with the syllable *wo* – Cantonese for 'harmony' – such as Wo Sing Wo (Harmony, Victory, Harmony) and Wo On Lok (Harmony, Peace, Happiness). Legend has it that the organization came into being at a grand meeting of disparate and antagonistic guilds and associations in Hong Kong in 1909, called by the founder to bring everyone into one big happy family. The Chinatowns of America, Europe and Australia have all been infiltrated by Wo members, and many a gangster in San Francisco or New York will have cut his teeth on a Wo operation in Hong Kong.

Outclassing them all these days, in age, size and aggressiveness, are the Teochiu (pronounced Chiuchow in Cantonese) triads. The attitude of the Teochius to outsiders has largely been prickly and suspicious, and triads drawing their membership from speakers of this dialect are probably the most clannish and exclusive of all the regional secret societies.5 The chief Teochiu triad is the Sun Yee On (New Righteousness and Peace), an extraordinarily well-organized society into which new members are still initiated in accordance with triad ritual. With a membership standing at 33,750 at the last count, in 1978, the Sun Yee On is presided over by a cabal of about 1,300 office-bearers. These are truly global, and into all the drug markets of the world, from Thailand to Holland, the Teochiu triads have long made their way. Their activities are unreservedly excoriated, and their reputation among the law-abiding is entirely nefarious.

It would be wrong, though, to assume a Hong Kong pedigree in all of the Chinese criminal syndicates operating in the West, because some of them have originated elsewhere, in Singapore, Malaysia, Vietnam or Taiwan. The ones from Singapore and Malaysia go by the name of Young Turks, and as yet not very much is known about them, except that they are active in Australia's Chinatowns. The Vietnamese gang, called Saigon Cowboys, harks back to the days of the Vietnam War, when there was no shortage of opportunities for racketeering, and young hoods lurked in the streets of what would one day be called Ho Chi Minh City to peddle drugs and operate the thriving black market. Some of these hoodlums are now in the West, having got there as refugees; and we hear of a gang called the Frogmen in New York, a one-time Vietnamese underwater demolition team. A good many of these refugees have Chinese antecedents, but they are fiercely nationalistic, and loudly disclaim all feelings of Chineseness.

There is nothing equivocal, on the other hand, about the ethnic identity of the Bamboo Union, the most powerful of the seven hundred or so Chinese gangs in Taiwan. A triad group, the gang got its name, so the story goes, from the bamboo thickets where it held its earliest secret meetings. Supreme at home, the syndicate controls, along with the next largest gang, the Four Seas, something like sixty per cent of the country's gambling, prostitution and protection rackets, and its presence is particularly felt in the entertainment industry. Abroad, its overseas ventures have earned it international notoriety. It maintains close links with the Japanese underworld, and this is not surprising, given the close historical and economic links between Taiwan and Japan. The Bamboo Union has been much involved in the illicit trade in speed, *the* drug of abuse in Japan; and it was Japanese chemists despatched to Taiwan by the yakuza who taught the Taiwanese gangsters to produce it.[6]

Like the yakuza too, the Bamboo Union enjoys powerful political links, and it is often difficult to tell where its criminal activities end and its espionage missions begin. Unlike the 14K and the Sun Yee On, the Bamboo Union is still in some ways a secret society in the old sense, with a political purpose. What happened in Daly City, San Francisco, in October 1984 certainly gave that impression. A fifty-two-year-old American-Chinese writer named Henry Liu, the biographer of the late President Chiang Ching-kuo and an outspoken and vehement critic of the Kuomintang government, was murdered in his garage by two members of the Bamboo Union just as he was about to obtain documents which, according to his widow, would prove embarrassing to the Taiwan government. In the dock in California, one of the two assassins testified that the murder had been ordered by a leader of the gang, Chen Chi-li, otherwise known as 'Dry Duck'. Chen, a strange figure who wore his hair long, down to his shoulders, is known to be intimate with the intelligence bureau of the Taiwan Ministry of Defence. Indeed, said Chen, he had been doing the bidding of high-placed military officers and the intelligence service – a claim vehemently denied by the government.[7]

There is a political dimension, too, to the society's subtle infiltration of Hong Kong, the arena of Communist Chinese ambitions and expanding influence. The syndicate tried to stage a comeback in 1985, throwing a lavish dinner party at a restaurant in the North Point district of Hong Kong, a sort of summit of the bigwigs (some 350 of them, according to one story) of all the local triad societies.[8] But a good many of the conspirators were pounced upon by the police, and the society suffered a setback in its attempt to gain a foothold in the British colony.

It was a temporary setback, though, and when we next hear of the Bamboo Union it is to learn that the society has successfully mounted a huge recruitment drive to enlist local triad lieutenants as its part-time agents. Paid a handsome retainer, these 'ghost members' work freelance for the Taiwan syndicate, helping to further the society's criminal and political purposes in Hong Kong, sometimes as racketeers, sometimes as spies. It made sense for the Bamboo Union, which has long protected Taiwan singers and film stars invited to perform in Hong Kong, to enter into an agreement with a triad in a complementary line of business – the Sun Yee On, protector of Hong Kong pop and film stars who perform in Taiwan.[9]

The engraved invitation cards the gang sent out to its dinner party guests are said to have declared WE ARE ALL ONE FAMILY, but these sentiments of fraternity are unlikely to have embraced the Big Circle Boys, a group of Cantonese immigrants who turned to crime during the severe recession of the mid-1970s. The Big Circle Boys have come directly from China, but this is not the only thing which sets them apart; less like a secret society than a band of desperadoes, the Big Circle Boys go in for violent crime and armed robberies (of goldsmiths and watch shops), and provide local triads with some of the toughest competition they have ever faced. Indeed, the threat they pose is said to be one reason the latter are looking to establish footholds abroad. The gang is so named because in underworld parlance the word 'circle' stands for the city, and the older generation in Hong Kong, migrants from neighbouring Kwangtung, still know the provincial capital of Canton as the Big City.

Many of the Big Circle Boys were wanted men in China, hardened criminals who had sneaked into Hong Kong as illegal migrants, or ex-Red Guards with a history of violence and frustration behind them. Some of them had even had military training in China, and are adept at handling firearms and at hand-to-hand combat. A reckless breed with far less to lose than the established triads – and thus far less to fear – they have managed to overawe even those gangs which greatly outnumber them. New arrivals from the mainland periodically swell their ranks, and they have been known, when they have a big job coming up, to send for extra help from China – delinquents who are only too pleased to come to Hong Kong. Given a fake identity card and provided with board and lodging, these visitors – known among Big Circle members as 'volunteers' – easily melt into the criminal underworld.

What do people generally think of when they think of a triad official: a leery thug, a po-faced psychopath, a sinister sybarite who collects *objets d'art*? Does he turn out to be the model son, the ideal dinner guest, the perfect host? Triad officials come in all kinds of course, but even so the identity of the Dragon Head of Sun Yee On, the 489 of this most ruthless of secret societies, came as a surprise to most people in Hong Kong. When, after a series of successful police raids, Heung Wah Yim was brought before the High Court of Hong Kong in the autumn of 1987, a spectator might indeed have thought himself in the presence of a rather dull bank clerk, a conscientious and unassertive plodder who leads a life of respectable and humdrum monotony. The last word a spectator would use of him would be 'forbidding'. Fifty-four years old, dressed in a business suit and tie, the bespectacled Heung Wah Yim wore his hair with a side parting and looked the solicitor's clerk that he was. It was at his office in the law firm he worked for, the court learnt, that he interviewed prospective office-holders of the secret society.

His father, Heung Chin, had been Dragon Head before him, and Heung the younger assumed control of the syndicate when Heung the elder was deported to Taiwan in the 1950s. Heung Chin was the Chairman of the Yee On Industrial and Commercial Guild, the predecessor of Sun Yee On, deregistered in 1946 on account of its criminal activities. It was presumably because of the authority he exerted over his followers that the elder Heung was able to organize neighbourhood patrols in Hong Kong when the allies re-occupied the territory after the Second World War – a service for which he won a commendation from the Commander of the British Forces.

Heung Wah Yim's fellow conspirators included his eldest son, a 426 or Red Pole, and son-in-law; extraordinarily, the latter turned out to be the son of a member of Hong Kong's law-making body, the Legislative Council. (Equally extraordinarily, Heung has another son studying to be a lawyer in England.) If there is such a thing as a triad type, it is certainly not self-evident, for of those brought before the High Court with Heung Wah Yim, one was a butcher, another a hardware-store owner and a third a Buddhist temple director.[10]

The records seized in the police raids showed the Sun Yee On to have been led by 1,267 office-bearers, of whom twenty-one were listed as being based abroad – twelve in Macao, one in Australia, one in New Zealand, three in Britain, and four in the United States.[11] This is as good an indication as any of the international character of the secret society. As if their own criminal gangs were not headache enough, a number of Western countries are reluctant hosts of the overseas members of Hong Kong's triad societies.

Britain, for instance, was home to a good deal of triad activity in the late 1960s and early to mid-1970s, when much of the trade in Southeast Asian heroin was in Chinese hands. In 1978 BBC Television Birmingham showed a six-part thriller in which a rich Chinese businessman and his bad but beautiful daughter Lily Li Tang set up a base for triad activities and drug-trafficking in the Midlands. This is a hackneyed enough theme, and the serial might have given the impression that a triad boss lurked behind the counter of every Chinese takeaway in the country; and yet truth is very often stranger than fiction, and in Britain a covert police operation in the mid-1970s did uncover a heroin-smuggling outfit with an alluring Chinese girl at its head. She was May Wong, a Malaysian Chinese model who had been educated at, of all places, Roedean, one of Britain's best known girls' schools. Also called 'Golden Butterfly', May Wong was a 432, or Straw Sandal, in the Wo Sing Wo society, as was her Singapore boyfriend and fellow drug trafficker Li Jafaar Mah.

Less surprising, but no less the stuff of television serials, was Georgie Pai, a Wo Sing Wo Red Pole who menaced Chinese businesses in England in the mid-1970s. Georgie's real name is Yao Lap Leung – *pai* is 'to limp' in Cantonese, so that his English name is actually Georgie

Limp. He was born in the New Territories in 1946, and had two years in prison for robberies and mayhem before he emerged as a Wo Sing Wo leader in England, where his parents owned a Chinese restaurant, in 1975. In those days the 14K considered Britain its bailiwick, and it was Georgie Pai who, by gathering about him a group of 49s and Blue Lantern probationers, made the Wo Sing Wo a name to be reckoned with in such cities as Portsmouth, Manchester and Birmingham. As the Wo Sing Wo got into its stride, so the demands for protection money became more widespread, with Chinese businesses receiving messages like 'Meet the big man from London [Georgie] at the Slow Boat Club – or else', and 'Georgie wants £2,000'. Although the sums extorted got bigger as Georgie Pai grew greedier and better established, more often than not they were a permutation of the numbers 336, familiar triad figures. The businesses, only a few of which felt bold enough to report the threats to the police, were Chinese restaurants, gambling clubs and organizers of late-night Chinese movies at Odeons and other British cinemas.

Georgie Pai's ambitions did not stop at protection, however, and the police were soon convinced that he was heavily involved in heroin-trafficking. It turned out that his circle of intimates included not only May Wong and Li Jafaar Mah, but a number of other characters in the heroin connection. One of these, a Thomas Chung, had been arrested by the British police but had jumped bail and escaped with his Irish girlfriend Julie to Amsterdam, a favourite transit point for drug cargoes bound for the Liverpool and London markets. It was Thomas Chung who, with Julie acting as the courier, kept Georgie Pai supplied with regular shipments of heroin.

It must have been a source of some chagrin to the police that they were unable to pin anything on Georgie Pai, but they did manage to deport him in the end, not because of any evidence coming to light, nor because of any slip-up in his operations, but because, by an unfortunate lapse of memory, the Red Pole had neglected to renew his visa for Britain. So it happened after all that Georgie Pai was arrested not for drug-trafficking, not for extortion, but on a tiny immigration technicality. Once he fell into the hands of the police, those of his nervous victims who took no chances before came forward and told their stories. By no means everything people said of him was uncomplimentary, however, for he seemed to have been a popular individual, the very model of the old-school secret society man, the sort who will never betray a triad brother. One rarely had a dull evening with

Georgie Pai, for he had a way with words, and one could always rely on his being witty and entertaining. Those who were slow in coming up with the protection money he demanded might find themselves very roughly manhandled or brutally wounded, but while some Chinatown residents shivered to hear his name mentioned, here is how the wife of a fellow gangster described him: 'He was one of the most gentle and considerate men I've ever known. He always knew how to turn on that extra little charm.'[12]

The Chinese traffickers suffered a slump in trade in the late 1970s, when Southeast Asian heroin was supplanted by heroin from Iran and Pakistan. They went quiet for a good many years, but the police in London sensed trouble ahead when a secret summit of European-based gang leaders took place in 1987, presumably to lay plans for a comeback. What reinforced the impression of a renewed triad interest in Britain's drug market was the reappearance of Georgie Pai, who had succeeded in smuggling himself into Britain via Ireland the year before. He was deported a second time, but, popping up yet again, he was spotted in London in 1987.[13]

The principal source of heroin trafficked by Chinese drug pushers is the famous Golden Triangle, a border region of northern Thailand, Burma and Laos. Opium and jade are the two high-value exports of this lawless country. Subsistence farmers there are richer for their cultivation of opium poppies, as are the people who control the place: the Chinese drug kingpin Khun Sa and his private army, and the remnant Kuomintang troops stranded here since the 1950s and augmented by CIA-backed intelligence bands from Taiwan.[14] The drug cartel is mixed up with the jade business, and the same people run both.[15]

The place where the jade is mined, the Kachin tribal area in northern Burma, is the home of a most curious group of Chinese; led by a Liu Ping-hung, an escapee from China when the country fell to the Communists, these are all members of a strange secret society. This goes by about seventy-two names but is best known as I-kuan-tao. The Communist Chinese describe the society as one which, 'under the cover of religious activities, served the Japanese invaders and the Kuomintang'; certainly if Liu hadn't escaped to Burma he would have been had up as a collaborator and a counter-revolutionary. In Burma, however, he is a law unto himself, going with the grain of the local economy by engaging in smuggling and black-marketeering. He also seems to be a man of predatory and empire-building tendencies, and over the years has been seeking to extend I-kuan-tao's influence throughout Burma's Chinese community, building a 'Buddhist' hall here, a school there, and despatching missionaries everywhere. To enrole in Liu's schools is to enrol in the I-kuan-tao religion, whatever that may be.

When his expansionist tendencies bumped up against Khun Sa's territorial instincts in the early 1970s, the latter kidnapped him and exacted a high ransom before releasing him. Only a little worse for wear, Liu moved the society's headquarters to Mandalay and there continued his extraordinary range of activities – which, apart from proselytizing, encompass agricultural and industrial undertakings and giving help to the Kuomintang's special agents. Earnings from farms, textiles factories, bakeries, noodle shops, drugstores and a string of commercial businesses in northern Thailand keep the secret society in funds, as do offerings made to acquire merit by its followers and an annual grant (so the story goes) from the Japanese embassy in Rangoon. When to all this are added the profits of the jade and drug business, it can be seen that the I-kuan-tao does not want for money.[16]

Various efforts sponsored by the US government and the United Nations have been made to choke off the drug supplies, but nothing short of napalming the area is likely to have the desired effect. In any case, the drugs business is hydra-headed; as soon as one source of supply is curtailed, another opens up. New York's heroin market, for example, used to be fed by supplies from Iran, Afghanistan and Pakistan; but imports from Thailand, Laos and Burma by gangs operating in Hong Kong and Bangkok have shot up dramatically, from an insignificant four per cent of the market in the early 1980s to seventy per cent in just five years.[17] Drugs go through cycles of popularity, official suppression and relative oblivion; in America heroin lost its power to provoke newspaper scares in the sweep of the Colombian cocaine menace. But South Americans are not the only people to cash in on the seemingly insatiable appetite for self-destruction in the United States. There is still enough demand for heroin for Chinese syndicates to do very well out of drug-trafficking.

The Chinese had stepped in sharply when the Mafia decided to reduce its narcotics interests. Extraordinarily, the Chinese expansion was traced to just one family. The head of this family, Johnny Kon, was a remarkable figure of the heroin connection, a holder of six passports (including the Costa Rican one he was carrying when he was arrested in Manhattan in early 1988) and a fan, so he himself had declared, of Al Capone. Born in China, Kon moved to Hong Kong before beginning his life as an international gypsy, keeping one step ahead of the law as he zigzagged from fleshpot to fleshpot, casino to casino, in Japan, the Philippines, Taiwan, Thailand and South America, often with an entourage of bodyguards, hangers-on and beautiful women. His wife and two children made a home in America; she, together with his brother and sister, was an accomplice in the business.

The heroin that would eventually end up in the streets of New York had been shipped there in suitcases, vases, T-shirts, wall plaques and ice-buckets. Shipments were usually picked up in the Hilton Hotel in Manhattan by John Routollo, a retired New York police sergeant Kon had met when he applied for a gun licence some years before, and who had become not only his supplier of weapons and firearm permits but also his drug distributor. Once money had changed hands – and the sums involved were staggering – couriers would take the proceeds to Hong Kong to be laundered. The profits had bought Kon not only the cooperation of the likes of John Routollo, but expensive status symbols and desirable properties in San Francisco and New York. He worked through numerous fronts, businesses like his watch firm in Paraguay and his fur company in Newark, New Jersey. To catch him, it is said, members of the US Federal Drug Enforcement Administration sought the help of several countries and posted agents at the United States consulate in Hong Kong.

Drug-trafficking is the most internationally aggressive of the typical mob businesses; were it not for heroin and the corruption it spawns, Chinese crime would not impinge upon other ethnic groups in the host country. The other criminal enterprises – extortion, gambling and loan-sharking – are a menace to only the Chinese community, and thus highly resistant to in-depth probing by American law enforcement agencies. It is hard to breach the language and cultural barriers, and the small number of Chinese informants compounds the difficulties. None of this is helped by the fact that some police officers take the attitude once adopted towards the Mafia, that it was best to let them fight among themselves and kill each other off.

American Chinatowns have changed, not only as all things change but as a consequence of new waves of immigration. The two hundred thousand Hong Kong immigrants who arrived in the United States after immigration restrictions were lifted in 1965 had among them many young unfamilied greenhorns who, looking to gang affiliation for shelter and support in the hurly-burly of a suddenly expanded Chinatown, were easily enrolled as henchmen and street toughs by the traditional associations, themselves mere fronts for criminal organizations. The violence with which fiefdoms came to be fought for by street gangs made Chinatown residents think back on earlier times as halcyon days of order and godliness. Now, there were even thugs specially recruited from Hong Kong, smuggled into Canada and brought down to US cities to swell the ranks of the gangs.

In New York the Chinese need gangs, just like the Italians, the blacks and the Hispanics – and the Jews too, in the days of Arnold Rothstein (the gangster who was mythologized in *The Great Gatsby* as Meyer Wolfsheim). The two most powerful Chinatown street gangs there are the Ghost Shadows and the Flying Dragons, one owing allegiance to the On Leong Tong, an association of restaurant owners and other businessmen; the other to the Hip Sing Tong, a working man's association originally founded for the benefit of railroad labourers. More than heads were broken when there was a falling-out between members or a power struggle. In one famous incident five shots were fired at Nicky Louie, the Hong Kong-born head of the Ghost Shadows, as he walked down a street in Chinatown. The assassins were a breakaway faction backed by the On Leong Tong. Louie survived the attempt on his life and fled with some of his men to Toronto, where his brother Eddie was chief of the Ghost Shadows. Toronto deported him, however, and Nicky Louie relocated to Chicago. There his bully-boy activities and extortion schemes – chiefly directed at businessmen linked to the On Leong Tong, his new enemy – were interrupted when eight Ghost Shadows thugs commanded by the On Leong Tong were despatched to put a stop to them. A shoot-out followed in Chicago's Chinatown, with the gunmen firing at Nicky Louie's cronies from the balcony of the On Leong Tong. The driver died, but although the hitmen were arrested and brought to trial, the judge had to dismiss the case for lack of concrete evidence – declaring in open court, however, that he was certain the defendants were guilty of murder.[18]

The breakaway faction had the On Leong Tong lord Eddie Chan Chi-chiu behind it. Chan was everybody's idea of the Chinese gangster. A restaurant owner who sat on the board of a Chinatown bank, Chan was, before he relocated to New York and took out American citizenship papers, a detective sergeant in the Royal Hong Kong Police Force. Chan was a rich man, and this was not surprising, for the Hong Kong police was a sink of corruption: 'In North America,' a sergeant with the Metropolitan Toronto Police has noted, 'a common denominator among high level Chinese organized crime figures is a former affiliation with the Hong Kong Police.'¹⁹

Soon after he arrived in New York, Chan opened a funeral parlour and joined the Chi Kung Tong, a pro-Nationalist organization of which he was presently to become Chairman. People in Chinatown looked up to Eddie Chan, the self-styled champion of Chinese public interest; if in trouble you went to see him at his office in Mott Street. It was Chan the hawkers went to, for example, when their business was threatened by New York's Sanitation Department. Through him, you felt, as through no other possible channel, your grievances reached the attention of the city administration. Scarcely a week went by without his picture – showing a balding man entertaining prominent municipal figures and glowing in the idealizing light of his public persona – appearing in one of the Chinese newspapers.

He performed his role to perfection. He liked to be seen to be on good terms with American politicians. It was in the hope that she would help ease Chinese immigration into the US, he said, that he donated $10 million to Mrs Geraldine Ferraro's election campaign. When, in the autumn of 1984, the President's Commission on Asian Organized Crime named him a gangster and linked him to the Chicago murder, he gave a press conference to protest his innocence – 'I have nothing to hide,' he said; 'I have a clear conscience.'²⁰ Later he disappeared into South America, and, in the way of Chinese banditti, entered fiction. Only this was American fiction: *The Year of the Dragon* by Michael Daly, later made into a film which provoked protests by indignant Chinese from New York to London. It is true that the film did nothing for the image of the Chinese minority, buttressing as it did the once-popular stereotypes of Chinese villainy. Nevertheless, its portrayal of New York's powerful and venal Chinatown boss as an ex-Hong Kong policeman and proprietor of a funeral parlour rings a bell with anyone who has heard of Eddie Chan.

Just as the Asian gangland scene in New York is divided into Ghost Shadows and Flying Dragons, into Chinese and Vietnamese, so the Asian underworld on the west coast is a complicated patchwork of Hong Kong and Vietnamese Chinese, the Hop Sing Boys and the Viet Ching, the Wah Ching and the Bamboo Union, the pro-Kuomintang groups and the anti-Kuomintang. The complexity of the rivalries, schisms and networks is further compounded by the web of alliances – the Wah Ching (the gang which dominates San Francisco's Chinatown) with the Bamboo Union, the Californian-based gangs with the Hong Kong triads, the Chinese gangs with the Japanese yakuza, and so on. Heads of different gangs have been known to team up in order to start up and operate joint businesses, a good example being the Oriental Arts and Promotional Corporation, a company which organizes tours by Chinese entertainers from the Far East. This company was represented in New York and Montreal by the head of the Ghost Shadows, in Los Angeles by a lieutenant of the Wah Ching, in San Francisco and Los Angeles by another lieutenant of the Wah Ching, in Hong Kong by a triad, in Toronto by another triad, and so on.

The Hong Kong report on organized crime speaks of 'the proven connections between overseas Chinese organised crime in the United States and Australia with Hong Kong gangs', and of the visits made by 'infamous gangs from the United States, such as the "Ghost Shadows" . . . with known triad office-bearers to assist, most probably, in arranging drug deals'.[21] It is a two-way traffic, and when the Sun Yee On of Hong Kong, for example, began to widen its connections in North America, one contact its officials looked up was Eddie Louie, the brother of Nicky and the chief of the Ghost Shadows in Toronto. Eddie Louie did the visitors proud, entertaining them lavishly and, at the same time as he wound down his activities on behalf of the Ghost Shadows, opening a restaurant called – for the benefit of those who need to take note of such things – Yee On.

If any gangster is a match for the Chinese gangster, it is the Vietnamese one. Adding to the mayhem on the west coast are the acts of violence and even of murder which Vietnamese gangsters have perpetrated against fellow Vietnamese in southern California, where a sizeable community of these refugees has sprouted in the city of Garden Grove in Orange County. Over the years the Vietnamese have been strengthening their position in the commercial life of the city: one family buys over one business in a shopping centre and before long all the businesses in the centre are Vietnamese. They have a reputation for fiddling welfare, and as tough, raw immigrants hardened by their war experiences in Vietnam, some of them make violent criminals. His fear, his ignorance of the strange country in which he has found himself, his distrust of alien authority and his vulnerability to the resentments of the settled communities make the Vietnamese greenhorn the perfect victim of extortion, torture, arson, car theft and armed robbery. There is no doubt that the community harbours a dangerous element; and while the residents of Garden Grove seem to huddle together closely enough, below the surface the place is shot through with deadly rivalries. A militant anti-Communism, it is thought, binds some of the gangsters; certainly the police do not rule out political motivation when a mysterious murder is reported or a case of arson comes to light.[22]

The Vietnamese have been muscling in on the rackets in Toronto too, taking over the control of gambling, for example, from the Kung Lok, the chief Chinese mob in that city. The Kung Lok was started by a triad from Hong Kong, and is a secret society in the old mould, honouring Hung Men traditions for conducting initiation ceremonies. A sergeant of the Metropolitan Toronto Police testifying before the US President's Commission on Asian Organized Crime said that it owned a gambling casino in the Dominican Republic and one in Puerto Rico. It knows very well which side its bread is buttered, and has long cultivated friendships with Canadian government officials, the ones in the Immigration Department in particular.[23]

It would be nice to think that Chinese gangsters were cut off from the world beyond the ghetto; the fact that they mostly prey upon their own people happens to point that way. Yet, as the Kung Lok shows, Chinese gangsters appreciate the advantages to be had from knowing what goes on in the larger world. They have no wish to be caught unprepared by external forces. Here is an illustration. Vincent Jew, a Wah Ching mobster whose business cards showed him to be the Marketing Director of the Hong Kong TV Video Program Inc. in San Francisco and the President of the Grandview Production Company on Sunset Boulevard in Los Angeles, was once taken in for questioning by the Hong Kong police. Among his seized possessions was a copy of the record of the hearings of the President's Commission on Asian Organized Crime, with the relevant bits about the Wah Ching underlined in red.[24]

Often the underworld shows its interest in the wider political arena by making unrefusable offers to politicians and policemen who get in the way. An enquiry into Brisbane's Chinatown in early 1988 shocked both Chinese and native Australians with its revelations of police corruption; even the knighted Queensland Police Commissioner was said to be on the take. The largesse stemmed from a Malcolm Sue, a Chinese racketeer with interests in drugs, bookmaking and brothels disguised as escort agencies and massage parlours. Sue was born in Kwangtung province and brought over to Australia by his parents shortly after the Second World War. He helped in the kitchen of the restaurant his parents ran and honed his martial-arts skills on fighting off thugs who tried to leave without paying. He presently set up a martial-arts school in an old warehouse and laundry building and made a name for himself as a kung fu master with supernatural powers – he could turn one hand hot and one hand cold at will, reported people who knew him. Plenty of business came the way of the security services company he also ran, for restaurants naive enough to think they could manage without his protection were wont to catch fire and burn. He made frequent trips to Papua New Guinea – for his drug deals, it was strongly suspected, though the ostensible purpose was to instruct the police force there in martial arts. An underling who travelled with him revealed that they never carried passports which bore their own names, and that Sue's method for faking passports – visiting cemeteries and taking down the names and dates of dead people – came out of Frederick Forsyth's novel *The Day of the Jackal*. Many illegal immigrants were brought into Australia on such passports. To judge by the staggering amounts he paid to his friends in the police force, Sue's ill-gotten gains were enormous. He was not one to throw his money about, but he had an incautious fancy for horse-racing, and this cost him dear, his gambling debts mounting up so alarmingly that, three years before the enquiry started, he had to do a disappearing act – to China, it was believed.[25]

It is appropriate that Malcolm Sue should be a kung fu master, for martial arts and secret societies have traditionally gone together. In the old days it was a rare martial artist who did not have some kind of triad affiliation – even today, it is generally assumed that the leading men in kung fu films made in Hong Kong or Taiwan, martial artists in their own right, are triad members, if usually inactive ones. This goes also for the performers of lion or dragon dances, spectacles which are traditionally staged at festivals in south China and overseas Chinese communities; these dances have spun off from kung fu, and in Hong Kong the troupes which perform them are appendages of triad societies. The association of triads with the entertainment business goes back to the days when actors and actresses were classed with the demi-monde, bracketed with kung fu practitioners, roving quacks and healers, and socially dubious people in the itinerant professions.

These people formed a sort of anti-society, a counter-culture as it were. They were men of the *chiang-hu*, or 'rivers and lakes', people who lived by their wits and a rough justice which reflected the sense of right and wrong of ordinary Chinese rather than the morality of the courts and statutes. It was in the company of these men, always on the move, that one found the *hsia*, the knight; the fugitive from corrupt law; the martial artist – the heroes, in other words, of kung fu stories.

A martial artist does not easily resist heroicization, and for this reason it is hard not to romanticize the triad, since, in folklore and in fact, the two are sometimes one. This poses a problem for those whose job it is to combat secret societies, for there is no exterminating them so long as citizens keep the idealized image alive. As a certain police inspector I spoke to in Hong Kong put it, the triads are only as powerful as society will allow them to be; the Chinese are not, he said, conditioned to think in terms of cops and robbers the way Westerners are. He gave the example of a well-known Chinese businessman who, in spite of the fact that the Commissioner of Police was somebody he had had to dinner, reacted to the news that his daughter's boutique was receiving the unwelcome attentions of some local thugs by picking up the telephone and dialling not the number of the police but that of Heung Wah Yim, the Dragon Head of Sun Yee On.

Because the secret society continues to be a strand in overseas Chinese communities, people might suppose that Chinese immigrant life as a whole is tainted by it, that the forces of mob crime are ubiquitous. This is clearly not the case, however, and most Chinese who live abroad do so in happy ignorance of the existence of triads and protection rackets, worrying far more about being robbed or mugged by the criminals of other ethnic groups than by those of their own. If there is a streak of criminality in the Chinese minority, there is criminality just as bad or even worse in the larger society. In America attempts have been made by the Italian American Civil Rights League to secure the suppression of the terms 'Mafia' and 'La Cosa Nostra' and their replacement by such ethnically neutral words as 'organized crime'. To use the word Mafia, it has been argued, is to distort the public's view of crime and to make it representative of a special kind of wrongdoing, one that is peculiarly Italian.[26] The danger that criminal secret societies and the Chinese will become synonymous in the thinking of the masses has been less of an anxiety to the Chinese in America than to the Italians, but it is felt all the same, as is demonstrated by their sensitivity to the screening of *The Year of the Dragon*. It is in the nature of multiracial societies for the issue of crime always to be tied to the perpetually simmering, if sometimes submerged, issue of ethnicity.

High on the list of the usual assumptions about the Mafia, along with its alien origin, is its limitless geographical spread. Chinese criminal syndicates, too, are said to be spinning networks that encompass the globe. So far the evidence suggests that the Chinese underworld does represent a source of contacts for the gangs of different countries, but to call this an organized global conspiracy would perhaps be an exaggeration. Some of the new arrivals would no doubt be happy to enter into joint ventures with those already established, but the latter have two ways of looking at them, either as helpful partners or as deadly competitors – and to respond accordingly.

CHAPTER EIGHTEEN

Hong Kong

The chuppie, or Hong Kong yuppie, has much in common with his counterpart in the West. He makes money out of money, riding the crests of the stockmarket to fuel his flashy style of living. In one particular, though, the Chinese Urban Professional is different: unlike the European yuppie, who is quite happy where he is, the Hong Kong chuppie is a potential émigré. Between January 1986 and March 1989, 134,182 of the British possession's 5.7 million people left Hong Kong for Canada, the United States, Australia and Britain.[1]

Emigration is nothing new in Hong Kong, which has been losing people to Europe, North America and Australia for decades, but the exodus of the 1980s is something different from the normal outflows of people leaving to better their lives or to join their relatives, for it is the flight of anxious people from the prospect of life under Communist rule. At midnight on 1 July 1997, British administration will come to an end and Hong Kong will revert to the People's Republic of China. It had been agreed between the two powers that Hong Kong, as a Special Administrative Region of the People's Republic, should retain its capitalist practices and its 'lifestyle' for another fifty years after that, until 2047. The Sino-British Joint Declaration on the future of Hong Kong, applauded at the time of its conclusion in September 1984 as a triumph of diplomacy and the best deal that Britain could have got, was offered to the people of the colony as a Hobson's choice and a jolly good thing, accompanied by a promise that political reforms would be undertaken to ensure that the citizens would be electing their own leaders by the time the place was surrendered to China.

But in the years that followed, it became only too apparent that the settlement was potentially disastrous, and that the British would not be leaving the colony with honour. For a start, Peking, through its shadow administration in Hong Kong, made it more than clear that Britain was not to do anything in Hong Kong that would displease the colony's future masters, such as introducing the locals to parliamentary democracy and leaving them with a government of their own, composed of Hong Kong people, elected by Hong Kong people, which would have the authority to stand up to the People's Republic if it should rat on its promises. Everyone was agreed that Hong Kong should continue to boom after 1997, but the Communists in Peking cannot see how a political system in which a different party can be voted into power at each election can be at all good for maintaining stability (in their own case you always end up with the Communist Party however you voted). What is more, their belief that the people of Hong Kong are far better off leaving politics to their elders and betters while they concentrate on making money is reinforced at every turn by the local lickspittles who are only too ready to see things from Peking's point of view.

There are Hong Kong citizens who, even if their loyalties are not to Peking, are genuinely pleased that the British are going, that orientals are supplanting occidentals at last. Such expressions of patriotism have been cynically used by both Peking and the British government to convince the people of Hong Kong that their affinity with their mainland cousins amounts to an agreement that they have more in common as ethnic Chinese than they are at odds as Marxists and capitalists. But there are also those who feel the resentment of the host whose guests try to make over his way of living with an effrontery all the more insufferable by reason of their economic and social inferiority. To these people, their free press, their civil liberties, and above all the fact that they are almost thirty-five times richer than their mainland cousins, are sign enough that they are superior. Besides, seven out of every ten of them either fled from the China of Chairman Mao in the first place, or have at least one parent who did; so it isn't as though they don't know what it is to live in a Communist state. They knew, long before the world woke up to the fact on 4 June 1989, that Communists are Communists, however hard they might have worked in the past decade to make their country more prosperous, more stable and more open to the outside world.

The fourth of June 1989 was the day the People's Liberation Army was ordered to turn its guns on the people, unarmed civilians who had been calling for less corruption and more democracy. In a spectacular surge of political dissatisfaction, patriotism and nationalism, thousands of student demonstrators, supported by the Peking citizenry, had occupied the symbolic heart of Chinese state power, the Square of Heavenly Peace (Tiananmen), and had frightened the Communist Party into declaring martial law and sending heavily armed columns of the Army to enforce it. Hong Kong Chinese, feeling themselves umbilically tied to the destiny of the democracy movement in China, were gripped by the drama from start to finish, sending student sympathizers up to Peking with material and moral succour, doing what they could to protect the wanted students and to get them out of the country when the purges and executions began. In a way the Communist Party was right when it accused the people of Hong Kong of taking part in 'illegal activities aimed at subverting the Chinese government'.

The true politicization of Hong Kong, whose people were said to be interested only in making money, and who wanted nothing to do with politics, may be dated to 21 May 1989, when more than half a million citizens took to the streets to demonstrate their support of the student revolt on the mainland. In the succeeding days and weeks protest marches, processions, mass rallies and even a Band Aid-style concert kept up the show of solidarity. The British colony had never seen anything like it before. At a stroke, it seemed, the people of Hong Kong had found their pride and their sense of community. China with its poverty and tyranny had not been a country worthy of their loyalty, but the idealism, heroism and patriotism of the students in Peking was something they could identify with; and when they took to the streets it was to demonstrate not only their love of liberty, but also their renewed sense of Chineseness. 'There has never been a moment in history', proclaims an issue of *Democracy Tides*, a paper which began publishing in May, 'when we have felt ourselves more completely a part of China, more completely Chinese.'

The irony of it is that the strength of feeling, so different from the apathy with which Hong Kongers had responded to home-grown campaigns for democracy, only goes to show how profoundly they could be moved by what goes on in China, and how much they remain, for all their insistence on autonomy, emotionally a part of China. Democracy was their cause, but their protests were shot through with feelings of a more elemental and primordial kind – tribalism, pride of race, love of country. The people of Hong Kong had been touched in their Chinese core; and when, marching, they broke into slogan or song, it was often to chant 'We are Chinese'. In the brief euphoric moment that was brought to an end on 4 June, there were hopes that the students marching, singing and fasting in Tiananmen Square were a portent of a better China.

After 4 June everybody thought again. Outrage apart, the people of Hong Kong were racked by fear and insecurity. What better proof was there that the Chinese regime was not to be trusted, that China was a deeply unstable country, subject to a political convulsion every ten years or so? At the next spasm, Hong Kongers will be among the victims. Queues of applicants for immigration visas not only lengthened at the consulates of the most popular destinations (Canada, America, Australia and New Zealand), but even the Paraguay Consul received four to five times more enquiries than previously.[2]

The emigration business is well developed in Hong Kong; and there is no shortage of emigration law specialists, foreign tax experts, foreign investment managers and foreign business planning consultants to advise a family set on acquiring a new nationality. Advertisements like this frequently appear in the local dailies: 'IMMIGRATE TO CANADA Our newly revised self-help guidebook will maximize your chances of success. This is the definitive guidebook for independent applicants. *Discover if your occupation is in demand.* Step-by-step advice on how to apply. And much more. Author has 26 years experience in immigration affairs. Only HK$105. Order now, or pick up at our office.'[3] And if you don't meet Canadian qualifications, you can look to immigration agencies like Chih-wei for help with acquiring Belize nationality, but it is probably best to shop around because there are about ten other foreign passports you could buy for between US$15,000 and $60,000 apiece.[4]

It is not that the Hong Kongers want to live in Belize; what they want is an insurance policy, a bolt-hole and an escape route in the event of an 'Armageddon scenario'. Eager seekers of foreign passports, the people of Hong Kong have habitually returned to the colony to live once they have been granted right of abode elsewhere. There are thousands of Canadian Chinese living and working in Hong Kong, for instance, and the biggest alumni society of the University of Manitoba is not, as might be expected, in Winnipeg, but in Hong Kong. Similarly, it was argued by those who campaigned for the right of residence in Britain following the brutal crackdown in Peking that the mass of the 3.25 million people who are British subjects at law – but who were deprived of their right of abode in Britain by successive Immigration Acts – want to stay in Hong Kong, but only if they can be assured the right of residence in Britain as a last resort; granting them that right, it was argued, would make it less likely that they would want to leave. It was indeed to keep them in Hong Kong that the French government decided to give citizenship to the hundred Hong Kong Chinese executives who worked in French banks and corporations in the colony. And ironically, a quarter of the five hundred thousand citizens of Hong Kong's neighbour, Macao, were promised proper European Community passports by Portugal –

passports which will allow them, if they so choose, to live in Britain after 1992, when the people of the EC will be free to work and reside in each other's countries.

A section of British public opinion supported the cause of the campaigners for the right of residence in Britain – had it no honour, many commentators asked of Her Majesty's government, no sense that it had a moral duty to its colony? Others shared the view of the Conservative politician who said, 'After ten years of controlling immigration into this country, we would have all the nasties back . . . all those hideous people we used to see at election time. And that is a heavy price to pay.'[5] It is perhaps a measure of the country's intolerance, or crowdedness, that an offer to let in fifty thousand heads of household, or 225,000 people in all, caused a row in Parliament when it was announced by the government. The Hong Kong populace was reproachful, but which imperial power withdraws from a colony without leaving a sense of betrayal behind?

Where would they all go? A Mr Douglas Mason of Britain's Adam Smith Institute suggested moving Hong Kong to a remote part of the west coast of Scotland. A Mr Albert Cheng, the spokesman of Hong Kong's Right of Abode Delegation (or ROAD), said that Britain could consider leasing an area the size of Hong Kong near Darwin in Australia. But the Promised Land remains the United States, to which nearly forty thousand migrated between January 1986 and March 1989. Larger numbers have gone to Canada, which has kept its door hospitably open to rich foreign investors, and as I write Hong Kongers are streaming into Vancouver at the rate of a hundred a day. You know their class by the huge houses and condominiums they live in (in smart neighbourhoods such as Kerrisdale and Shaughnessy), and by the name the Canadians give them, 'the yacht people'. These are people to whom tax laws matter, and one reason Canada has been such a lure is that it allows an immigrant, once he has become a citizen, to live abroad without paying Canadian tax. The rich of Hong Kong have been snapping up expensive Vancouver properties, very often sight unseen, in a way which recalls the profligacy of those Arabs who bought up slabs of Hyde Park and Knightsbridge in London. This rankles with the locals, many of whom have been heard to say that they do not want Vancouver to become another Hong Kong or Tokyo.

Immigration to Australia has intensified too – the number of immigrant visas issued to Hong Kong residents between 1986–87 and 1987–88 nearly doubled, from about 5,200 to ten thousand.[6] Australia is a popular choice with not only the Chinese of Hong Kong, but with those of Malaysia, Singapore and other Asian countries; and the influx from the British colony is only a small part of the country's total Asian immigration, numbering some 47,500 in 1987. The figures do not include the many 'illegal' immigrants from China itself, the ones who entered Australia for the purpose of studying English, but who are to be found washing dishes in Sydney's Chinatown or working for sweatshop wages in local factories. An unfounded rumour that Australia would grant an amnesty to its illegal immigrants on its two-hundredth anniversary in 1988 had run like wildfire in China's cities, and many of these 'students' had thronged the Australian embassy and consulate in Peking and Shanghai in the hope of an Australian future. Most of these newcomers to Sydney are too busy picking up a living to attend any classes; but the schools, interested only in taking their money, ask no questions. They melt easily enough into the city's Chinese community, which is large and is getting larger, making its presence felt in the suburbs, where Chinese, Vietnamese, Thai and Indonesian restaurants already outnumber the pubs.[7] Most Hong Kong immigrants choose to settle in Sydney or Melbourne, while Perth, right at the other end of the country, is favoured by Chinese Malaysians and Singaporeans.

The Australians never used to think they had much in common with their Third World neighbours, pursuing a White Australia policy to exclude the teeming coloured peoples on their doorstep. But they are being goaded by some of their politicians into redefining their place in the world, and into coming to terms with the fact that about a third of the country's new immigrants are Asian. The greater part of Australia's trade is now with Asia, and economic realities are obliging Australians to adjust their social attitudes. All the same Aussies are by and large uneasy Australasians, and the tide of Asian immigration discomforts many a white suburbanite of Perth and Sydney. These feelings are sometimes expressed in a graffito scribbled on a wall – CHINKS HIRED, YOU'RE FIRED – and sometimes in a call for a curtailment of Asian immigration. In Western Australia Chinese immigrants were alarmed by the appearance in 1987 of hundreds of hate posters put up in and around Perth by the Australian Nationalist Movement, saying ASIANS OUT, OR RACIAL WAR. The purchase of large slabs of property in Sydney by rich Chinese has, in the eyes of the resentful indigenes, a feeling of takeover about it, and tough new legislation restricting the buying of Australian residential property by aliens has had to be enacted to quell aggrieved complaints of real estate prices being driven beyond the reach of the average Australian family by speculative overseas money.[8] The swagger of opulent Chinese from Hong Kong brings out the bigot in the Aussie, and back in the British colony, an eavesdropper can sometimes hear a returned immigrant wife complaining to her friend over tea and cakes at the Hilton coffee shop that she had to stop using her Rolls-Royce for her trips into downtown Melbourne for her morning's shopping because the natives somehow made her feel that she was overdoing things.

It is easy to forget, so obsessively does life revolve around emigration, that Hong Kong is a classic immigrant city, a recipient as well as a despatcher of refugees and migrants, a departure point and a destination. Ever since it fell into British hands in the mid-nineteenth century, both in- and out-migration have been a constant of life in Hong Kong. Down the years, a ceaseless flow of Chinese emigrants, refugees, merchants and students has moved through its port in and out of China and over the seas. It was a hub and place of transit of the coolie trade; and it was the sea outlet of Kwangtung, the jumping-off point for the hundreds of thousands of peasants who left China dreaming of a better life in the New World.

Its own population has grown by immigration rather than by natural increase, and it was not until 1981 that it was established, for the first time, that more than half its people had been born in the colony. Huge numbers had begun life outside the colony, in Kwangtung province chiefly, but also in Shanghai and other points of origin in the Chinese hinterland. What turned Hong Kong into a great manufacturing centre was the influx in 1949 of immigrant industrialists from Shanghai, and the stream of refugees from across the border who supplied, cheaply and plentifully, the necessary labour in the factories. To Hong Kong over the decades have come successive waves of illegal immigrants from the People's Republic, sneaking across the border by land and sea, and escaping repatriation only if they are lucky. Hong Kong without its energetic migrants would not be the Hong Kong that people know, the economic prodigy and the place of perpetual striving. It has all the hallmarks of an immigrant Chinese community – the organization into dialect and clan groups, the division into secret societies. (In preparation for my research trip to Bangkok, where I knew speakers of Teochiu, pronounced Chiuchow in Cantonese, to predominate, I called at Hong Kong's Chiuchow Association in Western District to get some names and contacts and to get plugged into the worldwide Teochiu network.) Because it flies a foreign flag, it has always been the place to which Chinese have fled to escape troubles on the Chinese mainland, be they uprisings, wars, changes of government or reversals of policy or ideology.

Countless immigrants have made good in Hong Kong. Many migrants have found the city an avenue to fame and success, and its rich are in the league of the internationally wealthy, on a par with sultans and sheikhs. The richest of all is Li Ka-shing, who has been listed by America's *Fortune* magazine as one of the world's wealthiest billionaires, with a personal fortune coming within the first third of the top forty, well ahead of those of Rupert Murdoch and Donald Trump.[9] The embodiment of the classic rags-to-riches story, he is one of those people whom it is a little difficult to see clearly because their reputations are apt to be enlarged almost annually.

It is tempting to say that he is just one of those people who simply cashed in successfully on Hong Kong's abundant opportunities; but while his spectacular rise did have its share of luck, it was also compounded of hard work, energy, flair and above all a near-perfect sense of timing. A small man but of great presence, conventionally bespectacled and attired, with a lean face and a shiny forehead positively radiating with self-assurance and energy, K.S., as he is known to his friends, was born a Teochiu in the port of Swatow, the eldest of three children. Arriving in Hong Kong in 1940 as a twelve-year-old refugee from China's civil war, Li Ka-shing learnt early the meaning of responsibility, for he had barely had two years of schooling in the British colony when his father died suddenly, and he found he had to support his mother and younger siblings. He went to work in a plastic watchband and flower factory. A family breadwinner at fourteen, Li did as much overtime as he could cram into a day; and to visit him at his daily work would have been to see at once yet another of those Chinese to whom one could apply the superlatives of industry. He became first a salesman, then a general manager; by the time he turned twenty he was well on his way to starting his own company. This happened two years later, in 1950, when Cheung Kong was established.

Cheung Kong, one day to become the flagship company of his sprawling business empire, began life in the plastics business; but, early bird that he was, Li Ka-shing was soon catching the worms that he really wanted. Mr Li was an eager purchaser of properties, and it was on the quick speculative profits to be made from the buying and selling of these that he founded his success. In this he exemplifies many expatriate Chinese, whose taste for real estate comes from deep well-springs – something to do perhaps with their sense of uprooting.

From property development he moved on to other pastures, and his acquisition in 1979 of a nearly twenty-three per cent stake in Hutchison Whampoa, a British trading giant, gave Cheung Kong the jewel in its crown. If one were to sum up what he owned in the latter half of 1987, one would find that in Hong Kong alone his interests extended from the wharf to the market-place to encompass the city's main container-ship terminal, its largest supermarket chain, its largest drugstore chain, and its electric utility. Abroad, he had forty-three per cent of Canada's Husky Oil Limited; an interest in Pearson, the parent company of Penguin books and the *Financial Times*; a share in Britain's multinational telecommunications conglomerate Cable and Wireless; a little over a fifth of Britain's Cluff Oil; and numerous skyscrapers and apartment blocks in Canada and the United States. His is the single biggest corporate entity in Hong Kong, and this is gratifying to many of the colony's Chinese, who have waited for years to see Jardine Matheson upstaged.

As 'the man with the golden touch', Li is like a share-tipster to the many small investors who hope to rise with his fortunes, so that everything he does, from putting in a bid at a land auction to responding to the lurches of the stockmarket, is of avid interest to the business columnists. Like royalty, the very rich engender their own mystique, or have it thrust upon them. In the press reporting of his corporate moves, there often hovers the innuendo that there is more to his deals than meets the eye, an uncertainty as to what else he has up his sleeve. Hearing his deals described as 'unpredictable', 'secretive' and 'mysterious', you may think that that is just the journalist speaking, but still it is true that Mr Li seldom feels the need to explain himself, and that whenever he can he avoids undue publicity. His moves into oil and telecommunications are no exception to the rule that what he does intrigues and puzzles his audience; and because not all his investments have paid, time and again he has people wondering if what they are about to see is the end of his winning streak.

The suspicion that his forays into Canada heralded his own desertion of Hong Kong gave these speculations an ominous undercurrent; to a public sensitive to any sign of ebbing confidence in Hong Kong's future, a bid for a Canadian company signified capital flight, not the caution of a man who doesn't want all his eggs in one basket. Once, answering the question that was in everybody's mind, Li told an assembled group of reporters in 1986 that he and his wife held Hong Kong-British passports, and that he thought this good enough.[10]

It is often difficult to know whether an immigrant Chinese is a patriot or an opportunist. He may be staunch enough in his loyalty to Chinese culture, but he would hardly be an émigré if he did not prefer his host government to the regime in Peking. Li does business with China, sharing, as do so many of Hong Kong's tycoons, various self-interests with Peking. Both his obvious importance to Hong Kong's economic life, and his donation of some US$30 million to build a university in his native Swatow, have won him audiences with Peking's top leadership, including Deng Xiaoping; but one doubts if he flew to Peking in any real spirit of affinity.

His is the world of *laissez-faire* capitalism, and a speculator's world at that. In that world, race and nationality can sometimes appear almost immaterial. The heads bent confidentially together at a cocktail party, the looks exchanged meaningfully across a negotiating table, the hands shaken suavely over a clinched deal – these are encounters on neutral ground as it were, untouched by feelings of cultural difference. In reply to a question about his relations with Westerners, Li Ka-shing said, 'I have numerous Western friends who have become intimates', and that the quality of such relationships was no different from what he enjoyed with his Chinese friends.[11] It tells something about him that the man he placed at the head of Hutchison Whampoa is English; Simon Murray he met when the Englishman was selling air-conditioners and lifts for a Jardines subsidiary, about ten years before he invited him to be head of Hutchison. Born to an Army family, Murray had come to Hong Kong by way of the French Foreign Legion.

But Li is not a natural cosmopolitan, all the same, and he is no exception to the rule that East and West mingle only so far in Hong Kong. His social tastes are those of a conventional Chinese businessman, and to go by what he says of his aspirations, he seems to fall pat into the tycoon-philanthropist mould so characteristic of overseas Chinese – 'I would like to devote my energies', he replied, when asked to say where he was going, 'to make more money for my shareholders as well as for myself. Then I will use my money, my position, energy and experience to benefit the community.'[12] He does donate enormous sums to charity, most of it anonymously. He craves social respectability, and when he was found guilty of insider trading by a government tribunal in the spring of 1986, he was stung to the quick. Insider dealing is no crime in Hong Kong, and what divides the private from the corporate there is not a line but a blur; but just the suggestion of skulduggery was enough to upset him, for he had worked hard at his image of an honest tycoon.

Life offered him a single purpose when he was poor – to become rich. He is now fabulously rich, but his future biographer would detect no wish at this stage of his life to be anything other than what he is, a man who strives for still greater fortune, not because of the money as such, but because as yet there is no other criterion of excellence. His past struggles he considers meaningful, but 'What I am doing now', he tells me in his written answers to my questions, 'is also very meaningful indeed.' Yet he would reiterate that money does not buy happiness – 'One can only derive a sense of security from it.' 'You need to have an objective,' he continues, doing his best to define his idea of happiness for me; 'Otherwise the higher you get the lonelier you will feel.' He himself is not lonely: 'Perhaps,' he adds, with maybe a stab at humour, 'it is because I am not wealthy enough.'

Hong Kong is also the place where flotsam and jetsam Chinese, many of them migrants twice or even three times over, fetch up in escapes from inhospitality elsewhere – the Vietnamese Chinese expelled from Saigon, the Indian Chinese made uneasy by India's border war with China, the Malaysian Chinese disaffected by their country's discriminatory policies, the tens of thousands of Indonesian Chinese who were repatriated in the 1960s and who, disenchanted with life in Mao's China, migrated a second time to Hong Kong when they realized that their patriotic enthusiasm had been a terrible mistake. To the casual observer these may seem an indistinguishable part of Hong Kong's Chinese mass, but actually they are anything but unified, one group set apart from another by what each has absorbed of the culture of its previous country of residence.

Nor has it only been people who have found a haven here; from time to time a great whoosh of money comes in from Southeast Asia to be deposited in Hong Kong for security and quick returns, propelled by fears of anti-Chinese feeling, Communist insurgency or plain political instability. Partly it is its preponderant Chineseness, and partly the shelter afforded by the Union Jack for pursuing unfettered business opportunities, that makes Hong Kong so special to Chinese domiciled elsewhere.

There are Nanyang Chinese for whom Hong Kong is a second home or pleasure haven, the place where the shopping is better, the diversions more stimulating, the food more to their taste. Such an overseas Chinese is Vicwood Chong, also called Julian T. Santillan, a third-generation Hokkien owner of timber mills in the Philippines' Muslim south. Mr Chong may not, at first glance, impress the average citizen of Hong Kong as an important man, for he lacks the polish of the colony's entrepreneurial grandees, being of the rough-hewn Nanyang variety whom it would be hard to imagine looking neat and dapper in a pin-striped suit, shooting elegant spotless cuffs or sipping vintage French wine. But he conducts a thriving little empire from his office in the unfashionable end of Queen's Road, and the trail of his business dealings leads all the way from Mindanao in the southern Philippines to Oregon in the United States.

Flying an average of 250 hours a year, he divides his time between the Philippines, Hong Kong and America. But while it is common to find the very wealthy of many nationalities responding most warmly to the sophistication of northern metropolises and European pastimes, putting behind them the more parochial pleasures of home, Mr Chong is like those Hong Kong people who return from their trips to Europe or America relieved to be back in their native surroundings after the tedium of all those Western recreations. He makes no bones about it; 'Hong Kong', he says, 'is the best place in the world.' There is no pretence at cultivation, no wish to appear other than what he is, a man to whom, as he puts it, 'Money is the only measure of value; nothing else is real.'[13] In Hong Kong more than in any other place, his confidence in the correctness of this judgement is reinforced at every turn by the visible evidence of what his wealth can do.

In Hong Kong one is always coming across Chinese who, though settled abroad, have come to live here because it offers them opportunities, satisfactions and challenges denied them elsewhere – there are few places in the world, Jan Morris rightly notes in her book *Hong Kong*, 'where such a large proportion of the population is at least doing what it wants to do, where it wants to be'.[14] Such a Chinese is Po-chih Leong, a film maker born and brought up in England.

Po-chih Leong was born the son of a Chinese merchant sailor who jumped ship in London, and who became a legal immigrant because he ran a laundry in Northampton for the British Army during the war. He also opened one of the first Chinese restaurants in London's West End, and it was on the floor above this, in Denmark Street, that Po-chih Leong lived as a child. Later he went to a Quaker prep school in Reading, then read Philosophy at Exeter University – not to please himself, but to please his mother (his father had died), who was Chinese enough to insist he got himself a degree before he indulged his love of film-making. He married an English girl who in fact came to know more about his ancestral country than he, for she went to China to teach, and saw something of the Cultural Revolution at first hand.

He joined the BBC as a trainee assistant film editor, but it was difficult to get into the movies in England in the 1960s, the talk of mortgages and cars among his colleagues got him down, and when he found work with a television station in Hong Kong he emigrated. Finding himself surrounded by people of his own race who spoke a language he didn't understand was a culture shock; and yet 'it was a real adventure too', he later recalled, for there was in the Hong Kong of the mid-1960s all the fluidity and opportunity of a rapidly changing society. There, after a stint as a producer, he established his own production company, shot commercials for a living, and eventually made his mark as a feature film director. He returned to London to make his ninth feature, *Ping Pong*, a film about English-Chinese cultural differences, and instantly ran into a typically British difficulty over casting; there were people he would like to have used but couldn't simply because they were not members of the actors' union.[15]

The film turns on the question of how you remain yourself when you are bounced about, as one of the characters puts it, like ping-pong balls between the demands of conflicting cultures and identities, and what it means to belong. As a product of two cultures, these are questions Po-chih Leong will have pondered in relation to himself. Once upon a time he had no doubt at all that he was as English as the next Londoner, but though his nickname in Hong Kong, he claims, is *gweilo*, Cantonese for 'foreign devil', it would be strange if twenty years in Hong Kong had not made him bicultural. He may not exactly have discovered his *métier* in Hong Kong, but it was in Hong Kong that he came into his own; and can a man call himself an outsider to a place that has given him the chance of fulfilment?

Hong Kong is the Hollywood of the Greater Chinese world, its superstars more familiar to the mass of overseas Chinese than a Streep or a Redford. Impervious to the stimulations of the West, many Chinese abroad look to distant Hong Kong to satisfy their cultural tastes. You can see this by picking up a local Chinese newspaper in London, New

York, Paris, Bangkok, Manila, or any city where one is published, for hardly an edition is complete without some mention of the latest goings-on of Hong Kong's pop singers and movie celebrities. Hong Kong is the world capital of overseas Chinese popular culture, the heart of a whole climate and ambiance of thinking. There are Chinese girls in London and Paris whose notion of fashion is shaped far more by women's magazines from Hong Kong than by the trend in their adoptive city, and while their European neighbours tune into the latest episode of *Dallas* on TV, they are likely to be watching the Hong Kong approximation on home video.

Malaysia and Singapore are, with Taiwan, the biggest consumers of the video movies generated in Hong Kong, but they are exported to wherever there is a sizeable Chinese community, and this means that they go to every continent. If you missed an episode of *The Feud Between Two Brothers* in Hong Kong, you could probably make up for it in Fiji, and you could watch the entire sixty-one-part *The Rise of the Great Wall* in London as easily as you could in New York. Made in Cantonese, the dialect of Hong Kong, the videos come dubbed into several languages, from English and Mandarin to Thai and Vietnamese. On top of the soap operas and drama serials of Hong Kong television, audiences in many countries lap up feature films made specially for the export market, and 'specials' such as the Christmas and New Year variety shows and the Miss Hong Kong beauty contest.[16]

It was from Hong Kong that the kung fu craze was extended into the cinemas and consciousness of other countries, and Hong Kong is the nursery of the new kind of martial-arts movie, the contemporary kung fu comedy. The lowbrow comedies with their quick-fire dialogue in regional dialect and local references, and the action-packed movies with their dizzy special effects and stomach-churning stunts, give pleasure to Chinese viewers in nearly thirty countries, offering the common man in distant parts and alien cultures a form of entertainment he enjoys and understands.

There is almost no Chinese community where the popular myths of kung fu, taking form in story, strip cartoon and film, have not seeped into the minds of the Chinese young. The heroes are freelance do-gooders fulfilling a solemn mission – exacting revenge, righting wrongs, challenging tyranny, pursuing the vendettas of the widows and orphans of murdered men. They are bound by a strict moral code which stresses loyalty and fraternity, but they have something of the freedom of the hoboes of interstate highways in American 'road movies': they are always doing their own thing and being their own men. They are figures of romance, and their stories play to favourite old sentiments, the ones called up by loyalty and chivalry, patriotism and honour, the kind of uplifting emotions that make a man feel he is justified in what he is doing as he fights to kill. It is hard for Chinese parents to know whether their children's appetite for such stories is to be encouraged, because it is often impossible to tell a hero from an assassin, or where chivalry ends and murderous vengefulness begins. Fight scenes are central to kung fu films and stories, and the *frisson* comes with the climaxes of violence, in gore and head-breaking. In martial-arts movies much of the killing and dying takes on a balletic quality, which makes it easier on the eye but ultimately more appalling.

In the cinema the kung fu movie is an established genre, like the Western from which it has consciously borrowed elements. In the 1970s it gained an audience in the West with films like *Enter the Dragon*; this starred Bruce Lee, the best known of the kung fu actors of his time.[17] Bruce Lee was born in 1940 in the Chinese Hospital of San Francisco, the son of a Eurasian mother and a Cantonese opera singer who just happened to be performing in America. He was christened Bruce by a doctor in the hospital; later he was also to be known by his screen name Hsiao-lung, Young Dragon. His cinema career began early, with an appearance in a film called *Golden Gate Girl* when he was only three months old. As an adolescent in Hong Kong he was, as he himself put it, 'a punk who went looking for fights', a street-smart kid who had been receiving instruction in kung fu since he was twelve and who was once nearly arrested for his part in a gang fight with a rival martial-arts school.

Advised by his mother to claim his American citizenship, he left for San Francisco when he was eighteen. He was to stay in America for thirteen years, attending high school in Seattle, studying for a degree (in Philosophy and Psychology) at the University of Washington, and teaching martial arts at a club he founded in Seattle's Chinatown. He married, and upon graduation moved with his American wife to Los Angeles, where he played bit-parts in Hollywood movies and continued to give instruction in kung fu.

It was only when he returned to Hong Kong that he won his recognition. He did this with four films – he died mysteriously while making his fifth, when he was only thirty-two – of which the most accomplished is generally taken to be *The Way of the Dragon*. As in all such films, the story is simple: our hero arrives in Rome from Hong

Kong to help protect his relatives, owners of a Chinese restaurant, from harassment by a gang leader. The first half of the film follows the young hero as he displays his greenhorn gaucheness, provoking racist jokes about 'Chinese naiveté' and inciting ridicule for his inability to read a menu and his unfamiliarity with Western lavatories. He starts on his way gently, but the seeming diffidence turns out to be a trap for his enemies. The audience waits for the imago of the perfected martial-arts master to burst forth in a spasm of power and skill . . . and burst forth he does, in a series of fight scenes which reaches its climax in an electrifying sequence in which our hero takes on and kills an American of almost equal prowess in the Coliseum.

Bruce Lee was a small man, sickly as a child; and it is tempting to see his strenuous pursuit of muscular perfection as a way of compensating for this physical meagreness. It was when he was fighting, he wished his audience to believe, that he was most himself. He took undisguised pride in his body, and there is a scene in *The Way of the Dragon* in which he wakes up early and exercises himself with great self-absorption – with narcissism even. Bruce Lee drove himself hard, and part of this drive, one critic has suggested, came of his feelings of personal and racial inferiority. His racial pride, a motif which runs through his films, was fuelled, so the argument goes, by his failure in Hollywood and the discrimination he encountered in America as a member of an ethnic minority.[17]

Hong Kong is the largest node of the Greater Chinese network, its connections and influences extending across the seas like the circles of a pebble dropped in a pool, to kinsmen, classmates, friends, business partners, fellow provincials and to all the secondary ties these have forged until, farther and farther out, they come to encompass all the world. Not an immigrant Chinese community I have described in these pages but has some ties with Hong Kong, whether it be a business link or a bond of consanguinity.

It also stands at the heart of another network, the network of what Peking would term a counter-revolutionary conspiracy, an expatriate Chinese movement to support the democratic cause in China. Certainly it has become a repository of opposition to the regime in Peking, a place where China's fugitive student leaders have become popular heroes, and where countless people have subscribed to funds to support the democratic movement and to help those activists who succeeded in escaping abroad to carry it on in exile. If expatriate Chinese nationalism (coalescing this time around the idea of patriotic-democratic protest, for the sake of a better and freer China) were to enjoy a resurgence, not only will Hong Kong Chinese be among its chief champions, but Hong Kong itself will be a prime nursery. In fulfilling this function it stands in the classic line of the treaty port, in the line of cities like inter-war Shanghai, whose foreign concessions served as a sanctuary for Chinese (including early Communists) who found themselves unwelcome elsewhere in China, and as a refuge for heterodoxy and political subversion.

Paradoxically, if Chinese all over the world look to Hong Kong as their metropolis, it is partly because of its proximity to China: Hong Kong is the threshold and outlet of the motherland, the junction of diaspora and homeland. It is the place where China meets Greater China. It is an immigrant city, yes, but one where the populace do not feel themselves to be an uprooted or transplanted community, cut off from the old country; its affairs have been too entangled in China's for that. And while Chinese in Southeast Asia have had to transfer their political and emotional allegiance from China to their adopted homeland, Hong Kong Chinese never really had a new homeland to which to reorient their loyalties. Certainly the colonial government has never demanded it of them.

But this is not to say that Hong Kong Chinese are without their own identity. The city has evolved a generation of what I shall call 'treaty-port Chinese', a type last seen in pre-1949 Shanghai, a type of which, in Shanghai as in Hong Kong, history has had time to produce only one generation. Treaty-port Chinese are those who succeed in becoming truly bicultural, behaving in a Western mode without a debasement of their own. They are different from the Anglicized subjects of the British Empire in Southeast Asia; for one thing, they are not creolized in their speech, and for another, their emotional pole remains China. And yet, while Peking calls Hong Kong Chinese 'compatriots', to suggest a closer relationship than that which links it to the 'overseas Chinese' of Nanyang, the treaty-port Chinese of Hong Kong are a world away from the people of China; while their Chineseness is denied by nobody, it is unlike anything you will find in China proper. It is *sui generis*, fitting neither the overseas Chinese nor the ancestral Chinese mould. There is not the sense of distance from origins that one feels in an overseas Chinese proper, but neither is there the feeling of being hopelessly bogged down by that inescapable fabric of existence in China itself – a past that imprisons the present. The treaty-port Chinese are better able to do that difficult thing, snap the tough thread of Chinese history and achieve the happy balance which has always eluded their cousins in China: the balance between modernity and Chineseness, between moving with the times and remaining themselves.

In a way Hong Kong is the last remaining specimen of that historical genus, the treaty port. And when it ceases to be that, come 1997, so we shall see the last of the treaty-port Chinese – who, if they haven't done so already, will emigrate and bring forth a generation of American, or Canadian, or Australian, or British Chinese.

Inevitably, now that all is at risk, the good life that Hong Kong offers, its stimulations, its superiority to anything to be found in the West, enter many conversations. Regarded for so long in only the most utilitarian terms, simply as a place in which to make money, Hong Kong is at last evoking the affection it deserves. Even those least emotionally committed to the colony say that they are leaving it under protest, and in the Hong Kong of the late 1980s one senses poignantly among many of its people a new readiness to identify with it, a new willingness to call it home.

Almost every other day some long-time resident leaves for a second start upon another shore, with handshakes and poses for photographs at Kaitak Airport, and a sense of chapters closing. Left behind is a presentiment of encroaching death in persisting life, and a thunderstorm feeling of foreboding. Writing of Hong Kong in the autumn of 1988, Jan Morris notes that the talk there of 'the loss of friends, the emigration of the young, the clever, the highly educated and the ambitious' was 'an early chill premonition of 1997 – rather like Aids in San Francisco'.[18]

Epilogue

A thousand years ago there were no Irishmen in Australia; no Thais in Bangkok; no white, nor black, Americans in America. Migration is the great travel saga of all time. People have always moved to find land and work; and to flee from war, famine and oppression. They have also, at times, been forcibly relocated; for several centuries people were transported into slavery from one part of the world to another by Europe's imperial powers, and when the slaves were freed a substitute was found in Indian and Chinese indentured labour. The scale of the population relocations flowing from voluntary movement, mass transportation or expulsion has been immense. Since 1800 no fewer than twenty-eight million people have migrated to America. The First World War displaced nearly a million people; the Second World War, forty-five million. Today about four to five million foreign workers from South and Southeast Asia live abroad, supplying cheap labour to the world's richer countries. And an estimated twelve million refugees, a third of them in Africa, are awaiting resettlement or seeking asylum.

The Chinese dispersal across 109 of the world's countries[1] is part of that saga; the near-ubiquitousness of Chinese overseas, who are said today to number thirty million,[2] is an index of how much they have been part of the universal population flows of the nineteenth and twentieth centuries. The hegira continues, and theirs is not a story to which we can set a conclusion. An epilogue summarizing the main modes of migration must suffice.

The doyen of overseas Chinese scholars, Wang Gungwu, has said that, historically, there have been four main varieties of migrant Chinese.[3] The earliest to appear was the migrant of commercial calling: the trader, the artisan, the miner and the skilled worker. The seaports and cities of Nanyang were thickly settled with their kind – the Hokkiens in Batavia and Manila, the Teochius in Bangkok, the Hakkas in West Borneo – and it was they who developed the great trading networks of Southeast Asia. Theirs was the dominant pattern of migration in the eighteenth and nineteenth centuries, and, before the industrial revolution and the age of European imperialism, the only significant and indeed the only possible pattern of migration.

The second type of migration was represented by the contract labourer or the coolie of peasant origin. More like today's guest workers than true settlers, most of those who went abroad in this way returned to China when their contracts ended. Batches went to Sumatra and the Malay peninsula, but as an immigrant category they figured less importantly in Southeast Asia (where they were ancillary to the commercial migrant) than in North America and Australia (where they became familiar as gold rushers and railroad workers). If there was a fundamental difference between the American and Southeast Asian movements, it lay chiefly in this, that the former was predominantly working-class, while the latter was strongly mercantile. Falling within the era of quickened transformation by the rapid expansion of plantation economies and mining, and by growing Western wealth and industrialization, the movement to the Americas came to an end by the close of the nineteenth century, and to Southeast Asia by the 1920s.

The third type was the *hua-ch'iao*. The term is almost always rendered as 'overseas Chinese' and employed to refer broadly to all Chinese living outside China, but its epitome or model was a sojourner who enjoyed the protection of the Chinese government (through its embassies or consulates), and who lived in spirit in China, politically, culturally and emotionally attached to his mother country. The notion was of comparatively recent coinage, and the pattern it embodies had its heyday in the period between about 1900 and 1950, the years of overseas Chinese nationalist upsurge. The archetypal hua-ch'iao was Tan Kah Kee, the very model of the patriotic overseas Chinese, one who, in spite of having made most of his money in British Singapore, gave his primary loyalty to China.

When a Chinese called himself a hua-ch'iao, he did so with pride, for it signified his inclusion in the great Chinese political family; he was somebody that the Chinese government recognized for one of its own and, what was more, somebody whose money and expertise China needed and courted. Chinese settled in America were especially happy to call themselves hua-ch'iao, because the attributes and advantages that went with the name – national pride, official Chinese recognition and consular protection – gave them the self-respect which, as a despised and persecuted minority of coolie origin, they had so far lacked.

The Chinese in Southeast Asia, on the other hand, had less to gain from a fervid embrace of the hua-ch'iao ideology. Here their social status was higher, here many mixed on easy terms with the local authority (whether native or colonial), and here fewer needed nationalism to shore up their sense of purpose or dignity. But because China took a hand in raising their Chinese consciousness, people who had been totally removed from Chinese influences – the peranakans of Java, for instance – were encouraged to re-sinicize themselves and to recover the Chinese heritage they hadn't thought they possessed. All this gave the Southeast Asian Chinese a reputation for unassimilability, and made them, in the eyes of the government of their adopted country, politically untrustworthy. And after the left wing of the nationalist movement triumphed, to the envy that they aroused in being commercially successful was added the suspicion that they might be Communists. Though in time the force of Chinese nationalism dissipated, to give way to the realization that the adopted country and not China was home, anti-sinicism lingered, so that even those who wished to integrate were constantly reminded of their origins and treated as second-class citizens.

The newest of the Chinese immigrant types is the *hua-i*, the naturalized foreign national of Chinese origin, a category which embraces not only the foreign-born descendants of immigrants but educated professional re-migrants from Hong Kong, Taiwan, Malaysia, Singapore, and other countries of Southeast Asia. Many of these will have been immigrants twice or three times over, originating in China, and going on to the United States, Canada or Australia after a spell in East or Southeast Asia. Malaysian Chinese in Perth, Taiwan Chinese in Monterey Park, Laotian Chinese in Paris, Hong Kong Chinese in Toronto – these are all representatives of the breed. They are the people who have shifted the focus of Chinese migration from Southeast Asia to America, Australia and Western Europe. Cosmopolitan, very often Western-educated, they are 'cultural Eurasians' who think that 'it would be more satisfying to be Eurasians among Westerners than among Asians' like Taiwanese or Malays – perhaps because they are 'too Western to be comfortably Chinese and yet too Chinese to accept conditions where Chineseness is being penalized'.

Much of this book has been concerned with how overseas Chinese have adapted to life abroad, and it remains to fit them into the scheme of things at home. Historically, that scheme began with the fact (though it doesn't end with it) that China was a country of continental land mass, with an exposed frontier that was perhaps the world's longest.

For some two thousand years, the security problem of the empire has been to guard the Inner Asian frontier against the incursions of the nomads of the grasslands beyond the Great Wall. For two thousand years China looked inwards to the steppes and deserts of Asia, and more and more perhaps to itself. It habitually turned its back to the sea, and when troubles came from there, as they did in the form of piracy during the seventeenth century, the court reacted not by looking outwards but by closing the frontier, banning foreign trade and travel, and depopulating the coast.

It little knew that it would be faced with its greatest challenge when the gunboats of imperial Britain forced it open to oceanic influence. Out of this clash came maritime China, consisting partly of the coastal treaty ports, partly of the overseas Chinese communities of Nanyang. The port cities became gateways and centres of Western enterprise, part of the swirl of forces that were reshaping the lands of the Far East and bringing their economies into the system of Western commerce.

The vigour of the Western incursion was a cruel blow struck at Chinese self-esteem. Forced to look at themselves anew, as one nation among many, rather than as All Under Heaven, a universe synonymous with civilization, the intelligent and patriotic young of China wondered how their country might stand its ground in the international struggle for existence. And as they tried to come to terms with history, so modern Chinese nationalism was born, compounded partly of the old pride of race and cultural superiority, and partly of the Social Darwinian concern, then fashionable, with the competition for survival. To 'save' China from being weeded out in that competition came to be a nationalist resolve, one that the overseas Chinese were urged to share. Political and social change was seen to be the key to the success of this enterprise, and the overseas Chinese were persuaded – successively by K'ang Yu-wei, Sun Yat-sen, Mao Tse-tung, and the brave idealists of Tiananmen Square – that the means to this change was, respectively, constitutional government, republicanism, Communism, and democracy.

All down the years the Chinese abroad have hoped that China might yet regain its lost vigour, and to that end they have consistently set themselves against the old and stood with the new, siding invariably with those they saw to be the champions of reform and revolution. They have been a kind of foil to earthbound China, part of the oceanic influence pulling the country into the ambit of modern exchange systems, values and technology. Of all migrant Chinese types the trader-entrepreneur has been the most robust, and it has been in the arena of business, too, that emigrant Chinese have made their deepest impression on China.

Not philosophy but money and methods have been the chief contribution of the emigrant Chinese to China – money to start industries and the techniques to run them, the wherewithal to plot revolution or other political conspiracies. Nowadays they like to think of themselves as the agents of enlightenment, projecting modern styles of thought and ideology into the medieval bog of the mainland, but actually it has always been the other way round, and China has ever been the spur of their intellectual life and the catalyst of their political awakening. It was the students demonstrating for democracy in Peking, for example, who raised the political consciousness of the people of Hong Kong, not the other way round.

China has repeatedly dashed their hopes, and remains to this day a country to occasion despair, a country to get away from, so limited still are its material and social possibilities, so harsh and despotic its political exactions. Even so, the millions who live outside it will never cease to wish it well, to want for it a place among the great nations, not only for the sake of their own pride and dignity, but because they find it hard to resist its power to compel tribal feeling. If they revolt against it, that itself is a reference and a tribute to the potency of what has been left behind.

Each time they visit it, they ask themselves, 'Why are we here? Why do we keep coming back?' Why must they return to this cruel, tormented, corrupt, hopeless place as though they still needed it? Could they never achieve immunity? And yet had China meant nothing to them, any other place thereafter would have meant less, and they would carry no pole within themselves, and they would not even guess what they had missed.

When they leave it after their visit they feel that they have left something of themselves behind, yet they also realize that they could never live there. Deep in their hearts they know that they love China best when they live well away from the place.

Notes

Chapter One: Pioneers

1. Chin-chiang, 54–5.
2. Ta Chen, 1923, 4.
3. Fairbank, 1969, 29–38.
4. MacNair, 4.
5. Meskill, 20–21.
6. Skinner, 4–5.
7. Purcell, 181.
8. Struve, 116–19, 156–59.
9. Chin-chiang, 76–81.
10. Ta Chen, 1923, 42.
11. qtd Skinner, 15–16.
12. *Ta Tsing Leu Lee, Being the Fundamental Laws and a Selection from the Supplementary Statutes of the Penal Code of China*, translated by Sir George Staunton, London, 1810, 543–44.
13. Mote in Drake, 153.
14. Li Chi, 127.
15. Li Chi, 127.
16. Schafer, 1967, 7.
17. Meskill, 17.
18. Chin-chiang, 77.
19. Freedman, 10.
20. Schafer, 1967, 9.
21. Lach, 753.
22. Ta Chen, 1939, 24.
23. Shirokogoroff, 50–51.
24. Ta Chen, 1939, 31.
25. Schafer, 1970.
26. Ward, 106.
27. Skinner, 40.
28. Wu Tse, 122.
29. Skinner, 48.
30. Wickberg, 172.
31. Freedman, 4.
32. Freedman, 6.
33. Freedman, 105.
34. qtd Freedman, 8.
35. qtd Freedman, 106.
36. qtd Freedman, 106–7.
37. Fairbank, 1978, 134.
38. Meskill, 64.
39. Ward and Stirling, vol. 1, 61–63.
40. qtd MacNair, 9.

Chapter Two: East Meets West

1. Lach, 593.
2. Lach, 633.
3. Steinberg, 45.
4. Wickberg, 83–84.
5. Ta Chen, 1923, 55.
6. qtd MacNair, 52.
7. Fang, 30.
8. qtd Moore, 82.
9. Steinberg, 143.
10. C. P. Fitzgerald, 171–72
11. Fang, 121.
12. Snow, 43.
13. Fang, 120, 122.
14. Wang Gungwu, 25.
15. Skinner, 1957, 13.
16. Purcell, 104.
17. Purcell, 426.
18. Purcell, 507.
19. Wickberg, 9, 155.
20. Ta Chen, 1923, 100.

21. Purcell, 524.
22. Purcell, 511.
23. Ta Chen, 1923, 100.
24. Purcell, 514.
25. qtd Purcell, 514.
26. Purcell, 519.
27. Purcell, 522.
28. qtd Johannes T. Vermeulen, 'The Chinese in Batavia and the Troubles of 1740', *Journal of the South Seas Society*, ix, 1, 1953, 1–68.
29. Wen, 161.
30. Vermeulen.
31. A. R. T. Kemasang, 'The 1740 Massacre of Chinese in Java: Curtain Raiser for the Dutch Plantation Economy', *Bulletin of Concerned Asian Scholars*, xiv, 1, 1982, 61–72.
32. Vermeulen.
33. Kemasang.
34. Ward, 105–19.
35. Yen, 44.
36. qtd Payne, 22.
37. Runciman, 124.
38. Craig Lockard, 'The 1857 Chinese Rebellion in Sarawak: A Reappraisal', *Journal of Southeast Asian Studies*, 6, 1 March 1978, 85–98.
39. qtd Payne, 94.
40. Payne, 92.
41. qtd Payne, 86.
42. St John, 312.

Chapter Three: Floodtide

1. Wang Sing-wu, xi.
2. Fairbank, 1978, 109.
3. qtd Fairbank, 1978, 195.
4. Fairbank, 1978, 264–75.
5. Campbell, 3.
6. Wang Sing-wu, 5–6.
7. Tsai, 8; Wang Sing-wu, 111.
8. Stewart, 16.
9. Fairbank, 1978, 236.
10. Campbell, 89.
11. qtd Campbell, 90.
12. qtd Campbell, 129.
13. Wang Sing-wu, 48.
14. qtd Wang Sing-wu, 72.
15. Wang Sing-wu, 39–40.
16. Anthony Chan, 40.
17. reproduced in Wang Sing-wu, 43.
18. Campbell, 118.
19. Cuba Commission, 7.
20. Cuba Commission, 9.
21. Campbell, 4, 156.
22. Conrad, 31.
23. Wu Tse, 25; Cuba Commission, 12.
24. Cuba Commission, 16.
25. Jerome Ch'en, 245; *Bulletin of Chinese Historical Society of America*, Sept 1988.
26. MacNair, 16.
27. Fairbank 1978, 256.
28. Campbell, 120.
29. Ta Chen, 1923, 17.
30. Ta Chen, 1923, 173.
31. Tsai, 7.
32. Campbell, 153.
33. Skinner, 43.
34. Tchen, 4.
35. Tchen, 4.
36. qtd Tsai, 12.
37. Anthony Chan, 48–49.
38. qtd Tsai, 17.
39. Tsai, 27.
40. qtd Lydon, 64.
41. Lydon, 9.
42. qtd Wang Sing-wu, 266–67.
43. Wang Sing-wu, 261.
44. Wang Sing-wu, 308.
45. Bickleen Fong Ng, 15.
46. Travers, 40.

Chapter Four: Shores

1. Snow, 55.
2. qtd Snow, 56.
3. Fang, 69.
4. Fang, 207.
5. Fang, 70.
6. Fang, 74, 215
7. Snow, 61.
8. Snow, 56.
9. qtd Snow, 45.
10. Snow, 46.
11. Ta Chen, 1923, 129.
12. qtd Snow, 47.
13. Ta Chen, 1923, 138; Snow, 49
14. Ta Chen, 1923, 139.
15. qtd Tuchman, 354.
16. qtd Ta Chen, 1923, 129.
17. Ta Chen, 1923, 131.
18. Ta Chen, 1923, 132.
19. qtd Ta Chen, 1923, 140.
20. Fang, 241.
21. Ta Chen, 1923, 137.
22. qtd Summerskill, 12.
23. Tuchman, 351.
24. MacNair, 96.
25. MacNair, 102.
26. Cuba Commission, 17.
27. Cuba Commission, 19.
28. Cuba Commission, 20.
29. Cuba Commission, 18.
30. Cuba Commission, 43.
31. Cuba Commission, 80.
32. Wu Tse, 79.
33. Stewart, 17.
34. Stewart, 78.
35. qtd Stewart, 81
36. qtd Stewart, 90–91.
37. qtd Stewart, 93.
38. Stewart, 101.
39. Stewart, 122.
40. Stewart, 221.
41. Stewart, 217.
42. qtd Stewart, 226–27.
43. Stewart, 225.
44. Nicholas Bodington, personal communication.
45. Glick, 2.
46. Glick, 2.
47. London.
48. Glick, 53–54.
49. David Wu, 19.
50. David Wu, 21, 52,
51. David Wu, 63.
52. qtd David Wu, 28.
53. David Wu, 28.
54. qtd David Wu, 34.
55. Summerskill, 47.
56. Summerskill, 225.
57. Ta Chen, 1923, 142.
58. qtd Summerskill, 56.
59. Summerskill, 90.
60. Ta Chen, 1923, 148; Summerskill, 100.
61. Summerskill, 93.
62. Ta Chen, 1923, 144.
63. Summerskill, 158.
64. qtd Summerskill, 94.
65. qtd Summerskill, 132.
66. qtd Summerskill, 122.
67. Summerskill, 163.
68. Summerskill, 121.
69. Summerskill, 117.
70. Summerskill, 127.
71. Wilson, 250–51.
72. *Evening News*, 7 Oct 1920.

Chapter Five: Limehouse and San Francisco

1. Ng Kwee Choo, 17.
2. *Notes and Queries*, 25 April 1886; 9 May 1886.
3. P. J. Waller, 'The Chinese', in *History Today*, Sept 1985, 8–15.
4. S. Craggs and I. Loh Lynn, 'A History of Liverpool's Chinese Community', Merseyside Community Relations report, 1985.

5. qtd Virginia Berridge, 'East End Opium Dens and Narcotic Use in Britain', *The London Journal*, vol. 4, 1, 1978, 3–28.
6. qtd Berridge.
7. qtd Berridge.
8. *The Times*, 25 Nov 1913.
9. qtd Berridge.
10. Annie Lai and Pippa Little, 'China Annie: The East End Opium Trade, 1920–35', *Oral History Journal* xiv, 1, 1986, 18–30.
11. qtd Berridge.
12. qtd Berridge.
13. *The Times*, 24 and 28 Aug 1918.
14. Lai and Little.
15. *The Times*, 21 Dec 1918.
16. Berridge.
17. qtd Berridge.
18. qtd Isaacs, 116.
19. G. Wallas qtd Tuchman, 352.
20. Waller.
21. Waller.
22. *Cardiff Maritime Review*, 8 July 1911, qtd J. P. May, in Holmes, 116.
23. Cutting attributed to *The Evening News*, Jan 1901, in the Tower Hamlets Borough Library Collection.
24. qtd J. P. May in Holmes, 119.
25. *The Evening News*, 14 Oct 1920.
26. *The Evening News*, 7 Oct 1920.
27. Bret Harte qtd Isaacs, 114.
28. Stevenson, 131.
29. Stevenson, 130.
30. James G. Blaine, Republican of Maine, qtd Tsai, 59.
31. Tchen, 7.
32. *The Blue and Grey Songster*, 1877, qtd Perrin, 32–34.
33. qtd Tchen, 7.
34. Jack Chen, 140.
35. Tsai, 68.
36. Tsai, 57.
37. Tchen, 8.
38. qtd Isaacs, 100.
39. *Annales d'Extrême Orient*, qtd *The Times*, 22 Nov 1878.
40. Tchen, 8.
41. Tchen.
42. Otis Gibson qtd Jerome Ch'en, 258.
43. qtd Tchen, 85.
44. qtd Tchen, 123.

Chapter Six: Immigrant Society

1. Siu, 299.
2. Daniels, 81.
3. Tsai, 99.
4. Lai, Lim and Yung, 66.
5. Benton, 114.
6. Tsai, 183.
7. Siu, xx.
8. Jack Tchen in Siu, xxiii.
9. Bryce, 880–81.
10. Siu, 156.
11. Sherry, 180.
12. Sherry, 179.
13. qtd Warren, 14.
14. Warren, 205.
15. Warren, 242.
16. Andaya and Andaya, 138–39.
17. qtd Vaughan, 88.
18. Yen, 200.
19. Kohl, 94.
20. Kohl, 111.
21. qtd Skinner, 139.
22. Yen, 177.
23. Yen, 113–14.
24. Skinner, 142.
25. qtd Vaughan, 40.
26. Skinner, 120.
27. Jerome Ch'en, 244.
28. Yen, 224.
29. Cocteau, 49, 37.
30. Yen, 224.

31. Yen, 225.
32. Stewart, 102.
33. Jerome Ch'en, 244.
34. Tchen, 96.
35. Vaughan, 8.
36. Stewart, 103.
37. Yung, 19.

38. Yung, 19.
39. Yen, 253.
40. Spence, 42.
41. Grieder, 166.
42. Grieder, 167.
43. Spence, 72.

Chapter Seven: The Jews of the East

1. Young, 173.
2. Bird, 201.
3. Skinner, 418.
4. qtd Young, 9.
5. qtd Purcell, 395.
6. Purcell, 418.
7. Bird, 257.
8. De Wit, 52.
9. De Wit, 55.
10. qtd Ch'en Ching-ho, 93.
11. Ta Chen, 1923, 105.
12. Skinner, 104.
13. Ta Chen, 1923, 89.
14. Vaughan, 15.
15. Skinner, 117.
16. Bird, 257.
17. qtd Purcell, 409.
18. Vaughan, 44.
19. Vaughan, 43.
20. De Wit, 48.
21. Kipling, 275.
22. qtd Purcell, 410.
23. Vaughan, 2.
24. Bird, 190.
25. Ch'en Ching-ho, 94.
26. Wickberg, 72.
27. Wickberg, 71–72.
28. T'ien, 65n.
29. Cator, 19.
30. qtd Purcell, 408.
31. qtd Cator, 21.
32. qtd Purcell, 408.
33. Purcell, 431.
34. qtd Ta Chen, 1923, 60.
35. Purcell, 7.
36. Skinner, 103–5.

37. qtd Skinner, 104–5.
38. Light, 23–44.
39. Skinner, 101.
40. Godley, 85.
41. Cheng Min, 117.
42. Godley.
43. Cheng Min, 121.
44. qtd Ta Chen, 1923, 18.
45. Godley, 156, 178.
46. Godley, 94.
47. Cheng Min, 122.
48. Godley, 346.
49. Godley, 178.
50. Queeny Chang, 51.
51. Queeny Chang, 143.
52. Huang, 7; Wright, 893.
53. C. P. Fitzgerald, 171.
54. Steinberg, 198.
55. Mary Turnbull, 'Western Colonialism and the Chinese Diaspora', inaugural lecture delivered on 4 March 1988 at the University of Hong Kong.
56. Yen, 267.
57. C. A. Middleton Smith qtd Godley, 45.
58. *Straits Times*, 2 and 26 July and 3 Aug 1904.
59. Liao Chien-yu (Leo Suryadinata), 'Yin-ni hua-i fu-hao ch'u t'an', *Ya-chou wen-hua*, 9 April 1987.
60. Koo, 71.
61. Koo, 28.
62. Godley, 52.
63. Koo, 77–78.
64. Koo, 43.

65. Koo, 27.
66. Koo, 50.
67. Koo, 44.
68. Godley, 52.

69. Cheng Min, 120.
70. Koo, 45.
71. Koo, 48.
72. Skinner, 163–64.

Chapter Eight: Hybrids

1. Roland Bayhon, 'Cojuangco Genealogy', paper delivered at a conference on Local Source Materials of the Asia-Pacific Region, in Hong Kong, 6–9 April 1989.
2. Wickberg, 32.
3. Crisostomo, 80.
4. Fu-chien sheng T'ung-an hsien wei-yuan-hui, *T'ung-an wen shih tzu-liao*, 1986.
5. qtd Ta Chen, 1923, 77.
6. Bickleen Fong Ng, 124–25.
7. qtd Stewart, 225.
8. qtd Snow, 60.
9. Snow, 60.
10. S. Craggs and I Loh Lynn, 'A History of the Chinese Community', Merseyside Community Relations report, 1985.
11. Wright, 160.
12. Skinner, 27.
13. qtd Skinner, 3.
14. Antonia Tan in Carino.
15. qtd Wickberg.
16. Wickberg, 32.
17. qtd Ta Chen, 1923, 109.
18. Wickberg, 181–82.

19. Steinberg, 166.
20. Wickberg, 174.
21. Steinberg, 167–8.
22. Wickberg, 148.
23. Wickberg, 144.
24. Coates, xxix.
25. Coates, 304.
26. Esteban A. de Ocampo in Liao.
27. Rizal (a), 45.
28. Rizal (a), 122.
29. G. William Skinner, 'Change and Persistence in Chinese Culture Overseas: A Comparison of Thailand and Java', *Journal of South Seas Society*, 16, 1960, 86–100.
30. Clammer, 1980, 20.
31. Chia, 2.
32. Tan, 48.
33. Bird, 181.
34. Vaughan, 2.
35. Yao Souchou, 'Ethnic Boundaries and Structural Differentiation: An Anthropological Analysis of the Straits Chinese in Nineteenth-Century Singapore', *Sojourn*, August 1987, 209–29.
36. qtd Tan, 43.
37. Purcell, 413.

Chapter Nine: Three of the Men

1. Datin Aw Kow, tape recording of interview in Archives and Oral History Department, Singapore, Ref: A 000041/04.
2. K'ang, 45.

3. *Straits Times*, 9 Oct 1971.
4. *Straits Times*, 27 Nov 1987.
5. Vaudine England, 'The Aws: Remnants of An Empire', *Asia Magazine*, 28 July 1985.

6. Datin Aw Kow, recording.
7. Aw It Haw, tape recording of interview in Archives and Oral History Department, Singapore, Ref: 1 000051/05; *Straits Times*, 18 Mar 1987.
8. *Straits Times*, 10 Dec 1961.
9. Datin Aw Kow, recording.
10. K'ang, 84, 184.
11. *Daily Telegraph*, London, 1 Nov 1975.
12. K'ang, 110.
13. K'ang, 108.
14. Vaudine England.
15. *New Nation*, Singapore, 23 July 1971.
16. Slater.
17. *New Nation*, 31 May 1976.
18. *Asiaweek*, Hong Kong, 22 May 1987.
19. Yang, 7.
20. Yong, 44.
21. qtd Yong, 66.
22. Yang, 81.
23. Yong, 328.
24. Lee Poh Peng, personal communication, 1987.
25. Lady Percy McNiece, tape recording of interview in the Archives and Oral History Department, Singapore, Ref: 000190/04.
26. *Straits Times*, 25 Nov 1960.
27. Loke, 15.
28. Loke, 15.
29. Loke, 106.
30. *Straits Times*, 25 Nov 1960.
31. Loke, 15.
32. Loke, 14.

Chapter Ten: **Some of the Women**

1. Lethbridge, 74.
2. Yung, 18.
3. Lethbridge, 82.
4. Lethbridge, 82, 95.
5. *South China Morning Post*, 16 Sept 1971.
6. Yen, 257–58.
7. Stockard.
8. Marjorie Topley in Wolf and Witke, 262.
9. qtd Topley in Wolf and Witke, 255.
10. Topley in Wolf and Witke, 256.
11. Lai Ah Eng, 15.
12. Topley in Wolf and Witke, 264.
13. Lai Ah Eng, 79.
14. qtd Lai Ah Eng, 86.
15. Koo, 100.
16. qtd Koo, 123.
17. *Pai-hua chou-k'an*, March, 1988.
18. Leyda, 33.
19. Leyda, 82.
20. McCunn, 28–30.
21. Yung, 80.

Chapter Eleven: **Trojan Horse?**

1. Stephen Fitzgerald, 211.
2. Ta Chen, 1939, 113.
3. Ta Chen, 1939, 101.
4. Stephen Fitzgerald, 121–22.
5. MacNair, 11.
6. MacNair, 121–22.
7. Stephen Fitzgerald, 141.
8. Williams, 48.
9. Steinberg, 252, 332.
10. Comber, 26.
11. Comber, 28.
12. Heng, 25.
13. Suhaini Aznam and Rodney Tasker in *Far Eastern Economic Review*, 23 Nov 1989.
14. Barber, 27.

15. Alexander, 112.
16. Barber, 26.
17. Richard Harris qtd Stephen Fitzgerald, 235.
18. Steinberg, 407.
19. Barber, 238.
20. Comber, 39.
21. Stephen Fitzgerald, 70–71.
22. Ben Kiernan in Cushman and Wang, 211.
23. Stephen Fitzgerald, 146.
24. Suryadinata, 1986, 136.
25. Wang Gungwu in Mackie, 204.
26. Mozingo, 153.

27. Mozingo, 154.
28. Mozingo, 168.
29. qtd Mozingo, 171–72.
30. Wu and Wu, 71, 87.
31. Wu and Wu, 77.
32. Mackie, 117.
33. qtd Alexander, 4.
34. Alexander, 5.
35. Mozingo, 250.
36. Purcell, 568.
37. qtd Yung, 83.
38. Tsai, 134.
39. Tsai, 135.
40. von Brevern, 6.

Chapter Twelve: Crooks or Capitalists?

1. Botan, 123.
2. Yoshihara, 58–59.
3. Jesudason, 149.
4. Jesudason, 159.
5. Yoshihara, 129.
6. David Wu, 35.
7. Robison, 45.
8. Robison, 231.
9. *Lien-ho tsao-pao*, 8 Nov 1987; Liao Chien-yu (Leo Surya-dinata), 'Yin-ni hua-i fu-hao ch'u t'an', *Ya-chou wen-hua*, 9 April 1987; Ian Vechère, 'Lim Sioe Liong, Suharto's Secret Agent', *Insight*, May 1987, 9–17; Robison, 296–303.
10. Robison, 240–41; Guy Sacerdoti in *Far Eastern Economic Review*, 1 Aug 1980.
11. Anthony Rowley in *Far Eastern Economic Review*, 7 April 1983; Robison, 297–315.
12. *The Times*, 29 Aug 1988.
13. Vechère.
14. Kevin Hewison, 'The Financial Bourgeoisie in Thailand', *Journal*

of Contemporary Asia, xi, 4, 1981, 395–412; Prasartset.
15. *Lien-ho tsao-pao*, 29 Nov 1987; Rob Salamon, 'Chin Sophonpanich, The Bangkok Connection', *Insight*, June 1978, 8–18.
16. Hewison.
17. Paisal Sricharatchanya in *Far Eastern Economic Review*, 28 July 1983.
18. Phipatseritham and Yoshihara, 29.
19. Jonathan Friedland and Paul Handley in *Far Eastern Economic Review*, 13 Apr 1989.
20. Limlingan.
21. G. L. Hicks and S. G. Redding, 'Uncovering the Sources of Southeast Asian Economic Growth', *Euro-Asia Business Review*, ii, 4, Oct 1983.
22. Lim and Gosling, vol. 1, 5–6.
23. Lim and Gosling, vol. 1, 245–73; 1–9.
24. Burgess, 433.
25. Burgess, 36.

Chapter Thirteen: **Cultural and National Identities**

1. Mackie in Cushman and Wang, 220.
2. Lim and Gosling, vol. 2, 4.
3. Christina Blanc Szanton in Lim and Gosling, vol. 2.
4. Robert O. Tilman, 'The Chinese of the Philippines: Between the Scylla and Charybdis', *Solidarity*, v, 11, Nov 1970, 38–46.
5. See Chin-bee in Carino.
6. Skinner, 1957, 365–73.
7. qtd Comber, 12.
8. qtd Diane K. Mauzy and R. S. Milne in Gale, 99.
9. Gale, 87.
10. Judith Nagata, 'The New Fundamentalism', *Asian Thought and Society*, vol. 5, 1980, 128–41.
11. Judith Nagata in Gale, 123.
12. Naipaul, 45.
13. Theroux, 84.
14. *Financial Times* Special Survey, 22 Nov 1982.
15. Minchin, 3
16. George, 23.
17. qtd Drysdale, 118–19.
18. qtd George, 29.
19. Josey, 115.
20. qtd George, 17.
21. Minchin, 256.
22. *Straits Times*, 24 Nov 1979.
23. qtd Minchin, 262.
24. Goh Keng Swee qtd *Straits Times*, 24 June 1976.
25. Lee Chiaw Ming qtd *The Mirror*, 8 Jan 1973.
26. Clammer, 1983, 112.
27. *The Economist*, 10 Sept 1988.
28. Ward, 41–42.
29. Clammer, 1983, 108.
30. qtd *The Mirror*, 4 Sept 1978.
31. qtd Minchin, 254.
32. George, 17–20.
33. Minchin, 35.
34. Minchin, 311.
35. George, 19.
36. qtd Minchin, 309.
37. qtd Minchin, 277.
38. qtd Minchin, 41.
39. qtd George, 38.
40. qtd Minchin, 66.
41. Lee Kuan Yew, 16.
42. qtd George, 28.
43. qtd Minchin, 306.
44. George, 17.
45. qtd Minchin, 280.
46. Minchin, 254.
47. George, 169.
48. George, 176.
49. qtd Minchin, 265.
50. Minchin, 286.
51. Minchin, 304.
52. Minchin, 333.
53. Minchin, 261.
54. *The Economist*, 19 Sept 1987.
55. *Straits Times*, 26 Sept 1987.
56. qtd *Far Eastern Economic Review*, 29 Jan 1987.
57. qtd George, 25.
58. Minchin, 303.
59. qtd George, 30.
60. George, 30.

Chapter Fourteen **Melting Pot**

1. Burgess, 37.
2. Joel Kotkin and Yoriko Kishimoto, 'America's Global Advantage' in *California Business*, Sept 1988, 26–53.
3. US Immigration and Naturalization Service, qtd *Christian Science Monitor*, 25 Oct 1985.
4. US Bureau of Census, 1980.

5. Kwong, 4.
6. Glazer and Moynihan, 16.
7. Tsai, 164.
8. Frank Viviano in *Far Eastern Economic Review*, 24 Mar 1988.
9. Kotkin and Kishimoto.
10. qtd *Time*, 31 Aug 1987.
11. *Straits Times*, 7 Dec 1987.
12. *The Economist*, 18 Feb 1989.
13. House of Commons Home Affairs Committee, 'Chinese Community in Britain', 1985, xii.
14. House of Commons Swann Committee, 'Education for All: The Report of the Committee of Enquiry into the Education of Children from Ethnic Minority Groups', 1985, 666.
15. Taylor, 229–89; *Times Educational Supplement*, 29 Jan 1988.
16. *Financial Times*, 15 June 1987.
17. *The Economist*, 3 Dec 1988.
18. qtd Halberstam, 229.
19. Halberstam, 230.

20. *Financial Times*, 15 June 1987.
21. An Wang, 33.
22. Howe, 645.
23. *The Economist*, 9 Dec 1989.
24. Kingston, 1981, 85.
25. Margaret Loke in *New York Times*, 30 April 1989.
26. Le Anne Schreiber in *New York Times Book Review*, 23 Apr 1989.
27. Kingston, 1989, 27.
28. Frank Chin in an interview with Robert Murray Davis, *Amerasia Journal*, vol. 14, 2, 1988, 91.
29. Kingston, 1989, 5.
30. Le Anne Schreiber.
31. Glazer and Moynihan, 289.
32. *The Economist*, 11 June 1988.
33. *Sunday Times*, 16 April 1988.
34. Kuo, 82.
35. Daniels, 342–43; *Who Killed Vincent Chin?*, a film directed by Christine Choy and Renée Tajima, 1988.
36. Howe, 641.
37. Howe, 642.

Chapter Fifteen: **Chinatowns**

1. Buckley, 83.
2. Gillenkirk and Motlow.
3. Wu Tse, 386–94.
4. Tsou, 176.
5. Skinner, 106.
6. Skinner, 81.
7. Smithies, 63.
8. Paisal Srichratchanya, personal communication, 1987.
9. Report to the Fourth Teochiu International Convention, 1987, *T'ai-kuo Ch'ao-chou t'uan-t'i kai-k'uang pao kao shu.*
10. Bhamorabutr, 52.
11. Kwong, 25.
12. Douglas Martin, *New York Times*, 20 Feb 1988.
13. qtd Howe, 124.
14. Jones, 24.

15. Kwong, 24.
16. Kuo, 122.
17. Watson, 1975, 116.
18. Watson, 1977, 183.
19. Watson, 1977, 188.
20. 'Vietnamese Refugees in Britain – A Housing Report', Refugee Action Paper, 30 Oct 1984; papers of the Chinese Association of Tower Hamlets.
21. 1981 Census, qtd Alfred Chan.
22. Shang, 34.
23. Ng Kwee Choo, 74.
24. Taylor, 189.
25. 'The Chinese Community in Tower Hamlets and the Lack of Social Services to Them', paper submitted by the Chinese Welfare Project, July 1985.

Chapter Sixteen: **Food**

1. Schafer, 1963, 167.
2. *Encyclopaedia Britannica*, 15th edition, 1980.
3. Tom and Barbara Harrison, 'The Prehistory of Sabah', *Sabah Society Journal*, vol. 4, 1969–70.
4. Newbold.
5. Skinner, 346; Wu I-lin, 74.
6. Skinner, 346.
7. Lin and Chuang, 95–113.
8. McCunn, 33–39.
9. Lydon.
10. Lin Hai-yin, 125.
11. Tchen, 94.
12. Burgess, 72.
13. Driver, 80–81.
14. Shang, 27.
15. Orwell, 69.
16. Bernard, 82–83.
17. Mo, 29.
18. *Siyu*, 19, Nov 1987.
19. Tower Hamlets Chinese Youth Organization Gazette, 1 Oct 1987.
20. Shang, 27.
21. *Time Out Guide to Eating Out in London*, 1984, 96.
22. Yu Renqiu, 'Chop Suey' in *Chinese America: History and Perspectives*, Chinese Historical Society of America, 1987, 87–99.
23. *Boston Globe*, 9 May 1988.
24. Ch'en Pen-ch'ang, 75.

Chapter Seventeen: **Triads**

1. *Asiaweek*, 11 Nov 1989.
2. Morgan, 103.
3. Chang Sheng, 68.
4. *The Economist*, 9 Apr 1988.
5. Hong Kong Organized and Serious Crime Bureau, personal communication, 1988.
6. Kaplan and Dubro, 272.
7. *South China Morning Post*, 6 July 1986 and 18 March 1988.
8. Kaplan and Dubro, 272.
9. *South China Morning Post*, 6 July 1986.
10. *South China Morning Post*, 27 and 28 Oct 1987; *Asiaweek*, 11 Nov 1988.
11. Shown to author by Hong Kong Organized and Serious Crime Bureau, 1988.
12. *Bangkok Post Sunday Magazine*, 13 Nov 1977.
13. *Sunday Times*, 26 July 1987.
14. McCoy.
15. Bertil Lintner in *Far Eastern Economic Review*, 24 Sept 1987.
16. Kung-an pu, 11–13; Bertil Lintner's letter to author, 5 May 1988.
17. *South China Morning Post*, 27 Feb 1988.
18. President's Commission, 448–51.
19. President's Commission, 435.
20. *Chiu-shih nien-tai*, Dec 1984.
21. *South China Morning Post*, 19 April 1986.
22. President's Commission, 484.
23. President's Commission, 439.
24. Martin Cowley, personal communication, 1988.
25. *South China Morning Post*, 21 Feb 1988.
26. 'How One Family Stamps Out the M—', *Newsweek*, 5 Apr 1971.

Chapter Eighteen: **Hong Kong**

1. *Sunday Times*, 9 July 1989.
2. *South China Morning Post*, 26 June 1989.
3. *South China Morning Post*, 12 Sept 1987.
4. *Pai-hsing*, 10 Feb 1987.

5. *The Economist*, 23 Dec 1989.
6. *South China Morning Post*, 5 Feb 1988.
7. Robert Elegant, 'Urban Images on the Pacific Rim', *Discovery*, Jan 1988.
8. *South China Morning Post*, 4 Oct 1988.
9. *The Times*, 19 Aug 1988.
10. *Asian Wall Street Journal*, 5 Dec 1986.
11. Li Ka-shing, written answer to author's questionnaire, 1987.
12. Li Ka-shing, written answer to author's questionnaire, 1987.
13. Interview with author, 1987.
14. Morris, 72.
15. Interview with author, 1988.
16. *Asiaweek*, 9 Oct 1987.
17. Tony Rayns in Hong Kong Urban Council, 110–12, 175.
18. Jan Morris, *Independent*, 18 Sept 1988.

Epilogue

1. Cheng Min, 199–208.
2. *Fa-chih Jih-pao*, Peking, 22 Feb 1988.
3. Wang Gungwu, Keynote lecture given at an international conference on Chinese Emigration held at the University of Hong Kong, 14–16 Dec 1984.

Works Cited

Alexander, Garth, *Silent Invasion*, London, Macdonald, 1973

Andaya, Barbara Watson, and Andaya, Leonard V., *A History of Malaysia*, London, Macmillan Education, 1982

Barber, Noël, *The War of the Running Dogs: Malaya, 1948–1960*, London, Collins, 1971; Fontana Books, 1972

Benton, Barbara, *Ellis Island*, New York, Facts on File, 1987

Bernard, Jeffrey, *Low Life*, London, Pan, 1987

Bhamorabutr, Abha, *The History of Bangkok*, Bangkok, Somsak Rangsiyopas, 1987

Bird, Isabella L., *The Golden Chersonese: Travels in Malaya in 1879*, London, John Murray, 1883; Kuala Lumpur, Oxford University Press, 1967

Botan, *Letters from Thailand*, Bangkok, Editions Duang Kamol, 1982

Brevern, Marilies von, *Once a Chinese, Always a Chinese? The Chinese of Manila*, Manila, Lyceum Press, 1988

Bryce, James, *The American Commonwealth*, vol. 2, New York, Macmillan, 1911

Buckley, Charles Burton, *An Anecdotal History of Old Times in Singapore 1819–1867*, Kuala Lumpur, University of Malaya Press, 1965

Burgess, Anthony, *The Malayan Trilogy*, London, Heinemann, 1956, 1958, 1959; Penguin, 1972

Campbell, P. C., *Chinese Coolie Emigration to Countries Within the British Empire*, London, P. S. King and Son, 1923

Carino, Theresa (ed.), *Chinese in the Philippines*, Manila, De La Salle University, 1985

Cator, W. J., *The Economic Position of the Chinese in Netherlands India*, Chicago, University of Chicago Press, 1936

Chan, Alfred, *Employment Prospects of Chinese Youth in Britain: A Research Report*, London, Commission for Racial Equality, 1986

Chan, Anthony B., *Gold Mountain: The Chinese in the New World*, Vancouver, New Star Books, 1983

Chang, Queeny, *Memoirs of a Nonya*, Singapore, Singapore Eastern Universities Press, 1981

Chang Sheng, *Hsiang-kang hei-she-hui huo-tung chen-hsiang* (The True Face of Secret Society Activities in Hong Kong), Hong Kong, T'ian-ti t'u-shu, 1987

Ch'en Ching-ho, *The Chinese Community in the Sixteenth-Century Philippines*, Tokyo, The Centre for East Asia Cultural Studies, n.d.

Chen, Jack, *The Chinese of America*, San Francisco, Harper and Row, 1980

Ch'en, Jerome, *China and the West*, London, Hutchinson, 1979

Ch'en Pen-ch'ang, *Mei-kuo hua-ch'iao ts'an-kuan kung-yeh* (The Overseas Chinese Restaurant Industry in the United States), Taipei, Yuan-tung t'u shu, 1971

Chen Ta, *Chinese Migrations. With Special Reference to Labour Conditions*, Washington, Government Printing Office, 1923

  Emigrant Communities in South China: A Study of Overseas Migration and Its Influence on Standards of Living and Social Change, London, Oxford University Press, 1939

Cheng Min (ed.), *Hai-wai ch'ih-tzu – Hua-ch'iao* (Overseas Offspring – Hua-ch'iao), Peking, Jen-min ch'u-pan-she, 1985

Chia, Felix, *The Babas*, Singapore, Times Books International, 1980

Chin-chiang Overseas Chinese History Society Preparatory Committee (ed.), *Hua-ch'iao shih* (Overseas Chinese History), vol. 2, 1983

Clammer, John R., *Straits Chinese Society*, Singapore, Singapore University Press, 1980

  Singapore: Ideology, Society and Culture, Singapore, Chopman, 1983

Coates, Austin, *Rizal*, Hong Kong, Oxford University Press, 1968

Cocteau, Jean, *Opium: The Diary of a Cure*, translated by Margaret Crosland and Sinclair Road, London, New English Library, 1972

Comber, Leon, *Thirteenth May 1969: A Historical Survey of Sino-Malay Relations*, Kuala Lumpur, Heinemann, 1983

Conrad, Joseph, *Typhoon and Other Stories*, London, William Heinemann, 1903; as *Typhoon and Other Tales*, Oxford University Press paperback edition, 1986

Crisostomo, Isabelo T., *Cory: Profile of a President*, Kuala Lumpur, Pelanduk Publications, 1987

Cuba Commission, *Chinese Emigration: Report of the Commission Sent by China to Ascertain the Condition of Chinese Coolies in Cuba*, Shanghai, The Imperial Maritime Customs Press, 1876; reprinted Ch'eng-wen Publishing, Taipei, 1970

Cushman, Jennifer and Wang Gungwu (eds.), *Changing Identities of the Southeast Asian Chinese since World War II*, Hong Kong, University of Hong Kong Press, 1989

Daley, Robert, *Year of the Dragon*, London, Coronet Books, 1982

Daniels, Roger, *Asian America: Chinese and Japanese in the United States since 1850*, Seattle, University of Washington Press, 1989

Drake, F. S. (ed.), *Proceedings of a Symposium on Southern China, South-East Asia and the Hong Kong Region*, Hong Kong, Hong Kong University Press, 1967

Driver, Christopher, *The British at Table 1940–1980*, London, Chatto and Windus, 1983

Drysdale, J., *Singapore: Struggle for Success*, Singapore, Times Books International, 1984

Fairbank, John King, *Trade and Diplomacy on the China Coast: The Opening of the Treaty Ports 1842–54*, Cambridge, Mass., Harvard University Press, 1953; reprinted Stanford, Stanford University Press, 1969

Fairbank, John King, *The Cambridge History of China, vol. 10: Late Ch'ing 1800–1911*, Part 1, Cambridge, Cambridge University Press, 1978

Fang Chih-ken (ed.), *Fei-chou hua-ch'iao shih tzu-liao hsuan-chi* (Selected Materials on the History of the Overseas Chinese in Africa), Peking, Hsin-hua, 1986

Fitzgerald, C. P., *The Southern Expansion of the Chinese People*, London, Barrie and Jenkins, 1972

Fitzgerald, Stephen, *China and the Overseas Chinese: A Study of Peking's Changing Policy 1949–70*, Cambridge, Cambridge University Press, 1972

Freedman, Maurice, *Lineage Organization in Southeastern China*, London, Athlone Press, 1958

Gale, Bruce (ed.), *Readings in Malaysian Politics*, Selangor, Pelanduk Publications, 1986

George, T. J. S., *Lee Kuan Yew's Singapore*, Singapore, Eastern Universities Press, 1973; revised edition, 1984

Gillenkirk, Jeff and Motlow, James, *Bitter Melon: Stories from the Last Rural Chinese Town in America*, Seattle, University of Washington Press, 1978

Glazer, Nathan and Moynihan, Daniel Patrick, *Behind the Melting Pot: The Negroes, Puerto Ricans, Jews, Italians and Irish of New York City*, Cambridge, Mass., MIT Press, 1963; second edition, 1970

Glick, Clarence E., *Sojourners and Settlers*, Honolulu, Hawaii University Press, 1980

Godley, M. R., *The Mandarin-Capitalists from Nanyang: Overseas Chinese Enterprise in the Modernisation of China 1893–1911*, Ph.D. Thesis, Brown University, 1973

Grieder, Jerome B., *Intellectuals and the State in Modern China*, New York, The Free Press, 1981

Halberstam, David, *The Reckoning*, London, Bantam Books, 1987

Heng Pek Koon, *Chinese Politics in Malaysia: A History of the Malaysian Chinese Association*, Singapore, Oxford University Press, 1988

Holmes, C. (ed.), *Immigrants and Minorities in British Society*, London, Allen and Unwin, 1978

Hom, Ken, *Ken Hom's East Meets West Cuisine*, New York, Simon and Schuster, 1987

Hong Kong Urban Council, *A Study of the Hong Kong Martial Arts Film*, The Fourth Hong Kong International Film Festival, 1980

Howe, Irving, *World of Our Fathers*, New York, Harcourt Brace Jovanovich, 1976

Huang Yao, *Ma-Hsin hua-jen chih* (Annals of Malayan and Singapore Chinese), Kuala Lumpur, 1966

Isaacs, Harold R., *Images of Asia: American Views of China and India*, New York, Harper and Row Torchbook edition, 1972

Jesudason, James V., *Ethnicity and the Economy: The State, Chinese Business, and Multinationals in Malaysia*, Singapore, Oxford University Press, 1989

Jones, D., *The Portrayal of China and India on the American Screen 1869–1955*, Cambridge, Mass., MIT Press, 1955

Josey, Alex, *The Struggle for Singapore*, Sydney, Angus and Robertson, 1974; revised edition, 1976

K'ang Chi-fu, *Hu Wen-hu chuan* (Biography of Aw Boon Haw), Hong Kong, Lung-men wen-hua shih-yeh

Kaplan, David and Dubro, Alec, *Yakuza*, London, Futura, 1987

Kingston, Maxine Hong, *The Woman Warrior: Memoirs of a Girlhood Among Ghosts*, London, Allen Lane, 1977; Picador, 1981
   Tripmaster Monkey: His Fake Book, New York, Knopf, 1989

Kipling, Rudyard, *From Sea to Sea and Other Sketches. Letters of Travel*, vol. 1, London, Macmillan, 1900

Kohl, David G., *Chinese Architecture in Straits Settlements and Western Malaya: Temples, Kongsis and Houses*, Kuala Lumpur, Heinemann, 1984

Koo Hui-lan, *No Feast Lasts Forever*, New York, Quadrangle, 1975

Kung-an pu i-ch'u (ed.), *Fan-tung hui-tao-men chien-chieh* (Introduction to Reactionary Secret Societies), Peking, Ch'un-chung, 1985

Kuo Chia-ling, *Social and Political Change in New York's Chinatown: The Role of Voluntary Associations*, New York, Praegar, 1977

Kwong, Peter, *The New Chinatown*, New York, Hill and Wang/Farrar, Straus and Giroux, 1987

Lach, Donald F., *China in the Eyes of Europe*, Chicago, University of Chicago Press, 1985; Phoenix edition, 1968
   Southeast Asia in the Eyes of Europe, Chicago, University of Chicago Press, 1965; Phoenix, 1968

Lai Ah Eng, *Peasants, Proletarians and Prostitutes: A Preliminary Investigation into the Work of Chinese Women in Colonial Malaya*, Singapore, Institute of Southeast Asian Studies, Research Notes and Discussion Paper, 59, 198

Lai, Him Mark, Lim, Genny and Yung, Judy, *Island: Poetry and History of Chinese Immigrants on Angel Island 1910–1940*, San Francisco, San Francisco Study Centre, 1981

Lee Chin Koon, *Mrs Lee's Cookbook: Nonya Recipes and other Favourite Recipes*, Singapore, Eurasia Press, 1974

Lee Kuan Yew, *The Battle for Merger*, Singapore, Ministry of Culture, 1961

Lethbridge, H. J., *Hong Kong: Stability and Change*, Hong Kong, Oxford University Press, 1978

Leyda, Jay, *Dianying: Chinese Shadows*, Cambridge, Mass., MIT Press, 1972.

Li Chi, *The Formation of the Chinese People*, Cambridge, Mass., Harvard University Press, 1928

Liao, Shubert, *Chinese Participation in Philippine Culture and Economy*, Manila, University of the Far East, 1964

Light, Ivan H., *Ethnic Enterprise in America: Business and Welfare Among Chinese, Japanese, and Blacks*, Berkeley, University of California Press, 1972

Lim, Linda Y. C. and Gosling, L. A. Peter (eds.), *The Chinese in Southeast Asia*, vols. 1 and 2, Singapore, Maruzen Asia, 1983

Limlingan, Victor Simpao, *The Overseas Chinese in ASEAN: Business Strategies and Management Practices*, Manila, Vita Development Corporation, 1986

Lin Chin-chih and Chuang Wei-chi, *Chin-tai hua-ch'iao t'ou-tzu kuo-nei ch'i-yeh shih-liao hsuan-chi* (Selected Historical Materials on Modern Overseas Chinese Investments in Enterprises in China), Fu-chou, Fu-chien Jen-min, 1985

Lin Hai-yin (ed.), *Chung-kuo tou-fu* (Chinese Tofu), Taipei, Ch'un wen-hsueh, 1971

Loke Wan Tho, *A Company of Birds*, London, Michael Joseph, 1958

London, Jack, *The House of Pride and Other Tales of Hawaii*, London, Mills and Boon, 1912

Lydon, Sandy, *Chinese Gold: The Chinese in the Monterey Bay Region*, Capitola, Capitola Book Company, 1985

McCunn, Ruthanne Lum, *Chinese American Portraits: Personal Histories 1828–1988*, San Francisco, Chronicle Books, 1989

McCoy, Alfred, *The Politics of Heroin in Southeast Asia*, New York, Harper and Row, 1972

Mackie, J. A. C. (ed.), *The Chinese in Indonesia*, Singapore, Heinemann, 1976

MacNair, F. H., *The Chinese Abroad*, Shanghai, Commercial Press, 1924

Meskill, Johanna Menzel, *A Chinese Pioneer Family: The Lins of Wu-feng, Taiwan, 1729–1895*, Princeton, Princeton University Press, 1979

Minchin, James, *No Man Is An Island: A Study of Singapore's Lee Kuan Yew*, Sydney, Allen and Unwin, 1986

Mo, Timothy, *Sour Sweet*, London, André Deutsch, 1982; Sphere Abacus, 1983

Moore, Donald, *The Magic Dragon*, St Albans, Panther Books, 1975

Morgan, W. P., *The Triad Societies of Hong Kong*, Hong Kong, Government Printer, 1960

Morris, Jan, *Hong Kong, Xianggang*, London, Viking, 1988

Mozingo, David, *Chinese Policy Towards Indonesia 1949–67*, Ithaca, Cornell University Press, 1976

Naipaul, V. S., *The Middle Passage: Impressions of Five Societies – British, French and Dutch – in the West Indies and South America*, London, André Deutsch, 1962; Penguin, 1969

Newbold, T. J., *British Settlements in the Straits of Malacca*, Singapore, Oxford University Press, 1971

Ng, Bickleen Fong, *The Chinese in New Zealand*, Hong Kong, Hong Kong University Press, 1959

Ng Kwee Choo, *The Chinese in London*, London, Oxford University Press for the Institute of Race Relations, 1968

Orwell, George, *Down and Out in Paris and London*, London, Gollancz, 1933; Penguin, 1966

Payne, Robert, *The White Rajahs of Sarawak*, Singapore, Oxford University Press, 1986

Perrin, Linda, *Coming to America*, New York, Delacorte Press, 1980

Phipatseritham, Krirkkiat and Yoshihara, Kunio, *Business Groups in Thailand*, Singapore, Institute of Southeast Asian Studies, Research Notes and Discussion Papers, 41, 1983

Prasartset, Suthy, *Thai Business Leaders: Men and Careers in a Developing Economy*, Tokyo, Institute of Developing Economies, Joint Research Programme Series, 19, 1980

President's Commission on Asian Organized Crime, Record of Hearing iii, 22–25 October 1984

Purcell, Victor, *The Chinese in Southeast Asia*, London, Oxford University Press, 1951

Rizal, José (a), *El Filibusterismo*, translated by Charles Derbyshire as The Reign of Greed, second edition, Manila, Philippines Education Co., 1912
  (b) *Noli Me Tangere*, translated by Charles Derbyshire as The Social Cancer, second edition, Manila, Philippine Education Co., 1912

Robison, Richard, *Indonesia: The Rise of Capital*, Sydney, Allen and Unwin, 1987

Runciman, Steven, *The White Rajahs: A History of Sarawak from 1841 to 1946*, London, Cambridge University Press, 1960

St John, Spencer, *The Life of Sir James Brooke, Rajah of Sarawak*, Edinburgh, Blackwood and Sons, 1879

Schafer, Edward H., *The Golden Peaches of Samarkand*, Berkeley, University of California Press, 1963
  Vermillion Bird: T'ang Images of the South, Berkeley, University of California Press, 1967
  Shore of Pearls, Berkeley, University of California Press, 1970

Shang, Anthony, *The Chinese in Britain*, London, Batsford Academic and Educational, 1984

Sherry, Norman, *Conrad's Eastern World*, London, Cambridge University Press, 1966

Shirokogoroff, S. M., *Anthropology of Eastern China and Kwangtung Province*, Shanghai, Commercial Press, 1925

Siu, Paul C. P., *The Chinese Laundryman: A Study of Social Isolation*, ed. by John Kuo Wei Tchen, New York, New York University Press, 1987

Skinner, G. William, *Chinese Society in Thailand*, Ithaca, Cornell University Press, 1957

Slater, Jim, *Return to Go*, London, Weidenfeld and Nicolson, 1977

Smithies, Michael, *Old Bangkok*, Singapore, Oxford University Press, 1986

Snow, Philip, *The Star Raft: China's Encounter With Africa*, New York, Weidenfeld and Nicolson, 1988

Spence, Jonathan, *The Gate of Heavenly Peace*, London, Faber, 1982

Steinberg, David Joel, *In Search of Southeast Asia*, revised edition, Sydney, Allen and Unwin, 1987

Stevenson, Robert Louis, *The Amateur Emigrant*, London, Chatto and Windus, 1895; Hogarth, 1984

Stewart, Watt, *Chinese Bondage in Peru: A History of the Chinese Coolie in Peru 1849–1874*, Westport, Greenwood Press, 1970

Stockard, Janice E., *Daughters of the Canton Delta: Marriage Patterns and Economic Strategies in South China 1860–1930*, Stanford, Stanford University Press, 1989

Struve, Lynn A., *The Southern Ming 1644–1662*, New Haven, Yale University Press, 1984

Summerskill, Michael, *China on the Western Front: Britain's Chinese Work Force in the First World War*, London, Michael Summerskill, 1982

Suryadinata, Leo, *Pribumi Indonesians, the Chinese Minority and China*, Singapore, Heinemann, 1978; second edition, 1986

Tan Chee Beng, *The Baba of Melaka: Culture and Identity of a Chinese Peranakan Community in Malaysia*, Kuala Lumpur, Pelanduk, 1988

Taylor, Monica, *Chinese Pupils in Britain: A Review of Research Into the Education of Pupils of Chinese Origin*, Windsor, National Foundation for Educational Research – Nelson, 1987

Tchen, John Kuo Wei, *Genthe's Photographs of San Francisco's Old Chinatown*, New York, Dover, 1984

Theroux, Paul, *Sunrise With Seamonsters*, London, Hamish Hamilton, 1985; Penguin, 1986

T'ien, J. K., *The Chinese of Sarawak*, London, London School of Economics Monographs on Social Anthropology, No. 12, 1953

Travers, Robert, *Australian Mandarin: The Life and Times of Quong Tart*, Kenthurst, Kangaroo Press, 1981

Tsai, Shih-shan Henry, *The Chinese Experience in America*, Bloomington and Indianapolis, Indiana University Press, 1986

Tsou T'ao-fen, *Tsou fen wen-chi* (A Tsou Anthology), vol. 2, Hong Kong, Joint Publishing Company, 1978

Tuchman, Barbara, *The Proud Tower: A Portrait of the World Before the War 1890–1914*, London, Hamish Hamilton, 1966; Macmillan, 1980

Vaughan, J. D., *The Manners and Customs of the Chinese in the Straits Settlements, 1879*, Singapore, Oxford University Press, 1971

Wang, An, with Eugene Linden, *Lessons: An Autobiography*, Massachusetts, Addison Wesley, 1986

Wang Gungwu, *A Short History of the Nanyang Chinese*, Singapore, Eastern Universities Press, 1959

Wang Sing-wu, *The Organization of Chinese Emigration 1848–88*, San Francisco, Chinese Materials Center Inc., 1978

Ward, Barbara, *Through Other Eyes*, Hong Kong, The Chinese University Press, 1985

Ward, J. S. M. and Stirling, W. G., *The Hung Society, or the Society of Heaven and Earth*, 3 vols, London, Baskerville Press, 1925–26

Warren, James Francis, *Rickshaw Coolie: A People's History of Singapore (1880–1940)*, Singapore, Oxford University Press, 1986

Watson, James L., *Emigration and the Chinese Lineage: The Mans in Hong Kong and London*, Berkeley, University of California Press, 1975

(ed.), *Between Two Cultures: Migrants and Minorities in Britain*, Oxford, Blackwell, 1977

Wen Kuang-i et al., *Yin-tu-ni-hsi-ya hua-ch'iao shih* (The History of Indonesian Chinese), Peking, Hai-yang, 1985

Wickberg, Edgar, *The Chinese in Philippine Life 1850–1898*, New Haven, Yale University Press

Williams, Lea E., *The Future of the Overseas Chinese in Southeast Asia*, New York, McGraw Hill, 1966

Wilson, Angus, *Late Call*, Harmondsworth, Penguin, 1968

De Wit, Augusta, *Java: Facts and Fancies*, The Hague, W. P. van Stockum, 1912; reprinted, Singapore, Oxford University Press, 1985

Wolf, W. and Witke, R. (eds.), *Women in Chinese Society*, Stanford, Stanford University Press, 1975

Wright, A., *Twentieth Century Impressions of British Malaya*, London, Lloyds Greater Britain Publishing, 1908

Wu, David Y. H., *The Chinese in Papua New Guinea 1880–1980*, Hong Kong, The Chinese University Press, 1982

Wu I-lin, *Hsien-nan pieh lu* (Separate Records of Southern Thailand), Taipei, Shang-wu, 1985

Wu Tse, *Hua-ch'iao shih yen-chiu lun chi* (Collected Research Papers on Overseas Chinese History), Shanghai, Hua-tung shih-fan ta-hsueh, 1984

Wu Yuan-li and Wu Chun-hsi, *Economic Development in Southeast Asia: The Chinese Dimension*, Stanford, Hoover Institution Press, 1980

Yang Kuo-chen, *Ch'en Chia Keng* (Tan Kah Kee), Peking, Jen-min ch'u-pan-she, 1987

Yen Ching-hwang, *A Social History of the Chinese in Singapore and Malaya 1800–1911*, Singapore, Oxford University Press, 1986

Yong, C. F., *Tan Kah-kee: The Making of an Overseas Chinese Legend*, Singapore, Oxford University Press, 1987

Yoshihara, Kunio, *The Rise of Ersatz Capitalism in Southeast Asia*, Singapore, Oxford University Press, 1988

Young, Ernest, *The Kingdom of the Yellow Robe*, London, Archibald Constable, 1898; Kuala Lumpur, Oxford University Press, 1982

Yung, Judy, *Chinese Women of America: A Pictorial History*, Seattle, University of Washington Press, 1986

Index